OUR CHILDREN'S FUTURE: CHILD CARE POLICY IN CANADA

Edited by Gordon Cleveland and Michael Krashinsky

Since 1997 Quebec has offered licensed child care services for five dollars per day to its entire population. British Columbia has begun its own program of universal subsidization of licensed child care services for five- and six-year-old children. With these developments in mind, and with the belief that governments and the public in Canada are ready to contemplate making a major investment in improving child care services, Gordon Cleveland and Michael Krashinsky have assembled many of the key experts and activists in the area of child care policy and asked them to consider a number of important questions.

Based on a symposium on the topic held in 1998, *Our Children's Future* makes a significant contribution to understanding how Canada, with its particular institutions, history, politics, and values, should design a national child care strategy. Presenting a healthy and vigorous debate among child care experts, policy analysts, and key policy makers, this book attempts to answer how we are to make the transition to a future with substantially more public involvement in child care and offers suggestions as to what that child care system should look like.

GORDON CLEVELAND is Senior Lecturer, Division of Management, University of Toronto.
MICHAEL KRASHINSKY is Professor of Economics, Division of Management, University of Toronto.

Our Children's Future:
Child Care Policy in Canada

Edited by
Gordon Cleveland and
Michael Krashinsky

UNIVERSITY OF TORONTO PRESS
Toronto Buffalo London

© University of Toronto Press Incorporated 2001
Toronto Buffalo London
Printed in Canada

ISBN 0-8020-4695-9 (cloth)
ISBN 0-8020-8275-0 (paper)

Printed on acid-free paper

Canadian Cataloguing in Publication Data

Main entry under title:

Our children's future : child care policy in Canada

ISBN 0-8020-4695-5-9 (bound)   ISBN 0-8020-8275-0 (pbk.)

1. Child care – Canada.   2. Child care – Government policy – Canada.
3. Child care services – Government policy – Canada.   I. Cleveland,
Gordon   II. Krashinsky, Michael, 1947–   .

HQ778.7.C3097 2000   362.71'2'0971   C00-932079-2

The University of Toronto Press acknowledges the financial assistance to
its publishing program of the Canada Council for the Arts and the
Ontario Arts Council.

University of Toronto Press acknowledges the financial support for its
publishing activities of the Government of Canada through the Book
Publishing Industry Development Program (BPIDP).

Contents

Acknowledgments

The contributions that make up this book were originally presented at a symposium entitled 'Good Child Care in Canada for the 21st Century: Preparing the Policy Map.' The book includes edited papers, comments on those papers, summaries of the floor discussions at the symposium, and introductions and conclusions by the editors.

We owe a debt of gratitude to many people whose cooperation, enthusiasm, and dedication to advancing child care policy in Canada have made this book a reality. Money was a necessary, though not a sufficient, condition for the success of this enterprise. The Atkinson Foundation, and its determined executive director, Charles Pascal, deserve considerable credit for their efforts to keep child care on the political agenda, and to make certain that it deserves to be there. The Atkinson Foundation were enthusiastic supporters of the symposium with money and suggestions, and they have our thanks.

Human Resources Development Canada has recently received considerable bad press for their funding practices. On the basis of our experiences, we suspect that this reputation is undeserved. We can attest that Child Care Visions, part of Employability and Social Partnerships at HRDC, has played a very valuable role in stimulating research and development projects in the child care field. In particular, CCV was willing to provide funds to support the production of several of the contributions for the Symposium. A relatively small amount of seed money has brought forth, we believe, a bumper harvest. We thank Carol Levesque, in particular, for her unfailing helpfulness and attention to detail in monitoring our use of these funds.

We would be remiss if we did not warmly thank all of the presenters of papers and speeches, discussants, session chairs, and symposium participants for creating the swirl of ideas that fill this volume. As you will see, Bob Rae, Martha Friendly, Hillel Goelman, Gillian Doherty, Penny Milton, Susan Prentice, Anne Gauthier, Maureen Baker, Gina Browne, Jane Bertrand, and Annette LaGrange all consented to do research and make presentations on the topics we had chosen for them. Joanne Roulston, Bonnie Ewart, Michael Schuster, Joey Edwardh, and Louise Boily became co-authors of Gina Browne's contribution. Helen Penn and Jocelyne Tougas delivered eloquent and thoughtful speeches about how child care thinking has flowered in other places. Tom Kent, Alfred MacLeod, Ellen Vineberg Jacobs, June Pollard, Judy Bernhard, Pat Corson, Jane Beach, Julie Mathien, Shelley Phipps, Kathy O'Hara, Donna Lero, Michael Goldberg, Richard Budgell, Douglas Hyatt, and Marta Juorio were all willing to carefully consider the thoughts of those who had contributed papers and provide constructive and provocative criticisms of them. Margo Greenwood and Perry Shawana made extensive comments about Aboriginal perspectives on child care and generously agreed to write them up for inclusion in this book. Rita Chudnovsky wrote an afterword to one of the chapters and collaborated in the genesis of the original paper on which it is based. Another group of talented individuals were willing to chair sessions and shepherd the discussion along productive lines. This included Charles Pascal, Mab Oloman, Judy Rebick, Barbara Cameron, Lynne Westlake, and Laurel Rothman. We thank all of you for your profound labours of love.

Beyond money and ideas, there are the people who make the railroad run. Michele Glassford was the chief engineer, but she also had to stoke the engines, act as conductor, and perform emergency repairs en route. Almost all of the myriad details of staging the symposium were placed in Michele's capable hands. From time to time, she called on her trusty assistant, Maria Amparo Jardine, who did yeoman service, too. Our thanks to you both.

One of our biggest debts, for uncompensated labours, is to the referees who met one weekend in February, 1998, to pore over the original versions of the papers. This team included Kathy Teghtsoonian, from the Faculty of Human and Social Development, University of Victoria; Lynne Westlake, who is a senior policy analyst with the Social Policy Directorate, Strategic Policy, Human Resources Development Canada; Doug Hyatt, who is with the Division of Management and the Centre for Industrial Relations at the University of Toronto; and Martha Friendly, who is the indefatigable executive director of the Childcare Resource and Research Unit, Department of Urban and Community Studies, University of Toronto. These four worked closely with us to form a symposium team of reviewers. An anonymous reviewer examined the entire manuscript and provided useful feedback. We think it is obvious, from the chapters in this volume, that they did this work of criticism and suggestion most effectively.

Virgil Duff is the gatekeeper for University of Toronto Press. He responded warmly to our initial idea, pitched to him many moons ago. He provided encouragement when we needed it, and always found a way to pull strings to make the right things happen. Kate Baltais has ruthlessly edited this text making everything right that we could not or would not. The whole is more readable because of Virgil's and Kate's efforts. Without their support, you would not be reading these words.

It is customary for authors to thank their families. We are happy to discharge this apparent obligation. Sue, Tara, and Julia deserve Gordon's love and affection for all the support they have provided, and sometimes they even get the love and affection they deserve. Kathie, Harry, Jon, and Susan tolerated Mike's occasional absences in body and frequent absences in spirit during the work on the symposium and on this volume. Both of us want to acknowledge in public what we have stated many times in private – that what seem like individual accomplishments such as this book truly have a collective responsibility that our families share. We both want to express how much we have learned from Sue and Kathie about child care over the years, and how remarkably educational the experience of being fathers to our children has been.

Contributors

(in order of appearance in the book)

Gordon Cleveland is a senior lecturer in economics in the Division of Management at the University of Toronto at Scarborough.

Michael Krashinsky is a professor of economics in the Division of Management at the University of Toronto at Scarborough and at the Rotman School of Management at the University of Toronto.

Martha Friendly is an adjunct professor at the Centre for Urban and Community Studies at the University of Toronto and coordinator of the Child Care Resource and Research Unit at the University of Toronto.

Bob Rae currently practices law with Goodman, Phillips, and Vineberg, in Toronto, and was Premier of the Province of Ontario.

Tom Kent is now associated with the School of Social Policy Studies at Queen's University, and was policy secretary to the Prime Minister during the Pearson government.

Alfred MacLeod is a senior vice-president at EKOS Research Associates Inc. and served as a policy adviser in the offices of the Prime Minister and the Minister of Human Resources Development Canada.

Jocelyne Tougas is a child care researcher and consultant and, most recently, has been part of the research team working on the 'You Bet I Care!' study of wages, working conditions, and practices in child care.

Helen Penn is professor of early childhood at the University of East London, and a visiting fellow at the Social Science Research Unit, Institute of Education, University of London.

Gillian Doherty is a child care research and policy consultant, and an adjunct professor at the University of Guelph.

Hillel Goelman is a professor in the departments of educational and counselling psychology, and special education at the University of British Columbia.

Ellen Jacobs is a professor of early childhood and elementary education at Concordia University, and is co-editor of the *Canadian Journal of Research in Early Childhood Education*.

June Pollard is director of the School of Early Childhood Education at Ryerson Polytechnic University.

Judy Bernhard is a faculty member at the School of Early Childhood Education at Ryerson Polytechnic University.

Pat Corson is a faculty member at the School of Early Childhood Education at Ryerson Polytechnic University.

Penny Milton is executive director of the Canadian Education Association and has broad experience in public education at all levels.

Susan L. Prentice is an associate professor of sociology at the University of Manitoba.

Julie Mathien was a social policy consultant and teaches part-time faculty member of the School of Early Childhood Education at Ryerson Polytechnic University. She is now a Policy Development Officer with responsibility for children's policy at the City of Toronto.

Jane Beach is a child care researcher and policy consultant, in Victoria, British Columbia.

Margo Greenwood is an assistant professor at the University of Northern British Columbia.

Perry Shawana is an associate professor and chair of First Nations Studies at the University of Northern British Columbia. He is also a barrister and solicitor in British Columbia.

Rita Chudnovsky teaches in Child, Family, and Community Studies at Douglas College and consults on a wide range of community-based projects.

Anne Gauthier is an assistant professor of sociology at the University of Calgary.

Maureen Baker is a professor of sociology and head of the Department of Sociology at the University of Auckland, New Zealand.

Kathy O'Hara has worked in the federal public service since 1973 and is currently assistant secretary of the Social and Cultural Sector in the Treasury Board Secretariat.

Shelley Phipps is Maxwell professor of economics at Dalhousie University.

Gina Browne is a professor of nursing and clinical epidemiology and biostatistics at McMaster University. She is also the founder and director of the System-Linked Research Unit on Health and Social Service Utilization, and co-director of the Community Linked Evaluation Aids Resource Unit.

Joanne Roulston is senior researcher and policy adviser for the National Council of Welfare.

Bonnie Ewart is associated with the System-Linked Research Unit on Health and Social Service Utilization and was Commissioner of Social Services for Halton Region, Ontario until 1998.

Michael Schuster is associated with the System-Linked Research Unit on Health and Social Service Utilization and was Commissioner of Social Services for Halton Region, Ontario, until 1999.

Joey Edwardh is associated with the System-Linked Research Unit on Health and Social Service Utilization and is executive director for the Social Planning and Research Council in Halton Region, Ontario.

Louise Boily is a research officer in the Childhood and Youth Division of Health Canada.

Richard Budgell is the national manager for Health Canada of the Aboriginal Head Start program for urban and northern communities.

Michael Goldberg is the research director at the Social Planning and Research Council of British Columbia.

Donna Lero is an associate professor in the Department of Family Relations and Applied Nutrition at the University of Guelph and is co-director of the university's Centre for Families, Work, and Well-being.

Jane Bertrand is a faculty member of the Early Childhood Education diploma program at George Brown College in Toronto.

Annette LaGrange is an associate professor in the Faculty of Education at the University of Calgary and is also dean of the faculty.

Douglas Hyatt is an associate professor of management, economics, and industrial relations at the University of Toronto at Scarborough, at the Rotman Faculty of Management at the University of Toronto, and at the Centre for Industrial Relations at the University of Toronto. He is also senior scientist at the Institute for Work and Health.

Marta Juorio is director of the YWCA Child Care Centre in Saskatoon and is also co-chair of the Child Care Advocacy Association.

OUR CHILDREN'S FUTURE:
Child Care Policy In Canada

Introduction

Most young Canadian children use non-parental care arrangements every week. The Canadian National Child Care Survey of 1988 found that 74 per cent of all children in Canada who are between eighteen months and six years of age are in regular non-parental care arrangements.[1] This statistic should give all of us considerable pause – the large majority of young children in Canada already use non-parental care. Given this reality, the endless discussion about whether non-parental care is optimal is beside the point. The key issues for policy makers to ask and answer are 'What kind of care could and should our children receive?' and, especially, 'What can and should governments in Canada do to encourage the use of good quality child care?'

The world of young children has changed dramatically in the past thirty years. First, most mothers of young children now work in the paid labour force. In 1967, of mothers with preschool children 17 per cent were in the labour force.[2] Today, over two-thirds of these mothers are in the labour force. This phenomenal growth trend does not appear to be slowing down.

Second, young women are more career-oriented and education-oriented today than their mothers were. A quick look at the proportion of undergraduates and graduates in virtually any university program will confirm this. So, mothers today are more likely to have a career and to be accustomed to working in full-time employment than mothers were a generation ago.

Third, fertility rates have fallen dramatically in the past forty years. From an average of 4.0 children per mother in the early 1960s, fertility has fallen to less than replacement level (about 1.6 to 1.7 children per female). Many children do not have siblings; for many of their early years, most Canadian children are 'only' children.

Fourth, the use of care by non-relatives and, in particular, licensed or regulated forms of child care and early education has grown dramatically. In 1967 only 2 per cent of preschool children having an employed mother used day care or nursery school (about 7,000 children).[3] By 1994–5 nearly 22 per cent of preschool children with a mother engaged in employment or studying used a child care centre, a nursery school, or a regulated family day care home (about 270,000 children).[4] Over the same period, the number of children using other forms of care by a non-relative approximately tripled. Over 500,000 preschool children now use kindergarten for several hours a day at age four or five.[5]

Fifth, most mothers stay at home with their children for a little while after they are born, but 'stay-at-home motherhood' is more likely a transitory status than it is a permanent life choice. Most first-time mothers are in the labour force at the time of their first delivery, and the majority are eligible for maternity benefits and parental benefits paid through Canada Employment Insurance. It is typical for parents to use nearly all the benefit weeks to which they are entitled. A large number of mothers are therefore at home for most of the first six months of their baby's life.[6] Some union or non-union contracts provide extended benefits for up to a year or even longer. The large majority of mothers taking maternity leave return to the labour force; in Statistics Canada's 1988 National Child Care Survey, 98 per cent of mothers currently on maternity leave indicated an intention to return, sooner or later, to their previous employer.

Sixth, mothers who decide to stay at home with their children nearly always decide to use senior kindergarten and junior kindergarten services where they are available, and those with higher family incomes are increasingly likely to use nursery schools and other forms of non-parental care as well. As a result, even many families with a mother at home use some form of early childhood care and education.

In sum, non-parental child care is a reality for most young children most of the time; this is often, but not always, associated with parental employment, and all the evidence suggests these trends will continue. Despite the radical changes in children's lives over the past thirty years, and despite the very considerable use of non-parental child care, most governments in Canada have done surprisingly little to affect the quality, affordability, and availability of early childhood care services that families use.

CHILD CARE POLICIES IN CANADA

Over time a variety of child care policies and programs in Canada has developed, introduced by different levels of government, and designed to achieve diverse objectives. There is no overarching vision of how child care ought to be provided and what the goals of the system ought to be. There are five types of public programs currently oriented towards providing early childhood education services in Canada.

Kindergarten

Kindergarten is not typically considered to be a program delivering child care services. In reality, however, it is the only program (with the partial exception of child care in Quebec) providing early childhood education and care that is universally available, regardless of income, labour force status, or other criteria. In any given year, virtually all Canadian children who are between four years eight months and five years eight months of age at the beginning of September will attend kindergarten in the public school system. In Ontario most children who are a year younger than this will attend junior kindergarten. Kindergarten is nearly always offered on a part-time basis (in the morning, the afternoon, or on alternate days). Several years ago, New Brunswick moved from having no public kindergarten to offering it on a full-day basis. In 1997 as part of wholesale child care reform, Quebec began to provide full-day kindergarten within the school system for five-year-olds.

Maternity Benefits

Maternity benefits are provided to eligible mothers through the Employment Insurance (EI) scheme. In effect, maternity is considered to be a legitimate cause of absence from work, like unemployment or sickness, and therefore eligible for payment of insurance benefits. One of the reasons for providing maternity benefits through the EI is that payment of unemployment benefits is constitutionally a federal responsibility; other maternity issues, such as eligibility for maternity leave, fall under provincial jurisdiction. However, because EI rules were designed to apply to those seeking unemployment benefits, they also affect maternity benefit claimants. For instance, there is a two-week waiting period for maternity benefits (out of seventeen weeks of leave, only the last fifteen are paid). Intended to discourage those who are unemployed for very short periods from making claims for unemployment insurance, this rule is completely inappropriate when applied to new mothers. Similarly, new eligibility rules for unemployment insurance restrict eligibility for maternity benefits in unfortunate ways.

It might be argued that maternity benefit policy and child care policy are quite distinct and different things. However, most new mothers do not medically require a full fifteen or seventeen weeks to recover from childbirth. Some of the time is designed to allow mother and child to bond, the mother to continue breastfeeding, and the mother to adjust the household arrangements to the arrival of the new family member. The child care function of this leave is even more obvious with the adjunct to maternity leave known as parental leave (or child care leave). Parental leave is, since 1991, available to either parent (with, however, an additional two-week waiting period if taken by the father) for ten weeks following maternity leave, also paid by EI. Improvements in the parental leave program have been announced as this book goes to press.

Child Care Expense Deduction

The Income Tax Act has, since 1972, allowed families with child care expenses related to work to deduct these expenses from taxable income before income tax rates are applied. Logically, the income used to pay these expenses is not properly considered to be part of discretionary income which should be subject to tax. Expenses are claimable only if they are required to earn income, so they can only be claimed by either a single parent who works or the lower-earning parent in a two-parent family if both spouses are in the paid labour force. A limit of $7,000 per child under seven and $5,000 per child between seven and sixteen is intended to ensure that only the necessary level of child care expenditures can be claimed. This does not cover the costs of licensed child care for infants and toddlers in some parts of Canada.

Many observers argue that the Child Care Expense Deduction reduces the cost of child care, but this is a misleading observation. The Child Care Expense Deduction is properly seen as part of the process of defining taxable income.[7] We allow families to deduct child care expenses from income for the same reason that we allow a self-employed person to deduct the cost of renting office space – both are necessary expenses of earning income. Put another way, it is only earned income net of child care expenses that would be available for discretionary spending by the family, hence it is only earned income net of child care expenses that should be taxed.

Child Care Subsidies

Families with sufficiently low incomes are eligible in all provinces and territories for child care subsidies which may reduce the price of licensed child care to zero or to a relatively small amount. Eligibility for child care subsidy is determined partly by family income, but also partly by social criteria. For instance, most subsidies are only available to families in which the parent(s) are employed or in training for employment. Subsidies are generally also available when children have specific developmental handicaps or when family functioning is impaired in specific ways. As may be obvious from the description, the origins of child care subsidy rules, and the primary functions of child care subsidy policies, are strongly related to welfare and social assistance objectives. In most provinces and territories, the income criteria ensure that only single-parent families will get full subsidy; child care subsidies are intended to permit eligible parents to be employed, or train for employment, in order not to establish long-term dependence on public assistance. The punitive, small-minded features of many social assistance programs are reproduced in child care subsidy rules in many jurisdictions; these are purported to ensure that adequate incentives to work exist for low-income parents. Approximately 163,000 children received subsidies for the use of regulated child care services in 1998.[8] Subsidies provide approximately 30 per cent of revenues in an average child care centre.[9]

Operating Grants

Some provinces and territories provide regular operating grants to licensed or regulated child care facilities (centres and family homes). The purpose of these grants may be to stabilize funding to these services and/or to enhance the wages and benefits of low-paid staff in this primarily parent-funded service. This operational funding for child care has been highly variable across provinces and territories and across time within individual provinces and territories. In 1998, operating and other grants from government provided approximately 18 per cent of revenues of an average child care centre.[10]

It may seem, to the casual reader, as if the sum of kindergarten programs, maternity and/or parental benefits, tax benefits, child care subsidies, and operating grants is a considerable amount of assistance to child care. However, in the case of child care funding in Canada, the whole is less than the sum of its parts. In other words, available assistance covers (some or many) newborn children until they are about six months of age, some children in poor families whose parents meet strict eligibility criteria, some reduction of taxes on income which is not truly disposable income in the first place, and nearly all children for two and a half hours per day once they reach age five.

This contrasts sharply with prevailing policies towards early childhood care and education in many other countries in the world. In France, Spain, Denmark, Sweden, Finland, and many other European countries (and, now, in Quebec), universal early education for children between three and five or between two and five years of age is the norm and low-cost publicly subsidized arrangements for large numbers of children younger than that is typically available. Unfortunately, the countries with predominantly Anglo-Saxon heritages (United States, Great Britain, Australia, New Zealand, and Canada) share the very weak development of public support for early childhood care and education. Although there are considerable differences among the Anglo-Saxon countries, their similarities in child care policy outweigh their differences.

CURRENT USE OF CHILD CARE BY CANADIAN FAMILIES

There is little uniformity in the child care arrangements made by different parents while children are young. In 1994–5, at the time of Cycle 1 of the National Longitudinal Survey on Children and Youth by Statistics Canada, there were 2.4 million children in Canada who were zero to five years of age inclusive. About 1.4 million of them had a mother who was employed or a student. Not including kindergarten, just over 900,000 of these children used non-parental care. Over 250,000 children were in regulated care, whether in centres or family homes. The rest were in unregulated care – about 200,000 were cared for by relatives, and 430,000 were in informal care by non-relatives. The patterns of use of child care arrangements vary strongly with the child's age, by the cost to parents of the care arrangement, by family income, and by other family characteristics. However, in every age and income grouping, there are many children cared for by their parents (e.g., by parents working off-setting shifts), many cared for by relatives, many cared for in unregulated arrangements, and many cared for in regulated arrangements.

Even among working parents, only about two-thirds use paid child care arrangements. One reason is that child care can be expensive. Across Canada, the typical cost of a regulated child care space for a three-year-old is between $4,000 and $6,000 per year (even higher in Ontario).[11] Many families do everything they can to reduce child care costs, which may mean reduced work hours, off-shifting, or recruiting relatives. Even so, parents with preschool children who purchased care at the time of the Canadian National Child Care Survey in 1988 were found to be spending about 8 per cent of the family's pre-tax income, or nearly 18 per cent of the mother's pre-tax income on child care costs. There is no reliable information on the quality and characteristics of care that most preschool children currently receive. Just as the amounts parents pay for care vary widely, it is likely that the quality of care received is also highly uneven. It may well be true that the majority of preschool children in Canada receive early care that is best described as custodial, rather than developmental.

Child development is a very young science and there is still considerable debate about research results. Very few issues – the importance of parental care in early years; whether there are critical periods of development that will determine later ability to learn; whether the quality of non-parental care matters and how good quality care is defined; whether children learn mainly from their parents, or from any caring adults, or from peers – are definitively settled. Yet all of us, as parents, must take key decisions affecting our children's futures. Parents have a strong tendency, in the absence of consensus with regard to the evidence on child development, to make child-rearing decisions based on instinct, experience, and socialization, and to rationalize and self-justify the decisions they have made.

One of the main cleavages in social values around child-rearing is related to the participation of mothers in the labour force.[12] Some believe that the mother's place is in the home while children are young. Others believe that family life will, as a whole, be improved by full- or part-time participation of both parents (or a lone parent) in the labour force even when children are quite young. Many parents are unsure about their values and suffer from considerable guilt no matter what decision they make about the care of children when they are young.

Differences in current child care arrangements, differences in preferred child care arrangements, and differences in values about child-rearing make it difficult to design child care policies for young children that will be politically rewarding for incumbent governments. Even though there are differences in values, however, we do not believe this should be an excuse not to act. Most European countries, and Quebec, enjoy the same divergences in values among their populations, but have been able to fashion popular child care policies. We need to design child care and family policies that will be widely acclaimed for providing good care for children in their early years and that will allow considerable latitude for parental choice about child care and employment issues. In most countries, highly subsidized child care services accessible to most families are a part of the menu of choices. So are maternity and parental leaves. The rationale for policy is typically centred on the interests of children in receiving good quality early education and care services, irrespective of parental decisions about employment.

WHY HOLD A SYMPOSIUM ON CHILD CARE POLICY?

The idea for the symposium began in the heads of the two editors – Mike Krashinsky and Gord Cleveland – about a week after the release of their study of the costs and benefits of a child care program for all Canadian children between the ages of two and five (Cleveland and Krashinsky, 1998). The positive public reaction to the study made apparent the considerable public appreciation of the potential benefits of publicly supported early education and care for children and highlighted the role of government policy inaction in providing funding and legislative support for services. Basic decisions on child care policy are overdue; successive Conservative and Liberal federal governments have shied away from providing a Canada-wide financial and legislative framework for progress. Quebec has initiated universal early care and education for $5 per child per day, but no other provinces have had child care near the top of their agenda for action. As this book goes to press, British Columbia has announced an ambitious child care program beginning with school-age children (and expanding to younger children over time). Most of the implementation takes place after the provincial election in 2001.

As is always the case, there are reasons for an absence in most of Canada of political will to act. One reason is a cleavage in social values over the type of care we provide to young children. A second is the relatively high cost of initiating a major new tier of the educational structure or a new social program (two alternative ways of viewing child care reform). However, one major reason for inaction is the lack of expert and informed consensus on the appropriate design of government programs to support developmental early childhood services.

There is disagreement among child care experts, policy analysts, and key policy makers about what are the next steps to take in expanding child care services. There is disagreement about whether federal or provincial governments should play the key role in initiating legislation and in financing. There is disagreement about the role of the education system versus private, non-profit child care providers, about whether care should be provided primarily through an extension downwards of the public school system or through a growing upwards of the network of private non-profit centres and family homes offering child care. There is disagreement about exactly what kind and quality of services we should be providing for children, both in two-parent and single-parent and/or disadvantaged families. There is disagreement about what kind of family policy we need as a complement to the child care services we plan to provide. There is disagreement about the appropriate training and compensation levels of workers who will provide child care services and about the role of worker organizations. Because of these disagreements, it is difficult for policy analysts and experts to play an effective, active role in recommending the next steps in child care to policy makers.

It appeared to the editors that an interdisciplinary, well-prepared, symposium of academics and child care policy experts would allow barriers to policy reform to be identified and alternative solutions debated. Seven key issues were defined (these are outlined below) and two major presentations were commissioned on each issue. In most cases, papers were written in advance, refereed by a committee of academics and policy experts, and then revised for the symposium. Several of the presentations were prepared speeches – Bob Rae's speech on federal-provincial issues in the first session, and two lunchtime speeches; these were not refereed in advance. There were two, and sometimes three, discussants in each session; in most cases they had received and reviewed authors' papers some weeks in advance of the symposium. After the symposium, discussants submitted written versions of their comments, and paper presenters were given an opportunity for rebuttal or reflection on these comments. The two editors of this volume summarized the floor discussion from their notes; in most cases the floor discussion was frank, open, and pointed.

It is important that the reader understand that, despite the disagreements and debates reflected in this volume, the participants in the symposium – and particularly the authors of the main chapters – hold similar general views about the desirability of a comprehensive public child care strategy for Canada. They believe that children benefit from high-quality child care and are hurt by low-quality and haphazard child care arrangements. They agree that there is a public interest in good care for children. They support a significant increase in the amount of public money flowing into child care. Despite disagreements on how subsidization of services should be structured, and how services should best be organized and provided, there is consensus that all Canadian children ought to be able to access good child care. Thus, they share the views of the editors that it is important for Canada to find its way around the obstacles that, so far, have impeded movement towards a Canada-wide program of early childhood care and education. In other words, the debates in this volume centre on how to achieve universally accessible child care, not on whether universally accessible child care services are desirable. This focus represents a conscious choice, made in organizing the symposium, not to include debates with token opponents of child care to provide a false sense of impartiality to the proceedings. Readers desiring these contrary opinions can, of course, find them elsewhere.

   This book, then, represents the current thinking on child care policy – and on how to advance that policy – of some of Canada's foremost academic experts and policy advocates. As such, it can make an important contribution to understanding how Canada, with its particular institutions, history, politics, and values, should design a national child care strategy.

THE SEVEN SYMPOSIUM TOPICS

This introduction concludes with the description of the seven key topics discussed at the symposium, each representing one part of this volume. This list and description is substantially unchanged from its original form in 1998 when the symposium idea was born. Not all of the questions were answered. Some were ignored. Some new ones arose. As anticipated, the symposium grew beyond the vision that spawned it. But this basic outline survived and formed the framework for what follows.

Part 1   Child Care and the Social Union: Who Should Do What?

Apparently, a major expansion of child care services would be the formal constitutional responsibility of the provinces. Quebec has already taken major strides, both within and outside the education system, to provide universal child care services at reduced fees to parents. However, other provinces show few signs of pursuing this initiative, and even Quebec may not have the fiscal capacity to achieve its child care objectives.

There has, in the past, been a tradition of federal initiatives and federal-provincial cooperation in this area. Under the Canada Assistance Plan, for instance, the federal government matched provincial expenditures on child care directed at low income recipients and children at risk. In recent years, the federal government has withdrawn from matching funding, while provincial governments have been suspicious of federal cost-sharing initiatives. Given the substantial fiscal capacity of the federal government, relative to the provinces, it seems likely that the federal government must play some role in any major expansion of child care services across Canada.

Given that a substantial expansion of good child care services across Canada is necessary, what should be the respective reponsibilities of the federal and of the provincial and territorial governments for this expansion of services and for funding programs? Do those levels of government have the necessary constitutional authority, the financial ability, and the public support to carry out these responsibilities? What should change to allow governments to carry out their responsibilities?

What are the first steps for governments to take, in 2000 and after, to build a system of good child care services in Canada? How should the funding be designed and what are the funding priorities? Will there be national standards governing the quality of care provided? Will these arrangements be politically acceptable (and fiscally acceptable) in Quebec and other provinces? What lessons about implementation can we learn from other countries that have implemented such programs over time?

Part 2   What the Rest of Canada Can Learn from Quebec and from Other Countries

Other countries have used a variety of different systems for delivering care to young children, and have addressed all the questions discussed in this book in a variety of ways. What evidence is there on how outcomes for children and families vary according to the choices that are made? And how did countries get from here to there – that is, how did they develop their child care systems, and what lessons can Canada draw on as it designs a more comprehensive child care system? Equally relevant, for Canadians outside Quebec, the Government of Quebec has embarked, since 1997, on a radical restructuring of its policies on child care and early education. Many preschool children now attend regulated services at a cost to parents of only $5 per day, and the system is gradually expanding to include all preschool children who wish to use it. How did Quebecers, and the Quebec government become convinced of the desirability and feasibility of these reforms? What can other provinces learn about child care program design from these innovations in Quebec?

Part 3   What Is Good Quality Child Care and How Do We Get It?

We all want good quality child care, but what does that mean? Does that mean structured or unstructured care for preschool children; will the care be educational, or oriented towards children's developmental stages? Is there a 'best' kind of programming for young children, or does this depend on the age of the child, the personality of the child, the family background and abilities of the child? What is the role of national (or provincial or territorial) standards? Should centres and family homes be allowed to try out different combinations of education of staff, staff-child ratios, group sizes, or should these be strictly regulated? What is the role of innovation and variety in serving the needs of children and parents? What is the role of parental choice in determining the quality of care for their children? How much 'quality' can we realistically afford? What trade-offs are conceivable and which ones are not?

**Part 4   How Will Good Child Care Services Be Delivered:
          Education System or Community Services?**

Canadian child care centres have largely been private, with an increasing predominance of non-profit providers; the non-profit or profit status of licensed family child care providers is unclear. Kindergarten services for five- and, sometimes, four-year-olds are provided through the public school system. How will any substantial expansion of child care services in Canada be provided – through the public sector, by non-profit organizations, or in some other way? How will public funding and public management of the new child care system ensure efficient, cost-effective, publicly accountable, and responsive provision of child care services? Are there important issues of incentives and management that we must be sure to 'get right'? Will child care centres 'compete' with each other to serve parents and children in the best way? If private non-profit centres are part of the system, how will religious-based or other interest-based centres and family homes fit in? What requirements will be placed on for-profit centres, if these continue to exist? If the system relies primarily on public provision, how will the transition be made? Will the existing public school system be expanded, or will new institutions be designed? Will the current division between public and separate schools be carried over into the child care sector? Will 'charter' day care centres be encouraged? What kinds of experimentation on provision will be permitted?

Part 5 What Family Policies Are Needed to Complement Universal Child Care?

Child care policy is only one part of a much larger group of social policies designed to help families thrive as they try to cope with the financial and time demands of children. There seems to be considerable agreement that organized, good quality child care for children two to five years of age is beneficial. There is less agreement about other aspects of the support governments should provide to families. For instance, should infant care be primarily out-of-home, or should extended parental leaves and other supports be primary?

The issue to be discussed in this part is 'family policy.' Different countries have adopted very different approaches to family policy. Sweden's family policy is strongly oriented to maintaining labour force attachment; France is oriented to supporting either labour force attachment or a decision to have substantial time off when children are young. Italy, Spain, Denmark, and the Netherlands all have different types of family policies, of which their child care policies are only a part. What should the general objectives and elements of Canada's family policy be? And how should eligibility for child care services, maternity or parental leave and benefits and financial assistance to single- and two-parent families be arranged to support these objectives?

In particular, how will family policy support families in making the most appropriate care arrangements for infants? And how will family policy support families in decisions about whether mothers will be regularly employed in the paid labour force when children are young, or at home providing intensive care for their own children? There is currently an ideological divide between those who champion mothers staying at home to care for children and those who favour continuous labour force attachment and good child care services. Yet most mothers play both of these roles at different times in their lives, and future child care services will probably have to address the needs of both groups. How should child care and family policy address the needs of parents to spend time with their children and to earn income as well?

Part 6   Single Parents, Child Poverty, and Children at Risk: What Special Child Care Policies Are Needed?

Much of the public funding to date has focused on children from poor families – largely those with single parents – and those at risk. This 'welfare' approach to child care funding is at odds with a system that extends funding to all parents. Yet the needs of disadvantaged children and of their parents may be different from those of other families. How can these needs be addressed within a comprehensive system? Will new child care policies provide appropriate incentives, encouragement, and support to ensure parents enter the job market, develop new skills, and get off social assistance? Should Head Start–type programs be providing more enriched child care and parental supports to certain families, while regular child care services provide a normal level of services? Should there be a range of different types of programming available for different families and/or children? What role should child care play in the National Children's Agenda (the federal-provincial-territorial discussions on policies for children due to culminate in December, 2000)?

Specifically, there are two general policy issues in this area. First, there is the issue of how general funding for child care is integrated with the welfare system. Welfare payments to single parents have high tax-back rates that implicitly assume that these mothers will not generally want to work. Yet day care funding is based on the premise that these mothers will have a continuing connection to the workforce. How then can these views be reconciled? How can the welfare system be altered so as to continue support to these families while expecting them to work? Second, comprehensive day care assumes that all children need similar types of care. Yet we have traditionally attempted to direct larger amounts of resources to children at risk. Are these two views compatible?

Part 7 Child Care Workers: What Qualifications, Pay, and Organizations Should They Have?

Child care is an extremely labour-intensive service. The skills, knowledge, experience, and efforts of the caregivers are primary determinants of the quality of the care and the developmental effects on children. The wages, benefits, and staff-child ratios are, at the same time, primary determinants of the public and private cost of care. What government policies and human resource policies are necessary in order to maximize the benefits from good child care while keeping costs within reason?

There is a trade-off between the educational expectations we have of day care workers and the salaries we pay. Specifically, day care workers have been paid dramatically lower salaries than kindergarten teachers in public schools, yet both work with the same children. The result is that while teachers usually remain in their profession for a long period of time, day care workers tend to be more transitory. This goes to the basic question of what kind of job we envision for workers in the child care sector.

What should the pay, benefits, and responsibilities of child care workers be? What should the 'occupational ladder' of child care workers look like, and what should be the educational and experience requirements of different levels? What is the role of unions and professional associations in determining compensation and other conditions of work? What is the role of child care workers and their organizations in defining and maintaining quality child care services, and what is the role of regulation, policy and funding initiatives? How will we address these issues, especially in a transitional period of change and expansion for child care services?

Notes

1 H. Goelman, A.R. Pence, D.S. Lero, M. Brockman, N. Glick, and J. Berkowitz, *Where Are the Children? An Overview of Child Care Arrangements in Canada* (Ottawa: Statistics Canada, Catalogue 89-527E), 1993, 35.

2 Special Parliamentary Committee on Child Care, *Sharing the Responsibility: Report of the Special Committee on Child Care* (Ottawa, 1987), Table A15, 151.

3 Ibid.

4 Special runs from Cycle 1, National Longitudinal Study on Children and Youth, by Prof. Douglas E. Hyatt, unpublished.

5 J. Beach, J. Bertrand, and G. Cleveland, *Our Child Care Workforce: From*

Recognition to Remuneration – A Human Resource Study of Child Care in Canada (Ottawa: Child Care Human Resources Steering Committee, 1998), Table 1, 3.

6 The federal government has recently announced plans to extend maternity and parental benefits to a full year.

7 The role of the Child Care Expense Deduction in creating horizontal tax equity between parents in one-earner and two-earner families is discussed in M. Krashinsky, and G. Cleveland, *Tax Fairness for One-Earner and Two-Earner Families: An Examination of the Issues* (Ottawa: Canadian Policy Research Networks, 1999), discussion paper no. F07.

8 Childcare Resource and Research Unit, *Statistics Summary: Canadian Early Childhood Care and Education in the 1990s* (Toronto: University of Toronto Press, 1999).

9 Gillian Doherty, D. Lero, J. Tougas, H. Goelman, and A. LaGrange, *Centre Resources and Expenditures* (2000), Preliminary Report from the You Bet I Care! project at www.cfc-efc.ca/docs/00001311.htm, p. 4.

10 Ibid.

11 Ibid.

12 See the excellent studies on social values related to child care published by the Canadian Policy Research Networks in Ottawa, e.g., K. O'Hara and S. Cox, *Securing the Social Union* (1998) and J. Michalski, *Values and Preferences for the 'Best Policy Mix' for Canadian Children* (1999).

PART 1

Child Care and the Social Union:
Who Should Do What?

Introduction

The first session of the conference dealt with the quintessential Canadian problem: how to develop and finance a coherent national child care policy in Canada when the Constitution clearly gives responsibility for education and welfare to the provinces. This is not an abstract academic concern. Several times in the past two decades, Conservative and Liberal federal governments have declared a strong interest in expanding direct funding of child care services, yet, in the end, have failed to act. Lack of consensus among provincial and territorial governments about the design of federal assistance has been cited as a key barrier to federal action.

In the past, child care policy evolved as a shared responsibility of federal and provincial or territorial authorities. Under the Canada Assistance Plan introduced in the 1960s, the federal government matched provincial and territorial expenditures on child care directed at children in low-income families and children at risk. But over the past decade and more, the federal government has withdrawn from this kind of shared-cost funding. And Quebec and other provinces have become increasingly wary of federal promises and federal involvement in areas traditionally under provincial purview.

On the other hand, it is clear that any major Canada-wide child care initiative would have to receive significant federal funding and encouragement. For one thing, there appears to be growing concern among federal politicians about societal effects of poor child development. Furthermore, the emerging federal budget surplus and the periodic federal interest in child care spending suggests that such an initiative would be politically possible and politically attractive. The importance to federal politics of the women's vote is another factor. And the federal government is already involved in children's issues through the Canada Child Tax Benefit, the Child Care Expense Deduction, and the income tax system in general.

At the beginning of the twenty-first century, direct federal funding for child care services would have to take place in the context of the 'social union,' a negotiated compact between the provinces and the federal government which requires the agreement of a significant number of provinces for any new national social program, and which allows opting out by provinces that already have committed funds in that area.

Because of the importance of this issue for child care in Canada, this first session was allocated more time than the other individual sessions, and an unusual format was chosen. Martha Friendly, a long-time expert in the child care policy field, and a frequent advocate of stronger federal child care initiatives, was invited to prepare a paper on how a national program might be developed within the context of the social union, and that appears as the opening chapter of Part 1. Bob Rae, the ex-premier of Ontario with a long-standing commitment to child care and a deep interest in federal-provincial issues, was invited to present on the topic, having seen the first draft of Martha Friendly's piece in advance. An edited version of his speech follows the Friendly chapter.

Two discussants, Tom Kent and Alfred MacLeod, offered comments on the Friendly paper and the Rae speech. Again because of the importance of the topic and because the discussants did not have the Rae speech in advance, they were given considerable latitude in the scope of their remarks. Tom Kent has a long experience in federal-provincial matters, having been the federal bureaucrat who more than thirty years ago designed the federal-provincial hybrid that became the Canadian medicare system. We anticipated that his expertise in negotiating with the provinces would help provide insight into how such negotiations might take place within the context of the 'social union.' Alfred MacLeod is currently a researcher and pollster with an interest in child care, and he has also served in recent years in senior policy advisory positions in the Office of the Prime Minister and of Human Resources Development Canada (HRDC). We expected that he might comment on both presentations with some sense of what public opinion might and might not tolerate.

The first session was chaired by Charles Pascal, the administrative head of the Atkinson Foundation, and former deputy minister from Community and Social Services in Ontario with a commitment to early childhood education and a sense of how negotiations between Ontario and the federal Government have taken place in the past.

The session was a lively one, as expected. Although the principal speakers did not agree on all issues, they did agree that the time was ripe for the evolution of child care in Canada. Martha Friendly suggested the need for and possibility of federal leadership. Bob Rae supported the spending of federal dollars, but was more concerned about the need for garnering support for child care from all levels of government.

Martha Friendly took the position that the social union does allow for the development of a national child care policy. Such a policy would require federal leadership (and money), but the social union provides a possible and useful framework for the negotiations that might take place. The provinces would each run their own child care programs, but these programs would have to meet pre-agreed national goals. Given the essential nature of child care at this point in time, Friendly suggests that our attempt to negotiate a national child care policy should and will be seen as a test of our ability to function as a nation in the years to come. In that sense, she argues that child care is the 'canary in the coal mine' – if child care policy evolves and takes on life, then it will suggest that the Canadian union is itself alive and well; conversely, the failure of the federal and provincial governments to negotiate a child care policy will signal the deep divisions within the country and raise serious questions about the viability of any national policy within the current context of federal-provincial relations.

Bob Rae indicated his general agreement on a number of issues with Friendly. He too suggested that a national child care policy was essential, and that its time had come. However, he cautioned against relying exclusively on the federal government. The provinces are unlikely to sign on to any new program without considerable financial commitments from the federal government, and the history of the past twenty years – years in which the federal government backed away from shared cost programs to block funding that itself was later cut – makes the provinces suspicious of any federal initiative. Rae suggested that what might further the child care agenda is a series of provincial initiatives that could then be picked up and advanced by the federal government and its dollars. Rae reminded the symposium that this model had considerable antecedents; the evolution of medicare in Canada followed the lead of Saskatchewan and the Tommy Douglas government.

Tom Kent and Alfred MacLeod reacted to both presenters not simply as critics of the papers, but by providing their own original ideas on child care. Tom Kent suggested that, in fact, the medicare example was leading us in the wrong direction. Cost-sharing was a 1960s phenomenon that arose out of a unique set of circumstances and was unlikely to be repeated. He suggested that federal leadership would have to occur in different ways. He proposed that the federal government might use the tax system to channel money to child care services, and invited the provinces to develop policies on child care that would use that money in certain ways.

Alfred MacLeod suggested that we would only get a national child care policy when there was clear public support for it. This requires showing the public not only why we need child care, but designing a specific proposal for how that child care assistance might be delivered. The most important shift in the past few years has been the emergence of the view that child care is an essential component of early childhood education and is not simply a support to mothers' employment objectives. However, there remain considerable cleavages within public opinion on the values surrounding the role of mothers, employment, child-rearing, and child care.

1. Child Care and Canadian Federalism in the 1990s: Canary in a Coal Mine

Martha Friendly
Centre for Urban and Community Studies, University of Toronto

INTRODUCTION

Why Early Childhood Care and Education Is a Matter of National Importance

By the end of the 1990s there was a convergence of ideas about why good quality child care is an issue of national importance for Canadians. A National Council of Welfare study is a good reflection of contemporary thinking about the importance of early childhood care and education not only for individual Canadian children and families but for Canadian society-at-large:

Good child care makes an enormous difference in the ability of poor families to find and keep jobs. Affordable child care supports those families that are not poor stay in the workforce. But beyond all this, good child care is an excellent opportunity to provide early childhood education and to ensure that all children have the same chances for good development. Good early childhood education has enormous benefits for children, their families and their communities. All the population health research tells us that early childhood experiences are among the most important determinants of a person's health ... Preventing problems and ensuring that children have the best possible early development makes good economic sense.

Many social programs support families but child care is the backbone of them all.[1]

Research and policy analysts in diverse fields – economics, health and medicine, education, and human rights – have come to support traditional advocates in feminist, social justice, and trade union circles to insist that action on child care is imperative. There is broad recognition that a strategy for developing early childhood services that offer both early childhood education to strengthen healthy development for all children and child care to support the participation of mothers in the labour force is in the public interest.[2]

This view that early childhood care and education is a public good is now advanced by experts from economics,[3] health,[4] education,[5] and with social perspectives.[6] At the same time, early childhood care and education is a fundamental part of a human rights agenda, both from the point of view of the child[7] and the parents (or mothers).[8]

That Canada does not provide adequate early childhood care and education has been well documented and is not in dispute. In the 1990s Canadian child care is as characterized by inadequacy, fragmentation, and incoherence, as it was two decades ago. The mishmash of services offers 'education,' mostly part-day kindergarten for almost all five-year-olds. However, as it is part-day, and of only one year's duration, Canadian preschoolers' early opportunities are more limited than those of their peers in most mainland European nations where virtually all three- to five-year-olds attend publicly funded full school-day programs. To fill this gap, some preschoolers younger than kindergarten age attend part-day nursery schools, regulated in most provinces as child 'care'– if their parents can afford to pay.

The labour force participation rate of Canadian women with children aged zero to six has been above 65 per cent for some years, and it is higher than in many other industrialized nations. Yet the availability of good quality care for their children has improved little in the past two decades with the vast majority of children cared for in informal arrangements that are by no stretch of the imagination 'early childhood education.' Child 'care' services to permit parents' workforce participation are in short supply, meeting only about 12 per cent of the need, and inadequately funded so that they are often too expensive for ordinary parents. Early childhood educators and other caregivers earn poor wages and believe that their work is not valued by the public.[9]

While most early childhood care and education services are under provincial aegis, several other early childhood programs with similar objectives are fully funded by and the responsibility of the federal government. The federal government also delivers a tax deduction directly to parents to cover the cost of work-related 'care.'

Every aspect of early childhood education and child care varies widely across Canada's provinces and territories – the range of services offered, eligibility, funding, statutory requirements for their provision, monitoring, and enforcement of standards – and there may be almost as much range within provinces as there is among them. The objectives of programs providing early childhood care and/or education range from 'providing opportunities for healthy child development' to 'ensuring that children are "ready to learn" at school-entry age' to 'providing a "head start" for children at-risk' to 'supporting the transition of single mothers from welfare to work' to 'supporting the workforce participation costs of parents with young children.'[10]

It is sometimes suggested that this wide variety is an appropriate response to regional diversity in community needs. In reality, however, early childhood care and education services in most of Canada have been developed so incoherently that although each province and territory has a tangle of programs, only a small minority of children and families have access to the services they need or that their parents want. A statement made by a 1988 Senate committee studying child care still rings true in 1999: Provincial child care programs resemble each other ... in what they lack ... our intention is ... to suggest how rudimentary [the] system really is.[11]

In 1988 the Canadian National Child Care Study defined 'child care' as 'any form of care ... while parents were engaged in paid or unpaid work, study, or other personal or social activities.'[12] Thus, the study's concept of 'child care' did not include kindergarten, nursery school, or other early childhood programs for socialization, education, or healthy development unless they were linked with parental activities.

Since then, however, the definition of child care has shifted so that it is now closely linked not only to parents' activities (usually employment or training) but to the idea that early childhood education is essential for optimal healthy development.[13] Thus, it is understood that it is possible and desirable to include both 'care' and 'early childhood education' within one inclusive service, as European nations do. The term 'early childhood care and education' or 'early childhood development' underlines a shift in emphasis away from segregated services – oriented or restricted to children with working parents, or to advantaged children whose parents want to provide optimal developmental opportunities, to poor children, children with disabilities, children whose mother is in a training program, or children at risk – to a coherent, well-designed, inclusive system of services that can provide both care and early education for all children, and support for their parents, both in and out of the paid workforce. A UNICEF education report sums up the contemporary wisdom about this when it says, 'There is a growing consensus that childcare and early education are inseparable.'[14]

What Is This Chapter About?

Given its importance, why has Canadian child care and early childhood education never developed beyond a rudimentary level but even deteriorated in the 1990s? Why has a nation able to create a national system of health care, at one time recognized as one of the best in the world, not been able to create a social program to support the healthy development of its youngest children? A number of analysts have examined this question (or related questions), putting forward rationales that draw conclusions about the strength of maternalism, beliefs about the role of government, how women's groups relate to government, and the nature of legal systems.[15]

However, it is apparent that at least on one level, part of the answer lies within the nature of Canadian federalism, especially as federal-provincial understandings have shifted in the 1990s.[16] For example, in their 1997 analysis, Bach and Phillips postulate that child care could be 'the first fatality of the construction by the Federal and Provincial governments of a New Social Union,'[17] and Boismenu and Jenson suggest that philosophies about social programs in Quebec and the rest of Canada have diverged so much that the creation of a pan-Canadian child care strategy may no longer be possible.[18]

Is this so? Will Canada never have the pan-Canadian national child care program that has been envisaged for so many years? As Quebec begins to develop its own program, will the rest of Canada ever have comparable child care services? Will our incapacity to provide for young children mean that child care is the 'canary in the coal mine' that signals that Canadian federalism is not working?

This chapter examines the federal-provincial jurisdictional obstacles to a national child care strategy, especially those that arose in the 1990s. The key questions I try to answer are: What jurisdictional barriers have hindered the formation of a national child care strategy in Canada? Can the barriers be overcome? What strategies are needed to overcome them? What issues need to be addressed to ensure that a national child care program – one 'as comprehensive and universally accessible as medicare and education'[19] is established in Canada?

This chapter begins with several assumptions. First, early childhood care and education is a matter of national importance. Second, it is in the public interest to ensure that these services become widely available to all children. Third, because provision of early childhood care and education is in the public interest, public policy is the appropriate delivery vehicle. Finally, it assumes that some of the answers to the questions I try to answer can be found in an examination of federalism in the past decade.

The chapter first examines how a national child care program has been envisioned over the years, and clarifies the roles and responsibilities of the various levels of government that have been proposed. Then, it examines the three failed attempts to secure a national child care strategy in the context of the shifting federalism over the decade between 1984 and 1995. The third part of the chapter is an analysis of child care within the concept of the 'social union' that began to be debated as the federal role in social programs waned in the 1990s. Finally, the Social Union Framework Agreement of February 1999 (between the federal government and all provinces and territories except Quebec) and the possibilities it offers for a national child care program are appraised. I take the position that the agreement's principles and stated objectives create not only a new imperative for a national child care strategy but provide new opportunities for implementation. I also argue that federal leadership is necessary for the success of any national child care strategy, and propose that because it is an issue of national importance, an effective national child care strategy should be used as a benchmark against which to evaluate nation-shaping political arrangements like the Social Union Framework Agreement.

MODELS OF CHILD CARE AND PATTERNS OF FEDERALISM: HISTORY, CONTEXT, AND FRAMEWORK

What Does 'A National Child Care Program' Mean? Who Does What?

Even after twenty years of public debate about child care, there remain misunderstandings about the proposed roles and responsibilities of the various levels of government in a national child care program. This is epitomized by the question sometimes posed to child care advocates:

'But you don't really think that the federal government should run child care centres, do you?'

Over the past two decades, many government task forces and many non-governmental groups have recommended a 'national child care program.' None of these has suggested that child care services be designed, managed, maintained, or delivered by the federal government.

The federal government's role has generally been seen as maintaining an overarching policy framework of national principles and providing financing, usually under a cost-sharing agreement. The role of provincial or territorial governments has been envisioned as optional participation in the program (as it is optional in medicare), and designing, developing and maintaining a provincial program with a variety of service possibilities (for example, part-day, full-day, flexible hours, centre-based, and family day care) under provincial regulation. The overall provincial program and the range of services would be designed to meet the requirements of the individual provinces but would fit within the overarching national principles. Finally, service development and delivery have almost always been viewed as local responsibilities with extensive participation of voluntary groups, community groups, and local government.[20]

Perhaps the best way to conceptualize a national child care program – as it has been proposed throughout the past decade – is to adapt Kent's description of medicare: We cannot have, constitutionally, a national health service. We have ten provincial medicare programs that are based on common principles, and are therefore consistent enough to provide the same kind of service to all Canadians.[21]

Common Ground

A national day care act was first proposed by the Royal Commission on the Status of Women in 1970, and between 1984 and 1995 there were three significant attempts to develop a national child care strategy. Each of these – the 1986 Task Force on Child Care (the Katie Cooke Task Force), the 1987 Special Committee on Child Care, and the 1993–5 Liberal/Axworthy proposals – was initiated and led by the federal government.[22] Analysis of these three child care projects suggests that although between 1986 and 1995 there was a shift towards a more assertive provincial role, a central position for the federal government continued to be part of the concept of a national child care program throughout the decade.

Although there were critical differences among the details of the three proposed child care strategies, they shared some common ground in the way they viewed the roles of the different levels of government. Each proposed that: (1) the initiative would be 'put on the table' by the federal government; (2) opting in by the provinces would be voluntary; (3) substantial federal funding would be provided through some sort of cost-sharing arrangement as an enticement to the provinces to partici-pate; (4) provincial funding would also play a key role; (5) developing and maintaining overarching policy would be the responsibility of the federal government; (6) the provinces and territories would be respon-sible for program design and development, service delivery, and man-agement; and (7) within the conception of a comprehensive (varied) delivery system, provincial (and local) variation would shape the de-tails of service delivery.

The advocacy and public interest groups that pressed governments to take action on child care throughout the 1980s and 1990s generally concurred with these proposed characteristics (although there was cer-tainly no solidarity with some governments regarding specific details). Thus, governments and non-governmental organizations perceived the roles of the respective levels of government in a relatively common way.

Throughout the years of federal activity on child care, there was constant debate about the respective roles of federal and provincial governments on child care. Striking a balance between federal govern-ment leadership and provincial autonomy was never simple but was always fraught with difficulty.

The fragility of this balance was explicitly captured in the 1995 an-nouncement that the federal government was embarking on its prom-ised child care strategy. Describing it as a 'partnership offer to the provinces and territories of $630 million over three to five years to be followed with on-going funding for the maintenance of the spaces that are developed,' the minister of human resources development com-mented that 'because this is very much in the jurisdiction of the prov-inces, we have to be sensitive and responsive to what their priorities are.' He said: 'This is a national program. We want to make sure that it is available to children right across Canada. I don't want to prejudge what the provincial responses will be. This is clearly within their juris-diction, and their right to respond.'[23]

Thus, throughout the decade ending in 1995, a decade of debate on a national child care policy, there was an awareness of the need to respect the roles of both the federal and provincial governments. While there were always significant tensions about the relative strengths of the federal government and the provinces, it was possible for the federal government to 'take the first step' on child care.

Three-Time Failure of a National Child Care Strategy

In 1984, 1986, and 1995 three successive federal governments announced that a national strategy for child care would be developed, and each time no such policy materialized. What dynamics ensured the three-time failure of child care, and what lessons can be learned from these past efforts?

1984: The End of the Liberal Legacy
Shortly before the 1984 federal election, the Liberal federal government announced that the Task Force on Child Care would 'examine ... the need for child care services and paid parental leave ... as well as the federal government's role in the development of a system of quality child care in Canada.'[24] By the time the Liberal task force's report was released in 1986, a Conservative government had been in power for two years. The report recommended that child care become a publicly funded program available to all children to be organized by the provinces and delivered locally. The federal role would be 'leadership in developing stable, available, affordable child care' and 'funding through the provinces'; the provinces were to 'retain jurisdiction and a funding role.'[25] It was no surprise that the report of the Task Force on Child Care was put on the shelf when it was released in 1986, two years into the new government's mandate.

1987: Child Care the Tory Way
Even before the Liberal task force's final report was released, the Conservative government of Brian Mulroney set up its own federal committee to study child care. The reasons this new committee failed are more complicated than a simple change of federal regime. This committee held cross-Canada public hearings to 'talk to the people.' But when the committee's Conservatives issued their majority report, *Sharing the Responsibility*, in 1987, the details of the recommendations aroused the ire of the social activists who had lobbied hard for universal, publicly funded child care services, and opposed the tax deductions for parents, and the for-profit services the Tories proposed. The recommendations

were widely criticized as reducing federal leadership, failing to establish federal principles or standards, and expanding the role of the minister of finance in a social program.[26]

At the time that the national child care strategy was debated, between 1986 and 1988, the intricacies of federal-provincial tensions and how they affected child care were not really understood (although the importance of the federal role was) by social activists. However, in retrospect it became apparent that the child care proposals both reflected and presaged the key policy directions of the Mulroney government, especially in its second term. Phillips's analysis of the 1987 child care strategy connects the contentious details of the proposed policy (the absence of national standards, expansion of tax deductions, and encouragement of for-profit child care) to 'the Conservative view of a collaborative, decentralized federalism.' Phillips contends that the child care strategy 'clearly emphasized the Conservative vision of a market system ... It both anticipates and reflects the Meech Lake Constitutional Accord because it deliberately and carefully avoided interfering with provincial jurisdiction to shape the nature of the child care system and represented a self-imposed restraint on the use of the federal spending power. Finally, the child care legislation shows the importance of expenditure restraint that will ever be central to the Conservatives in their second term.'[27]

Why did the Conservative's national child care strategy fail? The Mulroney government's public opinion polling showed that there was a public perception that the Conservatives were weak on social policy, and analysts believed that they wanted to pass the Child Care Act before an election was called – as a centrepiece of the campaign.[28] But the strategy provoked so much criticism that the unpopularity of the proposals may have made child care a no-win situation for the government.[29] Indeed, the Child Care Bill died as the 1988 federal election was called. It became evident later on that the legacy of the failed Mulroney child care strategy fuelled the growing mistrust of federal initiatives by the provinces and contributed to a negative view of child care's 'bad history' among senior federal bureaucrats. *Sharing the Responsibility* went onto the shelf beside the *Report of the Task Force on Child Care.*

1993: The Red Book
The Liberal's platform for the 1993 election was a departure from tradition. It spelled out, and even costed its promises, and then popularized them. Their *Red Book* promised to expand regulated child care dramati-

cally, adding an additional $720 million over three years to funds already spent through the Canada Assistance Plan. The cost would be shared in equal amounts by the provinces, with parents contributing an additional 20 per cent. The promise was contingent upon a 3 per cent annual increase in economic growth and provincial willingness to participate.

Following the Liberal victory, Human Resources Development Canada began to work to meet the child care commitment. A major review of social programs, the Social Security Review (SSR), was also announced. An SSR discussion paper was released in 1994 that identified child care as central to three areas: employment, learning, and security.[30] The government's supplementary paper on child care offered a vision for child care and development across Canada that addressed the common themes of quality, availability, affordability, and comprehensiveness. It recommended the 'incorporation of a framework of principles to guide and consolidate investments in child care and development,'[31] and concluded by restating the federal government's 'commitment to improving Canada's child care system, and to developing, with governments, parents, and the public, a national framework for child care and development.'[32]

It should be noted that during the travelling public hearings, it did not seem as though provincial governments were opposed to a review of national social programs by the federal government without their participation. The need for a national approach to child care arose again and again from the public at the hearings.[33] The final report of the SSR noted widespread support for a child care program with a 'more dedicated funding approach' and 'a need to revamp the way the federal government finances child care.' It posed the question: 'How do we move towards this new social vision for Canada?'[34]

The 1995 Federal Budget: The Turning-Point
The question asked in the SSR report was soon answered: the report joined the growing pile on the government's shelf. The federal government decided to take a radically different approach to reforming social programs. Two major issues absorbed the federal government in 1995: fiscal anxieties related to the deficit and tension about the possible separation of Quebec. The failure of the Meech Lake and Charlottetown accords (both of which advanced a larger role for the provinces in social programs) and diminishing federal dollars for health and social programs contributed to growing decentralist aspirations among all the provinces, not just Quebec. Some of the provincial governments, as

deliverers of health, education, and social programs, found that their own neo-conservative, cost-cutting predilections were a good fit with the national milieu of devolution and downsizing; others struggled to balance dwindling revenue with the expectations of their citizens, and, in some cases, their own ideologies.[35] Across the political spectrum, however, there was a pervasive atmosphere of mistrust by the provinces of the federal government, and this was reinforced as apprehension about the deficit took hold in 1995.

Although Canada's fiscal situation had been deteriorating for some time, concern about finances grew as Ottawa's ratio of revenue to spending fell and the size of interest payments on the debt rose in 1994–5.[36] Ottawa's reaction was to reduce its spending by downsizing the public service and downloading the costs of government programs to the next level, the provinces, as well as to individual Canadians through privatization. The 1995 federal budget made massive cuts in transfer payments to provinces and terminated the nation's last conditional cost-shared program, the Canada Assistance Plan (CAP). A new block fund, the Canada Health and Social Transfer (CHST) was created to encompass federal funds for health, social welfare, and post-secondary education. This new unconditional funding scheme marked withdrawal of the federal government from its role in shaping social programs through its spending power – a role that had been instrumental in shaping social programs over a thirty-year period. The end of the Canada Assistance Plan and the creation of the CHST was greeted with consternation by social policy experts and social activists. Child care advocates were particularly apprehensive because the sole federal funds for regulated child care had been contained in the CAP. The planning and negotiation for a new child care strategy by the federal government between 1993 and 1995 had been based on the presumption that the expanded child care services promised in the *Red Book* would be built on a core of existing federal CAP funds reimbursed to the provinces, then about $300 million annually. It was feared that the spending cuts, together with melding health, education, and social transfers into a block fund, would mean that the lion's share of the provinces' shrinking funds would likely go to the health care services so highly valued by the public,[37] so that the CHST would become the Canada *Health* Transfer.

1995 and After: On the Federal-Provincial Highway without a Road Map
It was unfortunate that what had seemed, in 1993, to be a genuine commitment to develop a workable plan for a child care strategy came

precisely at the time when what had begun as an evolution in federal-provincial roles became, in essence, a revolution.

Although the introduction of the CHST seemed to be a natural extension of the federal government's reductions and retreats since the 1970s,[38] it was a much more radical departure from the status quo than had yet occurred, even under the Mulroney Conservatives. Tom Kent has described federal policy as being characterized more by 'retreats than advances.'[39] The Caledon Institute identified the 1995 federal budget as introducing 'the most profound change to social policy since Canada constructed its social security system in the 1950s, 1960s and 1970s ... and [they pointed out] Mr Martin's social security reform went well beyond any options that had been publicly discussed or even considered as part of Mr Axworthy's Social Security Review. [The Canada Health and Social Transfer] gives licence to the federal government to get out of the health and welfare business.'[40]

For child care, this quite clearly meant the end of the vision of a national child care program like medicare with national principles, portability among provinces, and federal funding. In the 1995 budget the child care funds committed in the *Red Book*, and allocated in the 1994 budget (but not spent) disappeared while the conception of child care within Human Resources Development Canada mutated from 'lying at the heart ... of employment, learning and security'[41] to become one of the HRDC's new 'employability tools,' surrendering the concept of child care as a service related to healthy child development. This shift was significant because it had clear implications for how strategies for child care would be developed.

In October 1995 came the referendum on Quebec sovereignty. When a very bare majority of Québecois voted for the status quo within Canada, it shook all of Canada and its federal representatives profoundly. Child care as a potential new national program found itself in the middle of the newly all-consuming national unity agenda, and it was certainly not on the government's front burner. Therefore, it was remarkable, considering the whirlwind of transformations in governance that were under way, that child care remained even on a very faintly flickering back burner, perhaps because of the interest of the federal Human Resources Minister Lloyd Axworthy.[42]

In the late fall of 1995 officials from HRDC and the minister carried out another round of preliminary discussions about the child care program with their provincial counterparts. These exchanges suggested that, despite federal cuts and a national climate of uncertainty that approached hysteria, several provinces, at least, indicated that they would participate in a child care program. Based on this expectation, the federal minister held a press conference on 13 December 1995 in Ottawa to announce that an offer conforming to the *Red Book* commitment had been made to the provinces and territories as the first step to implementing a cost-shared national child care program.[43] The provinces and territories were invited to respond within six weeks.

The Rules of the Game

In the beginning of 1996 Axworthy was replaced as Human Resources Minister by Doug Young, and within a month, a federal 'exit strategy' from the child care announcement surfaced in the press. This strategy consisted of a claim that the initiative was at an end because 'sufficient' interest had not been generated among the provinces.[44] To be sure, the *Red Book* had identified 'obtaining the agreement of the provinces' as a condition for proceeding with the child care commitment.[45] But it had not said how many provinces had to commit for the strategy to be a 'go'; the presumption was that although opting-in was a provincial choice, the program would go ahead even if, initially, only a few provinces participated. This had been the model for building provincial participation in medicare and the Canada Assistance Plan: It seemed that the rules had changed in mid-game.

Media coverage of the exit strategy reported that three provinces had expressed clear interest in moving forward, and that formal federal-provincial bargaining had not yet taken place. However, the federal government insisted that the national child care program had been abandoned because of a lack of provincial interest.[46]

A statement in the Throne Speech of February 1996, reminiscent of the Charlottetown Accord, formalized ex post facto how many provinces 'sufficient' meant, namely, a majority: 'The Government will not use its spending power in areas of exclusive provincial jurisdiction without the consent of a majority of the provinces.'[47] After the exit strategy and the Throne Speech, the conventional wisdom in Ottawa was that a national child care program was 'dead.' Neither child care nor social policy emerged as issues in the 1997 federal election campaign. Child care did not even seem to be a strong contender in the new, emerging federal-provincial discussions of a children's agenda. Child poverty, child health, and then 'readiness to learn' were identified as the children's issues of the day.

CHILD CARE AND THE SOCIAL UNION

The Federal-Provincial Climate after 1995

This analysis examines the steady decline in the federal role in social programs as illustrated by child care policy over the past decade. With the 1995 budget cuts and the CHST as a signal, the social policy environment underwent a radical change as, in an environment of apprehension and concern about federal fiscal downloading, the provinces took the initiative.

In August 1995 the annual meeting of the premiers established the provincial Ministerial Council on Social Policy Reform and Renewal. In December the ministerial council's report to premiers was finalized with the concurrence of all the provinces and territories except Quebec. The report laid out the provinces' approach to national policy; its recommendations spelled out how the provinces and territories should cooperate to 'create a national agenda for social policy reform and renewal which is supported by all First Ministers,'[48] as well as the respective roles of the provincial governments and the Government of Canada. One of the significant elements of this proposal was that *all* responsibility for social services, including child care, would belong to the provinces. This report was to shape the social policy agenda for the next several years.

Although tension between provincial and federal governments is not a new feature of Canadian politics,[49] in the 1990s it grew, encompassing health care, the environment, labour force training, and other areas. What was different this time was that the federal government was not struggling very hard to retain its fiscal influence. In Parliament, the prime minister described his government's actions as: 'The first time a federal government has undertaken formally to restrict the use of its spending power outside a constitutional negotiation.'[50]

There was another way the orientation away from a vigorous federal government affected child care. While it may not be possible to attribute the realignment of roles and responsibilities to any one factor – concern about the deficit and debt, anxiety about the possibility of Quebec separation, or the ideological bent of various governments – a key effect of the realignment was a shift in emphasis from the welfare state to the private sector, from the collective to the individual, and from public services to the market.[51] Although this was not entirely new, in the mid-1990s the growing vacuum at the centre of governance fostered the shift from public to private as neo-conservative and neo-liberal ideology was embraced by governments all across Canada.

In child care, the less collective, more market-oriented ideology is realized through tax deductions, credits, or vouchers to parents (so they can purchase child care), increased reliance on parent fees, and deregulation. A study carried out for Status of Women Canada in 1997 suggests that, even at this early stage of 'devolution, downsizing, and decentralization,' child care services across Canada were already feeling the effects of the changes. The research found diminishing affordability and availability of regulated child care, that a majority of provinces had reduced, frozen, or stopped universal program funding to services (which was often tied to staff wages), that parent fees had risen in relation to family incomes while subsidies for low-income families failed to keep pace with costs, and that an inability to cover their operating costs meant that child care programs had closed or were not staffing spaces. Consistent with a general shift from public services to more privatized approaches to social welfare, the study also identified a re-emergence of the pre-1980s' concept that child care was a program for the needy (rather than a public service for all children).[52]

Six months after the ministerial report became public, a group of national organizations met to respond to the provinces' proposals (to which the federal government had not yet responded), producing a statement to first ministers and social ministers expressing their collective concerns. These were focused on four themes: the federal role; income security proposals, social services, and health; and the decision-making process. A chief concern about social services, especially child care, or early childhood development, was that the 1995 provincial premiers' report had identified 'complete control of human services ... as the quid pro quo ... for a larger federal role in income security.'[53] The statement said that as 'human services – especially investment in early childhood development – is fundamentally important, the federal government was urged to play a leadership role in setting directions for and supporting health and social services.'[54] The group also outlined its concerns about the behind-closed-doors process of decision making.

Experimenting with the Social Union

The term 'social union' began to emerge in the tussle over 'who does what' in Canada's social programs as early as 1996, although there is a wide range of opinion about its meaning. Boismenu and Jenson point out that 'at its origin, the notion of social union is the complement of the idea that Canada is an "economic union that was finally completed" with the Agreement on Internal Trade in 1994.'[55] They point out that while Biggs's version of the social union defines it rather benignly as 'the web of rights and obligations between Canadian citizens and governments that give effect and meaning to our shared sense of social purpose and common citizenship,'[56] it is Courchene's harsher view that the social union is social and economic, and an inevitable response to global economic forces, with the emphasis on the rights of the private sector in a free market, that has been most influential.[57]

In this climate – in which there was tremendous anxiety about the possibility of separation in the wake of the Quebec referendum, a strong pull from the other provinces to decentralization, and very strong pressure from fiscal and ideological conservatives towards downloading to lower levels of government and to individuals – it was inevitable that it would be less than desirable to pursue a national child care program, a concept that had always been identified with national principles and public spending on services.

The 1996 federal Throne Speech had not only formalized the new rules about the introduction of new national programs, it also set the direction for a new and different policy initiative on children. Following a recommendation from the Ministerial Council on Social Policy Reform about consolidating income support for children into a single program, the Throne Speech suggested that the federal government might be willing to discuss how to improve Canada's child support system as a joint initiative with the provinces. The joint initiative eventually emerged in 1998 as the National Child Benefit (NCB).

Characterizing it as 'experimenting with the social union,' Boismenu and Jenson describe the NCB: 'The deal agreed to by all governments, except Quebec, is that Ottawa will individualize its relationship with poor families and their children, via tax credits. This is not new, of course. However, the difference between this initiative and previous social policy decisions is that the reform was co-ordinated *in advance* with provincial governments. Thus, their engagement to "reinvest" the money they will save on social assistance is linked to Ottawa's tax spending.'[58] (The arrangement allowed the provinces to claw-back an amount equivalent to the new portion of the child benefit from the welfare checks of social assistance recipients, thus leaving the provinces some funds to 'reinvest.')

The NCB is very much in the model of the 1997-era social union. The provinces proposed the program. The program development process was joint, around a provincial-federal 'table.' As an income transfer program, the NCB is more clearly in the federal arena than are services, as per the ministerial council report. There are no conditions about how the reinvestment fund – the province's quid pro quo – can be used. Although child care has been chosen for reinvestment by six provinces,[59] there are no national principles that can contribute to a national, pan-Canadian early childhood care and education program.

Have hopes for child care been 'dashed by programs such as the NCB,' as Bach and Phillips suggest?[60] It is certainly true that, as child care was moved off the federal government's agenda, the National Child Benefit was proffered as an alternative. As the National Children's Agenda (announced in May 1999 as a comprehensive strategy to improve the health and well-being of all of Canada's children) has replaced the NCB as the next social union experiment, key policy makers continue to reinforce the notion that child benefits for the poor (income) are interchangeable with an early childhood care and education program for all children (services). As a federal cabinet minister said to the *Globe and Mail*: 'We cannot implement a national child care program. [The Liberal government had tried to initiate a child care program with the provinces but could not get their cooperation.] This is not something we have the ability to initiate. In lieu of that, we came up with the National Child Benefit.'[61]

At the same time, social activists and children's policy experts continue to urge policy makers to consider social policy for children holistically, suggesting that, to be effective, policy for children must include a number of elements. Most analysts include both income security programs, like the child benefit, and early childhood care and education services, followed by other programs like maternity and parental leave, housing, and good jobs for the parents.[62]

The Social Union Framework Agreement: A 'Race to the Top?'

The federal government and nine provincial governments signed the Framework to Improve the Social Union for Canadians on 4 February 1999.[63] This agreement may have some potential to play a role in promoting closure in an era of anxiety and frustration, uncertainty about directions and roles, and a behind-closed-doors approach to policy making that has excluded almost all Canadians. Although the agreement is general and vague, it may – at the least – provide guidance for what comes next, and – at best – facilitate the creation of a national child care program.

The agreement drew a variety of immediate responses, from 'a step backwards,'[64] to 'fudge wrapped up in incomprehensible language,'[65] to 'a step forwards.'[66] Mostly, the public was indifferent and, even worse, knew little about the social union.[67] It is noteworthy that child care has often been used to illustrate what the social union framework agreement could do ('If it had been in place a couple of years ago, we might even have a national child care program today'[68]) or won't do ('Before Thursday, it was hard enough to interest Ottawa in urgent social needs – home care, pharmacare, or child care. Now it will be even harder').[69]

Agreement to the social union framework may mean that we are 'once again on the constitutional merry-go-round,'[70] or it may be 'a promising vehicle, a potentially useful process, an empty vessel into which the meaning, policies, and programs can be poured.'[71] And it may offer new potential – the first since 1996 – for promoting a national child care program.

For child care, the framework agreement can do several things. First, it can provide a vehicle to establish new pressure for child care through its principle and review clauses. Second, it codifies the rules for how funds for social programs are available under the federal spending power, providing some clarity along with impediments. It outlines commitments to accountability, transparency, and collaboration. Finally, it retains the possibility of federal participation in services like child care which had been in question following the report of the ministerial council. The following sections assess the potential windows of opportunity for child care in the framework agreement.

Principles (Clause 1)

The beginning of this chapter describes why early childhood care and education is an issue of national importance. Assuming that it is, the principles agreed to by the first ministers help frame the case that action on child care is imperative.

The two main rationales for child care are, first, enhancing healthy child development and, second, supporting parents' participation in the workforce. Based on these two rationales, high-quality early childhood care and education services are integral to the fulfilment of a number of the agreement's principles – 'equality, individual dignity and responsibility, mutual aid, our responsibilities for each other, promot[ing] equality of opportunity for Canadians, respect[ing] the equality, rights and dignity of all Canadian women and men and their diverse needs, provid[ing] appropriate assistance to those in need, promot[ing] participation of all Canadian's in Canada's social and economic life.'

In addition to these general principles of equality and fairness, the specific commitment to 'ensur[ing] access for all Canadians, wherever they live or move in Canada, to essential social programs and services of reasonably comparable quality' is a very strong principle for child care. The inadequate patchwork of services described in the opening section of this chapter would have been a strong enough motivation to insist that this principle means that the child care situation must be improved. That Quebec has undertaken a program with a goal of universal early childhood education and care strengthens this case considerably, as Canadians outside Quebec lack Quebecers' access to an essential social program of comparable services.

Federal Spending Power (Clause 5)

The federal spending power shapes the funding mechanisms for social programs and, thus, is at the heart of the debate about the social union. In the 1990s the federal spending power was hotly defended as federal transfers diminished, and concern about its decline was key to the opposition of social activists to the Meech Lake and Charlottetown accords.

The federal minister of intergovernmental affairs describes the federal spending power: 'A vital element in social development in all developed federations. In Canada, it has been instrumental in building with the provincial and territorial governments the Canada-wide social programs which all Canadians value, such as Medicare. It has been essential in promoting equality of opportunity for all Canadians, helping to ensure access to basic social programs of reasonably comparable quality to Canadians wherever they live or move in Canada ... the Government of Canada believes that this new formula for intergovernmental cooperation, called "the race to the top" model, will enhance the quality of social and health programs throughout Canada.'[72]

The federal spending power includes two routes, social transfers and direct federal spending. The first, social transfers (cost-sharing and block-funding) have historically allowed the federal government to fund social programs in areas of provincial jurisdiction like health and post-secondary education; the second is through direct federal transfers to individuals and organizations. The spending power, and the activity of the federal government in areas under provincial jurisdiction, are precisely what the provinces, especially Quebec, have challenged, before and throughout the 1990s.

The concept of the federal spending power is well supported by constitutional opinion; it is primarily the specific details and degree of federal intrusion that are challenged. In 1984 the Task Force on Child Care, after an analysis of social transfers and consultation with constitutional experts, concluded that 'the federal spending power ... inferred from the federal power to levy taxes ... provides ample scope to both participate in and influence the design of a new system of child care.'[73] However, the task force was careful to recommend that 'the federal government act with restraint when considering the imposition of conditions on federal funding,'[74] suggesting that national principles (like universality, portability, or high quality) were more appropriate than national standards (like staff-child ratios).

The framework agreement codifies the rules for the use of the federal spending power, and it is apparent that while each presents its difficulties, both social transfers and direct federal transfers offer some possibilities for child care.

Social Transfers
Social transfers to provincial governments have traditionally been used to support programs of services. As already described, the impediment to a cost-shared child care program in 1995 was the requirement that a majority of provinces agree prior to a new national initiative. The framework agreement restates that agreement of a majority of provinces is necessary to initiate a new national program. This is precisely the statement that aroused so much ire at the time of the Charlottetown Accord, and alarm at the time of the 1996 Throne Speech, namely, a commitment to 'not introduce such new initiatives without the agreement of a majority of provincial governments.'[75] This aspect of the agreement led commentators like Thomas Walkom and David Orchard to call it a 'step backward,' ' Meech Lake 3,' and the 'implementation of the Charlottetown Accord by stealth.'[76] (It should be noted that the Charlottetown Accord, but not the Throne Speech, had an additional stipulation that the majority of the provinces must contain a majority of

the population, thus making it virtually impossible that there could be an agreement without either Ontario or Quebec. Thus, for those who support a strong federal government, the framework agreement seems to be a step forward when compared with the Charlottetown Accord because this requirement is missing.)

It does mean that the 'federal spending power' is, in effect, more a national than a federal spending power, as the federal government has formally agreed to cede its authority to use social transfers for new initiatives without provincial permission. It should be noted that although consultation, and even, in some instances, permission, prior to the launch of a new program is not a new phenomenon (even regarding direct transfers to individuals),[77] some of Canada's most significant programs were initiated with only a minority of provinces participating at the outset. Thus, for example, if there had been a requirement that a majority of provinces agree, medicare would probably not have been launched as a national program.

As this chapter has described, virtually all past proposals for a national child care program have recommended cost-sharing. However, the federal government has been phasing out cost-sharing since the 1970s; the Canada Assistance Plan, abolished in 1995, was the last cost-shared program. An important question for child care policy is: Will there be new cost-shared programs in Canada? Kent believes that cost-sharing 'is not the way that new programs of a continuing nature will be introduced.'[78] He goes on to say: 'Because that was how major programs were established, many people still think of it as the natural, almost automatic way to start new programs. It is not: too many politicians, for various but decisive reasons, now dislike it ... similar problems would apply now to the cost-sharing that has often been suggested for child care. In any event, it is not a form of cooperation that either federal or provincial politicians will willingly embrace. A new technique has to be found.'[79]

The social union framework agreement formalizes what has been the status quo since 1995: majority provincial agreement *prior* to initiating a national program that involves social transfers. It is possible that a majority of provinces, motivated by their commitment to the principles of the framework agreement as well by a new spirt of collaboration, would be willing to proceed on introduction of a national child care program, and could agree on principles strong enough to ensure the kind of high-quality early childhood care and education that are now widely understood to be essential. The experience of the past few years has not been encouraging, but perhaps Canada has entered a new era or a new solution will be found.

The use of some form of social transfer would be the traditional route for a child care program. Is it likely or possible that the governments could work collaboratively to 'identify Canada-wide priorities and objectives' for child care services? Could a majority agree? What could encourage them to agree? Would more provinces agree if federal financing were more advantageous?

Prior provincial majority agreement, is, of course, the innovation in mechanism that formally changes the way Canadian social transfers work. Whether it is capable of producing a 'race to the top,'[80] in child care remains to be seen.

Direct Federal Transfers

Another way that the federal government can exercise its spending power is through direct federal transfers to individuals and organizations. The framework agreement describes it as 'direct transfers to individuals or organizations for health care, post-secondary education, social assistance, and social services' (retaining the possibility of federally funded services). Tom Kent has proposed a new technique for child care funding through this route. He suggests that rather than seeking provincial agreement to cost-sharing, the federal government fully fund a national early childhood care and education program through the device of a $7,000 per child annual direct transfer to parents. This idea, which is the first innovative proposal on child care funding in some years, nevertheless has several problems.

There has always been strong opposition from non-governmental organizations to the idea of channelling public funds for child care to parents through vouchers, tax credits, tax deductions, or other 'demand subsidies,' for two reasons. First, an individual payment is connected to the idea that child care is a market-driven, not a public or collective, service. Second, on the practical side, it has never been shown to produce accessible, high-quality early childhood care and education services. Funding to individuals, in essence, has not been shown to be a 'best practice.'[81] Indeed, Kent's proposal includes a caveat that direct payments to individuals 'is certainly not the ideal way to provide the public service of early childhood care and education.'[82]

Another problem with this approach would be the potential political backlash from the provinces. Although the federal government technically has the capacity to make income transfers to individuals in an area of provincial jurisdiction, circumventing the provinces is likely to be considered a serious intrusion even with the consultation required by the framework agreement.

A variation on the theme of individual transfer to parents could be a fully federally funded direct transfer to organizations. Historically, direct transfers to organizations have been used primarily for infrastructure-type programs but there are precedents for direct federal transfers to organizations for child care: child care capital costs were occasionally funded this way as recently as the 1980s. There is a strong argument to be made for a proposal that organizations like municipal governments, school boards, and non-profit organizations – organizations that have contributed much of the innovation in child care services – should receive federal funds through this route, at least to kick-start the stalled child care situation and to motivate innovation.

Although this route may technically be possible, it could be seen to be even more intrusive than individual transfers. It would have the additional drawback of not permitting Quebec to benefit financially from its lead in creating a child care program. It should also be noted that the direct transfer route lacks the opting-out clause that the social transfer route allows.

In summary, under Canada's social union framework agreement, which codifies federal-provincial arrangements for social programs, there are several ways that the federal government could finance a national child care program. While all of these are technically possible, all have significant problems that are primarily political. Does this mean that it is not possible or likely that Canada has a way to organize and finance a national child care program? What is necessary to ensure that the mechanisms codified in the social union framework agreement are not impediments to the national child care program implied in the principles? This will be addressed in the last section.

Public Participation: Public Accountability and Transparency

The social union framework agreement's emphasis on public accountability and transparency adds to its utility for child care. Kent describes how poor governance, 'improvisation,' and about-faces on commitments mean that 'people of good-will have increasingly turned in contempt from party politics.'[83] Perhaps awareness of this climate of cynicism and mistrust of governments motivated the inclusion of fairly extensive possibilities for ensuring public accountability and transparency.

One of the most interesting commitments is to 'ensure effective mechanisms for Canadians to participate in developing social priorities and reviewing outcomes.' If governments are pressed to meet this commitment, it could have implications for child care, as public support for universal early childhood care and education has broadened and deepened. A good example of how this agreement could change government processes is with regard to the National Children's Agenda, a three-year, provincial-federal social union experiment that has, to date, been carried on almost entirely behind closed doors.

The participatory approach extends to the last clause of the agreement promising a full review in three years: the commitment is to 'significant opportunities for input and feedback from Canadians and all interested parties, including social policy experts, private sector and voluntary organizations.'

Quebec

The relationship between Quebec and the rest of Canada is central to the debate about federalism and, thus, to a child care program. One of the aspects of the current child care situation that makes post–social union framework federalism promising is that Quebec has begun to introduce its own national child care program. The Quebec government has promised that a full-blown universal early childhood care and education system will be in place by 2001. As Godfrey and McLean suggest: 'It is Quebec's very strength in the field of early childhood care and education that should encourage the rest of Canada to create a National Project. As Saskatchewan was the model for public health insurance in the 1960s, so too should Quebec be the model for early childhood development.'[84]

That Quebec has already begun to develop its early childhood program means that the social union framework agreement provides an opportunity to use it as a model. Furthermore, the commitment to 'ensure access for all Canadians, wherever they live or move in Canada, to essential social programs and services of reasonably comparable quality' as a principle of the agreement, calls for action on child care outside Quebec in order to meet it.

The agreement also provides a way to allow Quebec to benefit without technically participating through the opting-out provision for social transfer programs: 'A provincial-territorial government which, because of its existing programming, does not require the total transfer to fulfill the agreed objectives would be able to reinvest any funds not required for those objectives in the same or a related priority area.' This could allow Quebec access to federal dollars to expand its early childhood programs or to use for the enhanced maternity leave benefits they have promised or for another related purpose.

Review of the Framework Agreement

The final clause (7) commits to a review of the agreement and its implementation after three years. As the agreement's principles almost invite that child care be a test case for its success, it is obvious that a key advocacy strategy should be to insist that a successful national strategy for early childhood care and education for every child in Canada be a benchmark against which to judge its effectiveness.

There Is Room in the Social Union for Federal Leadership

When the scope for federal leadership today is compared with that of the 1960s and 1970s, the possibilities appear to be limited. However, when the post–framework agreement possibilities for a federal presence are compared with the social program limbo of the latter part of the 1990s, when the echoes of the Charlottetown Accord formed conventional wisdom, one can be grateful and maybe even modestly optimistic. A reasonable conclusion of this analysis of how the social union framework agreement could work on behalf of a national strategy for child care is that, while the routes are not clear, there does seem to be some room for the federal government to take appropriate leadership. Whether it will or not is related to factors like finances, political will, ideology, federal-provincial dynamics, and public pressure. Thus, whether the Government of Canada plays a role in shaping a national child care strategy is related not as much to whether it *should* (for the reasons presented in the Introduction to this chapter) or whether it *could* (as this analysis of the social union framework agreement suggests it can) but more to whether it *will* (or will not).

WHAT HAPPENS NEXT? PROPOSALS FOR ACTION

This chapter lays out some of the history and difficulties of securing a national child care program for Canada, and examines them within the context of evolving federalism. As the previous sections of the chapter illustrate, a set of key political design issues continues to emerge again and again. Unless these are addressed, they will continue to be sticking points.

Key Political Design Issues

Balance between National Principles and Provincial Flexibility
This issue is at the heart of the debate about federalism. The challenge will be to strike a balance between ensuring that national guiding principles are strong enough to 'ensure access for all Canadians, wherever they live or move in Canada, to essential social programs and services of reasonably comparable quality,' as the framework agreement stipulates, and assuring the provinces that their role is not usurped. The concept of best practices in early childhood education and child care policy may help in striking this balance as may the commitments in the framework agreement to public accountability, transparency, and the involvement of non-governmental players in the processes.

Financing
Financing is, of course, always a key political issue. As discussed earlier, child care last came to the table at precisely the wrong time when the deficit and debt were the issues of the day. The end of the 1990s and the beginning of the new decade, as the federal government shows a surplus, and some provincial economies are healthy, may be a better time financially. Concomitantly, financial health is a relative and ideological issue, and economic ideologies very much define how much public funding is available to pay for a public service. Whether governments cut taxes instead of reinvesting money in services for children will be important, and as a national child care program seems likely to arise only if political agreements can be reached between the federal government and the provinces, how the federal government defines its ability to spend money for children will be a key factor. Past experience with initiating social programs indicates that adequate federal financing can go a long way to ensuring that the provincial players want to play.

Convergence of Federal-Provincial Dynamics
From the perspective of federal-provincial dynamics, child care last came onto the agenda at precisely the wrong time, as anxiety about

Quebec separation and demands for power from the other provinces peaked in 1995–6. It will be interesting to see whether agreement to the social union framework by the other nine provinces and the federal government has improved these dynamics, and what other factors (like financing) will actually contribute to a more collaborative federal-provincial dynamic. The absence of Quebec as a signer of the framework agreement, but a potential beneficiary of a national child care strategy, may also be a positive factor in shaping federal-provincial negotiations.

The Backdrop of Expert and Public Opinion
As the Introduction to this chapter describes, expert opinion in a wide variety of areas has come to support the urgency of action on child care – for children, for parents, for women, for communities, for productivity, for health, for Canadian society at large, and for the human or citizenship rights of children. Public opinion endorses government support for child care.[85] The most recent public opinion poll, conducted in 1998 for HRDC, found that 88 per cent of Canadians polled said that they strongly agreed with more government support for a child care program.[86] One of the reasons that child care has garnered broad expert and public support is that, as the Introduction to this chapter describes, it is part of so many diverse agendas. It is for this reason that, however inconvenient it has been for governments, it has not disappeared from public view, but has come back again and again.

The Role of Social Activists
Historically, the social activists who loosely comprise the 'child care movement' have had a key role in the Canadian child care debate, influencing its content and, sometimes, even the outcomes.[87] The circle of those recommending improved child care has expanded considerably, and the rationales have grown and deepened. Whether or not the child care movement will be reinvigorated, new developments like, for example, the Quebec initiative and the opportunities presented by the National Children's Agenda, will be critical.

Federal Leadership
The concept of federal leadership is very much imbedded in all these other key issues. Almost all analyses of the child care situation have concluded that, to solve it, the federal government must take a leadership role.[88] The Task Force on Child Care pointed out more than a

decade ago that the provinces and territories clearly have the capacity and the constitutional mandate to act on child care. Indeed, 'were the capacity to act sufficient in itself, the necessary child care services might already have been provided by provincial governments, acting alone.'[89]

No social program has been developed in this century without a key federal role in making it a national program – health care, public pensions, unemployment insurance, and so on. Indeed, as O'Hara points out in her study of family policy in eight countries, the decentralized federal structure of government in the United States seems to have impeded development of their family policy, too.[90]

The Government of Canada should be prepared to play an active role in making early childhood care and education a pan-Canadian program. This does not mean that provincial jurisdiction should not be respected nor that the federal government should act unilaterally. As the framework agreement commits to 'collaboration on implementation of joint priorities when this would result in more effective and efficient service to Canadians ... 'ensur[ing] access for all Canadians, wherever they live or move in Canada, to essential social programs and services of reasonably comparable quality,' the challenge for the government of all of Canada is to use vision and ingenuity to create the environment necessary to find solutions for matters of national importance like child care. An important question is: Who will get the ball rolling? Which level of government will put child care 'on the table' with a serious commitment to making the social union work?

Proposals for Action: One Scenario

A federal government with vision, political will, and commitment to children could forge a collaboration to assist in developing provincial programs within a national vision. The next federal budget is an obvious opportunity for a demonstration of effective and appropriate leadership on child care. An environment to forge this kind of collaboration could be fostered with a well-designed national child care strategy. This kind of strategy would include:

- Federal commitment to a multi-year Early Childhood Development Services Fund, to be introduced in the first year with a $2 billion federal commitment.[91]
- Key essential building blocks for Early Childhood Development Services in each province and territory consisting of integrated and

holistic early childhood education, child care, and parenting programs. Provincial programs could be organized in any of a variety of ways. Additional services to be part of a coherent Early Childhood Development Service system would be optional.

- Federal consultation with the provinces concerning national guiding principles, taking into account the best available knowledge about best practices in child development and family policy.
- Existing program and financial resources currently in use in each of the provinces as a foundation for each province's Early Childhood Development Services program.
- Provincial design, management, and implementation of early childhood development services.
- Participation of non-governmental experts and advocates in the process.
- Recognition of the key role of players at the local level – community-based organizations, local governments, and school boards, who would deliver services and develop innovative models. This role of innovator could be facilitated through a grant program to these organizations.
- Research, evaluation, data collection and analysis, and public reporting to ensure accountability to the public.

The exercise would be guided by attention to the principles and practices laid out in the social union framework agreement. There are potential other scenarios, but the challenge is to develop and implement a scenario that will move the issue forward.

National Guiding Principles

A set of guiding principles, together with clear goals and objectives, is an important and useful point of reference for any social program. Best practices in early childhood education and child care policy as well as the commitments in the framework agreement to public accountability, transparency, and the involvement of non-governmental players in the processes will be useful in developing a set of principles for child care. An appropriate set of principles based on best practices would include: universal provision (including all children regardless of income, class, ability or disability, region, and parents' work status); high quality (reflecting the best available knowledge of children's and families' needs); comprehensiveness (a range of service choices); responsiveness

(reflecting community values and diversity as well as including community and parental input); accountability (services are responsible to
the community served and governance, public resources are well used,
and mechanisms to ensure good governance are present); coherence
(services ensure continuity for children and parents and use community resources well). Guiding principles for child care have been proposed many times; for a further discussion of principles, see Friendly
(1994).

Models of Service

Within overarching national guiding principles, a wide variety of models for provincial delivery of early childhood care and education services are possible. Exemplary models of service provision can provide
illustrations of the potential flexibility for the provinces.

The Quebec Model
Early childhood care and education services are within a family policy
framework with services for five-year-olds and older children delivered primarily through an education mandate and by education authorities; services for zero- to four-year-olds – blending centres and
family day care – are delivered by community-based organizations.
Parent fees of $5 a day (with the government paying most of the cost)
are being phased in over several years as is expansion of services to
achieve a universal supply. Services are for all children regardless of
parents' work status or income.

The French Model
Early childhood care and education for children aged older than about
two and a half are under an education mandate at the national level and
are delivered by local education authorities; services for younger children are the responsibility of the Ministry of Health and are delivered
by local governments. All older preschoolers may attend a full school
day, and virtually all do. There are modest parent fees for services for
younger children and for additional services. Some communities (those
with low-income families, for example) get additional resources.

The Danish Model
All services for children from birth to age seven are under a social
welfare mandate and are delivered at the local level by local govern-

ments and voluntary organizations. Parents and government share the costs with affordable fees for some services. Virtually all older preschoolers attend, and a higher proportion of very young children (one- and two-year-olds – about 40 per cent) than any other European nation.

The 'Seamless Day'
Variations on this program have been proposed in Ontario since the 1980s. It would provide full school-day services for all three- to five-year-olds under the Ministry of Education, delivered by school boards; children could attend part-day if their parents chose. Services for younger children, including organized family day care, and parenting programs would be delivered either by school boards, local governments, or community organizations. Parents would pay affordable fees for some services.

A Community-Based Model
Another possibility could be early childhood services under a human resources mandate at the provincial level, with service delivery by local community-based organizations. In a sense, this is the existing model in place for regulated child care throughout much of Canada, but in every province it lacks funding and policy coordination of the three building blocks – child care, early childhood education, and support for parenting.

The Challenge: 'Thinking outside the Box'

A hackneyed expression in vogue in business, 'thinking outside the box,' is applicable to Canada's dismal child care situation. This idea, which means that new ways of thinking are necessary to solve knotty problems, captures the child care challenge today. Can the social union framework agreement contribute to 'thinking outside the box'? If it cannot, what can? The challenge is not to say, 'It can't be done,' but to find a way to ensure that it **is** done. This is the challenge to all our governments but especially the Government of Canada.

As this chapter points out, the framework agreement does create new pressures for governments to find a way to begin finally to create a national child care strategy. It has, as well, a timetable, tied to the commitment to the three-year review. In addition, the National Children's Agenda, announced in May 1999, provides important and useful opportunities to reinforce the message of the National Council of Welfare that many social programs support families but child care is the backbone of them all.[92] Perhaps these activities will act as some motivation for 'thinking outside the box.'

Is Child Care a Canary in a Coal Mine?

As coal mines used to hang a canary in a cage to warn of a mine disaster, Canada's inability to provide public policy for early childhood development services that are now commonplace in other mainstream societies should be a signal about how the nation is functioning. The government of all Canadians – the federal government – has to be able to forge agreement on initiatives that are pertinent to all of us in every region, or the nation will become increasingly non-functional.

Over the past few years, there has been considerable political discussion about focusing on outcomes and achieving the best we can as a society. Many of us have put forward what we believe is a convincing case that a national approach to high-quality early childhood care and education is essential to many outcomes. But even more than that, we should ensure these services because it is the right thing to do for children, for parents, for mothers. We need vision, commitment, the political will, and action to make a national approach to child care a reality.

Notes

1 National Council of Welfare, *Preschool Children: Promises to Keep* (Ottawa: Author, 1999), 70 and 89.
2 M. Friendly, 'What Is the Public Interest in Child Care?' in *Policy Options* (1997) 18(1): 5–6.
3 For example, T. Kent, *Social Policy 2000: An Agenda* (Ottawa: Caledon Institute of Social Policy, 1999); G. Cleveland and M. Krashinsky, *The Benefits and Costs of Good Child Care: The Economic Rationale for Public Investment in Young Children* (Toronto: University of Toronto, Centre for Urban and Community Studies, Childcare Resource and Research Unit, 1998); and the *Economist*, 'A Survey of Women and Work,' in the *Economist*, 18 July 1998, 16.
4 For example, National Forum on Health, *Canada Health Action: Building on the Legacy* (Ottawa: Author, 1997); M. Townson, *Health and Wealth: How Social and Economic Factors Affect Our Well-Being* (Toronto: Canadian Centre

for Policy Alternatives and James Lormier, 1999), D. Keating and C. Hertz-man, eds., *Developmental Health and the Wealth of Nations: Social, Biological and Educational Dynamics* (New York: Guilford Press, 1999); G. Browne, C. Byrne, J. Roberts, A. Gafril, S. Watt, S. Haldane, I. Thomas, B. Ewart, M. Schuster, J. Underwood, S. Kingston, and K. Rennick, *Benefitting All the Beneficiaries of Social Assistance Is within Reach: A Report of the Two-Year Effects and Expense of Subsidized Versus Non-subsidized Quality Child Care/Recreation for Children on Social Assistance* (Hamilton: McMaster University, System Linked Research Unit, 1998); and British Columbia Ministry of Health and Ministry Responsible for Seniors, *A Report on the Health of British Columbians: Provincial Health Officer's Annual Report 1997 – The Health and Well-being of British Columbia's Children* (Victoria, BC: Author, 1998).

5 For example, F. Mustard and M. McCain, *Reversing the Real Brain Drain: The Early Years Study* (Toronto: Canadian Institute for Advanced Research, The Founder's Network, 1999); and Council of Ministers of Education, Canada, *Preparation for Learning: Preschool Education – A Discussion Paper for the CMEC Third National Forum* (Toronto: Author, 1998).

6 For example, P. Moss and H. Penn, *Transforming Nursery Education* (London: Paul Chapman Publishing, 1996); and National Council of Welfare *Preschool Children*.

7 For example, United Nations, *Convention on the Rights of the Child* (New York: Author, 1991); and Council of Europe, *The Rights of the Child: a European Perspective* (Strasbourg: Author, 1996).

8 United Nations, *Convention on the Elimination of All Forms of Discrimination against Women* (New York: Author, 1979).

9 J. Beach, J. Bertrand, and G. Cleveland, *Our Child Care Workforce: From Recognition to Remuneration – More Than a Labour of Love* (Ottawa: Child Care Human Resources Steering Committee, 1998).

10 Friendly, 'What Is the Public Interest in Child Care?'

11 Senate of Canada, *Report of the Subcommittee of the Standing Committee on Social Affairs, Science and Technology, 1988* (Ottawa: Author, 1988), 1.

12 D. Lero, H. Goelman, A. Pence, L. Brockman, and S. Nuttall, *Parental Work Patterns and Child Care Needs – The Canadian National Child Care Study* (Ottawa: Statistics Canada / Health and Welfare Canada, 1992), 17.

13 National Council of Welfare, *Preschool Children*.

14 C. Bellamy, *The State of the World's Children: Education* (New York: UNICEF, 1999).

15 For example, K. O'Hara and S. Cox, *Securing the Social Union* (Ottawa: Canadian Policy Research Networks, 1998); L. White, *Welfare State Develop-*

ment and Child Care Policies: A Comparative Analysis of France, Canada and the United States (Unpublished doctoral dissertation, University of Toronto, 1998); A. Timpson, *Driven Apart: The Construction of Women as Worker-citizens and Mother-citizens in Canadian Employment Policy, 1940–1988* (Vancouver: University of British Columbia Press, in press). P. Girard, 'Why Canada Has No Family Policy: Lessons from France and Italy,' in *Osgoode Hall Law Journal* (1995) 32(3): 581–611; and V. Tyyska, *The Women's Movement and the Welfare State: Child Care Policy in Canada and Finland, 1960–1990* (Unpublished doctoral dissertation, University of Toronto 1993).

16 G. Boismenu and J. Jenson, 'A Social Union or a Federal State?: Competing Visions of Intergovernmental Relations in the New Liberal Era,' in *How Ottawa Spends, 1998–99: Balancing Act–The Post-Deficit Mandate*, L. Pal, ed. (Toronto: Oxford University Press, 1998), 56–79; and G. Doherty, M. Friendly, and M. Oloman, *Women's Support, Women's Work: Child Care in an Era of Deficit Reduction, Devolution, Downsizing and Deregulation* (Ottawa: Status of Women Canada, 1998).

17 S. Bach and S. Phillips, 'Constructing a New Social Union: Child Care beyond Infancy?' in *How Ottawa Spends, 1997–98: Seeing Red – A Liberal Report Card*, G. Swimmer, ed. (Ottawa: Carleton University Press, 1997), 236.

18 Boismenu and Jenson, 'A Social Union?'

19 K. Cooke, J. London, R. Edwards, and R. Rose-Lizee, *Report of the Task Force on Child Care* (Ottawa: Status of Women Canada, 1986), 234.

20 Cooke et al. *Report*; Child Care Advocacy Association of Canada, *Child Care Campaign Materials, 1993* (Ottawa: Author, 1994); and M. Friendly, *Child Care Policy in Canada: Putting the Pieces Together* (Don Mills, ON: Addison Wesley, 1994).

21 Kent, *Social Policy 2000*, 6.

22 Timpson includes the Commission on Equality in Employment (the Abella Commission) in her comparison of the significant proposals for a national child care strategy. It is not discussed here because it did not focus solely on child care. For a discussion of this comparison, see Timpson (in press).

23 L. Axworthy, Human Resource Development Canada Press Conference Transcript (Ottawa: Stenotran, 13 Dec. 1995).

24 Cooke et al., *Report*, 23.

25 Ibid., 284–5.

26 S. Phillips, 'Rock-a-Bye Brian: The National Strategy on Child Care,' in *How Ottawa Spends: The Buck Stops Where?* K.A. Graham, ed. (Don Mills, ON: Oxford University Press, 1989), 165–208.

27 Ibid., 168.

28 G. Fraser, *Playing for Keeps: The Making of a Prime Minister, 1988* (Toronto: McClelland and Stewart, 1989).

29 Special Committee on Child Care, *Sharing the Responsibility* (Ottawa: Author, 1987).

30 Human Resources Development Canada, *Improving Social Security in Canada: A Discussion Paper* (Ottawa: Author, 1994), 2.

31 Human Resources Development Canada, *Child Care and Development: A Supplementary Paper* (Ottawa: Author, 1994), 2.

32 Ibid., 25.

33 Childcare Resource and Research Unit, Summaries of the House of Commons Minutes of Proceedings and Evidence of the Standing Committee on Human Resources Development (Unpublished, 1995).

34 Ministerial Council on Social Policy Reform, *Report to the Premiers* (St John's, NF: Government of Canada, 1995), 27 and 69.

35 Doherty, et al., *Women's Support.*

36 S. Dupre, 'Taming the Monster: Debt, Budgets and Federal-Provincial Fiscal Relations at the Fin-de-Siècle,' in *Provinces and Canadian provincial politics,* C. Dunn, ed. (Peterborough, ON: Broadview Press, 1996).

37 M. Friendly and M. Oloman, 'Child Care at the Centre: Child Care on the Social, Economic and Political Agenda in the 1990s,' in *Remaking Canadian Social Policy: Social Security in the Late 1990s,* J. Pulkingham and G. Ternowetsky, eds. (Halifax: Fernwood Press, 1996), 273–85.

38 Doherty et al., *Women's Support.*

39 Kent *Social Policy 2000,* 4.

40 S. Torjman and K. Battle, *Can We Have National Standards?* (Ottawa: Caledon Institute of Social Policy, 1995), 2 and 10.

41 Human Resources Development, *Improving Social Security,* 1. ·

42 Timpson (in press); and Doherty et al., *Women's Support.*

43 Axworthy, Press Conference.

44 *Globe and Mail,* 16 Feb. 1996, A1.

45 Liberal Party of Canada, *Creating Opportunity: The Liberal Plan for Canada* (Ottawa: Author, 1993), 40.

46 Bach and Phillips, 'Constructing a New Social Union'; and Liberal Party of Canada, *A Record of Achievement: a Report on the Liberal Government's 36 Months in Office* (Ottawa: Author, 1996).

47 Canada, House of Commons, *Debates,* 134 (Ottawa: Author, 27 Feb. 1996), 4.

48 Ministerial Council on Social Policy Reform, *Report,* 1.

49 D. Guest, *The Emergence of Social Security in Canada* (Vancouver: University of British Columbia Press, 1985).

50 Bach and Phillips, 'Constructing a New Social Union,' 245.

60 Martha Friendly

51 Boismenu and Jenson, 'A Social Union?'
52 Doherty et al., *Women's Support.*
53 M. Mendelson, *The Provinces' Position: a Second Chance for the Social Security Review* (Ottawa: Caledon Institute of Social Policy, 1996), 3.
54 Ibid.
55 Boismenu and Jenson, 'A Social Union?', 58.
56 M. Biggs, *Building Blocks for Canada's New Social Union* (Ottawa: Canadian Policy Research Networks, 1996), 1.
57 T. Courchene, *Social Canada in the Millennium* (Toronto: C.D. Howe Institute, 1994).
58 Boismenu and Jenson, 'A Social Union?', 63.
59 The seven provinces were Newfoundland, Prince Edward Island, Nova Scotia, New Brunswick, Quebec, Manitoba, and British Columbia. For more details see L. Pearson, *Children and the Hill* (Ottawa: Senate of Canada, Fall 1999), 16.
60 Bach and Phillips, 'Constructing a New Social Union.'
61 S. McCarthy, 'Ottawa Urged to Keep Promise on Daycare,' in the *Globe and Mail*, 13 April 1999, A7.
62 Campaign 2000, *Mission for the Millennium: a Comprehensive Strategy for Children and Youth* (Toronto: Author, 1997); Human Resources Development Canada, Subcommittee on Children at Risk, 'Blues' – transcript of the meeting of the Human Resources Development Canada Committee, Subcommittee on Children at Risk (Unpublished, 1999). Child Care Advocacy Association of Canada, *Child Care and the National Children's Agenda* (Ottawa: CCAAC, 1999). C. Freiler and J. Cesny, *Benefiting Canada's Children: Perspectives on Gender and Social Responsibility* (Ottawa: Status of Women Canada, 1998).
63 Government of Canada, *A Framework to Improve the Social Union for Canadians: An Agreement between the Government of Canada and the Governments of the Provinces and Territories* (Unpublished, 1999).
64 T. Walkom, 'Social Union Deal a Step Backwards for Canadians,' in the *Toronto Star*, 9 Feb. 1999, A2.
65 R. Gwyn, 'Trying to Swallow the Fudge of the Social Union,' in the *Toronto Star*, 7 Feb. 1999, A19. (On-line document: http://www.thestar.com/back_issues)
66 B. Cameron and J. Rebick, 'The Social Union Framework Is a Step Forward,' in the *Globe and Mail*, 8 Feb. 1999, A11.
67 Pollara Research, personal communication, 1999.
68 Cameron and Rebick, 'Social Union.'
69 Walkom, 'Social Union Deal.'
70 D. Orchard, 'Canada's Social Union, According to David Orchard,' in the

Toronto Star, commentary page, 1999. Feb. 25th (Thursday). Quotation obtained from the internet (www.thestar.ca).

71 J. Godfrey and R. McLean, *The Canada We Want: Competing Visions for the New Millennium* (Toronto: General Distribution Services 1999), 134.

72 S. Dion, *Collaborative Use of the Spending Power for Intergovernmental Transfers: The Race to the Top Model,* 5 Feb. 1999, 1. Obtained online at url: http://www.pco-bcp.gc.ca/aia/ro/doc/efeb0599.htm (Online document: http://www.pco-bcp.gc.ca/aia/ro/doc/efeb0599.htm)

73 Cooke et al., *Report,* 285.

74 Ibid., 287.

75 Government of Canada *Framework to Improve,* 6.

76 Walkom, 'Social Union Deal'; and Orchard, 'Canada's Social Union.'

77 Personal communication with B. Cameron, 1999.

78 Kent, *Social Policy 2000,* 11.

79 Ibid., 21.

80 Dion, *Collaborative Use of the Spending Power,* 2.

81 Friendly, *Child Care Policy*; B. Cameron, *Child Care: Whose Responsibility? Putting the Pieces Together: A Child Care Agenda for the 90s* (Toronto: Ontario Coalition for Better Child Care, 1994).

82 Kent, *Social Policy 2000,* 22.

83 Ibid., 5.

84 Godfrey and McLean, *The Canada We Want,* 135.

85 Friendly, 'What Is the Public Interest in Child Care?'

86 Environics Research Group Limited, *Child Care Issues and the Child Care Workforce: A Survey of Canadian Public Opinion – Summary Results* (Toronto, Environics Research Group Limited, 1998).

87 Timpson, 1997; Friendly, *Child Care Policy.*

88 For example, Cooke et al., *Report*; Doherty et al., *Women's Support*; Kent, *Social Policy 2000*; and National Council of Welfare, *Preschool Children.*

89 Cooke et al., *Report,* 288.

90 K. O'Hara, *Comparative Family Policy: Eight Countries' Stories,* CPRN Study No. F04 (Ottawa: Canadian Policy Research Networks, 1998).

91 This figure is derived from the Cleveland and Krashinsky study that forms the basis of the symposium. It represents a first step of funding early childhood care and education for all four- and five-year-olds across Canada. G. Cleveland and M. Krashinsky, *The Benefits and Costs of Good Child Care: The Economic Rationale for Public Investment in Young Children* (Toronto: University of Toronto, Centre for Urban and Community Studies, Childcare Resource and Research Unit, 1998).

92 National Council of Welfare, *Preschool Children,* 70 and 89.

2. The Politics of Child Care in Canada: Provincial and Federal Governments

Bob Rae
Goodman, Phillips, and Vineberg

My views are a little different from those of Martha Friendly, with her emphasis on the importance and centrality of federal leadership, but I do not think that I am at all antagonistic to what she sets out as her primary objective.

There is some very good news in the continuing evolution of Canadian public opinion regarding child care, where politicians are lagging behind the public. The good news is that eventually the politicians will catch up. Frankly, more have caught up in the past five years than had before, not because of anything that is terribly inexplicable, but because the increased need for child care flows from two dramatic and significant secular changes in our economy over the past twenty-five or thirty years.

The first obvious change is the dramatic increase in the participation of women in the workforce. This is one of the great social revolutions of our time. It has had a dramatic impact on women themselves, a huge impact on the very nature of the family, and a tremendous impact on the economy and the whole of our society. Despite what some dinosaurs and neanderthals would care to say, it is a change that is permanent as well as deep. Thus, in 1995–6, for example, there were newly elected cabinet ministers in Ontario making preposterous comments that there was no need for a day care system because the neighbour could take care of the kids. But this fails to recognize the simple fact that the neighbour is also at work. Life is changing and politicians are forced to respond. Thus, you tend not to find politicians saying dumb things like that (and certainly not during an election campaign) because they know that it has no resonance with voters.

The second change has to do with the nature of the modern economy.

The simple reality is that levels of education have everything to do with one's success in that economy. Therefore, investments in people (to use that awful catch phrase) are in fact essential. This has been documented very effectively by Martha Friendly, by Fraser Mustard's group, by the Atkinson Foundation, by the United Way, and by the significant studies commissioned by my own government (through the premiers' council) with respect to early childhood experiences and early childhood education. The evidence is overwhelming. What we do for children between the time they are born and when they start school, and what we do for the families that are sustaining those children, has everything to do with their success. And as this information becomes well known, it will become increasingly impossible for governments not to respond to this crying need for early education.

Early education is the best anti-crime program you can have in the Province of Ontario or across Canada. Dan Offord's work at McMaster University shows categorically that those kids who are neglected when they are born and as they grow up are those who are most likely to turn to crime. From a purely hard economic point of view, the cost of that crime to Canadians is enormous. And this is to focus in on only the most extreme benefit from early intervention. Tom Kent's chapter also makes this point – that we should not now engage in long philosophical arguments about why good child care needs to happen. We need instead to get into some detailed discussions about how it can happen.

First, I think that we need to look at the origin of the social union. Why did this social union agreement get drafted? The answer requires us to go back some fifty years. In the postwar period, the federal government ran steady surpluses. This led directly to the ability of Lester Pearson's government to produce a series of national shared cost programs. The critical assumption was that the federal government would be there to pay for the programs. For example, medicare began in Saskatchewan, but it became a national program only when the federal government took the successful model from one province and offered to fund 50 per cent of the cost for all provinces. This provided an irresistible incentive for the provinces to sign on. As a result, medicare is the one program that affects literally everybody. But the reality is that, steadily and systematically, the federal government has pulled away from funding those programs. There was deep frustration in provinces of every ideological stripe about what took place starting in 1977. In that year, the federal government announced that they would no longer fund programs at 50 per cent. They provided funding on a block basis, and the size of that block was to be determined unilaterally by the central government.

That first change took effect under Pierre Trudeau in 1977. The second change, under Brian Mulroney in 1989, affected Ontario and Alberta and British Columbia more than the other provinces, and Ontario most of all. In the latest federal budget, Paul Martin admitted that the cost of the cap on the Canada Assistance Plan (CAP) for the Province of Ontario was ten billion dollars. I can tell you as somebody who was on the receiving end of those cuts that they were painful and difficult. But even more to the point, they had the effect of breaking the trust and the sense of confidence that the provinces had in the federal government as a reliable partner. That trust was broken finally and conclusively in 1995 with the Martin budget that eliminated the Canada Assistance Plan and brought in the Canada Health and Social Transfer (CHST). In the end, the first problem is money, the second problem is money, and the third problem is money. If you do not understand that, you do not understand the basis for attaining a national child care program.

The provinces are not in need of intellectual leadership from the federal government. They are not in need of moral leadership, or studies, or more detailed analysis. What we do need is someone who is prepared to fund child care programs on a consistent and reliable basis.

To offer a constructive comment on Martha Friendly's chapter, it is necessary to understand the importance of financial trust and financial leadership. The social union did not start in 1995, but in 1992, when the province of Ontario said, 'We will not support the Charlottetown Accord unless there is a social charter.' That charter had to recognize the mutual obligation of the provinces and the federal government to work together to create a genuine Canadian social union. In that social union, Canadian citizenship means that you have certain substantive rights. It is not just a matter of being able to travel from one part of the country to another and get a job. It is not just a matter of knowing that the services that you have and the kind of quality of life that you are able to receive have substance across the country. The reason for the social union is that the provinces lost faith in the federal government's unique capacity to provide leadership for social programs. The federal government had become a kind of absconding debtor. As a result, the provinces insisted on having a place at the table.

In my view, to look exclusively to the federal government for child care policy is a mistake. I think it is also a bit of a fictional re-creation of our own history to suggest that that is how it happened in the past. Let us remember that medicare did not start as a thought out of the head of some wise boffin in Ottawa. It started because citizens fought for the program in community after community and because one provincial government was prepared to stand up and say, 'We want to do this.' And they did not do it in short order either: it took years to build it. My advice would be not to put all your faith in one federal budget, or one statement by a federal minister. Child care policies will emerge out of a long steady process of building a national program. It will not happen as part of a top-down process. Instead, it will happen because it comes out of the condition and the needs of the people, as those needs are articulated by community activists and by leaders of all kinds. Eventually, politicians will respond to the popular will. It is not just going to be one particular party or one particular group. Instead, it will bring all people together.

In summary, the social union started in 1992–3. Its genesis was in the growing frustration and sense of concern among provinces about how programs were being funded. In terms of child care, when people talk about the federal initiatives in 1993, they often quote the federal Liberals' argument that there was no provincial interest in child care. But in reality the provinces were being starved by the federal minister of finance. So when some other ministers came along and invited the provinces to participate in a shared-cost child care initiative, the provinces reacted predictably to this kind of 'pyramid sale.' Then in the 1995 federal budget, Ontario had their federal grants chopped by over $2 billion. How then could we have any faith in what was being proposed? In fact, what was being proposed was not part of a coherent federal strategy with respect to transfers to the provinces. Instead it was a mug's game – a public relations game. The federal government, on the one hand, asked for a leadership role in child care and, on the other, chopped off every source of funding that Ontario had to run the child care programs that we had already started.

Funding for child care had been increased in the Province of Ontario dramatically starting in 1991 and continuing through until 1995. The infrastructure is now in place for a national program in Ontario and in many other provinces. The fundamental question comes down to one of funding.

Martha Friendly is right when she argues that it is a matter of political choice. To initiate a new national program is not cheap. My own view is that the federal government is only going to proceed on a national program of this kind if there is substantial participation by the provinces. Some provinces have to come forward and commit their resources to child care. The federal government should be focusing its resources on affordability issues and on the financial position of lower- and middle-income families. Of course, the provincial governments could be supplementing these initiatives. But the provincial governments must also do more to ensure that the infrastructure of child care services is available in their provinces.

Child care is both a national issue and a provincial one. It is subject to provincial jurisdiction, and this fact is at the heart of Canadian policy making. We are a federal country. The provinces have jurisdiction over education and over the delivery of care and services to people. That is a fact of life in Canada. The federal government could not unilaterally exercise jurisdiction without causing a huge constitutional and legal conflict. But the federal government does have access to dollars, and the federal government can act as a useful coordinator of the development of national standards. Now when I say national standards, in fact, I mean federal-provincial standards and guidelines with respect to how services can be provided. The federal government has an overall financial responsibility to ensure that there is relative equality with respect to access to services in different parts of the country. That is a constitutional obligation of the federal government under Section 36 of the Constitution.

If the political will is there, our federalism can be a useful advantage in achieving a child care policy. Federalism allows us to take the examples in certain provinces and use those as benchmarks and examples for other jurisdictions. The federal government's key role, in my view, is to take the information, disseminate it, and provide the provinces with a real understanding of what is going on in different jurisdictions.

It is not the job of the federal government to run programs in individual provinces or to supplant what local groups and community groups are doing. That is not a useful role for the federal government and that is not what anyone intends by a national program. What we intend is a program funded on a federal-provincial basis, with standards and approaches that are shared across the country, and with a deep recognition that the future of our country depends very much on what we do for our children. Child care policy is about the kind of attention and care we pay to the needs of all children across the country.

The social union does present us with an opportunity. But at the same time, the fundamental political and economic challenge is money. What any provincial premier of any political stripe will say when the federal government starts talking about child care is: 'Show me the money.' And if the federal government cannot show us the money, then it need not bother giving speeches about it or talking about how children are the most important thing in the world and how we should do more for them.

Over time, the availability of federal money is going to be the test of whether or not Canada will have a national child care program. We have a continuing national program with respect to medicare, and pensions and unemployment insurance because periodically the people have risen up and told the federal government, as they did in health care, 'You've got to get back into the game.' Governments act when they see the extent to which the public is responding. And that is what will eventually create the momentum for change in Canada. These are political choices and these are economic choices.

To sum up, let me start with the good news again. The good news is that child care has always been on the agenda and it will be increasingly on the agenda no matter which political party has which political view at any given time. It is on the agenda because of two compelling reasons: Women are in the workforce to stay, and increasingly we recognize the need to focus on younger children as the key to success in the twenty-first century. Early education is the key to the new economy of the new millennium. If those two things are true, then the good news is that the momentum for child care is there.

It remains for us to focus political attention on the issue. This last point is the one concern I have. We cannot let the provinces off the hook. Do not put all your political lobbying eggs in one basket, looking for a federal program. We have seen how this can fail on the housing issue. Each government plays the issue off against the other. Each government claims that it is spending while the other is not, while overall we see the biggest exit from a social program that has occurred in the past twenty years. We are left as the only country now in the western world that does not have a social housing program at either the federal or the provincial level. Both levels of government have to be held responsible for that outcome.

In child care, we cannot make the mistake of thinking that if we can get the federal government to move, then that solves the problem. (I have tried to describe this a bit in my last book.) We live in a decentralized world. We live in a world in which local governments and regional governments and provincial governments are more important and are going to continue to be more important than they were in the past. Therefore, do not ignore the importance of focusing attention on child care needs as they relate to each province. Do not let the provinces simply say that it is a national program and therefore not their responsibility. That is the wrong strategy.

Instead, I believe that the right strategy is to target the local community, to target boards of education, to target local governments, to target municipal governments, to target provincial governments, and finally to target the federal government. We need to continue to focus on the needs of children and on the needs of their parents, and on the fact that this is not an issue for one class or another. It is increasingly a universal issue shared by every family, and one which will increasingly be true for the twenty-first century.

3. The Federal Imperative

Tom Kent
Queen's University

This chapter is confined to one question – the characteristically Canadian question – about the policy map for good child care. How can we achieve a nation-wide purpose through services that are under provincial jurisdiction? The problem is rooted in the diversity of the provinces: diversity in size, from Prince Edward Island to Ontario; diversity in ideology, from Quebec to Alberta; and an economic diversity that produces far greater differences in provincial finances than it is possible to remove by the measure of tax 'equalization' that is politically acceptable. Such diverse provinces cannot be expected to produce major program initiatives that are close in nature or in time. In many respects, there is no reason why they should. In many other respects, however, we can work as a national society and economy only if public programs are much the same for Canadians everywhere. And that is possible only if, in some areas of provincial jurisdiction, the federal government nevertheless takes initiatives, in policy and in finance.

Medicare is a conspicuous example. Popular though it quickly became and has remained, in the early 1960s there was little disposition among provincial politicians to follow Saskatchewan's lead. The governments of Ontario and Alberta, in particular, were then strongly opposed to medicare. They changed only when the federal government made an offer too good to refuse: it would provide, from federal taxes, half of the costs of provincial health programs conforming to certain national principles. Many people have long seen a parallel need for federal leadership in child care, nation-wide. The case does not require repetition by me. It requires action at last.

In the 1960s the same financial formula was used for other major legislation besides medicare. For a time, fifty-fifty cost-sharing seemed to be established as the natural Canadian way to operate social programs. Indeed, even after it has been abandoned for existing programs, claims for new national action are still put forward with an almost automatic assumption that the financial mechanism would be cost-sharing. In this volume, Martha Friendly recounts the successive disappointments to such plans for child care. Hope, however, dies hard. Some enthusiasts saw the beginning of a new era in February 1999, when the so-called framework agreement on the social union was signed by all but one of Canada's first ministers. Friendly, though too experienced to leap into easy optimism, cannot resist entertaining the possibility that the agreement paves the way for new cost-shared programs.

Certainly the agreement has merits. Against a background of federal-provincial conflict, it is useful to have the governments making a cooperative declaration of their good wishes for the Canadian people and of their good resolution to be more polite and considerate in their dealings with each other. The resolution is given immediate effect in the agreement's treatment of cost-shared programs. Not only are swords sheathed. No feelings are hurt. Most of the words might belong to an address to resurrect cost-sharing. Rarely has a funeral oration been so tactfully contrived as to be almost unrecognizable.

The agreement provides that the federal government may take new initiatives to fund social programs operated by the provinces, provided that six provincial governments agree; the six smallest and poorest, most eager for federal money, will do. That, however, would hardly constitute a nation-wide program; those six provinces together have only 20 per cent of Canada's population. Nevertheless, once there was agreement, all ten provinces would be entitled to their shares of the federal funding required for the program; the other four would need only to commit to meeting the same 'objectives' in their own way; and if they could do that without all their federal money, they could use the rest 'in the same or a related priority area.'

In short, as much as 80 per cent of the federal funding would go into provincial programs with which federal politicians had no identification, in which they had no say, for which they would gain none or hardly any of the political credit. No federal government in its right mind will transfer money to the provinces under the terms of this part of the social union agreement. Presumably that is what was intended by most, if not all, of the politicians and officials involved in the agreement. Whether the intent will stand, when the agreement has run its initial three-year course, may be a more open question.

It will stand, if Pierre Trudeau was right in an assessment made early in his prime ministership. He said that there would 'never' be another shared program such as medicare. For nearly thirty years, at least, he has been right. The reasons are fundamental to our politics. Shared programs require federal politicians to raise money that provincial politicians spend. That remarkable generosity came easily in the 1950s and 1960s. Public attitudes still reflected the years of depression and war. Everyone knew that, whatever the provinces might administer, it was the federal government that was running the country; and running it, for the most part, pretty well. Jurisdictional niceties did not prevent federal politicians from getting most of the credit, initially, for good things like medicare.

The political conjunction that made sharing easy for Ottawa, and irresistible for the provinces, is now long gone. Politicians are in much worse repute. The two lots of them, federal and provincial, are in far more direct competition for what little credit the public can see in either lot. For Ottawa, shared programs have therefore long lost their political appeal; hence the downloading of its financial troubles to the provinces. For the provinces, funding cuts were the betrayal of trust that stirred to anger what had always been their mixed feelings: liking for federal dollars, but resentment of federal arrogance.

The regrettable conclusion is, in my view, inescapable. If we want good child care, nation-wide, soon, we cannot realistically put faith in the old, direct approach to federal funding of provincial programs. Another way has to be found.

Bob Rae, it seems, would put his faith in lobbying the provinces. One – Quebec – is at present far in the lead in its public provision of child care. Its example has not yet been followed elsewhere. If, however, another province or two could be pressured into significant action, then public demand might in time mount to the point where the provinces collectively would challenge Ottawa to involvement in a Canada-wide program. That would be a reasonable scenario, employing a strategy of the 'fabian' kind, if we had plenty of time. We do not. Canada is a laggard in early childhood education. We need to develop it now. We need it because the wealth of a nation now depends most fundamentally on its human capital, on the understanding and knowledge of its people; and their capability is largely shaped in early childhood. We need it because otherwise the increasingly high-tech economy will produce an increasingly polarized society, with better and better opportunities for some and doors ever more tightly closed against others.

Those economic and social forces are already strong and growing stronger. Countervailing changes in our public institutions – early education, above all – ought to have been long under way. We do not now have leisure. We need decisive, not gradualistic, public action. It can be taken, within the terms of the social union framework. Effectively though the agreement hobbles federal transfers to provinces, it does not purport to limit the federal government's power to make payments directly to individuals and organizations.

Ottawa does now contribute directly, and generously, to the care of children with well-to-do, working parents. That is the effect of the deduction from taxable income allowed for child care expenses. Like all such tax allowances, it is greatly discriminatory: a substantial benefit for people with high incomes; of little or no value to people with low incomes. If we are serious about child care, that must be changed. The thoroughgoing change, for preschool children, would be to replace the expense allowance by a direct payment available to their parents as reimbursement for child care fees. The present maximum allowance, $7,000 a year, is close to the per child cost of high-quality, educational care. Like all such provisions, it should be indexed to the cost of living. Up to the maximum, and subject to a claw-back from high incomes, the payment would be universally available against evidence of child care fees.

Such a financial empowerment of parents would produce an outburst of new child care facilities. Public reimbursement of fees should properly be restricted to not-for-profit services, which a variety of community organizations could provide.

When I first put forward a proposal of this kind, I made the mistake of describing the entitlement to fees as a voucher, a word with some unfortunate and unintended associations. It should be clear that what is intended, in the context of Canadian federalism, is simply to base the federal role in child care on the undisputed power to make payments to individual Canadians. That, however, would be the start, not the end, of the affair. The offer should not and would not be a cold-shouldering of the provinces, still less a pre-emptive strike into their jurisdiction. They would immediately be invited to opt in, to take full responsibility for organizing the provision of child care. The net cost of the federal payments offered to parents would then be available to an opting-in province. It would be close to the province's full expense of making good care universally accessible. Some provincial budgets, particularly Quebec's, would be relieved of considerable costs they now incur for kindergarten classes and day care.

The terms of such arrangements would require complex negotiations, province by province. Varying provincial circumstances would produce considerable differences in the details of the agreements. Provided, however, that the claimed spirit of the social union holds, it is hard to see why any province, even including Quebec, would stand aside. The practical result could well be a series of provincial programs consistent enough in nature to be equivalent to a Canada-wide shared program.

It would, however, be different in one major respect from any previous shared program. Its financial basis would not be a negotiated funding of provincial programs. It would instead be rooted in the principle of a federal payment committed to individuals. Ottawa's identification with the program, and hence its share of political credit, would be clear and continuing; by the same token, the provinces could be confident of continuity in funding. If some provinces should stand aside, financial compensation would not go to their governments; the funding entitlement would remain with parents seeking good care for preschool children.

The cost to the federal government, when such a program is mature, can be reasonably estimated at $8 billion a year. That this is most, not half, of the cost of good child care will shock many people. It is, however, the consequence of past errors in dealings with the provinces as well as delays in policy.

No doubt the federal government could continue for some years to contain the pressure for good child care. It could engage in prolonged negotiations with the provinces, eventually producing some support for some improvements. Whether that conventional politics is good politics may be doubted. It seems probable that public opinion would respond enthusiastically to bold action for the early care and education of children. Certainly that is where the public good lies. Certainly the need is urgent, the hour already late. And certainly, it is a national need that will not be met, adequately, nation-wide and soon, unless Ottawa is creative, in leadership and with money.

Certainty does not, of course, extend to the particulars of the policy suggested here. Discussion is needed. Better plans and smarter strategies may well come forward. What matters is that the discussion be driven by the importance and the urgency of good child care.

4. Child Care and the Social Union Framework Agreement: Lament or Leverage?

Alfred MacLeod
EKOS Research Associates Inc.

SETTING THE STAGE

To date, the social union framework agreement leads a double life. In the real world of public memory and awareness it is an obscurity. Only about one in five Canadians clearly recall hearing or reading anything about the agreement. As a point of intersection between governments and the general public, however, while the agreement may be an anomaly, it is by no means an obscurity. Its clear emphasis on values and principles, public accountability and transparency, and partnership and collaboration mesh almost seamlessly with public sentiments, or at least the sentiments of the majority of the public. The proof of the pudding is in the tasting, and only time will tell what taste will be left in the public's mouth as the agreement moves from proclamation to practice. The best bet, in my view, is sweet rather than sour.

A focus on machinery and governance, present in the chapters by both Martha Friendly and Bob Rae, is absolutely significant. For about one year I had a screen saver on my work computer scrolling the words of a wise and wily friend of mine: 'Don't mistake process for progress.' In today's context of child care and federal-provincial relations, I am not sure that this slogan holds true. Good process can lead to progress. Martha Friendly describes well the flaws in the government program machinery over the past two decades as it served, or failed to serve, the interests of intelligent and comprehensive child care policy in Canada. Despite an apparent consensus among experts as to what had to be done, it did not happen. And this is all the more puzzling given what Tom Kent has described as a point of national convergence around the concept that 'the good society is a society in which all citizens start with opportunities for a good life.'[1] Perhaps the social union framework agreement, with its commitment and mechanisms for collaborative priority setting, will redress the deficit on coordinated, comprehensive approaches to getting our children off to the best possible start in life.

CANARY IN A COAL MINE?

Martha Friendly makes an important contribution to the public and expert discourse on child care in Canada and the evolving dynamic of federal-provincial approaches to social policy more broadly. Why, exactly, is her chapter important?

First, it is absolutely critical that the intellectual wheels of child care policy continue to turn. The chapter by Friendly provides stark evidence that the 1990s have not been years of great structural gains in the area of child care. This means that it is even more important that Friendly, and people with similar talents and insights, continue to build the intellectual case for a more enlightened, systematic approach to nurturing and caring for our children. As difficult as it is to keep the faith when objective indicators expose setbacks rather than advances, this perseverance is a precondition of making breakthroughs on child care.

Moving from the 'high road' to the 'middle road,' another reality must be acknowledged. Child care may be an obvious 'public good,' but it is not the only game in town. There is a lot of competition for space on the public policy agenda. Where does home care fit, what about enhanced supports for Canadians with disabilities, where does more funding for post-secondary education fit, and how about tax cuts and job creation and training programs? There is a sort of 'policy Darwinism' at play, as governments juggle public priorities. We see among governments a tendency to have 'funding of the fittest'; and fittest does not necessarily mean the best. To a certain degree, the fittest priorities are the ones that through a variety of channels, not always public, capture the most attention and create the most momentum.

Second, readers of the Friendly chapter find a select, yet rich, narrative built around an annotated chronology covering close to two decades of the high-water and low-water marks of child care policy and politics in Canada. While interpretation of these events and decisions is open to question, it is very useful to have this tight account of how child care fit, or did not fit, into the broader federal-provincial social policy and program dynamic over the period under discussion.

While not a major feature of the chapter, the cursory reference to how the very definition of child care has shifted since the 1980s is significant. Friendly informs us that 'the definition of "child care" has shifted so that it is now closely linked not only to parents' activities (usually employment or training) but to the idea that early childhood education is essential for optimal healthy development.' This observation helps to move the debate beyond the more limited domain of child care as a support for parents who work outside of the home and towards a more child-centred perspective, including children of parents who work in the home.

Third, Friendly also raises some key questions about the future of child care. For example, what levers are available to governments to push forward with an ambitious and comprehensive agenda for Canada's children? Can we ever get beyond the question of 'Who does what?' and on to the equally critical question of 'When will we do what should be done?' Despite the somewhat ominous metaphor used to frame the chapter (i.e., the canary in the coal mine), Friendly's is a positive perspective. She does a good job of balancing a lament for what might have been accomplished with a principled, yet pragmatic, call to seize the opportunities presented by recent developments in the machinery of federal-provincial relations and improved fiscal conditions.

Martha Friendly's chapter is a good point of departure for some elaboration of issues around funding, accountability, and the role and importance of public opinion, all of which are fundamental elements in the larger process of building the case for child care.

Fourth, with some notable exceptions (e.g., Gordon Cleveland and Michael Krashinsky's excellent work), elaborate costing models may not be the strong suit for child care policy thinkers. A case can be made that this is not necessarily a deficiency. But good ideas and good policy proposals must get over the costing bar before the conceptual becomes an actual program. In the real politics and real economics of government, within the political and bureaucratic arms, the policy and program–cost axis is critical. There is without doubt a 'catch-22' effect at play. Without the requisite costing work, a proposal is seldom taken seriously. With costing attached, however, it is easy for 'sticker shock' to obscure the policy objectives and the public good to be served. The best way to approach this dilemma is to present a funding range or band and show how to move towards the ultimate target in increments. This strategy is reminiscent of the riddle, 'How does the anchovy eat the whale? Answer: one bite at a time.'

Why not ask governments to take their cue from the little fish? When exasperated and sometimes indignant public officials (usually from departments of finance throughout the country) turn to child care advocates and ask, 'How are governments of modest means ever to afford such an expensive program?' the answer should be, 'Let us agree on a plan and build it one piece at a time.' Social policy activists often dismiss incrementalism as an inadequate response. In many cases they are right. The trick with this approach is to ensure that the increments are happening within the context of a coherent and comprehensive plan. One might refer to this as 'enlightened incrementalism.' Child care advocates in this country involved with governments in a serious and genuine debate about pace, rather than policy inertia, would be evidence of real progress.

Fifth, there is a growing constituency within government circles for a strong focus on measurement and evaluation and the public reporting of outcomes. It is no longer sufficient to have programs that look good on paper; the 'real world' results are the true test. My experience as a foot-soldier of sorts during federal-provincial negotiations on social policy initiatives showed me that this new emphasis truly is a promising area for action. The social union framework agreement, in fact, contains specific language on this point. It is in this very area that child care experts, those of you from the ivory towers and those of you from the front lines, have so much to offer governments. It is an area that lends itself to close collaboration and trust-building.

There are no more blank cheques from governments. While this statement may be a bit inflammatory in its implication for past practices, it is a feature of the public view of government that has important implications for future publicly-funded initiatives. Transparency and accountability clauses are prominent in the social union framework not by happenstance. These are now prerequisite conditions that Canadians want applied to government interventions. This is a positive development. It imposes a new discipline that should be welcomed by political actors across the ideological spectrum. Interestingly enough, governments and the public are asking many of the same questions (questions to be answered at the front end of the decision-making and judgment process, not after the fact): What is the public payoff? What does it cost? What are the results and for whom will these results be achieved? How will we know when we have achieved these results?

While we were driving to Toronto from Ottawa, a five-hour trek, in the backseat of the car my three-year-old son became a broken record of sorts. His two favourite tunes were: 'I have to go to the bathroom!' and 'Are we there yet?' It is his second tune that is applicable here. For my son, he knew we had arrived in Toronto when he saw the big buildings (the CN Tower to be precise). For me, the marker of choice was my watch. For others the markers might be different again from time and architecture. The point is that accountability, by the nature of the diversity of audiences, must take many forms. Governments, child care experts, and practitioners can serve all Canadians by working together in developing practical and reliable markers for tracking the progress of Canada's children and their families.

Sixth, Martha Friendly's chapter contains a passing reference to the finding that 88 per cent of Canadians who, when polled in 1998, indicated that they supported more government support for a child care program. But what does that really mean? More digging has to be done here – not a surprising conclusion from a person who makes his living by public opinion polling. There are critical and significant challenges in going beyond the surface consensus to understand the very real and deep cleavages that exist in Canadians' opinions around this issue. This process is at the heart of any effort to create legitimacy among the public for specific early childhood development tools and strategies.

The concept of ensuring that all citizens start with opportunities for a good life was presented earlier as a point of national convergence. This point of convergence, which I believe to be genuine, holds within it a number of complexities for child care. To fully appreciate the nature of the challenge one has first to appreciate that there is no linear link between the general consensus on whether to do something for our children and the more specific questions of what to do and by and for whom. Agreement on the desired outcome (i.e., well-adjusted children poised to move productively into adulthood and the associated roles of work and family and citizen) is no guarantee that there will be agreement on how best to achieve this outcome.

This is where values emerge as the salient feature of the debate on early childhood development programs and strategies. There is insufficient space here to explore this relationship in any detail: however, there has been much written lately about the state and form of Canadians' values and what these changes mean for our society and governments (e.g., Canadian Policy Research Networks, Frank Graves, Neil Nevitte, and others). This is a phenomenon that needs to be better understood by government. It is a phenomenon that must be clearly understood by those who advocate on behalf of children. More specifically, understanding the tangle of values that surround family, children, and work, and more broadly speaking, equity, will be as important to charting the way forward on child care policy as are clearer insights into government machinery and funding.

PULLING IT ALL TOGETHER

Bob Rae's contribution, in effect, provides a critique of Martha Friendly's chapter and serves to expand its context. By taking the chronology of federal-provincial cost-shared programs further back to the 1960s, Rae provides a valuable glimpse of how Canadian federal-provincial fiscal arrangements have evolved. The general and crucial feature of these arrangements has been their tendency to change. Sometimes gradually and on other occasions abruptly, as was the case in 1989 with the cap imposed by the federal government on the Canada Assistance Plan, which directed the federal government's contribution to provincial governments for welfare and other social assistance programs. The lesson to be learned is that change in and of itself is not the problem, but the process through which these changes are introduced is critical. Applied to the current approach set out in the social union framework agreement, the traditional arbitrary nature of the federal government's stance on fiscal arrangements stands to be moderated by commitments to predictability and stability in funding to its provincial partners.

Another feature of the social union framework, connected very closely to fiscal arrangements, is the commitment to establish common and shared priorities among governments. For some, this is a step backwards from a time when the federal government, on the strength and authority of its spending power launched national programs and helped to subsidize the costs for provincial governments. Bob Rae points out that over time, the proportion of the costs paid for by the federal government invariably declined, leaving provincial governments with a bigger bill to pay. By the 1990s, this feature of the arrangements and the added 'indignity' of dancing to Ottawa's tune in regard to establishing priorities, oftentimes falling into provincial jurisdiction, had tarnished the image of cost-shared programs within many, if not most, provincial capitals.

The federal government, for its part, became less willing to share the costs of programs that were driven by client demand and the respective provincial governments' fiscal capacities to roughly match the demand with a supply of programs. This situation was particularly troubling given the federal government's intent on reigning in program expenditures in the face of mounting annual deficits and accumulating national debt. The cap on the Canada Assistance Program, which held year-over-year increases in the federal contribution to 5 per cent in Alberta, British Columbia, and Ontario, was one mechanism employed to put a ceiling on cost-shared program budgets. There were to be more.

In its 1995 budget, the federal government announced its decision to consolidate the Established Programs Financing transfer to the provinces for health care and post-secondary education and the Canada Assistance Plan into a reduced block transfer to provincial governments – called the Canada Health and Social Transfer. The CHST became a lightning rod drawing the heat of social policy activists and provincial governments alike. Activists saw the new mechanism as a federal retreat on two fronts: funding and enforceable standards. Provincial governments, while welcoming the new flexibility of the transfer, mobilized their common opposition around the issue of reduced funding within the block transfer.

In defending the CHST, the federal government used three main points:

- The fight against the deficit was central to the country's capacity to recover the fiscal means necessary to support social programs in the future.
- The old arrangements with their rigid regulations and eligibility criteria actually resulted in perverse situations in which provincial governments lacked the flexibility they needed to serve the very people who needed help.
- Federalism was well served by a new transfer that backed the federal government away from certain areas that were the purview of provincial governments.

In many ways the social union framework agreement is a natural extension of the CHST, and it is the culmination of the situation described well by Bob Rae. In part, the skids along which the agreement moved were greased by a significant infusion of cash by the federal government into the CHST. While the agreement has a lot to do with money, it is not exclusively about money. To conclude that is to sell short both important symbolic and practical elements of the deal. Most strikingly, governments are seeing eye-to-eye on a process for collaborative action on social programs. Mutual priority setting is 'in,' and arbitrary decisions are less likely, at least prior to a prescribed period of notice. The experiment in more collaborative approaches among governments will be bolstered by input from citizens and the voluntary and non-governmental sectors. Added to this is the return to fiscal order among governments throughout the country. Although the public is unlikely to tolerate fiscal imprudence at any level of government, getting the machinery right at a time when most governments will have at least modest capacity to undertake new investments in social policy infrastructure is a propitious convergence.

To be certain, there has been a transformation in the relationship between the federal government and provincial governments. The nature of the new regime provides reason for optimism. There will be those who lament the passing of an era in which the federal government operated in a way that extended beyond its jurisdictional and fiscal grasp. Bob Rae helps to put this into a clearer semantic perspective. He asserts that it is critical to differentiate between national goals and objectives and federal goals and objectives. These may overlap, and in some cases be indistinguishable, yet they are not one and the same. Progress towards national goals does not have to be dictated by the federal government, nor must the goals be determined in isolation by the federal government. That the federal government must play a key role in advancing progressive social policies should not be seriously questioned. However, if the result of a more collaborative partnership approach is sustainable, relevant and effective social program interventions throughout the country, the role will have changed for the better.

It is on this point that Rae provides important insights. Provincial governments are not secondary players in the world of government. History has shown them in many instances to be veritable social policy laboratories (evidence medicare's roots in Saskatchewan and Quebec's new nest of family policies including measures to make child care more accessible and affordable). The social union framework, untested as it is, introduces a rational and functional guide for building the responses to Canada's social policy needs. If we believe that citizens benefit most when governments align their actions, as the majority of Canadians do, then the new agreement opens the door to progress on a range of fronts that need light shone on them. Some of that light will undoubtedly emanate from provincial capitals. To continue with this metaphor, when it comes to child care the federal government is more likely to reflect light than to generate light, which in a federation such as ours may be the way it should be. To repeat: It worked for medicare!

The individual and collective benefits of attending to the developmental needs of our children are more broadly discussed and understood now in Canada than ever before. When will this awareness and comprehension be transformed throughout the country into comprehensive early childhood development policies and programs, including child care? These are important considerations for all Canadians who want to build into our future a fuller range of opportunities for all of our children. The social union framework agreement brings us a little closer to making better things happen for Canada's children.

Note

1 T. Kent, *Social Policy 2000: An Agenda* (Ottawa: Caledon Institute of Social Policy, 1999), 2.

Discussion

The crisp and contrasting presentations generated significant discussion from the floor. One child care advocate clarified that no one in the child care community had ever expected that the federal government would directly run child care programs, but it was expected to be an active financial and planning partner with the provinces. At the time of the implementation of the Canada Health and Social Transfer, in 1995, the federal government had pleaded poverty. Now it is natural to look to the federal government for leadership on child care policy because of the federal surplus, and because of recent promises to direct some of that surplus towards social programs.

Bob Rae argued that for twenty years all the policy innovations in child care have occurred at the provincial level. We are not likely to advance now by relying on the federal government to provide dominant leadership in child care. Instead what is needed is for some province to come forward and lead by example, committing itself to the development of child care programs as a provincial priority.

One symposium participant, responding to Bob Rae, pointed out that we now have a model for child care policy in Quebec, yet it is not being picked up by the federal government. As supporters of child care reform, we should be publicizing and championing these Quebec initiatives. Tom Kent replied that while there was little preventing the federal government from running with the Quebec example, there was also a deep prejudice within the government against this kind of significant financial commitment. Martha Friendly suggested that what was needed was for some other province to pick up the Quebec model and run with it. Alfred MacLeod reminded the group that public goods are competitors for public funding; child care is thus competing with medical care and other social programs. A wise strategy may be to stress the links between child care and health outcomes, child care and educational outcomes, child care and decreased social expenditure, and so on.

Finally, Bob Rae suggested that Lucien Bouchard was no Tommy Douglas, and was thus not likely to champion the establishment of a new federal program. Rae suggested that the advantage of focusing attention on the provinces is that it allows us to draw strength from our diversity. The diversity of design of child care programs can be an important plus. The real problem, he suggested, is that not enough Canadians see child care as an 'us' program. Too many Canadians, instead, see child care as an 'us vs them' program. Health care has clearly become an 'us' program, so that all Canadians see expenditures in this area as benefitting all of 'us.' In contrast, if a program is seen as an 'us vs them' program, then taxpayers ask why they should pay taxes to support something that benefits someone else. We need to emphasize in our public presentations that child care benefits all of us.

The questions shifted to the mode of delivery. One questioner asked whether the type of 'vouchers' that Tom Kent had been suggesting would be restricted to spending on non-profit forms of child care. Another questioner, who has studied polling evidence about public support for child care, suggested that there remained significant disagreements and complexity on the question of just how support ought to be delivered to child care. There is considerable polling support for child care programs in general and some consensus that there is need for programs that would support parental efforts in child care. There is also consensus that child care should be jointly funded by governments and by parents. This led another questioner to raise the recent debate on tax disadvantages facing the stay-at-home parent, as evidence of divisions in public views of just how support for children should be delivered.

Tom Kent responded by stating his opinion that federal funding for child care must take place only through the non-profit sector. He suggested that the provinces would naturally implement policy in different ways. He reminded the symposium that Saskatchewan had moved alone on medicare and that other opposing provinces had only come on board when presented with federal funding.

Martha Friendly suggested that there is no guarantee that parents would direct federal money into non-profit care. Although directing federal money through parents has been presented as the only option under the social union, it poses problems for child care. Tom Kent responded that he saw no difference between the federal government giving the money to provinces with conditions, and giving the same money to parents with conditions. Friendly continued by suggesting that it would be difficult to get fifty funded parents together to set up a non-profit day care centre, so that some kind of funding to non-profit institutions would be needed. Tom Kent suggested that this was where the provinces would come in.

In response to a question of whether child care would have to wait in line for funding behind medical care, Alfred McLeod argued that child care should be linked with other priorities. Further, there would have to be some flexibility in what is considered to be an acceptable program design (province by province) so that the 'best' does not become the enemy of the 'good.'

After another set of questions that focused on details of implementing child care policy, the presenters and discussants offered some final remarks. Bob Rae reiterated that advances in social policy have never been easy and have often not been universally acclaimed at their inception. After all, three decades ago, John Robarts in Ontario had described medicare as a 'Machiavellian conspiracy' by the Federal government! We should not lose sight of the secular trend that has driven day care policy – the increasing entry of mothers into the labour force. This, and our own efforts, are what will turn child care into an 'us' issue, remembering that at various points in our lives we are all children, parents, and grandparents in need of good early care and education. Polling, which turns on how questions are constructed, tends to obscure this general shift in public support. Bob Rae went on to argue that building a coherent child care policy would be part of the process of recovering our sense of the 'public good' and of our collective quality of life.

Martha Friendly emphasized the need to continue efforts to educate the public on child care and develop markers to measure our successes. She suggested that we had to emphasize that our model of child care was not monolithic. Furthermore, the envelope for child care had to be expanded, so that one kind of program for children did not compete against all others.

Tom Kent closed the session by reminding us that early childhood education was a social right. Since under the Constitution it would have to be delivered by the provinces, innovative ways would have to be found to involve the federal government in protecting this social right.

PART 2

What the Rest of Canada Can Learn from
Quebec and from Other Countries

Introduction

The symposium also included two speeches delivered as lunchtime addresses. In each case, the intention was to explore the experiences of other countries and jurisdictions in dealing with the various problems being raised at the symposium. After all, Canada is not the first country to expand its child care system, so some valuable lessons can presumably be learned from what has happened elsewhere. In particular, we have going on within our own country a remarkable expansion of child care services in Quebec. The Quebec government is in the process of providing child care at $5 per day to all preschool and school-aged children in the province, making access to this subsidized system available by age, one year at a time.

How have other jurisdictions addressed the issues faced by the participants in this symposium? How do the outcomes vary according to the choices that have been made? And how did other jurisdictions get from here to there – that is, how did they develop their child care systems, and what lessons can Canada draw as it designs its own comprehensive child care system?

Jocelyne Tougas is a child care researcher and consultant who has been involved in the child care field for twenty years, largely in Quebec. She worked for ten years as executive director of Quebec's provincial association of family day care agencies, and from 1993 to 1996 she was executive director of the Child Care Advocacy Association of Canada. She is currently part of the research team working on the 'You Bet I Care!' study of wages, working conditions, and practices in child care, and she is also on the steering committee of 'Training in Family Day Care,' a research project sponsored by the Canadian Child Care Federation.

Tougas discussed recent developments in Quebec and tried to explain both why the population of Quebec has been so receptive to child care policy reforms and why the Government of Quebec has made these reforms a priority. She suggested that child care policy was positioned as part of an overall approach to families and to education. Thus, child care could not be attacked by its opponents in isolation. Furthermore, the policy was structured to be comprehensive and to offer benefits to a wide variety of different family needs and interests within Quebec. Nevertheless, the critical ingredients for success lay in the particular circumstances within Quebec. Because that province sees child care as being exclusively a provincial responsibility, there is a clear focus for political action. Perhaps more critically, there is a government with a clear direction in family policy that is favourable to child care and with dedicated women in positions of power able to push for child care policy. Not all of these conditions exist in the rest of Canada, but the main principles of Quebec's reforms have a universal application.

Helen Penn is professor of early childhood at the University of East London and a visiting fellow at the Social Science Research Unit, Institute of Education, University of London. She has been an academic for ten years, and before that was an administrator of Early Childhood Services in the United Kingdom. She has done considerable research on private sector child care in Britain, and her recent work has involved international comparisons, both within Europe, and among the developing countries. Her latest book is *Early Childhood Services: Theory, Policy and Practice* (Buckingham: Open University Press, 2000), and she has just completed an analytical review of child care provision in different countries (to be published by the Child Care Resource and Research Unit at the University of Toronto).

Helen Penn attempts to position Canada within the array of countries with child care policies. She emphasizes that policy making is complicated and that advocates and academics were welcomed only if they were in line with what policy makers were considering. Understanding Canada's position requires us to look at three separate areas of policy: educational policy, child care policy, and welfare policy for disadvantaged children. In each case, Canada can be seen as being at a turning-point, deciding between the European public sector approach and the American market-oriented approach.

In education, the issues are how far down the age profile public education should extend and how child care dovetails with education.

In child care, the issue is what kind of public support is to be given to working mothers. In welfare, the issue is how much inequality is to be tolerated as part of the market system. In all three cases, the United States chooses to rely strongly on the market. The choice for Canada is how far we will follow that lead.

5. What We Can Learn from the Quebec Experience

Jocelyne Tougas
Child Care Consultant

It is a tall order to explain how and why, despite having the same budgetary constraints and the same preoccupation with attaining zero deficit as elsewhere in Canada, the government in Quebec was able to introduce a major reform of child care services, injecting new funds and garnering the support of the entire population.[1]

This chapter begins with a discussion of the factors that contributed to creating a climate promoting progress and change in the field of early childhood education in Quebec. They are unique to Quebec, its history, and the Parti Québécois government. Then the early childhood and child care components of Quebec's new family policy are discussed more specifically, as well as how the proposed formula meets the different needs and expectations of the population. The last section examines the major principles underlying the reform of child care services in Quebec that seem to have been responsible for winning the support of most of Quebec's population.

FACTORS CONTRIBUTING TO THE CREATION OF A CLIMATE FAVOURABLE TO THE EXPANSION OF QUEBEC'S CHILD CARE SYSTEM

The Quebec government chose to strategically position early childhood and child care services in a much broader policy context: both as part of family policy and part of education.

Child care services were placed at the heart of Quebec's new family policy in January 1997. The objectives of this policy reflect 'the most important values of our society: the meaning of family and love of children,' to quote Premier Lucien Bouchard. The new policy combined an integrated child benefit for low-income and large families with a maternity and parental insurance plan granting greater numbers of parents access to maternity and paternity leave and more generous benefits. Thus, child care services were associated with policies to fight poverty, enable parents to work, and ensure equal opportunity. Furthermore, parents can take advantage of child care services regardless of their income or employment status. Child care services exist to support parents in their responsibilities – not to replace them.

Likewise, in Quebec the educational role of child care services has been validated and strengthened. Even if they were not integrated into the education system as such, in simultaneously promoting both full-time kindergarten for five-year-olds (in the education system) and early childhood multifaceted agencies for children four years and under, the Quebec government recognizes the central role child care services play in children's development, success in school, and social integration. Framework documents of the educational programs to be applied in kindergartens and child care services were published only a few months apart. There is to be no question of parking children in 'boring' child care until they are of school age. The concepts of educational services and stimulating child care services have been merged. Although each setting is to retain its own procedures, adapted to the environment and culture it serves, the guiding principles and objectives of the educational programs of kindergarten and early childhood centres both resemble and complement one another.

The Quebec Government Assumes Full Responsibility for Child Care Services

Whether one considers child care services to be a social program, an employability measure, or an educational service, in the eyes of the Quebec government and of the population of Quebec, they fall under provincial jurisdiction. Thus, all policies and decisions concerning child care must be initiated, determined, and implemented by the Quebec government. Responsibility to act resides with the province. There is no question of waiting for, much less wishing for, federal intervention. Leadership in this domain comes from Quebec.

Governments and child care advocacy groups elsewhere in Canada do not share this point of view. They believe that the federal government does have a role in child care, and in some cases one of leadership. The more conservative, provincial governments take comfort in this situation and use it to justify inaction in this domain, leaving the entire matter up to the federal government. As for less conservative governments, they concentrate on other areas that they consider to be just as important, but exclusively under provincial jurisdiction. Why should they inject the limited available funds into child care services when they can hand their role and responsibilities over to the federal government? The end results are the same: no progress is made. Child care services weaken and start to fall apart because everyone is waiting for outside intervention.

The Parti Québécois Government Promotes Values that Are Shared by a Majority of Québécois

Quebec moved onto the path of social democracy in a relatively short period, during the *Quiet Revolution*. This was as true of urban centres as of the outlying regions. The values of the Roman Catholic right, which had gagged and snuffed out change for generations, were rejected outright and replaced by the desire for greater openness to the outside world and modern ideas. The Parti Québécois emerged out of this openness to the rest of the world. Its fundamental objective, the sovereignty of Quebec was, and still is, part of a broader philosophy of justice, equality, and liberty. These great principles – justice, equality and liberty – resonate with the people of Quebec whether they support the government's sovereigntist objective or not.

The members of the National Assembly of the Parti Québécois were either active participants in the Quiet Revolution, helped extend its impact, or integrated the values and gains it brought about. They come from all fields of work, but, in order to become a candidate for the Parti Québécois, they first had to pass the social democracy test. They were required to prove that their values were in the right place. They had to have their credentials as activists in organizations and groups who promote social justice and solidarity. Those who transformed themselves into Péquistes overnight for an election without sharing any other party values besides that of Quebec sovereignty were quickly dismissed. Quebec's political and social leaders share common roots and move in the same power circles. Despite possible differences of opinion concerning tactics and strategies, overall, they share a common vision and are dedicated to the same social mission.

Thus, the decision to promote a policy concerning families and children corresponded to the popular will, and the proposed measures rallied the general public as much as the social leaders. The few, mostly right-wing, groups who demonstrated any significant resistance to the reform, had very little effect on the public debate. On the whole, the government ignored their grievances, no doubt considering that they represented marginal positions that would have no significant impact on the implementation of the policy. The government simply gave them no say in the matter.

The Parti Québécois Government and Its Relationship with Community Groups

The recent government policies concerning child care did not appear out of thin air, anymore than did the ones that preceded them. Parti Québécois governments have always maintained close ties with working-class and community groups. For one thing, this is where its roots lie, and for another, it allows the government to stay grounded in reality as much as possible. It goes without saying that this is also a way of guaranteeing the support of these groups, for the most part. The arrangements that the exercise of power dictates are never such as to result in a permanent rupture with the working-class milieux.

The multifaceted early childhood and child care agency model that was taken up by the Quebec government and integrated into its family policy, was developed by Concertaction, a very active lobby group composed of non-profit child care centres. Concertaction submitted its plan during the economic summit called by the provincial government in 1996 that brought together the principal socioeconomic stakeholders in Quebec. The government's main advisers in this area are, in fact, the same people who first developed the model for Concertaction – fieldworkers dedicated to the child care community and devoted to expanding the early childhood and child care system.

In Quebec, non-profit child care associations receive government funding. In principle, these funds are used to provide their members with services such as information, training, and support; in practice, they enable associations to establish an infrastructure that allows them to consult with the community, reflect on policies likely to improve the existing system, and write the briefs they submit to the government. The associations are regularly consulted by the government when preparing bills, regulations, and policies affecting child care and early childhood services. Given that the Quebec government supports through funding the advocacy groups lobbying for quality child care, one may assume that it shares their views on the importance of the role of child care services in the development and growth of young children.

Women Cabinet Ministers at the Helm of Child Care Reform

No matter how important a project, it takes dedicated, determined, and powerful individuals to see it through. In Quebec, the child care portfolio over the years has been carried by women cabinet ministers of great calibre. One that stands out, of course, is Pauline Marois.

Pauline Marois is the minister that brought forward the first child care act in Quebec twenty years ago. She has demonstrated exceptional determination in dire times and used every opportunity – from Camille Bouchard's report on Quebec's children to the reform in education – to raise the issue and make her colleagues in government, and other leaders in the community, understand the importance and role of early childhood and child care services for the future of Quebec.

Powerful women have played a major role in convincing key figures to support child care reform. Getting Premier Bouchard to say publicly that one of the actions undertaken by his government that has given him the most satisfaction is the family and child care policy was quite a feat. Having Gérald Larose, the outgoing president of the Confédération des Syndicats Nationaux (CSN), use child care as an example of the struggles progressive unions need to engage in, was, similarly, an impressive coup.

REALISM, PRAGMATISM, AND SPEED

History has made it such that, in order to preserve their language, culture, and values, the Québécois people have needed to demonstrate political realism and pragmatism. It has often been said that the Québécois are a people of contradictions. The strangest allies unite around a common cause. It is thus that Quebec manages to get all social, community, economic, cultural, and political stakeholders to sit down together at the same table to hammer out a national consensus. While consensus concerning means may not always hold, that regarding the ultimate objectives endures.

The Quebec government's early childhood and child care services scheme, as we have seen, was inspired by proposals developed by community groups (Concertaction) representing those concerned with child care. Furthermore, all stakeholders of the child care community – parents, unions, educational organizations, and business, to name but a few – came forward with recommendations. They expressed their opinions at discussion tables set up by the government, at forums held by organizations, and at the provincial socioeconomic summit. Clearly, unanimity was not reached on all aspects, but even if the proposed reform did not meet all the expectations of the different groups involved, and even if there had not been enough time to iron out all the difficulties and fix all differences, once the government had made up its mind and decided to table the proposed reform, the various parties formed a united front to ensure there would be no impediments to its implementation. The final objective was never lost from sight, nor did it ever lose ground to special interests. The speed with which the government moved on this issue galvanized the troops and stimulated the civil servants' creativity, the proliferation of ideas, and the development of new approaches. Reservations gave way before the need to act – to prove that this vision was the right one and that it could be achieved. Detractors could be allowed no sway, no matter how few in number.

A REFORM THAT SATISFIES DIVERSE INTEREST GROUPS

To begin with, let us remember that the Quebec government had the wisdom to place the early childhood educational services component at the core of its family policy, alongside the integrated child benefit and paid parental leave. These measures are bound together in such a way that it would be difficult to reject one without being seen as attacking all of them at once. If the government had chosen to isolate the issue of child care services and treat it as an independent portfolio – an early childhood policy, for example – the outcome might have been quite different.

This being said, in order to understand what rallied a majority of the population to the family policy, and particularly, the reform of child care services in Quebec, despite the disappearance of certain family assistance programs, the increased public funding, and the complications encountered in implementing the reform, one must examine how the new measures serve the interests and meet the expectations of the principal parties involved.

A Brief Summary of the Measures

A network of multifaceted early childhood and child care agencies was created out of non-profit child care centres and family child care agencies. Each agency is regulated by Bill 145 (Government of Quebec, 1997, Chapter 58 : An Act Respecting the Ministère de la Famille et de l'Enfance and Amending the Act Respecting Child Day Care, but is administered by a private, non-profit corporation; its board of directors is composed primarily of parents. The agencies are open to children ages zero to twelve. For the moment, these agencies offer two types of child care services: family and centre-based care. Eventually, they will be able to offer other types of child care programs such as drop-in centres, nursery schools, evening, night, and weekend child care as well as other family services in collaboration with community organizations.

An educational program has been implemented by all agencies, both family and centre-based; the educational program is adapted to the age of the children and the amount of time they spend in child care. Five-year-olds have access to full-time kindergarten, and part-time kinder-garten combined with in-school educational child care is available for four-year-olds in high-risk communities.

Regulated child care at $5 a day – both family and centre-based – has been offered progressively to four-year-olds, then three-year-olds, and then, in the year 2000, to children of all ages regardless of their family's income. Child care at $5 a day is available to all children attending these programs at least three days a week. Free regulated child care is available for four-year-olds in high-risk communities. Refundable tax credits and an exemption and financial assistance program are maintained for parents unable to take advantage of spaces at the reduced rate.

A permit, licence, or accreditation is compulsory for anyone wishing to offer child care services to seven or more children.

For the purposes of this chapter, I have divided the stakeholders concerned by the child care reform into two major categories which, while not absolute, represent fairly accurately two major schools of thought regarding Quebec's family policy: the early childhood community and the socioeconomic right.

The Early Childhood Community

The Quebec government cut the pear in two. The Ministry of Education was given responsibility for children aged five and up, while the Minis-try of Family and Children took those four and under. Historically, the education and child care communities were divided on this issue. There was a great deal of wrangling, and it was impossible to arrive at a consensus. Thus, while the government's decision was not welcomed by all, it did not provoke a collective uproar, especially as it established permanent structures for connecting the two sectors and avoiding useless and counterproductive duplication.

The government also decided in favour of *regulated and non-profit* early childhood educational services, thus adopting the position that those concerned with the issue had always endorsed, defended, and demanded. It would have been ill-advised for the early childhood community not to support the government's position. The child care field saw the creation of early childhood agencies, the implementation of the educational program in family and centre-based child care, the creation of $5-a-day spaces, and the renewed obligation to hold a permit, as ways of fighting the proliferation of illegal and commercial child care facilities and establishing a basis for a truly affordable and diversified network of quality child care services. Despite the irritants and implementation problems, how could one complain?

Another aspect supported by those who believe in the effectiveness of a comprehensive and integrated approach and who insist on the importance of early intervention, prevention, and detection especially with clienteles who are at risk was the possibility that the early childhood agencies would eventually incorporate all services offered to families and children and work in conjunction with other community organizations. Following the reform, the integrated structure will enable early childhood educators, all of whom are concerned with the well-being and development of children, to discuss and share information concerning a child and his or her family in order to better devise and coordinate interventions so as to guide the child's development and remedy the problems he or she may be encountering.

The reform brought hope to early childhood educators and child care providers. First, it recognized the importance and fundamental role in our society of quality child care services. It thus established a solid basis for increasing recognition of the value of the child care profession and obtaining commensurate remuneration. It points to significant expansion of the system, diversification of child care services, integration of new family services, and thus more jobs and opportunities in terms of both horizontal and vertical career paths. All of a sudden, a profession that seemed to have no future looks promising. Henceforth, the working conditions of child care providers in family and centre-based settings will no longer depend solely on parents and their ability to pay higher child care fees. It goes without saying that unions will make a concerted effort to organize as many workers as possible in support of their demands. The reform of child care services and the Quebec government's commitment to them raise the possibility of substantial improvements in pay and working conditions in the child care field, professionalization of the field, and increased levels of competency and qualifications of those working in the sector. The reform holds something for each of the key stakeholders, all part of the early childhood and child care infrastructure: training institutions, professional groups and associations, and unions.

Regulated, quality child care with trained staff, spaces at $5 a day in one's own neighbourhood at the child care centre of one's choice, with the promise that hours will eventually become more flexible and better adapted to the demands of the workplace – who could hope for more? Working parents support the program wholeheartedly. The only ones who criticize it, and with reason, are those who do not yet have access to spaces at the reduced rate. However, they can still take advantage of the financial exemption or benefit from a tax credit. In the meantime, the government has announced additional funding to create more $5-a-day spaces than initially planned.

The Socioeconomic Right

People with conservative political and economic views come from all fields of activity. It would be fairly safe to say that they usually identify with the following statements – although they do not necessarily support each and every one of them:

- They are not in favour of investing public funds in child care services.
- They consider child care to be a private matter – for which responsibility lies entirely with the parents.
- They believe that governments have other, more important priorities and simply do not have the means to invest in these types of services.
- They extol traditional family values in which the father is the breadwinner and the mother the best candidate to stay at home and look after the children's education.
- They want to keep government intervention in the field to a strict minimum, and they call for deregulation.

Although these people did express their views on the child care reform, they did so in a much less vehement fashion than usual – and with good reason. The announced measures preserve some elements of parental choice. Indeed, parents may take advantage of the refundable tax credit if they opt out of regulated child care. The policy includes a parental insurance program for parents wishing to stay at home with children during their first year. Moreover, the policy can be understood as a work and employability incentive, a way of countering social 'dependency.' As for large or low-income families, they will continue to receive a family allowance. The policy openly recognizes that the primary responsibility for children's education lies with their parents.

As for funding for the new regime, it has mainly come from the amalgamation of existing provincial programs: family allowances, benefits for young children, and the 'baby bonus,' as well as from the repatriation of Quebec's share of the federal government's Child Benefit Program. Moreover, the government has suggested that any new money invested into the program will be quickly offset by short-term savings on welfare, early intervention, and tutoring expenses. Public spending for the reform did not come up as a major issue, especially as the Quebec government was diligently working its way towards a zero deficit.

The business community and employers know first-hand what the lack of child care services costs them in terms of absenteeism. The stress their employees are under because of the constant search for adequate child care arrangements also has measurable repercussions on productivity. Problems related to child care services – the flexibility of child care hours, the cost, and proximity – are all part of business's daily routine. It is remarkable that the business sector, which usually objects to the implementation and expansion of all new social programs, had so little to say about this issue. While it is true that business did not take on the role of valiant promoter of the new regime, it should be noted that it did not oppose the reform either. One suspects that the emphasis on the educational aspect of child care services influenced the tacit approval of business. Business people are well aware that the children of today are tomorrow's workforce, and that society must ensure that children have all the necessary tools to graduate and acquire the skills enabling them to step into the twenty-first century.

Despite its resistance, the commercial child care sector, very active and critical of the government's decisions concerning child care services, also benefited from the reform to a certain extent. The government offered to convert their businesses, for a fee, into non-profit early childhood centres. A commercial child care centre could also choose to participate in the program on a smaller scale and receive subsidies for spaces at the reduced rate ($5) provided that certain conditions were respected. Finally, it could continue to function outside the reform as long as it respected the existing regulations, a kind of 'grandfather' clause. The commercial child care sector's protests – and there were protests – were dismissed by the government. The Parti Québécois government has never attempted to conceal its preference for a non-profit child care system.

Given the options they were offered, including the possibility of maintaining the status quo, and sensing that they did not have strong public support, the private commercial child care centres decided to abandon their protest movement, for the moment at least.

THE PRINCIPLES THAT UNDERLIE THE REFORM

All those concerned by the issue of early childhood and child care services and who are in favour of government intervention to ensure their support and development, attribute a fundamental social, cultural, and economic role to child care. Indeed, access to quality child care services is seen as a means of ensuring equity and equality, first for children who will benefit from a level playing field as they start off in life, and also for women who will be able to enter the workforce and stay active throughout their lifetimes, thus being assured professional opportunities and living conditions on a par with men. It is seen as a way of fighting poverty and enabling parents to work and obtain further training to gain access to jobs with a better salary. Child care is recognized as having an educational role which, while promoting children's growth and development in the short term, benefits society as a whole in the long term. Finally, quality child care services are seen as providing children with a safe environment where they can grow, benefiting from the caring and supervision provided by staff qualified to accompany them and guide their development.

This view of child care is based on principles that have long been put forward by the community as guarantees of a high-quality child care system: the principles of accessibility, affordability, and quality. Several reports and studies have been written describing these principles, examining their every detail, and have made it possible to establish their correlation to the struggle for equity, the fight against poverty, and the socioeconomic growth of society. Here is a brief examination of the form these principles take when applied to child care services.

Accessibility
A high-quality child care system must be comprehensive and include diversified and flexible child care services, available in sufficient number, and delivered either close to the family home or to the parents' workplace. Services must be available during the day, evenings, and weekends. They must be inclusive, welcoming children with special needs and children from different cultural and ethnic backgrounds. All children should have access to them, regardless of the parents' employment status or where they live.

Affordability
A high-quality child care system must allow all who wish to take advantage of it to have the means of doing so.

Quality
A high-quality child care system must have as its base qualified, well-paid, and caring staff with adequate working conditions. It must be supported by laws and regulations that create an environment promoting children's growth and development. It must provide a role for parents and involve them in decisions concerning the well-being and education of their children. Finally, child care services must be non-profit.

Assessing the child care reform put forward by the Quebec government in terms of these three main principles, one can see that the components leading to a good early childhood and child care system are in place.

Accessibility
The concept of early childhood agencies that integrate different child care and family services demonstrates the principle of accessibility. The agencies are an example of educational and child care services offered to young children of different backgrounds, welcoming children with special needs, and made easily accessible to families seeking quality child care services. Needs and priorities involving the consolidation,

development, and expansion of new services are determined by a regional joint action group that includes parties from all areas concerned with early childhood care services, such as the health, education, community, and economic sectors. Additional funding is available to meet the specific needs of targeted clientele. According to government projections, all children whose parents wish to avail themselves of early childhood educational services will find a place within the system by the year 2005.

Affordability
The policy regarding spaces at a reduced rate ($5) obviously reflects the principle of affordability. Given that the decision to chose one child care setting over another, or to withdraw from the job market while children are young, is closely linked to the cost of quality child care services, the $5 rate greatly enhances universal access to good child care and also promotes the expansion of a quality system.

Quality
Although certain groups maintain that reforms and changes to funding methods will be detrimental to the quality of child care, such a conclusion seems premature. Quebec has a regulation in place ensuring adequate standards with regard to group size, teacher-child ratio, physical environment, training of personnel, and educational programs. The province has shown no tendency to deregulate, and for it to do so would be surprising. Whatever happens, the foundations necessary to ensure quality child care services are in place, and advocacy groups will see to it that the government is reminded of its commitments in this regard, just as they have made sure that it is aware of the fundamental importance of child care workers in ensuring and maintaining the quality of the system, and making it work.

CONCLUSION

The hallmark of any good system lies in the value and relevance of its underlying principles, in its flexibility and openness, and in its ability to integrate a vision that strives for excellence and eliminates ideas hindering such a goal. A good system makes sure that its best assets grow, reach new heights and expand, while ensuring that weaker elements either are improved or disappear. When a system is sound, those who use it and those concerned, support it and promote measures that favour its expansion and the positive by-products.

It is too early to tell if the child care system put forward by the Quebec government includes all these criteria, but it is clearly based on sound principles. Will it, however, be able to stay its course and continue the good work? One thing is certain: with regard to child care policy the Quebec government has made a commitment and embarked on a course that sets it apart from the rest of Canada and the United States. It felt no need to delay any longer its decision to invest in early childhood care knowing full well that such an investment is a winning proposition, both in the short and the long term.

Note

1 I have received considerable assistance in filling this tall order from Brigitte Guy, Micheline Lalonde-Gratton, Michel Lanciault, and Claudette Pitre-Robin.

6. Getting Good Child Care for Families: What Can Canada Learn from Other Countries?

Helen Penn
University of East London

One of the processes that happen to you as you get older is that you tend to agree with Einstein – that is you feel you know more and more about less and less. Or put another away, rational explanation comes on a continuum between parsimony and complexity, and having started off at the parsimonious end of the continuum, which is the belief that all behaviour is basically straightforward and subject to rational explanation and prediction – essentially an economist's view – I now operate at the opposite end of the continuum, that is, I believe that everything is richly interlinked and irredeemably complex, and trying to explain, categorize, and predict – or even merely record – what happens in daily life, is, to use Einstein's famous metaphor, like trying to count grains of sand on the beach.

On the other hand, we must start somewhere. To parody Socrates' most famous remark, that the unexamined life is not worth living, unexamined phenomena are not worth having. We need critical research and analysis. So having positioned myself as an older and nearly obsolete Gaia-like researcher, what nuggets of wisdom can I offer about child care?

POLICY MAKING

We would be naive to suppose that policy making was straightforward and logical and simply a case of putting one's arguments to be judiciously heard by clear-minded men and women, and for it to be considered on its merits. We know, to our cost, that policy is more typically driven by circumstances and ideology, and to be heard we have to take part in the wider game of politics, and be opportunistic. Stephen Ball distinguishes between the notion of policy as text, that is, the stated (or hoped for) legislation, and policy as discourse, that is, the set of arguments and circumstances that surround a given (or hoped for) piece of legislation.[1]

From a political perspective, policy making is a never-ending parade of urgent events, most of which have financial implications. To be a politician is indeed to be a juggler, to keep not merely balls in the air, but a whole collection of awkwardly shaped items circulating, any one of which may explode in his or her face. The very difficult task of child care lobbyists is to introduce yet another item into this motley collection of issues that constitute the political discourse.

Issues may be resolved at one level, only to founder on another; the level of government, local, regional, and national, that is, the structure of the government itself also determines the nature of the debates that go on. Having a non-elected House of Lords with a veto has peculiarly skewed British political discourse. In Canada the federal Constitution imposes particular legislative constraints and determines where you make your pitch.

Policy making is complicated, and those who must formulate and administer it are already compromised in many ways. But can policies nonetheless advance? Can policy makers respond to changing times, and devise and administer policies that are more sensible and more relevant? In particular can they respond to changing concepts of the family and changing concepts of childhood? The answer is probably that activists and academics make a difference insofar as they contribute to shaping the wider political discourse, but their contribution is not always welcome or heeded if their message is too off-line. That caveat of opportunism underpins any policy debate.

In this chapter I want to look at how Canada might position herself against the United States, on the one hand, and against Europe, on the other, since the United States and Europe present very different policy options and policy routes. This distinction infuses the rest of my discussion. I want to consider three specific discourses, which are usually presented separately, concerning the provision of services to young children. These are: (1) education policy; (2) child care policy; and (3) welfare policies for vulnerable or disadvantaged children

I am not going to consider tax and benefit policies, although they are critical, because they are not my area of speciality. I can only observe that in some countries it is hard to be poor if you have young children; and in others it is difficult to avoid it. In general, as Shelley Phipps (this volume) shows, where finance goes directly into services for children, rather than into people's pockets to buy services, children benefit directly. But here I will confine myself to discussing the direct provision of services and the rationales that underpin different kinds of provision.

Education

All countries in the world, in theory at least, have an agenda of public education; they have defined a body of knowledge and skills that children must acquire to become functioning adults, and accept a public responsibility for providing it, or at least making sure that someone provides it. How far should that public agenda for education extend downwards, when should it kick in, where is the crossover point between looking after and caring for children and educating them? If learning new knowledge and acquiring new skills, and learning how to learn them, in particular learning the skills of numeracy and literacy, are so important, how long should we wait before officially inculcating them? We know that young children possess an extraordinary potential for learning, but we are less sure about the epistemology: what exactly should young children be learning, and how should that learning be acquired?

Different countries have addressed these questions in different ways. In some European countries, most notably Nordic countries, children are not regarded as ready for schooling, or any kind of formal literacy or numeracy until they are at least seven years old, and they do not usually enter the education system before then (although this situation is currently under revision).[2] Where services are provided for young children – and they are provided generously – they are provided by pedagogues, with four years of post-secondary education, but trained as care rather than education workers. They offer laissez-faire, relaxed regimes; they emphasize creative activities such as dancing and storytelling and domestic and outdoor activities. There is no pressure on young children to learn; they are rather encouraged to 'be' rather than to 'become'; the present is regarded as more important than the future.

By comparison, in the United Kingdom the education system is extending downwards. The argument is, put crudely, you cannot start learning reading, writing, and arithmetic too early. The Department of Education and Employment has now assumed almost all administrative responsibility for the provision and regulation of the education and care of young children. The formal education system is competitive. There is a national curriculum, and children are tested on it at ages seven, eleven, and sixteen, and schools are singled out for praise or blame depending on the results the children achieve. Most children in England, although not in Scotland (which has a slightly different system), now start formal school at age four. At four, children have an entitlement to part-time free nursery education, but for various complex reasons this is mostly offered within schools rather than as a separate nursery experience. Soon this entitlement is to be extended to three-year-olds. A new national curriculum is to be introduced for children aged three to six that stresses the accomplishment of set learning goals, including very basic literacy and numeracy, by age five, with accelerated targets for brighter kids.

The education system in the United Kingdom could be described as swallowing up ever younger children, without modifying or tempering the educational ethos of a competitive system designed for older children. This educational experience does not include child care; so children who also need child care will typically switch between several forms of care within a single day, although, since the current government came to power, the provision of child care is subject to oversight and regulation by the educational administrators.

The Spanish have also addressed the problem of the overlap between care and education – through the Spanish Education Reform Act (LOGSE) of 1990. This is a comprehensive piece of legislation that reviewed the entire education system and its goals. Among other duties, the Ministry of Education assumed responsibility for planning and providing for children aged zero to six years. From earliest infancy children are offered education and care, but there is a careful distinction between the different cycles of education. Infant education is regarded as recognizably different from the education offered at primary level. It encompasses two cycles from zero to three years and from three to six years of age, with a very broad curriculum, set by the ministry; the curriculum is sensitive to regional and local community concerns. At the same time as reforms in early childhood services were introduced, higher education reforms introduced training for teachers to work with these young age groups.[3]

These reforms in Spain were preceded by five years of careful experimentation, research, and debate in all aspects of education policy. I remember attending a conference in Madrid at which the reforms of early years were discussed, just prior to the passing of the reform act, and the atmosphere was magical. More or less the entire preschool community was involved in the discussion and in the realization that their ideas and plans were going to be inscribed in the legislation. Spain in this sense offers an exemplary example of an inclusive and systematic policy process, prompted, I think, by a widely held conviction among politicians and others, that after the thirty-five years of stagnation under the fascist regime of General Franco, policy making had to entail democratically arrived at, serious, and well-thought strategies.

The initial spirit of reform has now been dissipated, and the education act, although a model piece of legislation, has not been fully implemented. But changes have certainly happened.

New Zealand is another country that has introduced educational administration of preschool provision. In New Zealand there was a plethora of different kinds of provision: kindergartens, playgroups, community-based child care, private child care, and so on. In the early 1980s these were brought together under the jurisdiction of the education ministry, which established a common funding structure, common training requirements for staff, common management or 'chartering' structures, and a common curriculum for children aged zero to five years that was supposed to apply to all establishments of whatever kind. A major expansion of the system, particularly for infant care, was planned. The main lobbying impetus for these reforms came from the teachers' trades union, and the Labour government embraced them fully; the Prime Minister David Lange authored and signed the booklet *Before Five* which introduced the reforms.

These reforms, and the money allocated to them were subsequently badly undermined by right-wing governments, but some aspects are still retained. In particular there is a common education based on three years of post-secondary school training for all those who work with children in their early years, including teachers, and a very good common curriculum. Both of these are extremely sensitive to Maori traditions and culture, Maori and Pacific island peoples comprising nearly 20 per cent of the New Zealand population.[4]

Other countries have staked out various positions in regard to the education of young children, both in terms of organization and in terms of curricular activities. Most countries in Europe now offer a free educational entitlement to all children three, four, and five years of age, mostly for four or more hours, although the type of regime offered, and the definitions of learning that apply within it, differ greatly. The questions remain for many systems, how does the educational system dovetail with child care for working parents, and what happens with younger age groups who are not entitled to education?

In the United States, by contrast, one of the determining features of education is the assumption of the validity of a market model. It is assumed that both the private and public sectors can offer comparable services and the provider is of little consequence per se. No European country, except possibly the United Kingdom, would make such an assumption – a point to which I shall return.

Child Care

The discourse on child care for young children has usually arisen from feminist, employment, and equality issues, and has been distinct from the educational arguments. Even in a European context this has been so. However, it is an incontrovertible argument that in order for women to work, someone must care for their children. The employment of women presupposes adequate child care, and if women's access to employment is to be taken seriously as a policy issue, child care must be provided. The question is, who should provide it? Can a market framework deliver appropriate services?

Unlike education, child care, at least in Anglo-American countries, is not usually perceived as a state-provided service, free or heavily subsidized, for users. Instead, child care is viewed as a commodity that women must purchase for themselves, should they decide to use it. Some women may be given assistance in the form of vouchers or credits, to make their purchase, but essentially this presumes a market where child care is bought and sold.

This market, in turn, requires regulating, hence all the discussion about quality standards, to make sure that the products of the market are not substandard. The child care advocates refer to the notion of 'good quality,' although quality is a very elusive notion.[5] One of my most salutary moments was when, in Scotland, through the local authority, I took a private nursery to court, because I argued that its standards were so poor. The case was dismissed by the judge on the grounds that the local authority did not have a sufficiently robust definition of quality. The case cited as a precedent for this legal decision was that of a firm of meat packers. Their meat was of a somewhat suspect quality, but there was not a sufficiently tight understanding of what constituted rotten meat, and so the meat packers were let off. So it was with the nursery; they had been handling children badly, but the

local authority had not defined its regulatory or procedural requirements in a watertight way.

The child care market in this sense is no different from the meat
market. It, too, is a rough place, with its substandard products as well
as the top-of-the-range items, and it needs regulation to safeguard
consumers' interests. The trouble with regulation and regulators is that
they cannot take risks or exercise much discretion. As my Scottish
experience suggests, regulation can only succeed where it is most prescriptive. Those people who argue for 'good quality' child care are
caught in this dilemma. They want to prevent bad practice, and in
doing so they must be very specific in defining what quality is. But, if
you want a living, growing, developing system, one that is innovative
in response to new demands, then you are also trapped by definitions
of quality, which, by their very nature, are arbitrary and fixed.

By contrast, most European countries do not regard child care as a
market phenomenon. They see it as essentially a public service, as an
entitlement for children – even for children under age three – and as an
entitlement for women. Regulation does not arise, since the state sets
the framework for policy, training, curriculum, and so on. Services are
not determined by what parents can afford; children are not dependent
on their parents' income for a high-quality place.

Vulnerability and Disadvantage

The third discourse concerns young children who are vulnerable, either
because of disability or because of very stressed family circumstances.
At any one time, it is estimated, about 20 per cent of children need help,
about a quarter of whom (that is, 5 per cent of children) are likely to
have long-standing disabilities or problems.[6]

Traditionally such children have been dealt with by welfare agencies,
usually in separate programs. There is an increasingly powerfully articulated view, expressed in international agreements such as the *World
Conference on Special Needs Education: Access and Quality*, in Salamanca in
1994, that children with disabilities should not be segregated from
mainstream education. However, there is much more ambiguity about
what should be done about vulnerable or disadvantaged children in
child care settings.

Part of this ambiguity has to do with the rhetoric of early intervention. Jerome Kagan, the eminent Harvard psychologist, calls it 'the
allure of infant determinism' – the idea that infancy represents a critical

period of development, and if there is some kind of benevolent intervention before the age of five, children's life chances will be enhanced.[7] There is now almost an army of psychologists trying to prove this point through ever more elaborately refined methodologies. Kagan pours ridicule on the idea and suggests that the actual evidence, either physiological or psychological, that early intervention makes a difference is very slight, but that the ideology that justifies it is overwhelming. Early intervention protects the myth of equality in a society that, like the United States, is profoundly unequal. Social class, and one might add, cultural context, are the most powerful predictors of future performance: 'So many people believe in infant determinism [because] it ignores the power of social class membership. Though a child's social class is the best predictor of future vocation, academic accomplishments and psychiatric health, Americans wish to believe that their society is open, egalitarian, without rigid class boundaries. To acknowledge the power of class is to question this ethical canon.'[8]

In a society like the United States, where the government favours market solutions and cannot acknowledge that an egalitarian system means that the same kinds of resources are available to all children regardless of their parents' circumstances or income, a targeted or segregated early intervention program for vulnerable children is a neat solution. It costs relatively little but avoids heartlessness; it shows society still has a remnant of responsibility towards children who are patently disadvantaged by virtue of their families' poverty or by some disability.

Are there other models? Economists like Amartya Sen argue that social disorder is partly a function of the gini coefficient; in other words, the more unequal society is, the more problematic the lower classes become, and the more costly it becomes to control them.[9] Ethics and economics go hand in hand. In those countries where there is access to comprehensive and universal basic services that are democratically run, there are less likely to be so many social problems (which in turn incur heavy law-and-order costs). So in the Nordic countries, although of course there are social problems, they are far less acute than anything experienced in the United States, where child poverty is higher than anywhere else in the developed world, where the prison population per capita is also the highest in the world, and where the life expectancy of an African American man is less than that of a male in Bangladesh – one of the world's poorest countries.[10]

Translated into early childhood services, this means that there are likely to be far fewer traumatized children in egalitarian societies. In my book *Comparing Nurseries*, I commented on northern Italy. North Italy is prosperous, homogeneous, and egalitarian, and its state-run nurseries are available to all children whose parents want to use them.[10] It was extremely rare to come across a child in a nursery who was in a bad way. Whereas in the United Kingdom, which is much less egalitarian, we have targeted welfare nurseries or family centres that cater exclusively to children who are in a bad way. Not only are there more vulnerable children in the United Kingdom, but they are segregated into not very good, specialized provision. Jack Tizard, an eminent academic in the United Kingdom, who was, in his lifetime, profoundly concerned with vulnerable children, said that 'a service for the poor is inevitably a poor service.'[12]

Targeted services are in effect a kind of ghettoization. They are a deliberate segregation of those children who have, possibly arbitrarily, been defined as disadvantaged. Such ghettoization, instead of relieving disadvantage and difference, serves to confirm it.

Although it represents something of a continuum, the argument concerning the integration of children with physical or learning disabilities is a slightly different one, because physical or learning disability can and does cut across social class. The argument is that children with disabilities – as opposed to disadvantaged children – need specialized help that is not routinely available in 'normal' provision. However, as various people have suggested, definitions of physical or learning disabilities can also be suspect, and both diagnosis and treatment can be shown to have changed over time and according to fashion.[13]

There are some carefully documented examples of the integration of services for children with disabilities in the early years.[14] I was myself involved in a nursery in Scotland which, as well as having 'normal' children, also catered to some of the most profoundly disabled children (non-ambulant, with little if any responsiveness to sound, touch, or any other stimuli). These severely disabled children could not be integrated into the daily life of the nursery, and they were placed in a separate room, although visited by the other children. But their parents could be and were integrated. What happened was that other parents helped them out. There were all sorts of extracurricular activities for adults alongside those of the children, in which everyone took part. The parents of the disabled children were not ashamed or embarrassed about their children in company, and the non-disabled children and their parents saw and accepted disability as a normal part of life.

Children with disabilities can be integrated, and services can adjust in such a way as to make their integration painless; specialist services such as physiotherapy can be brought to the nursery rather than hauling the child to a specialist. Services that extend themselves in this way have to be more thoughtful about what they provide, and thoughtfulness is usually the prerequisite for better, more flexible, and more imaginative services.[15]

CONCLUSION

In this chapter, I have discussed three strands of early childhood services: education, child care, and welfare services for vulnerable children. If I were to give advice, which I only do reluctantly as an outsider, I would say that any serious attempt to provide services for young children must address all three issues: education, child care for working parents, and the inclusion of vulnerable children. There are many models for doing it, but not to do it is to invite yet more angst.

The most powerful argument for action in North America, because it has so much immediate political appeal, has been that of early intervention; the notion that children are much more receptive to societal manipulation, albeit beneficial, before the age of five, and therefore it is much cheaper to intervene when they are young than when they are older. But this is a suspect argument on a number of counts, as I have already indicated. Moreover, it has not been used in any of the countries, European and further afield, where there are widespread early childhood services and where the notion of entitlement has proved more persuasive, both entitlements for children and entitlements for women.

A further characteristic of many European countries is that policy reforms have not only been value based, they have been comprehensive. A coherent policy on early childhood services has to take on board a tranche of reforms, legislative, administrative, and financial, curricular, and training, which relate to and derive from one another as essential and indivisible components. The European Child Care Network, which is a European Commission working group of experts from European member states has summarized how such comprehensive policy frameworks might be developed in their document entitled *Quality Targets in Services for Young Children*.[16] It provides a useful benchmark and serves as a contradistinction to a U.S. market-based model.

One last point to make is that there is a more recent set of arguments developing the notion of entitlement for children and how it can be measured.[17] These are derived from the U.N. Convention on the Rights of the Child. The argument is that children are people with rights, and they have legitimate thoughts and feelings about the circumstances in which they find themselves that should be given voice.[18] There is now a considerable and increasing body of academic work around this issue of children as a distinct and oppressed social group,[19] and the most recent government-sponsored research in Nordic countries,[20] in Italy,[21] and even in Scotland,[22] highlights the need to regard young children not as incomplete and inarticulate beings who we adults must shape with our early intervention programs, but as consumers of services in their own right, who must be consulted about how they are treated. The international journal *Childhood* is a useful reference point for this debate. If children themselves can provide informed comment on what they experience, then this too should influence the nature and shape of provision. Children presumably do not want to be crammed into small places for long hours with unsympathetic adults, but their preferences seem not to be taken into account; they are consumers without choices. It is no coincidence that the United States, along with Sudan, are the only countries in the world that have not signed the Convention on the Rights of the Child. One is inclined to ask, how can it, given the gross inequalities and violent culture that it perpetuates?

Canada is perhaps at a turning-point. Do you look south to the United States or across the pond to Europe? They are very distinct routes drawing on very diverse societal models and calling upon very specific research assumptions; they imply very different policy routes.

Notes

1 S. Ball, *Education Reform: A Critical and Post-Structural Approach* (Buckingham: Open University Press, 1994).

2 Children in Scotland, *Services to Young Children: Study Visit to Denmark and Sweden* (Edinburgh: Children in Scotland, Fact Sheet no 48, 1998).

3 M.M. Garriga, 'The Spanish Education Reform Act and Infant Education,' in *Early Childhood Services: Theory, Policy and Practice*, H. Penn, ed. (Buckingham: Open University Press, 1999).

4 M. Carr and H. May, 'Te Whariki: The Making of the New Zealand Curriculum,' in *Early Childhood Services: Theory, Policy and Practice*, H. Penn, ed. (Buckingham: Open University Press, 1999).

5 G. Dahlberg, P. Moss, and A. Pence, *Beyond Quality* (London: Falmer Press, 1999).

6 The Salamanca Statement and Framework for Action on Special Needs Education, from the World Conference on Special Needs Education: Access and Quality, Salamanca, Spain, 7–10 June 1994. The statement was published by UNESCO and the Ministry of Science and Education, Spain.

7 J. Kagan, *Three Seductive Ideas* (Cambridge, MA.: Harvard University Press, 1998).

8 Ibid., 147.

9 A. Sen, *Inequality Re-examined* (Cambridge, MA: Harvard University Press, 1995).

10 De Vylder, *The Economics of Childhood* (Stockholm: Radda Barna, 1997).

11 H. Penn, *Comparing Nurseries* (London: Paul Chapman, 1997).

12 J. Tizard, *Conference Paper, Sunningdale Conference on Low-Cost Care* (London: HMSO, 1976).

13 P. Alderson and C. Goody, *Enabling Education* (London: Tufnell Press, 1998).

14 S. Wolfendale, ed., *Special Needs in the Early Years: Snapshots of Practice* (London: Routledge, 2000).

15 J. Holdsworth, *Lao Integrated Education Programme* (London: Save the Children, 1994).

16 European Childcare Network, *Quality Targets in Services for Young Children* (Brussels: European Commission, 1996).

17 J. Qvortrup, M. Bardy, G. Sgritta, and H. Wintersberger, eds., *Childhood Matters: Social Theory, Practice and Politics* (Aldershot: Avebury Press, 1994).

18 P. Alderson, *The Rights of Children Under Five* (London: Save the Children, 1999).

19 A. James and A. Prout, *Constructing and Reconstructing Childhood* (London: Falmer Press, 1998).

20 STAKES (Finnish Welfare Ministry), *Conference Proceedings on the Voice of the Young Child* (Helsinki: Author, 1998).

21 Dahlberg et al., *Beyond Quality*.

22 Scottish Office, *Tender Specifications for Three- and Four-Year-Olds in Daycare* (Edinburgh: SOEID, 1999).

Discussion

The two lunchtime speeches left little time for discussion, but generated enormous interest. After Jocelyn Tougas's speech on the Quebec innovations, there was some concern expressed by two questioners. One suggested that although Quebec seemed to have designed a utopian policy for child care, it had been implemented too quickly. The high demand for $5-a-day spaces created considerable problems in providing them on relatively short notice. Staff could not be trained quickly enough, and the eight-month training program provided in Quebec was simply inadequate. The short-term measure of increasing child-staff ratios could not work over any significant period of time. Thus, there had been considerable growing pains, and the program was as yet unproven. A second questioner asked how family home care would fit into the Quebec plans in the long run.

Other reactions were more positive. One questioner suggested that the short-run problems in Quebec would disappear in the long run. A second urged critics to maintain some perspective on these growing pains, and suggested that child advocates in other provinces would love to have some of Quebec's problems!

Jocelyn Tougas responded by admitting that there had been some problems. However, she suggested that the policy provided a firm base on which to build a child care system in Quebec. She also suggested that the speed with which the policy had been implemented had some significant advantages, because it involved all advocates working together to address any problems. Tougas admitted that the long-run evolution of family day care was as yet uncertain.

After Helen Penn's speech, comments from the floor pointed out the difficulty in moving beyond an early education paradigm for child care and in enlisting children in the decision process. One questioner suggested that it was difficult for Canadians to look beyond the U.S. experience in child care.

PART 3

What Is Good Quality Child Care and
How Do We Get It?

Introduction

The second session of the conference turned to a discussion about what the word 'quality' means when considering child care. Everyone is, of course, in favour of 'high quality' child care. Everyone at the symposium was in general agreement that achieving higher quality was going to require spending more money per child than is currently being spent in most day care centres across Canada. In fact, the monograph by Cleveland and Krashinsky, which stimulated the symposium, suggested that child care should cost about $8,500 per year for each child between the ages of two and five years of age, which is significantly more than what governments are paying for that care right now. What is seldom laid out is exactly how that extra money might be spent and how the inevitable policy trade-offs should be resolved.

For example, many would agree that child care staff require a post-secondary education, at least at the college level. What kind of education should be mandated? Should the program last for two years or three, and should a university degree be required for all staff in the centre, or a majority, or some, keeping in mind that salaries will have to rise if training requirements are raised? Furthermore, it is generally agreed that children benefit when staff-child ratios are kept high. How high should they be, and should they depend on staff education levels, or staff experience? Children are hurt when there is frequent staff turnover, so keeping staff will require some kind of salary grid that rewards experience and makes possible a career in day care. What kinds of pay increase would be required to accomplish this, and do pay increases mean staff-child ratios will have to be lower for child care to be kept affordable?

Agreeing, in a general sense, on what is desirable is not enough. With a budget that will undoubtedly be too low to have everything (e.g., $8,500 per child), choices will have to be made. Is it better to increase staff-child ratios or to increase the training of staff and the wages they would have to be paid, or a bit of both? If we agree that training is important, should we insist that all staff receive the same training, or should we train some staff more and have them assisted by staff with lower levels of training? Should devoting additional resources to staff take precedence over directing resources to physical plant? Is education more important than experience, or vice versa? Should the first scarce dollars be spent on getting better-prepared directors in child care facilities, or better front-line staff?

It is also unclear how a national child care program would treat in-home child care. Currently, more children are cared for in homes than in centres, although centre-based care is predominant among licensed and regulated facilities. Most family day care is unsupervised, and even when it is supervised, training levels are generally lower than in child care centres. Would the $8,500 that was discussed in the monograph by Cleveland and Krashinsky be available for in-home regulated child care, and if so, what standards would apply?

These issues are rarely confronted directly. There is a fear that any compromises made on child care quality could have significant negative effects on the development of some children. Although it is widely recognized that someone will eventually have to make compromises in designing a radically expanded child care system, nobody wants to be the one to recommend those compromises. Still, it is important to explore, even in a preliminary way, which trade-offs are worth considering, and which are too risky to contemplate.

Not being specific about program design and program quality has its own risks. If the demands for additional funding per child are unlimited, then politicians may be less willing to commit additional funds (since any increase could simply generate additional demands). If child care experts are unwilling to provide a guide to acceptable and unacceptable trade-offs in policy design, these choices will be made haphazardly if and when reforms are initiated.

The focus of the symposium was on moving the debate about universal child care services from 'why' to 'how.' For that reason, we devoted the second session to examining just how good quality child care might be achieved. The two presenters were chosen because of their long-established interest in this question. Hillel Goelman is a professor in the departments of Educational and Counseling Psychology and Special Education at the University of British Columbia. His research interests include the impact of child care on children and the formation of child care policy, and he has been a co-investigator on both the Canadian National Child Care Study and the 'You Bet I Care!' project. The latter focused on wages, working conditions, and quality in child care centres and family day care homes.

Gillian Doherty has a doctorate in child and clinical psychology. She has worked for the Ontario Ministry of Community and Social Services as both a regional director and a director of policy services. She is now an independent child care research and policy consultant, principal investigator on the You Bet I Care! reseach study, and an adjunct professor at the University of Guelph.

The two discussants, Ellen Jacobs and June Pollard, commented directly on the two presentations. Ellen Jacobs is a professor of early childhood and elementary education at Concordia University. She has written extensively in the field of school-age child care and is co-editor of the *Canadian Journal of Research in Early Childhood Education*. She consults with day care centres on quality issues. June Pollard is the director of the School of Early Childhood Education at Ryerson Polytechnic University, and she has recently been involved in two Child Care Visions projects related to quality issues.

Hillel Goelman presented on the importance of training in generating quality. His chapter suggested that the best use for additional funds in child care would be to improve the training of staff, and he suggested that a program involving a minimum of two years of post-secondary education should apply to all staff working with young children. His focus was principally on child care centres. Gillian Doherty examined the various determinants of quality and concluded that the emphasis ought to be on increasing the remuneration available to child care workers in both centres and family child care. Higher salaries would reduce turnover and allow for more training. A second priority was providing more support to family child care providers. Doherty argued that the large role served by family child care was not likely to disappear as we move towards more universal use of child care services and thus that improving care in this sector was a key priority.

Ellen Jacobs discussed why training for child care workers was so low, and suggested that achieving uniform standards would not be easy. She also questioned why different standards should persist for workers in centres and in-home facilities. June Pollard suggested that the emphasis on training had hidden dangers, including being a potential threat to diversity and erecting a barrier between those with training and those without (including many workers in family child care).

7. Moving towards Achieving Quality Child Care

Gillian Doherty
Child Care Consultant

The monograph that served as the inspiration for this publication suggests that Canada can afford to spend between $5 and $6 billion annually for a child care program for children aged two to five.[1] Although an expenditure of this size would assist in the development of a high-quality program, it is not sufficient to do everything that would be desirable. Therefore, hard decisions must be made about priorities. This can only be attempted after clarification of what is meant by 'good quality child care' and identification of the current situation. After defining 'quality' and looking at the current situation, this chapter concludes that the priorities for any new funds should be increasing remuneration levels in both centre- and family-based settings and providing additional supports to family child care.

WHAT IS GOOD QUALITY CHILD CARE?

Defining good quality child care involves addressing three basic questions. First, what does the child's family and community value for its children – what are their perceptions of a desirable child care experience? Second, what does the society want its children to become – what skills, knowledge, and abilities are valued by it and required for its survival? Third, what does the family need to support its child-rearing role – what type of care, when, what can it afford to pay?

Family and Community Values

In 1998 the Canadian Child Care Federation sponsored a series of ten community workshops across Canada to explore the issue of quality environments for young children. The workshops involved parents, child care providers, representatives from other services for children and families, health professionals, and municipal politicians. There was widespread agreement about the characteristics of a desirable experience for young children both across workshop participants and across sessions. High value was placed on protection of children's health and their physical and emotional security, adult behaviour that is supportive and respectful of the child, acknowledgment of the uniqueness of each child, and the provision of experiences that foster the development of good communication and social skills.[2]

Desired Developmental Outcomes

Daniel Keating, at the Ontario Institute for Studies in Education, suggests that there is broad agreement in Canada regarding desirable developmental outcomes for children. These include the ability to make effective social connections with others, good coping skills, the ability to handle stress in an adaptive fashion, a sense of psychological well-being, and good self-esteem.[3] If Canada is to prosper in the high technology international economy, it needs people who can think creatively, are adaptable, have good problem-solving skills, have high literacy and numerical skills, and are able to master new technologies as they emerge.[4]

Meeting the Needs of Families

The labour force participation of women with young children has steadily increased over the past two decades. In 1975, 31.2 per cent of all mothers with a child under age three, and 40.0 per cent of those whose youngest child was age three to five were engaged in paid work. By 1997 the percentages had risen to 64.1 per cent and 68.8 per cent respectively.[5] It is now rare in Canada for one parent in a two-parent family to remain at home to care for the children, do the housework, and attend to the myriad other tasks related to daily life. Not surprisingly, a survey of 22,000 Canadian families found that 50 per cent of working mothers and 36 per cent of working fathers reported high levels of stress.[6] A major source of this stress is the difficulty parents experience finding reliable child care that will support their child's development, is available for the hours needed, close to home or work, and affordable.[7]

In summary, there are three aspects to good quality child care:

1 Meeting the child's needs. This requires physical environments that minimize the risk of accidents, injury, or infection and promote

children's physical health and well-being. Also required are interactions with warm, caring adults who respond promptly and sensitively to each child and provide daily experiences that are stimulating and appropriate to the child's developmental level. This type of care is much more likely to occur when child and care provider are in a long-term relationship. In Canada's multicultural society, there is a particular need for child care that provides a measure of cultural and linguistic continuity, especially for infants and toddlers.[8]

2 Meeting the needs of families. This requires care that the parents feel comfortable with, is available at the hours required by the family, in reasonably close proximity to the parent's home or workplace, and affordable.

3 Meeting the needs of the community and the larger society. This requires working in partnership with the family to assist the child to develop the skills, knowledge, and abilities valued by the community and required to succeed in the larger society. In a multicultural society such as that of Canada, there may be inconsistencies between the values and needs of the larger society and those of the child's culture of origin. Recognition of this has led to the concept of helping children to become 'bi-cultural,' that is, equally comfortable and competent in both cultures.

FACTORS ASSOCIATED WITH GOOD QUALITY CHILD CARE

Twenty years of child care research provide considerable information about what enables and encourages, though does not guarantee, safe, healthy environments and care provider behaviours that facilitate child well-being and development.[9] This research identifies five key factors, which will be discussed below: (1) a limited number of children per care provider; (2) specialized training related to child development and/or early childhood care and education; (3) adequate remuneration levels for care providers; (4) social support for care providers – this is particularly important for family child care providers who usually work alone with a group of children; and (5) staff consistency.

THE CURRENT SITUATION IN CANADA

Ratio

The Canadian Child Care Federation recommends optimal care provider–child ratios for centres that have been adapted from those recommended by the U.S. National Association for the Education of Young Children and are based on research findings.[10] The regulations in every province and territory in Canada fall short of meeting these, though usually only by one or two children, for example, allowing a ratio of 1:8 instead of 1:7 for three-year-olds. The only ratio of real concern is Quebec's provision for a ratio of 1:5 for children age zero to eighteen months rather than the recommended 1:3.[11] When one caregiver has five children still in diapers and having to be fed or assisted with feeding, the likelihood of children having to wait for their needs to be met is high.

The Canadian Child Care Federation does not specify the desirable number of children per care provider in family child care. Instead, it indicates that the number and age of the children should permit evacuation by the care provider should this be necessary.[12] Provincial and territorial regulations, except in the Northwest Territories, limit the number of children under age two years cared for by one provider to two or three at the same time. Most also limit the number of children under age five years.[13]

The Proportion of Care Providers with Specialized Training Related to Child Development and/or Early Childhood Education

A Canada-wide survey of centre-based staff conducted in 1998 reports that 11.4 per cent of all child care staff have no specific training related to child development or early childhood education. The majority of staff do, however, have Early Childhood Care and Education training; 10.4 per cent have completed a one-year ECCE training course; 42.1 per cent have completed a two-year course, and 29.2 per cent have a higher ECCE credential. Thus, 71.3 per cent of all centre staff who responded to the survey have a two-year ECCE credential or more.[14]

The available information suggests that formal ECCE credentials are more rare in family child care. A Canada-wide survey of the regulated sector conducted in 1996 collected information about general educational levels but not training related to early childhood education. It reports that 35.9 per cent of the respondents had obtained a post-secondary school certificate, diploma, or degree.[15] A companion study on unregulated family child care conducted in 1997 did seek information about ECCE training. Six percent of the respondents reported having an ECCE diploma from a two-year program; 4 per cent said they had an ECCE certificate from a one-year program, and 1 per cent reported having an ECCE degree.[16]

Remuneration Level

A Canada-wide survey of centres conducted in 1998 found that nationally the median highest hourly rate found in centres was $10.00 for assistant teachers, $11.98 for teachers or supervisors, and $14.25 for head supervisors or teacher-directors.[17] Since this is the median highest rate, many centre staff have wages below these levels.

Remuneration levels are lower in family child care, whether it is regulated or unregulated. Nationally, regulated caregivers, who provide care for a full year for an average of 5.4 children, earn an annual gross income of $15,600. However, after deducting expenses related to providing child care services this annual income drops to $8,400 before taxes.[18] Caregivers in the unregulated sector on average care for four children. Their average annual gross income is about $10,400. This drops to a national average of $6,400 before tax when child care–related expenses are deducted.[19]

The low levels of remuneration for both centre- and family-child care providers are completely inconsistent with the complexity of the work and the responsibility associated with supporting and fostering young children's development.

Social Support

Staff in centres work with at least one other person in the centre, even if not in the same classroom, and often have several co-workers. In contrast, the family child care provider generally works alone. Regulated family child care providers in Alberta, Nova Scotia, Ontario, and Quebec are affiliated with an agency that is legislatively required to provide in-home visits on a regular basis. Some agencies go beyond this, for example, setting up provider peer support networks, arranging professional development opportunities, and/or providing regular play groups for caregivers and the children for whom they are responsible. Other agencies provide only the minimum support required by legislation.

It is much harder for independently licensed or unregulated family child care providers to link with support services. Such programs are only widely available in two provinces. British Columbia funds non-profit organizations (Child Care Resource and Referral Programs) to support and train both licensed and licence-not-required family child care providers. In Ontario, government funding supports Family Resource Programs which have a specific mandate to support the unregulated child care sector.

Staff Consistency

A Canada-wide study conducted in 1991 reports a national annual turnover rate of 26 per cent among centre teaching staff.[20] Reported caregiver turnover rates in regulated family child care are higher. Family child care agencies in an Alberta study reported a province-wide turnover rate of 51 per cent within the previous twelve months.[21] In Ontario, a survey conducted in 1989 found that the average rate of agency-sponsored caregiver turnover was about 45 per cent.[22] Both reports note considerable variation in turnover rates across agencies within their respective provinces. This may reflect the influence of factors such as the level and type of support provided by the agency to its caregivers. For example, one Ontario agency that provides a range of support services reports that 55 per cent of its caregivers have been with the agency for five years or more and 24 per cent for ten years or more.[23]

WHERE ARE THE CHILDREN?

In 1994–5 an estimated 67 per cent of children under age six years and 69 per cent of children age six to twelve receiving regular non-relative care outside their own home obtained this care in a family child care home.[24] There are a number of possible reasons for this heavy use of family child care, reasons that would suggest it is likely to continue. These include:

1 In 1988 only 55 per cent of working parents had a standard work week (Mondays to Fridays only, with fixed daytime hours).[25] Since then the incidence of non-standard work patterns has increased significantly.[26] However, for staffing reasons, it is difficult for centres to accommodate a parent's need for irregular or changing hours of care. Family child care homes have greater potential flexibility in their hours because they usually only involve one caregiver or one caregiver and an assistant.
2 Many parents prefer family child care for infants and toddlers because of its familylike setting and smaller number of children.[27]
3 Some parents particularly value having their child remain with the same caregiver for the whole of the child care day, which typically is longer than the eight-hour shift worked by centre staff.[28]
4 Experts in the child care field note that cultural and linguistic continuity between home and alternate care is particularly desirable for

infants and toddlers from cultures other than that of the dominant society. Cultural consistency makes it more likely that young children will become firmly rooted in their own culture and can use this rootedness to become comfortable in the dominant culture as well.[29] Parents who are recent immigrants or from a culture other than the dominant culture sometimes prefer having a care provider from their own background. Finding a care provider from the child's own culture is often more feasible in the family child care sector.

5 Family child care homes are a more practical approach to child care provision than are centres in situations of sparse, scattered populations such as found in many parts of Canada.

It is interesting to note that significant use of regulated family child care occurs in countries with a well-established, affordable network of child care centres. For example, in Denmark, 61 per cent (56,690) of the children under age three years receiving child care are in family child care homes; however, about 90 per cent of older children attend centres.[30] Family child care in Sweden cares for 27 per cent of children between age zero and three years, and 22 per cent of children age three to seven.[31]

IDENTIFYING PRINCIPLES, SETTING PRIORITIES

As noted earlier, $5 to $6 billion a year from the government would not be sufficient to fund everything that should be done to develop a universally accessible high-quality child care system. Therefore, hard decisions must be made about values and priorities. The priorities suggested in this chapter are based on three principles:

1 All child care must be safe and the activities provided must support child development. A distinction is being made between care that purposefully seeks to enhance development through a planned 'curriculum' and care that sets the stage for development to unfold in the course of daily activities. For example, while purposeful programming to stimulate language development might be desirable, increasing the time caregivers talk with (not at) children may be a more realistic first goal.
2 Available funds should be used to bring the whole system to the level of quality that sets the stage for development to unfold, not to enhance parts of the system that are already stronger.

3 Child care must meet the needs of the parent and family by being reasonably close to home or work and available during the hours needed.

On the basis of the four key factors associated with quality noted earlier, the current situation is better in centre- than in family-based care. Formal ECCE training is more common, turnover is lower, and most teachers have some social support through co-workers and/or supervisors. Ratios, with the exception of Quebec's permitted ratio for infants, are not significantly out of line with those recommended by advocacy groups.

However, the largest proportion of children are in the family child care system. For the reasons already identified, this is likely to continue. Of particular concern is the fact that 69 per cent of children under age six in family child care are in unregulated situations that do not have to meet even basic health and safety standards.[32] For all the reasons noted above, enhancing quality in the family child care system would appear to be more crucial than addressing factors associated with quality in centres. The exception is the need to address the low remuneration levels in centre- as well as in family-based child care.

Research has repeatedly found an association between low salary level and negative care provider behaviours in centres. It has also found that salary level is a better predictor of overall program quality than ratio or teacher ECCE qualifications. Poor remuneration is associated with high turnover in both centre- and family-based care and therefore impedes the development of consistent relationships between child and adult.[33] In the family child care field, it impedes recruitment.[34] While there does not appear to be research on the issue, low remuneration may well be a disincentive to seeking college training. This is especially true if obtaining such education requires taking out a loan that then has to be repaid. Given the pervasive negative impact of current low remuneration levels across the whole child care system, addressing the compensation level must be the top priority in both sectors. The potential positive effect of increasing training levels or reducing the number of children per caregiver would be lost if turnover remains high and/or recruitment is difficult.

Priority One: Addressing Current Low Remuneration Levels

As a first step, remuneration should be increased for all providers in both the centre- and family-based child care systems. These basic increases should not be dependent on formal ECCE credentials but instead should be an acknowledgment of the complexity of the job being done. However, the opportunity should be taken to use increased remuneration levels to encourage people to seek experiences that will increase their knowledge and skills. Therefore, all persons with an ECCE credential should be paid a bonus in addition to the basic increase given everyone. In the family child care field, as argued below, current ECCE certificates and diplomas may not be the most appropriate preparation. However, the same principle should be applied. The bonus in this case might be tied to successful participation in professional development activities and/or a certification process that requires the person to demonstrate a certain knowledge base and skill level. Maintenance of salary differentials based on ECCE education or demonstrated competence would encourage people to broaden their knowledge and abilities.

If money was used to increase remuneration levels across the board, could 'savings' be made by making changes in other areas? In France, a ratio of 1:28 is permitted for three- to- six-year-olds in centre-based care, though in practice the actual ratio is closer to 1:22. Teachers for this age group have the equivalent of a Master's degree in early childhood and elementary education.[35] There has been some speculation in Canada that increased educational requirements for centre staff would enable a teacher to be responsible for more children than currently permitted.[36] If the above suggested bonus for an ECCE certificate or diploma were successful in increasing the number of centre staff with at least a two-year ECCE diploma, could they be made responsible for more children? The answer is probably no, especially in regard to children under age six years. The decision to increase remuneration should not be conditional on some future saving made through changing ratios.

The ability of a teacher in France to provide what is considered to be quality care for twenty-two preschoolers must be considered in context. In Canada all adult classroom staff are counted in the ratio, regardless of their educational background. There is little job differentiation. Instead each adult works with the children, gets involved in serving snacks, tidies up, and does whatever else may be required. However, in France, only the professionally trained teacher is counted in the ratio. She usually has an assistant who is responsible for helping children dress, serving snacks, supervising nap, and so on. This allows the teacher to concentrate on developing and implementing program activities. Centres have cooks and maintenance workers who relieve the assistants of some tasks they might otherwise have to do.[37] As a result, when the whole staffing pattern is taken into account the French ratio for preschoolers is much better than 1:22. Similarly, in infant and toddler rooms only the person responsible for the group is counted in the ratio. However, there are usually 'floating' infant staff who help with changing and feeding. This makes the actual ratio better than the official ratio of 1:5.[38]

The French staffing pattern, with a highly trained professional assisted by a less-trained person and clear task differentiation, raises the question of whether all staff in a centre involved with children need a college ECCE credential. Some saving might be achieved by requiring only one person in a classroom to have post-secondary school ECCE training and providing them with a less-trained assistant so that they could focus on programming. This would create more of a career ladder than currently exists and permit differential salary levels.

Priority Two: Supporting Family Child Care

As illustrated by the reasons already cited for the current high use of family child care, a system that aims to meet child and family needs must include this sector. This holds true in spite of concerns that may exist about the isolation of care providers, the lesser likelihood of their having college-level ECCE education, and current turnover rates. Two longitudinal studies conducted in different cities in Sweden demonstrate that quality in family child care can be equal to that in centre care. Regulated family child care in Sweden is embedded in a support infrastructure that enables it to be of high quality. In both studies, developmental outcomes when the children were in elementary school were equally good whether the child had been in centre- or family-based child care as an infant or toddler.[39] Concerns about provider isolation, turnover rates, and presumed poorer understanding of child development and child care provision can and must be addressed. For example, caregivers can be assisted to develop routines to ensure that older children understand and practice what is to be done if a child must go to hospital or a home has to be evacuated. Linkages with other caregivers can reduce stress, as can opportunities to go to a drop-in centre or play group for caregivers and children. In-service education can expand a caregiver's understanding of what is realistic to expect from a child at a given developmental level. Increased remuneration might go a long way towards reducing turnover rates.

When reviewing the current situation with respect to factors associated with good quality child care, the main pressure points specific to the family child care field appear to be access to appropriate educational opportunities and lack of support services.

Educational Opportunities for Family Child Care Providers
It has been suggested that ideally centre child care providers should have at least a two-year college ECCE credential.[40] This chapter has suggested that this might not be necessary in centres if there were more task differentiation. The requirement for a two-year credential is, anyway, impractical for family child care. The decision to become a family child care provider is often made after the person has her own children. Thus, she is no longer able to attend a daytime college program. After a ten- or eleven-hour working day, the provider may experience difficulty finding the time and energy to attend evening courses for several years to obtain a certificate.

In addition, two factors call into question the appropriateness of the traditional two-year ECCE college course for preparing family child care providers. The first relates to the characteristics and situation of the providers themselves. The second relates to the effectiveness of classroom teaching with this population.

Unlike the college student who enters an ECCE course immediately after leaving high school, many family child care providers have experience with their own children. As a result, they have some knowledge of what young children are like. Others have experience as elementary school teachers or as nurses. All are in the midst of providing care. They need information that addresses the issues they are facing right now presented in a way that can be easily applied to the real-life home child care setting. There is also a growing recognition that family child care differs in fundamental ways from centre-based care. It involves sharing a real home and the usual activities of a home with children. Usually the age group is mixed and providers have a much closer relationship with the parents than is usual for teaching staff in a centre.[41] Acknowledgment of this uniqueness is illustrated by the development of specific family child care quality criteria through a three-year process of field consultation by Thelma Harms and her colleagues.[42] Training must address both the diversity of experience among family child care providers and the specific realities of providing care in a home setting.

Only a small percentage of family child care providers have specialized training in ECCE before starting to provide care. Therefore, of necessity, increasing their knowledge and understanding of children must depend on in-service educational opportunities. After reviewing the research on the the extent to which short-term classroom courses change caregiver behaviour or improve practice, Susan Kontos concluded that this approach has limited effectiveness.[43] A recent study of once-a-week training sessions totalling fifteen to twenty-five hours of classroom time reports modest improvement in global quality in the homes in two of the three training sites. However, 'providers' interaction with children did not improve at any site.'[44]

If formal classroom education, presumably offering the same curriculum to all participants, is of limited usefulness, are there other more effective approaches for improving practice? The agency model in Canada uses home visitors to supplement workshops and other professional development opportunities. Kontos notes that there is some evidence that home visits do improve quality.[45] In the United States, most of the thirty-two Family-to-Family training projects for family child care providers have developed formal mentoring programs. These use experienced caregivers as role models and providers of support tailored to match the less-experienced providers' immediate needs.[46] There is some indication that mentoring is helpful as a support mechanism in family child care but whether this translates into improved quality has not yet been researched.[47]

Both home visitors and mentors permit a more personalized training that can build on each provider's existing knowledge and practices. Intuitively this would seem to be a promising approach for expanding providers' knowledge base and improving practice in the family child care field. A proportion of any new monies invested in family child care should be used to set up and explore the effectiveness of an individualized approach, such as home visitor and/or mentoring programs, as a means of sharing information that will improve caregivers' knowledge and encourage self-reflection.

Other Support Services
Social support services reduce feelings of isolation and stress. Networking with other caregivers provides an opportunity to get ideas from others who may have successfully dealt with a problem that a provider is facing. In Denmark, such mutual support is deliberately fostered by grouping homes in neighbourhood clusters of five or six. Once a week

each cluster of caregivers and their respective children spend the day together in a mini-centre fully equipped with a variety of toys and materials. This reduces the isolation of the individual and encourages friendships within the cluster. If a caregiver is ill or goes away on vacation, each of the other caregivers in the cluster is permitted to take on an extra child, a child who already knows the caregiver and children he or she will be joining.[48] It would also seem worthwhile to invest some resources in exploring the feasibility of this approach in Canada.

Canadian family child care agencies, family resource programs, and child care resource and referral programs provide various forms of support such as toy and equipment lending libraries, drop-in programs, professional development activities, and opportunities for bulk buying. However, as noted in the section on the current situation in Canada, such support programs are only widely available in some provinces. The Quality 2000 Initiative in the United States, a consortium of over 250 child care researchers, advocates, and practitioners, viewed the provision of community-based support organizations to be so important that it recommended there be 'an organization in every community for supporting all family day care providers.'[49] Of interest, is the emphasis on all, not just those who are regulated. The development of an infrastructure of family support services for all caregivers in all provinces and both territories should be a priority in Canada as well.

CONCLUSION

The definition of quality in child care must be expanded beyond the traditional child-centred focus to include consideration of its role in family and community support. In some respects family child care is better able to address these roles than is centre-based care. Yet in many ways family child care is the hidden component of the child care field even though it serves the greatest number of children. The time has come to establish enhancement of family child care as a top priority. Improvement of remuneration levels in both family- and centre-based care must also be a priority. The current low levels impede the recruitment and the retention of providers and may influence care provider behaviour to the detriment of quality.

Notes

1 Gordon Cleveland and Michael Krashinsky, *The Benefits and Costs of Good*

Child Care: The Economic Rationale for Public Investment in Young Children (Toronto: University of Toronto, Centre for Urban and Community Studies, Childcare Resource and Research Unit, 1998), 76.

2 Ruth Chapple and Marilynn Kuhn, *Partners in Quality: Lets Talk about It!* (Ottawa: Canadian Child Care Federation, unpublished background paper, 1999).

3 Daniel P. Keating, *Developmental Determinants of Health and Well-Being in Children and Youth* (Toronto: Premier's Council on Health, Well-Being and Justice, 1993), 1.

4 Gillian Doherty, *Zero to Six: The Basis for School Readiness* (Ottawa: Human Resources Development Canada, Applied Research Branch, 1997), 4–10.

5 Cleveland and Krashinsky, *Benefits and Costs*, 41.

6 Linda Duxbury and Christopher Higgins, 'Families in the Economy,' in *Canada's Changing Families: Challenges to Public Policy*, Maureen Baker, ed. (Ottawa: Vanier Institute of the Family, 1994), 30.

7 Ibid., 31.

8 Janet Gonzalez-Mena and Judith K. Bernhard, 'Out-of-Home Care of Infants and Toddlers: A Call for Cultural Linguistic Continuity,' in *Interaction* (1998) 12(2): 14–16.

9 For comprehensive reviews of the research see Gillian Doherty, *Elements of Quality*, background paper prepared for the Canadian Child Care Federation's Partners in Quality Project (Ottawa: Canadian Child Care Federation, 1999), and Gillian Doherty-Derkowski, *Quality Matters: Excellence in Early Childhood Programs* (Don Mills, ON: Addison-Wesley, 1994).

10 Canadian Child Care Federation, *National Statement on Quality Child Care* (Ottawa: Author, 1991), 9.

11 Childcare Resource and Research Unit, *Early Childhood Care and Education in Canada: Provinces and Territories, 1998* (Toronto: University of Toronto 2000, Childcare Resource and Research Unit, 2000).

12 Canadian Child Care Federation, *National Statement on Quality*, 25.

13 Child Care Resource and Research Unit, *Early Childhood Care and Education in Canada.*

14 Hillel Goelman, 'Training, Quality, and the Lived Experience of Child Care,' this volume.

15 Goss Gilroy *Providing Home Child Care for a Living: A Survey of Providers Working in the Regulated Sector* (Ottawa: Canadian Child Care Federation, 1998), 11.

16 Ibid., 13.

17 G. Doherty, D.S. Lero, H. Goelman, A. LaGrange, and J. Tougas, *You Bet I Care! A Canada-wide Study on: Wages, Working Conditions, and Practices in*

Child Care Centres (Guelph: Centre for Families, Work, and Well-Being, 2000).

18 Gilroy, *Providing Home Child Care*, 31.

19 Ibid., 28.

20 Canadian Day Care Advocacy Association and Canadian Child Care Federation, *Caring for a Living* (Ottawa: Canadian Child Care Federation 1992), 87.

21 Malcolm Read and Annette LaGrange, *Those Who Care: A Report on Approved Family Day Home Providers in Alberta* (Red Deer, AL: Child Care Matters, 1990), 26.

22 Norpark Computer Design, *A Survey of Private Home Day Care in Ontario, 1988* (Toronto; Queen's Printer for Ontario, 1989), 32.

23 Elsie Chan, Executive Director, Andrew Fleck Child Care Services, Ottawa. Personal communication with Gillian Doherty.

24 Jane Beach, Jane Bertrand, and Gordon Cleveland, *Our Child Care Workforce: From Recognition to Remuneration* (Ottawa: Canadian Child Care Federation, 1998), Table 1, 3.

25 Donna S. Lero, Hillel Goelman, Alan R. Pence, Lois M. Brockman, and Sandra Nuttal, *Canadian National Child Care Study: Parental Work Patterns and Child Care Needs* (Ottawa: Statistics Canada, 1992), 13.

26 Gordon Betcherman and Richard Chaykowski, *The Changing Workplace: Challenges for Public Policy* (Ottawa: Human Resources Development Canada, Applied Research Branch, 1996), 7–9.

27 Kathy Modigliani, *Promoting High-Quality Family Child Care* (New Haven, CN: Yale University, Quality 2000 Initiative, 1994), 2.

28 Malene Karlsson, *Family Day Care in Europe* (Brussels: European Commission Network on Childcare, 1995), 56.

29 Gonzalez-Mena and Bernhard, 'Out-of-Home Care of Infants and Toddlers,' 15.

30 Karlsson, *Family Day Care*, 25.

31 European Commission Network on Childcare, *A Review of Services for Young Children in the European Union, 1990–1995* (Brussels: Author, 1996), 116.

32 Beach et al., *Our Child Care Workforce*, Table 1, 3.

33 For comprehensive reviews of the research, see Doherty, *Elements of Quality*, and Doherty-Derkowski, *Quality Matters.*

34 Modigliani, *Promoting High-Quality Family Child Care*, 25.

35 Carollee Howes and Elisabeth Marx, 'Raising Questions about Improving the Quality of Child Care: Child Care in the United States and France,' in *Early Childhood Research Quarterly* (1992) 7(3): 354.

36 Beach et al., *Our Child Care Workforce*, 13.
37 Howes and Marx, 'Raising Questions,' 353–7.
38 Ibid., 357.
39 Bengt-Erik Andersson, 'Effects of Day-Care on Cognitive and Socio-emotional Competence of Thirteen-Year-Old Swedish Schoolchildren,' in *Child Development* (1992) 63: 32; and also Anders Broberg, C. Philip Hwang, and Susan V. Chace, *Effects of Day Care on Elementary School Performance and Adjustment*, paper presented to the 60th Anniversary Meeting of the Society for Research in Child Development, 25–8 March 1993, New Orleans, 6.
40 Goelman, 'Training, Quality, and the Lived Experience of Child Care,' this volume.
41 Modigliani, *Promoting High-Quality Family Child Care*, 4.
42 Family Child Care Quality Criteria Project, *Quality Criteria for Family Child Care* (Chapel Hill, NC: University of North Carolina at Chapel Hill, Frank Porter Graham Child Development Center, 1995).
43 Susan Kontos, *Family Day Care: Out of the Shadows and into the Limelight* (Washington, DC: National Association for the Education of Young Children, 1992), 139.
44 Susan Kontos, Carollee Howes, and Ellen Galinksy, 'Does Training Make a Difference to Quality in Family Day Care?' in *Early Childhood Research Quarterly* (1996) 11: 441–2.
45 Kontos, *Family Day Care*, 137.
46 Amy Dombro and Kathy Modigliani, *Evaluation of Family-to-Family, 1993* (New York: Families and Work Institute, 1993).
47 Gillian Doherty, *Mentoring as a Strategy for Promoting Quality in Child Care* (Ottawa: Canadian Child Care Federation, in press).
48 Valerie Polakow, 'Who Cares for the Children? Denmark's Unique Public Child-Care Model,' in *Phi Delta Kappan* (1997) April: 605.
49 Sharon L. Kagan and Nancy E. Cohen, 'Vision for a Quality Early Care and Education System,' in *Reinventing Early Care and Education*, Sharon L. Kagan and Nancy E. Cohen, eds. (San Francisco: Jossey-Bass, 1996), 313.

8. Training, Quality, and the Lived Experience of Child Care[1]

Hillel Goelman[2]
Faculty of Education, University of British Columbia

In a recent advertisement for laser eye surgery, one company dispar-aged the qualifications of its competitor by suggesting that an appropri-ate sales slogan for the competitor should be, 'Our staff skipped medical school and we pass the savings on to you!' The not-so-subtle message is clear: Professional training makes a significant difference and our staff is much better trained than our competitors. A similar argument is presented in this chapter: The levels of overall education and of Early Childhood Care and Education (ECCE)-specific training play a critical role in the provision of quality child care programs, and, for this reason, training and education must be a very high priority in the quest for better quality child care. This chapter first reviews the research on the effects of training and education of the child care workforce[3] and then briefly summarizes the state of ECCE training programs in Canada. Data are presented on the current education and training levels of ECCE staff in Canada. Finally, suggestions are made as to how training can be improved and arguments are given as to why training should be assigned such a high priority in the quest for child care quality in Canada.

THE IMPORTANCE OF TRAINING IN THE
LIVED EXPERIENCE OF CHILD CARE

As the depth and breadth of the contributions in this volume demon-strate, 'quality' in child care is a many-sided Rubik's cube. Many in the research literature[4] have identified both structure and process variables that impact on the quality of child care programs. Structure variables include such regulatable features as group size, adult:child ratio, the number and type of specific age-appropriate materials and equipment in the centre. The Early Childhood Education Rating Scale is a widely used checklist and rating scale that focuses on the number and availability of different kinds of early childhood materials and equipment, but not necessarily the *use* of the materials in the centre.[5] Perhaps the most important structural feature of child care that impacts on quality is the wage paid to ECCE staff. Wages are strongly associated with higher levels of education and lower levels of staff turnover. While child care wages and working conditions are unacceptably low for all staff, for many of the better educated staff the discrepancy between their levels of training and salary leads to lower morale, higher dissatisfaction, and, subsequently, higher rates of turnover.

Process variables are those that relate to the lived experience of child care, the day-to-day learning and caring interactions in child care settings. This chapter is based on the assertion (and the empirical data supporting the assertion) that while structure variables might provide useful minimal regulatable standards for acceptable levels of child care, it is in the training of individuals who work in child care that contributes much more significantly to the nature of the process, the lived experience that characterizes high-quality child care programs. The major thrust of this chapter is that the child care provider plays the most important role in ensuring that children are provided with learning and caring interactions in safe, responsive, and stimulating settings and that the child's language, social, emotional, cognitive, and physical growth are all facilitated by appropriate activities and interactions. Well-trained staff are far more likely to provide this level of quality care than are poorly trained staff. Further, although some research indicates that staff training is a more powerful predictor of quality than structure variables,[6] most studies show that it is the combination of training, group size, and favourable ratios that together contribute to quality in child care programs.

There is a robust research literature in both Canada[7] and the United States[8] that reports the relationships between training levels and program quality. Several studies reported that in both child care centres and in family child care homes, settings with better trained staff were characterized by developmentally appropriate, stimulating, and responsive activities and interactions.[9] The children in these higher quality settings – and particularly those from at-risk home environments – scored higher on measures of expressive and receptive language development.[10] Specifically, better trained caregivers were found to engage children in appropriate and stimulating language interactions using the kinds of questioning, listening, and reflecting strategies that facilitate children's expressive and receptive language development.

The U.S. National Child Care Staffing Study (NSS)[11] found that formal levels of education and professional preparation specifically in early childhood education and care resulted in measurably superior levels of structural and process quality. Compared with poorly trained staff, better trained staff provided higher levels of 'appropriate caregiving,' higher ratings of 'sensitive' and 'responsive' interactions with infants, toddlers, and preschoolers, and significantly lower ratings of being 'harsh' or 'detached.' The NSS study found that both the overall level of caregiver education and the specific level of ECCE training were more significant predictors of child care quality than experience alone, especially in the case of infant and toddler care. The most optimal 'package' of training in terms of child care quality and child development outcomes was the combination of the overall level of formal education coupled with specialized training in ECCE. Staff with lower levels of formal and specialized training provided lower quality child care in lower quality child care environments. The *Cost, Quality, and Child Outcomes* study also reported that training is a significant predictor of child care quality,[12] which in turn was a major predictor of child development outcomes in language ability, mathematics, self-esteem, social skills, and teacher-child relationships.[13]

It has been demonstrated that training makes a significant contribution to the lived experience of child care. However, there is less agreement as to what constitutes the ideal content, sequence, length, breadth, and depth of ECCE training programs. Spodek and Saracho, for example, identify what they see as the necessary knowledge, skills, and attitudes that are needed at six different levels of professional work in ECCE from the most basic level (decision maker) to the most advanced (counselor/adviser).[14] They do not, however, propose specific education and training guidelines. In contrast, the National Association for the Education of Young Children (NAEYC) has generated fairly specific curriculum content guidelines for ECCE training programs in terms of both general education and ECCE-specific knowledge and competencies.[15] While the NAEYC claims that a basic, minimal level of competency might be attained in two years of full-time study, it strongly endorses the idea that the desired levels of expertise and effectiveness can be expected only after the completion of a four-year degree program. Pence and Griffin provide a nice synthesis of the NAEYC and

Spodek and Saracho approaches by identifying specific levels of knowledge and responsibility and suggesting the specific levels of education and training needed to achieve those levels of expertise.[16] Despite the differences among and within the various professional, governmental, and academic communities regarding the optimum levels of ECCE training, there is broad agreement on at least three major issues regarding ECCE training:

1 There is an important and substantial body of knowledge that must be learned.
2 It takes time, study, practice, and mentoring to develop the necessary knowledge, understandings, attitudes, and skills needed to work effectively in child care settings.
3 Almost all current training programs are much too short for the required material to be covered in a satisfactory way.

In addition to these fairly broad issues, studies have identified a number of specific concerns regarding ECCE training in Canada.[17] They have documented the inconsistency in training requirements and the limited availability, accessibility, and affordability of training programs across provincial and territorial jurisdictions. There are differences across jurisdictions as to whether training regulations pertain to any, some, or all staff. Most (but not all) provinces and territories offer full- and/or part-time certificate and/or diploma programs, and about half of them offer distance education programs. Despite a continuing demand for trained personnel there are a limited number of places available in ECCE training programs and limited opportunities for part-time and distance education learning opportunities. Further, many governments and institutions have responded to the demand from the field by offering training in very short and compressed time frames. Administrators in post-secondary institutions often argue that given the low salaries received by graduates of ECCE, it would be inappropriate to ask students in these programs to spend more time and money to prepare for a profession in which they will be overworked and underpaid.[18]

Summing up, training makes a critical contribution to child care quality, and both training requirements and opportunities vary tremendously across Canada. This chapter considers two questions regarding ECCE training in Canada: How well prepared are ECCE staff, and what policies are needed to address current and future concerns about ECCE training in Canada?

HOW WELL-PREPARED ARE CANADIAN ECCE STAFF?

The data presented below were collected as part of the 'You Bet I Care!' project which was funded by Human Resource Development Canada.[19] Phase 1 of YBIC, from which the data in the report come, is a replication and expansion of the 1991 survey, reported in *Caring for a Living*, of the wages and working conditions of ECCE staff.[20] Phase 1 consisted of three surveys that were distributed to child care centres in all provinces and the two territories.[21] The Centre Survey addressed such issues as enrolments, fees, and centre policies and practices,[22] and the Director Survey focused on the personal and professional background of the centre director. The Staff Survey, from which the data in this chapter are drawn, addressed a wide range of issues relating to the wages, working conditions, benefits, and demographic characteristics of the child care workforce. Responses were received from 4,154 staff at 848 child care centres. Appropriate weighting allows us to use this sample to represent the true population of 38,021 staff at 4,636 child care centres.

Since different terminology is used in different jurisdictions, respondents were asked to use the following definitions in the survey in describing their current position in the centre: 'Assistant Teacher' refers to a person who works with children under the direction of another teacher, a supervisor, or the centre director. 'Teacher' refers to a person who has primary responsibility for a group of children. This person also may have supervisory responsibilities for assistant teachers. 'Supervisor' refers to a person who has primary responsibility for a group of children and also has supervisory responsibilities for teachers.

Based on these definitions, survey results provide information about the ECCE staff of whom 14.8 per cent were assistant teachers, 72.9 per cent were teachers, and 12.4 per cent were supervisors. The strength of this sample is in its size and representativeness. It should be noted that in the Centre Survey, child care directors reported a slightly different proportion of assistant teachers (22.3 per cent) and teachers (65.7 per cent) in their centres, although the percentage of supervisors (12.0 per cent) was the same as reported in the staff survey. These variations suggest that the sample that responded to the staff survey may have been slightly better educated and possibly better paid than the total population from which they were drawn. Implications of this are discussed below.

This chapter reports data on the education and training of the staff who responded to the Staff Survey. The data are presented for Canada as a whole and, when appropriate, by province and territory and by the respondents' position in the centre. Data from staff in commercial and non-profit child centres are compared but municipally sponsored centres are not included in these comparisons because all municipal centres in this sample were from Ontario and represented only 3.6 per cent of the sample. Because of the extremely small sample sizes, data from the Yukon (one child care centre) and the Northwest Territories (five centres) are only reported when the data are numerically meaningful. In addition to presenting data on the workforce as a whole, data are also presented on those staff working with infants and toddlers and those working with other specialized populations. Where appropriate, comparisons are shown between the findings of this 1998 study and the 1991 survey of wages and working conditions reported in *Caring for a Living*. In this chapter, no data are reported on directors' levels of education and training, a matter that also deserves consideration (and that has been dealt with elsewhere).[23]

Highest Levels of Overall Educational Achievement

The highest levels of overall educational attainment are reported by province in Table 8.1. For 3.3 per cent of all staff the highest level was 'some high school,' and for 11.0 per cent it was receiving 'a high school diploma.' These figures represent national averages, and there was tremendous variability across jurisdictions. For example, the percentage of respondents in the 'some high school' category were much higher than the national average in Alberta (9.6 per cent). The percentage of respondents in the 'high school diploma' category was much higher than the national average in Alberta (18.9 per cent), New Brunswick (23.5 per cent), and Saskatchewan (20.4 per cent).

Nationally, 10.4 per cent of all respondents completed a one-year community college credential,[24] yet provincial results ranged from a high of 43.3 per cent in New Brunswick to a low of 3.5 per cent in Ontario. Nationally, 37.8 per cent completed a two-year community college credential, ranging from 9.3 per cent in Quebec to 60.6 per cent in Ontario and 64.9 per cent in Prince Edward Island. The completion of a three-year college credential was reported by 13.2 per cent of the national sample, but by 39.4 per cent of staff in Quebec. Most ECCE staff in Quebec matriculate through three-year programs in the CEGEP post-secondary system (which follows on Grade 11 for Quebec students), and, as a result, 72.6 per cent of all three-year credential

Table 8.1. Highest overall education level, all staff (except directors), by province and territory (%)[a]

	Some high school	High school diploma	One-year college credential	Two-year college credential	Three-year college credential	Post-diploma credential	Bachelor's degree or more	All levels of education
British Columbia	1.3	6.2	32.5	34.4	4.7	5.1	15.8	100.0
Alberta	9.6	18.9	20.1	28.8	3.4	2.2	17.0	100.0
Saskatchewan	7.6	20.4	26.9	20.1	1.6	3.0	20.4	100.0
Manitoba	5.7	19.1	8.7	27.9	3.8	7.1	27.7	100.0
Ontario	0.7	7.7	3.5	60.6	5.8	5.8	15.8	100.0
Quebec	4.0	10.1	5.9	9.3	39.4	10.5	20.8	100.0
New Brunswick	7.3	23.5	43.3	13.5	NR	4.5	8.0	100.0
Nova Scotia	1.8	16.0	12.6	34.2	5.4	6.2	23.7	100.0
Prince Edward Island	2.3	7.2	4.5	64.9	NR	0.9	20.3	100.0
Newfoundland	1.0	6.0	21.9	59.5	0.7	2.9	8.0	100.0
Yukon	33.3	33.3	33.3	NR	NR	NR	NR	100.0
Northwest Territories	13.7	25.5	30.4	9.8	NR	NR	20.6	100.0
National	3.3	11.0	10.4	37.8	13.2	6.4	18.0	100.0

[a]NR = not reported; used when results fall below reportable levels.

Figure 8.1. Highest level of overall education in non-profit and commercial centres (all staff except for directors)

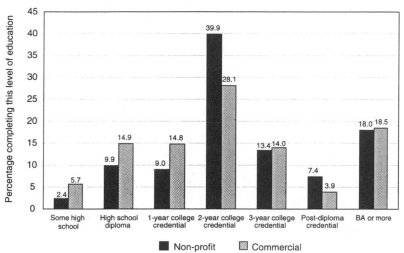

holders across Canada are from Quebec. A total of 57.4 per cent of all respondents held a two-year credential, a three-year credential, or a post-diploma college credential. For 18.0 per cent of respondents, the completion of a Bachelor's degree (or more) was the highest level of education attained.

Differences were found between staff in non-profit and commercial child care centres (Figure 8.1). Overall, higher proportions of staff in commercial centres than in non-profit centres were represented in the three lower categories of educational achievement: some high school, high school completion, and a one-year college credential. Conversely, higher percentages of staff in non-profit centres than in commercial centres were represented in the two-year college credential and post-diploma programs. Approximately equal proportions of commercial and non-profit staff members had completed three-year college programs and Bachelor's programs. As shown in Figure 8.2, higher proportions of assistant teachers were represented in the three lowest categories of overall education and higher proportions of teachers and supervisors were represented in the four higher education levels.

A comparison of data from the 1991 *Caring for a Living* and the 1998 *You Bet I Care!* studies reflect some measure of positive movement in the

Figure 8.2. Highest level of overall education for assistant teachers, teachers, and supervisors

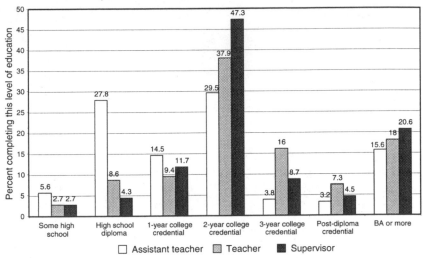

intervening years (Figure 8.3). Between 1991 and 1998 the percentage of staff with only 'some high school' education dropped from 6.1 per cent to 3.3 per cent while the percentage of staff with a high school diploma or 'some college' dropped from 25.4 per cent to 11.0 per cent. The percentages of staff with a one-year credential were virtually the same in 1991 (10.0 per cent) as in 1998 (10.4 per cent). Between 1991 and 1998 the aggregate of two-year, three-year, and post-diploma holders rose from 45.5 per cent to 57.4 per cent and the percentage of those holding a Bachelor's degree rose from 13.1 per cent to 18.0 per cent.[25]

Highest Levels of ECCE Education and Training

In 1998, 11.4 per cent of all child care staff in Canada had no specific training in early childhood care and education (Table 8.2). Those juris-dictions that were substantially higher than the national average were New Brunswick (36.0 per cent), Manitoba (21.9 per cent), and Saskatch-ewan (17.4 per cent). At the next level of ECCE-specific training, 6.8 per cent of all child care staff had completed a 'short course' in ECCE that lasted less than one calendar year. Much higher percentages were re-ported in Alberta (26.2 per cent) and Saskatchewan (22.6 per cent), where such courses are required by government regulation.

Figure 8.3. Highest levels of overall education, 1991 and 1998 (all staff except directors)

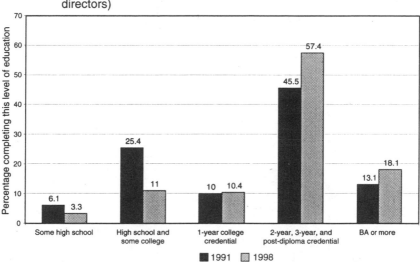

In Canada as a whole, 10.4 per cent completed a one-year ECCE training course. The 42.1 per cent of all respondents who held a two-year credential made up the largest single category in ECCE-specific training. Across Canada, 13.3 per cent of staff had completed a three-year credential compared with 40.8 per cent in Quebec. Taken together, 70.8 per cent of all staff were holders of one-year, two-year, three-year, or post-diploma credentials, an increase from the 58.0 per cent reported in the 1991 study. The percentage of staff holding an ECCE-related Bachelor's degree (or higher) rose from 7.0 per cent in 1991 to 10.9 per cent in 1998.

As shown in Figure 8.4, higher proportions of supervisors had completed two-year and ECCE-related Bachelor of Arts programs than had assistant teachers or teachers. Higher proportions of assistant teachers than teachers or supervisors had no ECCE training, a course lasting less than one year, or a one-year ECCE course. While roughly one in three assistant teachers (30.2 per cent) had completed a two-year ECCE training program, almost the exact same percentage (30.6 per cent) of all assistant teachers had no ECCE training at all. Staff in non-profit centres had, on average, higher levels of ECCE-specific education than staff in commercial centres (Figure 8.5). Higher proportions of commercial staff were represented in no training, less than one year, and one-year

Table 8.2. Highest ECCE education level, by province and territory (%)

	No ECCE training	ECCE course <1 year	One-year ECCE course	Two-year ECCE course	Three-year ECCE course	Post-diploma ECCE	ECCE-related BA or more	All levels of education
British Columbia	7.5	1.9	37.1	35.4	5.1	3.6	9.4	100.0
Alberta	9.2	26.2	20.2	30.9	2.0	1.6	9.8	100.0
Saskatchewan	17.4	22.6	24.8	16.8	0.9	1.9	15.6	100.0
Manitoba	21.9	11.0	6.3	29.5	4.2	6.5	20.5	100.0
Ontario	8.7	2.4	2.8	69.0	5.3	4.5	7.3	100.0
Quebec	12.9	4.6	6.9	11.5	40.8	8.1	15.1	100.0
New Brunswick	36.0	8.7	36.0	12.9	NR	0.4	6.0	100.0
Nova Scotia	9.8	6.2	14.4	38.3	6.1	7.6	17.6	100.0
Newfoundland	14.9	4.3	12.3	60.5	NR	2.9	5.1	100.0
Prince Edward Island	8.2	7.8	2.3	66.2	NR	0.9	14.6	100.0
Yukon	66.7	NR	33.3	NR	NR	NR	NR	100.0
Northwest Territories	42.6	11.9	33.7	4.0	NR	NR	7.9	100.0
National	11.4	6.8	10.4	42.1	13.3	5.0	10.9	100.0

NR = not reported; used when results fall below reportable levels.

Figure 8.4. Highest level of ECCE education for assistant teachers, teachers, and supervisors.

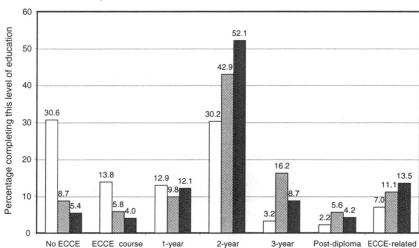

training programs, and higher proportions of non-profit staff had completed the two-year college, three-year college, or post-diploma college ECCE programs. Roughly equal proportions of commercial and non-profit staff had completed Bachelor's degrees.

While some positive movement has occurred between 1991 and 1998, the level of ECCE preparation of the Canadian child care workforce as a whole is still at an unacceptably low level, if we take a two-year ECCE diploma as the minimum standard. The proportion of staff with some post-secondary training has increased, and the field as a whole and the training institutions in particular must be commended for these increases in an era of downsizing and retrenchment. There has been some modest growth in the numbers of those considered to have entry-level competence to work as an ECCE professional. The training floor has been raised for many staff and the proportion of completely unqualified individuals staffing child care centres has decreased.

Caution must be used in interpreting these data which may reflect a slightly inflated level of training for the population of ECCE staff as a whole. While 70.7 per cent of all teaching staff who responded to the Staff Survey reported that they had completed at least two years of

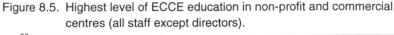
Figure 8.5. Highest level of ECCE education in non-profit and commercial centres (all staff except directors).

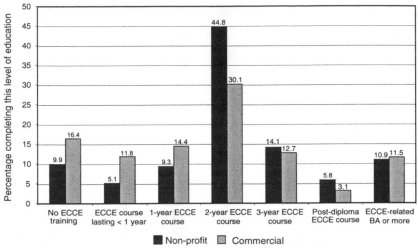

post-secondary training in ECCE, directors reported on the Centre Survey that only 61.5 per cent of teaching staff had attained this level of training. This may reflect a difference in the samples and/or a tendency for a higher proportion of the better educated staff to respond to the Staff Survey.[26] It is encouraging to see some modest improvement in staff training levels between 1991 and 1998 and to note that it appears that a majority of child care centre staff across the country have at least two years of post-secondary training in ECCE.

Staff with Additional Responsibilities

Most ECCE training programs and most provincial and territorial training regulations are intended to ensure a minimum level of competency for entry-level child care staff. The nature of child care work, however, demands that professionals develop skills and knowledge beyond those taught in these introductory programs. Many ECCE workers have additional supervisory and teaching responsibilities for which additional and more specific training is required. Yet, surprisingly few have that additional training. In this section, we examine the education and training levels of staff who supervise student teacher practica and those who work with more vulnerable populations of children and families.

Many instructors in ECCE training programs consider the student teaching practicum experiences to be the most valuable part of a student's ECCE education. The practicum experience allows students to observe professional staff at work in what are usually higher quality child care centres. In this way, practicum students can see the practical applications of information and material they learned in the classroom and can begin to apply some of their knowledge and skills in real-life situations. Students are usually supervised by both an instructor from their ECCE institution and by one of the staff in the centre. The guidance and support given by ECCE staff are critically important to the student's learning process, for it is through this supervision that students learn to reflect on their practice, to examine the decision-making processes that contribute to classroom practice, and to monitor their own growth and development.

Almost half of all respondents (46.0 per cent) had responsibility for supervising ECCE practicum students, although this varied depending on the position of the respondent: 58.7 per cent of all supervisors, 49.4 per cent of all teachers, and 18.5 per cent of all assistant teachers. The education and training levels for staff members who performed practicum supervision were compared with staff members who were not responsible for practicum supervision. Staff members who supervised student practica did not, as a group, have more extensive training or education to prepare them for practicum supervision. For 9.1 per cent of practicum supervisors, high school completion is the highest level of ECCE training; 7.9 per cent have a one-year ECCE credential, 52.8 per cent have a two-year credential, and 30.1 per cent have more than a two-year credential. A relatively small proportion of ECCE staff who provide supervision, guidance, and support to ECCE students have actually received the additional training needed to perform these tasks.

Child care centres and staff are also expected to work with a growing population of children and families, many of whom are considered to be 'vulnerable' or 'at risk.' Working with these children and families requires a more extensive knowledge base and a larger repertoire of professional practices in the areas of normative and atypical child development, communicating with parents, and liaison with other health care and social service professionals. The 1989 U.S. National Staffing

Study emphasized the importance of additional training for staff working with infants and toddlers: 'This finding highlights the importance of high level specialized training for infant and toddler teachers. It runs counter to the popular notion that any "grandmotherly" type can teach babies because all one needs to know is how to rock them and change diapers. We suspect that college-level specialized training for infant and toddler teachers provides them with basic child development knowledge essential for understanding and responding to the unique, rapid course of development during this early period of a child's life.'[27]

In Canada, however, only British Columbia requires special training to work with infants, and only British Columbia and Ontario have training requirements for staff who care for children with special needs. Despite this lack of training requirements Canadian child care centres do offer a variety of programs to specialized populations. The Centre Survey results indicate that 12.3 per cent of all centres provide at least one service for children at risk, and the percentages were higher in non-profit and municipal centres in specific provinces. The Staff Survey revealed that while 40.9 per cent of child care staff in Canada work with infants and/or toddlers and 24.4 per cent of staff work in a 'specialized' child care setting, these staff tend not to have any additional or higher levels of training than those of the child care workforce as a whole. Slightly more of the workforce caring for children under three years of age completed a two-year college program, and slightly fewer completed a Bachelor's degree. Staff in specialized programs are somewhat more likely than other staff to have a two-year college credential or Bachelor's degree. The programs themselves may be considered 'specialized,' but there is little to suggest that the training received by staff who work in these programs is similarly specialized.

HOW ECCE TRAINING CAN BE IMPROVED

These data raise serious concerns about the education and training ECCE staff in Canadian child care centres. These results are not presented as a criticism of the field or those who train ECCE professionals. There are indications that despite all of the systemic constraints and obstacles confronting ECCE training, there are fewer unprepared or poorly prepared staff in 1998 than there were in 1991. Yet, even though there has been movement in the right direction, there are still significant obstacles that are impeding further progress in the education and training of ECCE professionals in Canada. The obstacles include the fact that there continues to be tremendous variability across jurisdictional boundaries on the requirements for ECCE training and the availability of ECCE training. Within and across jurisdictional boundaries, ECCE training programs vary in length and content. There is little in the way of transferability or portability of ECCE training programs across institutions. There is little in the way of professional or financial incentives to encourage ECCE staff to undertake training beyond that required for entry-level positions. In this section we consider some possible policies and programs that may serve to encourage the continued pace of enhanced ECCE training in Canada. The urgency of the situation is that, despite some positive movement in recent years, the education and training levels of the Canadian child care workforce as a whole are still unacceptably low, and there are indications that morale is lower and turnover higher among better trained caregivers. Definitive measures must be taken to address this situation.

Child care quality is a Rubik's cube of different but interrelated pieces; enhancing child care quality in general and raising training levels in particular will require coordinated and complementary action by government, training institutions, and the child care community. These recommendations are based on the data presented in this chapter, and they also draw on the other recent and current work in this area.[28] These recommendations are not intended to pre-empt the current consultations but to contribute to those consultations. The proposals outlined below are based on a vision of child care training that has consistent training requirements and opportunities across jurisdictions and enhanced transferability of program credits across institutional and jurisdictional boundaries. In this vision individuals will be actively encouraged to pursue further training and education and governments and institutions will be actively encouraged to provide opportunities for training beyond the introductory level of competence. Creating this vision will involve the sustained and committed collaboration among different parties. It will also require a combination of incentives and regulations to encourage the various players to move towards this vision.

The Central Recommendation

Within ten years all jurisdictions in Canada should require that all child care staff at the rank of 'teacher' must complete at least (the equivalent of) a two-year training program in ECCE. (As above, the definition of 'teacher' is 'a person who has primary responsibility for a group of children and ... also may have supervisory responsibilities for assistant teachers'.) If and when this goal is met, a second ten-year plan should be adopted to ensure that all 'teachers' will be required to complete (the equivalent of) a four-year training program. The increase in training time is necessary because of the increasingly complex and demanding nature of the job. The children in Canadian child care centres represent a broad spectrum of abilities and disabilities, languages, and ethnicities, demanding higher levels of knowledge and understanding to work successfully with such diversity. More time is needed for ECCE students to gain this knowledge both in classroom and lecture settings as well as in extended practicum experiences in diverse ECCE child care settings. More time is needed to train entry-level practitioners.

The recommendation that *all* teachers be required to achieve two years of formal training is critical because of the responsibility of the position and the combination of knowledge, skills, and understanding needed to perform this job well. Currently, most provinces stipulate that only some staff (either a specific number or those with specific responsibilities) be required to have the level of training recommended by the NAEYC,[29] Pence and Griffin,[30] and suggested by Spodek and Saracho.[31] Granted, the precise definition of a 'two-year training program' varies since academic years in different institutions may be eight, ten, or twelve months in length. Also, many students who wish to study part-time or through distance education may have difficulty working within the constraints of a two-year, full-time program of study. The intent of this proposal is not to specify a specific time frame per se, but to stress that there is much to learn in the process of becoming a competent, entry-level ECCE practitioner and that 100 per cent of practitioners should have this level of education within ten years.

The realities of the labour market, budgetary constraints on institutions, and the financial pressures on ECCE students to enter the workforce sooner rather than later all present serious obstacles to attaining this goal. Because of this, it will take a combination of carrots and sticks to encourage the various players to work towards this objective. One stick would be the adoption of provincial and territorial legislation (or regulation) mandating that (1) all staff must have a two-year ECCE credential; (2) the 'adult' in all adult:child regulations must be a teacher (not 'assistant teacher'); and (3) licensed child care centres can only hire individuals with the two-year credential. However, regu-

lation in the absence of resources to achieve these goals will be ineffec-
tual. In the first five years, a set of specific financial incentives should be
offered to training institutions, centres, and individuals through federal
and provincial and territorial cost-sharing. In the second five-year period these incentives would be coupled with a set of legislative and/or
regulatory vehicles to monitor the implementation of the proposed
training levels.

While the financial incentives should extend for all ten years, in the
second five-year period the incentives would be coupled with certain
disincentives intended to regulate and enforce compliance with legal
expectations. At the end of ten years the regulations and legislation
disincentives would continue to be enforced but the financial incentives available in the first ten years would be discontinued. The financial incentives would be available to the stakeholders only during the
initial ten-year period on a 'use it or lose it' basis. The purpose of the
financial incentives would be to encourage training institutions, centres, and individuals to work towards the ten-year goal in the following
ways.

ECCE Students

Financial assistance and incentives must be provided to students entering and graduating from ECCE training programs. On a cost-shared
basis, the two senior levels of government must develop and deliver a
new set of bursaries, scholarships, and/or loans to help offset the costs
of post-secondary ECCE training programs. Perhaps a special provision of the Millennium Scholarship fund could be devoted specifically
to this purpose. Current policies permitting the use of Employment
Insurance funds to be used by community college students should be
expanded to include more potential students and should also be made
available to ECCE students in university ECCE programs as well. During the first five years, all graduates of two-year ECCE programs would
be entitled to a special, one-time salary 'top-up' bonus when they are
hired for their first job in a licensed centre. The top-up would raise their
starting base salary. The bursaries and top-up hiring bonuses would be
available only during the initial ten-year period, and students without
the two-year credential would not be eligible to be hired for teacher
positions in centres.

Child Care Centres

Throughout this first five-year period centres would be encouraged to hire graduates of two-year ECCE programs, and beginning in the second five-year period they would be required to do so. Throughout both five-year periods, centres would benefit from the salary top-up awards to graduates of two-year programs which would help centres to recruit and hire staff. During both five-year periods, centres hiring graduates from two-year programs would be eligible to apply to a newly created package of operating and/or capital grants funded on a cost-shared basis by the two senior levels of government. Beginning in the second five-year period, centres might enroll children on child care subsidies only if all staff members are holders of a two-year ECCE credential.

Two-Year Training Programs
Program enhancement grants would be made available to training institutions that develop strategic plans for extending one-year training programs. Funds could be used at the discretion of individual provinces, for example, expanding distance education opportunities or learning programs to accommodate part-time learners or special programs for currently employed staff who do not have their two-year credential. Funds could also be used to expand course and program offerings in areas of advanced specialization such as infant care and the care of children with special needs.

All initiatives regarding the training institutions and professional associations should draw on and be informed by many of the recent and current initiatives regarding ECCE training.[32] These projects have begun to address many of the more difficult problems in ECCE training in Canada including the content of ECCE training programs, the mobility and portability of ECCE credentials, and the need for national clearinghouses on training standards and regulations.

Transfer from College to University
A major issue identified by Bertrand and Beach[33] and others is how to deal with the transition from college ECCE to university ECCE programs. This is another long-running debate that arouses much vigorous discussion from many different quarters. College ECCE programs argue that the academic quality and integrity of their courses are equivalent to those of university programs and, in some cases, are even more practical and applicable to the demands of providing quality child care than are university programs. University-based ECCE programs have been extremely reluctant to grant full credit to graduates of college ECCE programs. University programs argue that college admission

standards are lower than university standards and that the calibre of academic work at colleges is lower than at universities. Further, in some universities and particularly in some faculties of education, the professional training programs are restricted to those already holding a Bachelor's degree, thus further widening the gap between completing a college program and entering a university program.

In Quebec, there is a fairly smooth transition from the CEGEP programs in ECCE and university programs in faculties of education. Transfer of credit is also relatively straightforward at the universities of Manitoba and Victoria as well as at Concordia, Ryerson, and Carleton universities. In moving ahead towards broader and easier transfer from college ECCE programs to university ECCE programs, there will need to be a high degree of coordination and consultation, not just among university and college administrators and staff, but among the respective professional bodies within different and across different jurisdictions. Program development grants should be made available to universities and colleges working in collaboration to develop a more coherent articulation of credits across institutional boundaries. Consultations must also include respective professional bodies (e.g., teachers' federations), school boards, Ministry of Education representatives, and university leadership at its highest levels (e.g., Canadian Association of Deans of Education).

ECCE TRAINING AS A MAJOR PRIORITY IN THE QUEST FOR CHILD CARE QUALITY

There are really two questions here. One asks about the value of training as an absolute, and the other asks about the value of training relative to other factors in the quality equation. That training makes a critical difference in the quality of child care programs has been demonstrated extensively in a large number of large- and small-scale studies. Better trained staff are more empathetic, sensitive, and responsive to the children in their care; they plan more appropriate individual, small group, and large group activities and make better use of the materials and equipment in the centre. Training works, and Canada needs more and better trained caregivers.

Discussions on quality tend to dichotomize such factors as group size, ratios, and training, as if these are competitive or mutually exclusive in some way. Although there are data that do suggest that staff training levels are in fact more powerful predictors of quality and account for more of the variance in quality than group size and adult:child ratio,[34] most studies show that these factors tend to cluster together. Centres with well-trained staff also tend to have better paid staff, with smaller group sizes and more favourable adult:child ratios.[35] Many discussions of quality, however, tend to focus primarily on group size and ratios because, I believe, these features can be easily observed, regulated, and enforced. In and of themselves, however, they do not ensure that the lived experience of those smaller groups with favourable ratios is good quality child care. Goelman and Pence found that, while practically 100 per cent of all licensed child care centres in British Columbia reached the minimal standards required for government licensing, few exceeded the minimal requirements and very few reached levels of excellence.[36] By way of analogy, building codes set minimal standards of safety and durability; they do not, however, determine the kinds of quality interactions that occur within a completed building.

Quality in child care, like quality in any other commodity or service, does not come cheaply but it is not clear at this time precisely what raising required training standards would cost. Cleveland and Krashinsky have calculated that the annual cost for providing full-time care to 1,600,000 children two to five years of age in centres that operate within acceptable standards of group size and ratio would be $5.2 billion, or $8,500 per child.[37] These calculations are also based on the assumption that an additional 150,000 ECCE staff earning an average salary of $30,000 per person would be needed to make this system operational. While the proposal addresses the important questions of affordability, availability, accessibility, and wage enhancements, it does not appear to include the costs of training ECCE staff and it would be inappropriate to cut funds from it. It also does not ensure that those better paid staff in more accessible child care centres would be any better educated or would provide any improvement in the quality of the child care experience.

As in other service and health professions (e.g., social work, medicine, physiotherapy, or nursing) training budgets in ECCE are distinct from service delivery budgets. The costs of public schooling, for example, are calculated by schools, school boards, and ministries of education based primarily on student enrolment, but they are not in any direct way tied to the budgets given to universities for the training of teachers. While the delivery of child care services typically falls under ministries of health, social services, or human resources, the delivery and the cost of ECCE training programs are the responsibilities of ministries of higher or advanced or post-secondary education. One difficulty in estimating the impact of program changes on the costs of training is the tremendous variability in the length, content, and modes of delivering ECCE training across jurisdictions. The cost of training differs significantly based on the proportions of full-time versus part-time students, the relative availability and accessibility of distance education and on-site programming, differences in the costs of basic and specialized ECCE training programs, differing numbers of practicum experiences of different lengths, and other factors. Determining an accurate Canada-wide cost for the level of training called for in this chapter requires the collection, analysis, and synthesis of additional provincial and territorial data.

TRAINING, WAGES, AND MORALE

We have seen that even with the current minimal levels of support given to ECCE training programs, the percentage of staff with at least two years of post-secondary education rose from 45.5 in 1991 to 57.4 1998, an increase of 11.9 per cent in seven years or, on average, 1.7 per cent a year. When the additional 18.1 per cent of all 1998 staff with a Bachelor of Arts degree are added in, 75.5 per cent of the ECCE workforce can be considered to have attained the minimal entry-level education requirements called for in this chapter. If this 'natural' rate of growth could be further stimulated with the kinds of incentives cited above, it is not unrealistic to expect that an additional 20 to 25 per cent of staff could reach this level of training within a ten-year time frame.

These stimuli and proposals must be part and parcel of a major conceptual and political commitment to young children and to the professionals who work with them. As Cleveland and Krashinsky point out, similar issues arose regarding the value of public school programs for young children.[38] While the vast majority of all five-year-old children in Canada today attend publicly funded kindergartens, and while the vast majority of all public school teachers have a four-year post-secondary credential, this was not always the case. In 1960 only 13.2 per cent of all five-year-olds in the four western provinces were in public kindergarten, and the percentages rose to 18.7 per cent in 1961 and to 31.9 per cent in 1968.[39] By the 1970s practically all school boards in Canada offered public kindergarten programs.

Current discussions on the importance of training child care workers are strongly reminiscent of similar discussions in previous decades on the importance of training elementary school teachers. Just as kinder-garten programs expanded quickly, elementary teacher education pro-grams also experienced dramatic growth from the 1950s to the 1970s. Until the 1950s most elementary school teachers received their training through one- and two-year training programs in post-secondary nor-mal schools. In the 1950s many normal schools evolved into teacher colleges in which the professional preparation for teaching involved a strong emphasis on practical, classroom skills along with some addi-tional but limited course work in arts and sciences. Friction existed between teachers' colleges and universities because of their (mis-)per-ceptions of each other. Colleges typically felt that universities were sorely out of touch with the 'real world' of schools, classrooms, teach-ers, and children, while universities typically criticized the teachers' colleges for what they saw as lower admissions standards and less qualified instructional staff. These institutional barriers were slowly overcome as normal schools and teachers' colleges were merged into faculties of education in universities. Currently, public school teachers must be graduates of a four-year Bachelor of Arts or Bachelor of Educa-tion program, or they must complete a 'professional development pro-gram' after they have completed a four-year degree program.

The child care training programs of today face similar obstacles to those faced by elementary education training programs in the 1950s: the lack of professional status and recognition; the brevity and content of their training programs; questions about the needs, value, and im-portance of training; low salaries upon entering the field; and the overwhelmingly high percentage of women in their respective work-forces. While caution is needed when examining similarities between different occupations across a fifty-year time frame, the instructive power of the comparison is this: within a generation, major changes were effected in the ways in which society reconceptualized and responded to the needs of young children – enhancing and raising the training standards for professionals working with those young children.

If the recommendations for higher levels of education, acceptable group sizes, and appropriate adult:child ratios are adopted, the result will be a better educated workforce serving children in higher quality child care settings. But, unless funding for centres is increased, the more likely result would be a better educated but an even more under-paid workforce. To follow through on the analogy to kindergarten teachers, the combination of higher levels of required education resulted in greater professional status and a wage structure that reflected the level of education and responsibility that the job entails. Prospective ECCE staff who are required to take additional years of professional preparation have every right to expect a wage structure that reflects the level of education and responsibility their job entails. We see disturbing signs in the 1998 *You Bet I Care!* data that it is precisely the better educated staff who experience the highest levels of dissatisfaction with their work in child care.

In both the 1991 and 1998 surveys, ECCE staff were asked the following question: 'If you were choosing a career now, would you choose child care?' There was a sharp decline between the 62.4 per cent who answered 'yes' in 1991 and the 44.4 per cent who answered 'yes' in 1998. The percentage of those saying 'no' nearly doubled from 16.2 in 1991 to 35.2 in 1998. There is further cause for concern when we examine the pattern of responses by staff with differing levels of education. Staff whose highest levels of education were some high school, a high school diploma, or a one-year college ECCE credential were far more likely to say 'yes' (that they would choose child care as a career) than staff who held a university degree who were much more likely to say 'no' to the same question. The concern is that it is precisely these better trained staff who are reporting the highest levels of dissatisfaction with their work and the poorest trained staff who are indicating that they are prepared to stay in the child care workforce. There is much work to be done, not only to ensure that better trained staff are entering the ECCE workforce, but that these staff will also stay in the workforce. It is their knowledge, education, wisdom, and experience that are the most important contributions to quality child care.

Notes

1 Despite the obvious importance of family child care and school-aged child care, this chapter focuses exclusively on the training of ECCE staff who work in child care centres with children aged 0–5. There are two reasons for this focus, one conceptual and the other practical. First, precisely because family child care and school-aged child care are such unique and distinct forms of child care, the educational and professional development needs of caregivers in these sectors are also unique and are therefore in need of a fuller and more in-depth discussion grounded in the ecology of family child care. Second, the space limitations of this chapter preclude the possibility of providing an adequate discussion to these unique and distinct needs.

2 The author acknowledges the support of Mike Marshall, director, and Robert Taylor, associate director of Applied Research Evaluation Services at the University of British Columbia for their role in data collection. Also, many thanks to Barry Forer for his assistance with the statistical analyses of these data.

3 For ease of reference, simplicity and readability, the terms 'early childhood education,' 'child care,' and 'ECCE' are used interchangeably. Similarly, 'training,' 'education,' and 'professional preparation' are used interchangeably; the child care workforce is referred to alternatively as 'practitioners,' 'caregivers,' 'providers,' and 'early childhood educators.'

4 H. Goelman and A.R. Pence, 'Children in Three Types of Day Care: Daily Experiences, Quality of Care and Developmental Outcomes,' in *Early Child Development and Care* (1988) 33: 67–76.

5 R. Harms and R. Clifford. *Early Childhood Education Rating Scale* (New York: Teachers College Press, 1980).

6 S. Helbrun, J. Morris, M. Culkin, S. Kagan, and J. Rustici, 'Within Sector Comparisons and the Effect of Public Funding,' in *Cost, Quality, and Child Outcomes in Child Care Centres: Public Report*, S. Helbrun, ed. (Denver CO: University of Colorado at Denver, Economics Department, 1995), 11–34.

7 For example, G. Doherty and B. Stuart, 'The Association between Child Care Quality, Ratio and Staff Training,' in the *Canadian Journal of Research in Early Childhood Education* (1997) 6(2): 127–8.

8 For example, D. Phillips, ed., *Quality in Child Care: What Does Research Tell Us? NAEYC Monograph Series* (Washington, DC: National Association for the Education of Young Children, 1987).

9 Goelman and Pence, 'Children in Three Types of Day Care; and H. Goelman and A.R. Pence, 'Effects of Child Care, Family and Individual Characteristics on Children's Language Development,' in *Quality in Child Care: What Does Research Tell Us? NAEYC Monograph Series*, D. Phillips, ed. (Washington, DC: National Association for the Education of Young Children, 1987), 89–104.

10 H. Goelman, E. Shapiro, and A.R. Pence, 'Family Environment and Family Day Care,' in *Family Relations* (1990) 4: 251–70.

11 M. Whitebook, C. Howes, and D. Phillips, *Who Cares? Child Care Teachers and the Quality of Care in America – Final Report of the National Child Care Staffing Study* (Oakland, CA: Child Care Employee Project, 1989).

12 S. Helbrun, ed., *Cost, Quality, and Child Outcomes in Child Care Centres: Public Report* (Denver, CO: University of Colorado at Denver, Economics Department, 1995); C. Howes, 'Reconceptualizing the Early Childhood Workforce,' in *Cost, Quality, and Child Outcomes*, 159–70.

13 E.S. Peisner-Feinberg and M. Burchinal, 'Descriptive Analysis of Preschool Children's Developmental Outcomes,' in *Cost, Quality, and Child Outcomes*, 125–58.

14 B. Spodek and O. Saracho, 'Professionalism in Early Childhood Education,' in *Professionalism and the Early Childhood Practitioner*, B. Spodek, O. Saracho, and D. Peters, eds. (New York: Teachers College Press, 1988) 59–74.

15 S. Bredecamp, *Developmentally Appropriate Practice in Early Childhood Education Programs from Birth through Age 8* (Washington, DC: National Association for the Education of Young Children, 1987).

16 A. Pence and S. Griffin, 'Defining a Window of Opportunity, Part 1,' in *Interaction* (1991) 4(1): 24–9; and A. Pence and S. Griffin, 'Defining a Window of Opportunity, Part 2,' in *Interaction* (1991) 4(4): 12–17.

17 J. Beach, J. Bertrand, and G. Cleveland, *Our Child Care Workforce: From Recognition to Remuneration* (Ottawa: Human Resources Development Canada, 1998); and J. Bertrand and J. Beach, *Mobility of Early Childhood Care and Education Credits and Credentials in Canada* (Ottawa: Association of Canadian Community Colleges and the Canadian Child Care Federation, 1999).

18 H. Goelman, *Visions of Program Revision: The Early Childhood Education Review Project* (Victoria, BC: Ministry of Advanced Education, Training and Technology, 1992).

19 Information on the background, objectives, instrumentation, and sampling of *YBIC* is reported in Canadian Day Care Advocacy Association and the Canadian Child Day Care Federation, *Caring for a Living: A Study on Wages and Working Conditions in Canadian Child Care* (Ottawa: Canadian Day Care Advocacy Association, 1993).

20 Canadian Day Care Advocacy Association and the Canadian Child Day Care Federation, *Caring for a Living* (Ottawa: Canadian Child Care Federation 1992).

21 Phase 2 was conducted in the fall of 1998 in six provinces and the Yukon. It included the three survey instruments from Phase 1 as well as two observational instruments of the process quality in these centres. Phase 3, conducted in the spring of 1999, was a study of family child care homes in six provinces and the Yukon and included both survey and observational components.

22 These data are reported in chapter 9 of G. Doherty, D.S. Lero, H. Goelman, A. LaGrange, and J. Tougas, *You Bet I Care! A Canada-Wide Study on: Wages, Working Conditions, and Practices in Child Care Centres* (Guelph: Centre for Families, Work and Well-Being, 2000).

23 Ibid.

24 Since the terms 'certificate' and 'diploma' are used differently within and across jurisdictions, the 'one-year qualification' includes both.

25 There is reason to believe that the staff surveys for both *Caring for a Living* and *You Bet I Care!* had higher response rates among staff with higher levels of education and lower response rates among staff with lower levels of education. In making this comparison, we assume that the variations caused by sampling error are reasonably similar in the two surveys.

26 For further discussion of this point see Lero et al., 1999, *A Profile of Canadian Child Care Centres, 1998.*

27 Whitebook et al., *Who cares?*

28 For example, Association of Canadian Community Colleges and the Canadian Child Care Federation. *Program of Research on Post-secondary Training in Early Childhood Education and Care: Working Papers* (Ottawa: Canadian Child Care Federation, 1998); Beach et al., *Our Child Care Workforce;* Bertrand and Beach, *Mobility of Early Childhood Care;* Canadian Child Care Federation, *Towards Excellence in ECE Training Programs: A Self-Assessment Guide* (Ottawa: Author, 1995).

29 For example, Phillips, *Quality in Child Care.*

30 Pence and Griffin, 'Defining a Window of Opportunity.'

31 Spodek and Saracho, 'Professionalism in Early Childhood Education.'

32 See note 28.

33 Bertrand and Beach, *Mobility of Early Childhood Care.*

34 Helbrun et al., 'Within Sector Comparisons.'

35 N. Mocan, 'The Cost of Producing Center Child Care,' in *Cost, Quality, and Child Outcomes*, 261–78; and L. Phillipsen, D. Cryer, and C. Howes, 'Classroom Process and Classroom Structure,' in *Cost, Quality, and Child Outcomes*, 125–58.

36 Goelman and Pence, 'Effects of Child Care.'

37 G. Cleveland and M. Krashinsky, *The Benefits and Costs of Good Child Care: The Economic Rationale for Public Investment in Young Children* (Toronto: University of Toronto, Centre for Urban and Community Studies, Childcare Resource and Research Unit, 1998).

38 Ibid.

39 Dominion Bureau of Statistics, *Survey of Education in the Western Provinces, 1969–70* (Ottawa: Department of Industry, Trade and Commerce, 1971).

9. The Role of Caregiver Training

Ellen Vineberg Jacobs
Concordia University

The authors of the two chapters written for this part have focused their attention on the delivery of quality care. Prior to commenting on their particular approaches to achieving good quality child care, it is important to stress that there are many different ways to look at quality child care. One is the holistic, big-picture view presented by the European Commission Network on Childcare in 1996. The policy framework for Early Childhood Services drafted by the twelve countries of the European Union of Member States (EU) consists of forty targets grouped into nine target areas including (1) policy formation, (2) finance, (3) levels and types of services, (4) education and curriculum objectives, (5) staff:child ratios, (6) employment and training, (7) environment and health, (8) parents and the community, and (9) the measurement of performance.[1]

These target areas are substantive and are meant to be developed with respect to the needs and interests of individual countries. From the EU perspective, quality is viewed as 'a relative concept based on values and beliefs, and defining quality is deemed to be a dynamic, continuous and democratic process.'[2] There are those who would argue that by not defining quality in absolute terms one member state could apply an interpretation that might not be as beneficial for children as the one applied by another member state. However, if diversity is to be recognized and accepted then the member states of the EU have agreed to strike a balance between a completely open and relativistic approach and the recognition of core values and objectives in order to achieve good quality services for young children.

Quality of care can also be defined in terms of the North American model that looks at quality from the perspective of regulations and the actual service delivered. This model derives its support from empirical studies that the European perspective eschews. In the North American model, quality consists of (1) global environment variables (e.g., furnishings and activities), (2) structural variables (e.g., staff:child ratios, staff training, wages, and group size), and (3) process variables (e.g., staff-child interactions, staff-parent interactions, and staff interactions). Although the European and North American models are similar in content, the European model is more variable and comprehensive; however it is also more difficult to quantify and, therefore, harder to use as a measurement tool for researchers.

Hillel Goelman and Gillian Doherty are two researchers who refer to quality in child care in terms of the North American model. Further, they have focused on one factor in the list of structural variables – caregiver training. Although Doherty mentions family and community values, desired developmental outcomes, and meeting the needs of families as quality issues, the rationale for focusing solely on the caregiver as the determinant of good quality child care could be strengthened. Goelman mentions structural and process variables as being relevant to the 'lived experience of children in child care' and cites several studies that indicate that there is a strong and important relation between caregiver education and training and program quality. He uses these research findings as the springboard for this presentation that focuses on the findings of the You Bet I Care! study of caregiver education and training in child care centres across Canada.

Both authors indicate that the majority of the responsibility for the provision of high quality child care rests with the caregiver. Although they point to some of the other factors associated with the delivery of high quality care, both Doherty and Goelman have named the caregiver as the ultimate determinant of the quality of care the child will receive.

For many years now experts in the field of child care research have been pointing to the importance the caregiver plays in providing high quality care.[3] More particularly they have shown that specialized, extensive training in early childhood education at the post-secondary level is a key element in the caregiver's ability to provide high-quality lived experiences for children and meet the needs of children, their families, and their community.[4]

Given these findings we should question why Canadian child care regulations do not require all caregivers to have specialized training and education to work in child care settings. Goelman informs us that there has been a change in the right direction in the proportion of individuals with Early Childhood Care and Education (ECCE) instruction and training over the past seven years. In Canada as a whole 70.8 per cent of staff have one-, two-, or three-year or post-diploma credentials, which is an increase of 12.8 percentage points since the 1991 study.[5] There has been a decrease in the proportion of staff with only a high school diploma or with some college (25.4 per cent to 11 per cent) and a decrease in the proportion of staff with only some high school education (6.1 per cent to 3.3 per cent). However, on the cusp of the twenty-first century we should be shocked to find that 11.4 per cent of the staff working with children in Canadian child care centres do not have specific training in early childhood care and education.

It is important to note that the training statistics reported by Goelman are for staff working in child care centres. These statistics do not take into account the levels of training of the family child care providers, which Doherty reports are much lower than those in centres. She also cites a 1994–5 statistic that the majority (67 per cent) of children under six years of age who are in regular non-relative care out of their own home are enrolled in family child care. This translates into the frightening possibility that this large proportion of Canadian children are not being cared for by individuals who have received extensive, specialized training in ECCE.

This situation may be the result of government and policy makers dragging their heels to avoid raising the minimum training requirements, which would increase the likelihood that salaries would rise and child care costs would increase. However, as we all know, poor developmental outcomes for children are very costly for society. Goelman proposes a set of recommendations to increase the proportion of trained staff to 100 per cent and suggests ways to put four-year degree programs within the reach of all child care staff and to make this their ultimate goal. Some of these recommendations are realistic; others may not be easily achieved. For example, Goelman suggests that universities should offer graduates of two-year programs credit for the courses they have completed. Many universities will not grant equivalent credit for courses completed in a two-year college program, as the course content and credit hours may not be equivalent. However, a number of universities have worked out a system of exemptions whereby students who have completed two-year college programs are not given credit for introductory level courses, but are exempted from these courses and required to replace them with more advanced ones. In Quebec, students who have completed a three-year DEC (Diplome d'études Collegial) are sometimes given one university course credit for two college courses completed. Credit for internships seem to be the most contentious issue and a problem that has no easy solution. All post-secondary programs attempt to develop a particular signature for their internships and require the students to follow the prescribed set of courses. Therefore, Goelman's suggestions may require extensive negotiation to achieve. Simply willing that equivalent credits be granted may not accurately reflect the realities of academia.

Doherty presents a worrisome view of the quality of care that young Canadian children who are enrolled in family child care are receiving. She indicates that in a 1996 survey that examined general education levels, only 35.9 per cent of the respondents working in regulated family child care settings had a post-secondary school certificate, diploma, or degree.[6] A 1997 study of unregulated family child care revealed that 6 per cent had an ECCE certificate from a two-year program, 4 per cent from a one-year program and 1 per cent had an ECCE degree.[7] Doherty cites these low levels of specialized training as a problem, yet she does not view preservice or in-service training as a viable solution because of the particular situation of most family child care providers: they are usually mothers of preschoolers who have not planned to be care providers and so did not complete any preservice courses. After they begin to provide care, they are too fatigued to enroll in in-service courses in the evenings because they offer care for approximately ten hours per day.

These two situations are problematic, but not insurmountable. The reference made to the fact that these women were already mothers and that consequently they have some knowledge about children is an old-world view and perpetuates the myth that experience as a mother is all that is needed to enable women to care for other people's children. Another source of concern was Doherty's willingness to discard the idea of short-term classroom courses because one study found that this was ineffective in changing caregiver behaviour or improving practice.[8] Perhaps if a project fails, one might rethink the course content and the style of information delivery rather than dismiss the possibility of future success with other curricula.

Doherty did propose the home visit model; however, this process is labour intensive and reaches only one individual at a time. Quebec has proposed a community model whereby each family care provider is linked to an early childhood centre, and the centre director or the director's assistant is responsible for overseeing what transpires in the family child care programs that are linked to her centre. The actual process for doing this has yet to be worked out, and many in the field are particularly nervous about the workload associated with this plan. Nevertheless, it appears to be a model worth pursuing.

To return to the position presented by both Doherty and Goelman, both maintain that the caregiver is the ultimate determinant of the quality of care the child will receive. I would like to explore this assumption. Where the caregiver is concerned, a recent study of caregivers' displays of angry or affectionate behaviour has reported that specialized caregiver training serves as a protective factor for individuals working under adverse conditions.[9] Where children are concerned, all of the research to date (and for the past ten years) has shown that specialized caregiver education and training is a strong predictor of positive classroom interactions, verbal communication skills, cooperative behaviour, and cognitive abilities.[10] Therefore, although we might assume that a caregiver with specialized training and education will deliver high-quality care, the following questions should be considered before leaving readers with the impression that the responsibility for high-quality care rests completely with the caregivers:

1 Is this assumption correct regardless of the quality of the environment in which the caregiver is working?
2 Can caregivers who are well trained make a poor quality centre better?
3 Does specialized training help the caregiver understand what is needed in a centre and compensate for what is lacking?
4 How much control does a caregiver really have over structural and global features of a child care centre?

If research indicates that caregivers are the ultimate determinants of the quality of care the child receives, then the following question should be addressed:

5 Should we expect caregivers working in the centre to have specialized training and to insist upon the same for care providers in regulated family child care? This is particularly pertinent given that the family child care provider usually is in control of the child care environment.

Notes

1 H. Penn, *A Framework for Quality: A European Perspective* (Toronto: University of Toronto, Child Care Resource and Research Unit, 1999).
2 European Commission Network on Childcare and Other Measures to Reconcile Employment and Family Responsibilities, *Quality Targets in Services for Young Children* (Brussels: European Commission DG5 Equal Opportunities Unit, 1996), 9.
3 See, for example, J. Arnett, 'Caregivers in Day Care Centres: Does Training Matter?' in *Journal of Applied Developmental Psychology* (1989) 10: 541–52; T. Field, 'Preschool Play: Effects of Teacher-Child Ratio and Organization of Classroom Space,' in *Child Study Journal* (1980) 10: 191–205; C. Howes and J. Rubenstein, 'Determinants of Toddlers' Experiences in Day Care: Age of Entry and Quality of Setting,' in *Child Care Quarterly* (1985) 14: 140–51; R. Ruopp, J. Travers, F. Glantz, and C. Coelen, *Children at the Centre: Final Report of the National Day Care Study* (Cambridge, MA: Abt, 1979); P. Smith and K. Connolly, 'Experimental Studies of the Preschool Environment: The Sheffield Project,' in *Advances in Early Childhood Education and Day Care*, vol. 4, S. Kilmer, ed. (Greenwich, CT: JAI Press, 1986), 27–67; M. Whitebook, C. Howes, and D. Phillips, *Who Cares? Child Care Teachers and the Quality of Care in America – Final Report of the National Child Care Staffing Study* (Oakland, CA: Child Care Employee Project, 1989).
4 G. Doherty, 'Moving towards Achieving Quality Child Care,' this volume.
5 D. Lero, H. Goelman, A.R. Pence, L.M. Brockman, and S. Nuttal, *Canadian National Child Care Study: Parental Work Patterns and Child Care Needs* (Ottawa: Statistics Canada, 1992).
6 Goss Gilroy, *Providing Home Child Care for a Living: A Survey of Providers Working in the Regulated Sector* (Ottawa: Canadian Child Care Federation, 1998).
7 Goss Gilroy, *Providing Home Child Care for a Living: A Survey of Providers Working in the Unregulated Sector* (Ottawa: Canadian Child Care Federation, 1998).
8 S. Kontos, *Out of the Shadows and into the Limelight* (Washington, DC: National Association for the Education of Young Children, 1992).
9 D. Mill and D.R. White, 'Correlates of Affectionate and Angry Behaviour in Child Care Educators of Preschool-aged Children,' in *Early Childhood Research Quarterly* (1999) 14(1): 155–78.
10 T. Field, 'Preschool Play'; Howes and Rubenstein, 'Determinants of Toddlers' Experiences in Day Care'; Ruopp et al., *Children at the Centre*; Smith and Connolly, 'Experimental Studies of the Preschool Environment'; Whitebook et al., *Who Cares?*

10. The Professionalization Process in Child Care

June Pollard, Judy Bernhard, and Pat Corson
School of Early Childhood Studies, Ryerson Polytechnic University

Both Hillel Goelnman's and Gilian Doherty's chapters are excellent in that they give us hope. They are both based on a profound understanding of the current status of child care in Canada and are grounded in an optimistic view that we can improve and move towards a system of child care provision that is the best possible experience for young children and their families. Gillian Doherty provides sound arguments for working towards better family child care supports, increased public awareness, and improved training and salaries in ECE. Hillel Goelman focuses on the need to improve the expectations for training of child care staff, reaching for nothing less than four-year degrees for all child care staff within twenty years.

A major issue with Gillian Doherty's chapter has to do with diversity. Each of the problems outlined affects immigrants and non-Anglos more substantially than other groups and this needs to be recognized.

We do very much like the organizing questions early in Doherty's chapter concerning 'good quality child care' where the focus is on 'what does the child's family and community value for its children – what are their perceptions of a desirable child care experience? What does the family and community want its children to become? What skills knowledge and abilities are valued in the society required by it for its survival? What does the family need to support its child-rearing role?' These are excellent questions, and they provide a useful framework for examining quality. Yet, we do think these areas could be further elaborated. For example, when we talk about training, it is important to consider how to meet the needs of diverse groups and how to recruit diverse people. The issues of linguistic and cultural matching are not seen as a component of quality care, although family language maintenance may be very important to the community and key to supporting families.

The issue of diversity also needs attention in the Goelman chapter. Goelman does acknowledge 'that Canadian child care centres represent a broad spectrum of abilities and disabilities, languages and ethnicities, demanding higher levels of knowledge to work successfully with such diversity.' However, again, there is nothing on how an increase in expectations of formal training can be done in such a way that it does not exclude a diversity of staff backgrounds.

Our major concern with Goelman's chapter, however, relates to the extent to which his vision of increased formal training for all child care staff is a reproduction of the professionalization process of teaching and social work, a process whereby there is an increase in the number of years of formal training, a clearer delineation of the line between the expert child care teacher and others who are doing similar work but without the training. Those who have the training will be the experts in the care and education of young children. Those who do not have the training – home child care providers and parents – will not be the experts in the tasks they do. This kind of hierarchy of expertise and exclusionary process related to the care and education of young children does not serve us well and tends to value education and devalue caring. In our four-year degree program in the School of Early Childhood Education at Ryerson Polytechnic University, the majority of students come in to get a degree so that they do not have to do 'just day care' but can be 'real teachers.' Child care staff talk about not being 'just babysitters' like their mothers or the neighbours they assisted when they were growing up. This kind of thinking prevents us from having respect for and taking responsibility for the larger task of using all the resources we have to provide the kind of child care that is responsive to family and community values.

We need to have an inclusive process of defining quality and the best kind of training and education possible and accessible for all people who are providing care and education for young children. We should not be dividing and alienating our resources for the care and education of young children; these resources include parents, home, and centre-based caregivers and educators. All of these people need to be present in the decisions about the best ways to improve quality through training.

Discussion

The chapters on how to achieve high quality in child care generated significant discussion on two central issues. The first was the role of and the appropriate standard of education and ECCE-specific training for caregivers providing centre-based care. The second was whether these same expectations should be applied to providers of family day care.

On the first issue, some questioners suggested that better training might not be the magic bullet that would ensure high-quality child care. Training might well be only one of several inputs into high quality, and we might also have to look at improving the child-staff ratio and the physical facilities in the centres. Other countries, after all, choose different mixes of training, and we might look at some minimum percentage of the caregivers in a centre having certain levels of education. Furthermore, the emphasis on academic qualifications might be problematic in some rural areas and especially in the north. It was pointed out that the child care and education field was just developing guidelines for training and career development.

In response, other comments from the floor were more supportive of the emphasis on raising training standards for caregivers. It was pointed out that there was significant variation in needs of different age groups of children, something that needed to be taught to caregivers. Furthermore, higher educational requirements for caregivers would go along with higher salaries, and this would help to address the critical issue of retention of staff. Training for staff would permit the implementation of a career lattice in child care, with better trained staff being promoted (and thus paid more). This would also allow people to view child care as a valid career. Furthermore, training could provide the knowledge that might serve as a buffer against burnout.

In response to all these comments, Hillel Goelman reiterated his belief that training for staff was far more critical in ensuring high quality than group size or physical facility (at least within current ranges). Gillian Doherty supported the notion that higher levels of training were only practical if salaries were raised.

On the issue of family day care, one questioner asked whether a two-year or four-year educational requirement was practical, and, if it were not, what might be its equivalent? It was suggested that community-based training could work with family day care. In some jurisdictions, family day care providers have developed mentoring and networking arrangements with other caregivers to enhance their skills and the quality of care provided. Learning is, after all, a collaborative process, and peer-support could be vital in family day care.

There was some discussion about whether centres or family day care represented the most effective use of scarce dollars. Gillian Doherty forcefully reiterated her belief that money spent on family child care providers would deliver stronger returns in terms of improved quality of care. These people are currently much less likely than centre care providers to have specific ECCE training, and they are much more likely to be working in isolation from peers. Rather than guaranteeing that every worker in a centre has three or four years of ECCE, scarce dollars should be directed to improving family child care and salaries in centre care.

In conclusion, Hillel Goelman reminded those at the symposium that achieving high quality required us to start raising standards and that training was the natural focus.

PART 4

How Will Good Child Care Services Be Delivered:
Education System or Community Services?

Introduction

This session of the conference turned to a critical organizational issue: how should child care services be delivered? To date, Canadian child care centres have largely been private organizations. Some centres operate for-profit, but there has been an increasing predominance of non-profit providers. The emphasis on non-profit provision provides for a relatively decentralized community-based system. But there is an obvious alternative model available. The education of children in Canada is, of course, provided largely through the public school system, with direct public control through school boards. Kindergarten services for five-year-old children (and junior kindergarten in Ontario for four-year-old children) are a type of child care and early education provided free of charge in public schools, and care for school-aged children before and after school and at lunch time may be provided through the school system.

How then would we organize an expanded comprehensive childcare system, and what are the advantages and disadvantages in each way of doing this? What kind of transition would move us from where we are to where we want to be? To answer these and related questions, we devoted the third session of the symposium to examining how to best organize the delivery of early childhood care and education services. The two presenters were chosen because of their expertise and their different approaches to the issue. Penny Milton is executive director of the Canadian Education Association. She has broad experience in public education at all levels, and has served as chair of the Toronto Board of Education, executive assistant for the Federation of Women Teachers' Associations of Ontario, executive director of the Ontario Public School Boards Association, and deputy minister of the Premier's

Council on Health, Well-being, and Social Justice. She has considerable interest in day care in the schools, going back at least to 1982 when she chaired the Toronto School Board's Working Group on Comprehensive Care Programs for Children. Susan Prentice is an associate professor of sociology at the University of Manitoba. She has written about a range of child care policy issues, with a focus on the history and practice of child care advocacy, and has a commitment to community-based institutions.

The two discussants, Julie Mathien and Jane Beach, also have a long interest in child care in general and in these kinds of organizational issues in particular. Julie Mathien has twenty-five years of experience in Canadian social policy, particularly in education and programs for children and youth. She has worked for the Toronto School Board, where she developed an initiative that established non-profit community-based child care programs in over seventy public elementary schools. In 1987 she was seconded to the Ontario Ministry of Education to manage an initiative building child care space into new schools. At the time of writing she was working as a social policy consultant while teaching part-time at Ryerson Polytechnic University and completing graduate work at the University of Toronto. Jane Beach has worked in the child care field for more than twenty years, holding numerous positions in both government and the voluntary sector. She has been director of child care for the Province of British Columbia, leaving in 1995, and since then has worked as a child care researcher and policy consultant.

Although the two main presenters came at the issue from very different perspectives, they ended up with many similar ideas about the organization and delivery of child care services. Penny Milton suggested that the lack of seamlessness between schools and child care facilities made for problems for many parents. Thus, basing child care facilities in schools would serve the needs of parents. At the same time, the ubiquitousness of the public education system could provide an effective base for developing a national child care system. But Penny Milton did not see the educational system controlling child care. Instead, she envisioned a world in which each public school would be required to provide child care facilities that could be operated and controlled on a day-to-day basis by non-profit child care providers. Public schools would assist in setting up the centres, would provide services to those centres, and would provide some overall policy direction, but child care services would be community-controlled.

Susan Prentice also emphasized the need for local control, and suggested that this kind of child care system could not only care for children, but would serve to energize local communities and provide for diversity. She looked at social policy examples from Denmark and the Province of British Columbia to demonstrate that quite different models could be used that would still retain critical elements of local control of child care.

It was left to the discussants to suggest that centralized organizations could play a useful role in developing child care systems in Canada. Julie Mathien suggested that it would be useful to push schools to expand, since they have the advantage of being an existing universal system. She suggested that public services are the best protection against privatization, thus arguing against separate non-profit organizations within schools. Jane Beach emphasized the usefulness of working with the existing educational infrastructure, and raised the question of whether effective local control would fail in the absence of good local agencies. Furthermore, child care centres that were in schools but not part of the mandated educational system could easily be seen as a non-essential part of the schools, subject to attack when times were tough.

Margo Greenwood and Perry Shawana, co-principal researchers for 'First Nations Quality Child Care: A National Study,' gave a short view of the Aboriginal perspective on child care. Margo Greenwood is an assistant professor at the University of Northern British Columbia and Perry Shawana is chair of First Nations Studies at the University of Northern British Columbia and a barrister and solicitor in British Columbia. They pointed out that central control was problematic for a group that viewed child care as a critical way to communicate Aboriginal values and that the assimilating influence of the school system would make reliance on it a hard sell within the Aboriginal community. Local control was an essential value, since Aboriginal children need to be embedded within their own culture before they can easily move outside. Thus, community-based organizations were essential. However, good child care was an essential service, since both early education and support for mothers in the labour force were, for the Aboriginal community, matters of survival.

11. Education and Child Care: Confronting New Realities

Penny Milton
Executive Director, Canadian Education Association

In the event that schools cannot be kept open safely, boards would be required to provide payment of up to $40 per school day, per family, to help off-set the costs of making alternative arrangements to ensure care and supervision of children and to help parents with young children cope with this disruption.

Ministry of Education and Training[1]

The commitment from the Ontario Ministry of Education and Training, made during the 1997 province-wide teacher walk-out, illustrates the extent to which debate about the role of public schools in child care is carried out at arm's length from the reality of family life. By publicly acknowledging the school system's role in providing essential care, the Ontario government recognized that child care and public schools cannot be separated in the practical lives of children. It went even further, giving an implicit nod to the universal need for such a service, by waiving the requirement to provide proof of additional expenses; parents needed simply to demonstrate that they had a child under the age of thirteen enrolled in a school or a day care program located in a school that was closed by the teacher protest.[2]

This brief foray of a provincial government into direct reimbursement for lost child care services signals three important facts that policy makers must acknowledge: schools in fact provide both education and care for students aged four or five to thirteen years of age; care is an essential service for which the public bears the cost; and the loss of care provided by schools may be of greater short-term consequence to families than the loss of an educational program. In other words, we are not strangers to publicly funded and universal school-based child care.

Although we should not confuse the primary mandate of public schools with child care, we can certainly look to the schools for a universal service provision model that has proven effective.

We need an effective model. Two working parents is now the norm in Canadian families, so that the majority of young children require some kind of child care arrangement. Yet, 75 per cent of children requiring child care do not have access to licensed spaces, either because licensed spaces are in short supply in many localities, or because many families who do not qualify for subsidy are nevertheless unable to afford them.[3] Finding solutions to the growing child care crisis has become a matter of national urgency.

In this chapter I will argue that the integration of child care with education is both inevitable and desirable and that the most effective policy response to the crisis we face is to facilitate that integration. Three interlocking policy imperatives underlie this argument: the urgent need for significant expansion in the number of high-quality, affordable child care spaces; a growing recognition of the relationship between early childhood experiences and learning outcomes; and the commitment at all levels of society to raise the educational attainment of school leavers. Although each of these imperatives can be addressed in child care settings outside the public school infrastructure, the existence of that infrastructure in every community, its central place in the lives of virtually every Canadian family, and the significant overlap of services provided by schools and day care facilities make increased integration both convenient and cost-effective.

If governments required (and funded) school boards to provide child care where needed, with subsidized spaces available to eligible parents, and with flexible programming to include full child care, kindergarten, and nursery school, they could solve the crisis in child care spaces, improve the readiness of children to learn in the primary grades, and contribute to the long-term school success and educational achievement levels of graduates. This is not to say that the existing policy environment and public attitudes are conducive to such an approach. Indeed, the barriers are significant. They can only be overcome if policy makers commit to the development of a national child care strategy within the context of the changing nature and patterns of work and learning, with attention to the developmental needs of all children, and with support to parents for building their capacity to raise their children well.

THE ROLE OF CHILD CARE IN THE EDUCATION CONTINUUM

No discussion of child care, particularly as it relates to the public education continuum, can ignore the massive education reform initiatives sweeping the country. Governments and the public are responding to the changing nature of the workplace and opportunities for young people. Central features of their reform agendas include curriculum redesign, outcome standards, external assessment, indicator development, and attention to transitions between home and school, work, and post-secondary education.[4] Within the context of these reform initiatives, many education leaders are also calling attention to the preschool years, arguing that reforms to formal education alone will not deliver the results that society requires and children deserve.

The current focus on quality programs for young children arises from a shift away from the traditional notion of equal opportunity to the concept of equitable outcomes, a shift that underlies many education reform initiatives. As the connection between early childhood learning and later success becomes ever clearer, optimal levels of early development are being recognized as an economic as well as a social imperative. Structural changes to labour markets arising from globalization and rapid technological development have increased the importance of school success as the need for 'knowledge workers' has increased and the demand for low-skilled workers decreased.[5] Estimates of high school drop-out rates of between 15 and 18 per cent, together with below average literacy skills for 40 per cent of the population who complete high school, give some indication of the size of the problem.[6] Without doubt, this issue must be tackled by education departments and schools. However, rich learning environments for preschool children are also an essential part of the solution.

The economic and social context may be new, but the argument is not. For years, child care advocates have cited the benefits of high-quality programs to children's early learning and later school success. Their intuitive and observational data have been supported by longitudinal studies of early childhood program outcomes[7] and extended by recent findings of neuroscience.[8] To a considerable extent, the focus is on the children of disadvantaged families. The correlation between family socioeconomic status and school success, although not one of cause and effect, has been well documented. Children from low-income families are at a significant risk for limited school success.

The combined effects of preschool programs on the future success of students have been extensively studied in the United States. The High/ Scope Perry Preschool study, the longest and most intensive follow-up study of the effects of early childhood programs on later development, found that a comprehensive preschool experience resulted in increased commitment to school, better relationships with friends and neighbours, greater adult economic success, lower crime rates, and fewer teenage pregnancies for girls. It was estimated that every dollar invested in a high-quality comprehensive preschool program led to a future cost avoidance to the taxpayer of $7.[9] A more recent economic study prepared by Cleveland and Krashinsky broadens the financial analysis to include the dollar value of benefits to children, women, and the child care sector of the labour market. They found that the public provision of high quality child care for all two- to five-year-olds resulted in a cost-benefit ratio of 1:2. The annual new expenditure required to achieve this ratio would be about $5.3 billion or less than 1 per cent of Canada's GDP, an investment that compares favourably with several European countries.[10]

Such an economic analysis provides a powerful incentive for policy change, but not all advocates of state-supported services to young children favour an investment-based paradigm. Moss and Penn, for example, argue that policy development should be based on a paradigm that values young children for who they are rather than who they will become.[11]

THE FAILURE OF CURRENT POLICY FRAMEWORKS

Canadian children and families do not enjoy equal access to regulated child care across the country. Standards for child-staff ratios, staff training, group sizes, and family day care vary from province to province.[12] Statistics compiled by the Child Care Resource and Research Unit indicate that two provinces provide regulated care to fewer than 5 per cent of their children zero to twelve years old; five provinces experienced a drop in the supply of regulated spaces between 1990 and 1995; six provinces and territories spend less than $100 per year for each child up to the age of twelve; nine provinces require fewer than two years of post-secondary education for child care workers; and in eight provinces and territories income eligibility levels have remained largely unchanged since 1989.[13]

The situation is deteriorating. Doherty, Friendly, and Oloman report that the number of regulated spaces declined in four provinces during the 1990s and may be overestimated in others. Fees have increased while family incomes have decreased and government subsidies have remained almost static (with the exception of Quebec). Direct operating funds to child care centres have been eliminated in some provinces. Combined, these factors have contributed to the underutilization of existing licensed spaces.[14] At a time when the contribution of child care to meeting the social and economic objectives of healthy child development, women's equality, and job creation is well understood, access is becoming increasingly precarious as the affordability and availability of regulated child care decreases.

The national failure to provide a coherent child care service is exacerbated by the quintessential Canadian problem of competing jurisdictions. Child care falls under provincial or territorial jurisdiction with school boards, as potential players in the child care field, occupying a fourth level of government in the jigsaw puzzle. Furthermore, in the absence of national standards, and with the replacement of the Canada Assistance Program by the Canadian Health and Social Transfer in 1996, child care has come to be viewed in some quarters as a 'services market.'[15] The complex interaction of legislation, regulation, and funding among federal, provincial or territorial, municipal, and school authorities, combined with the private sector, presents enormous challenges to integration and coordination of program delivery. This situation is compounded at the provincial or territorial level by the separation of jurisdiction for education and care into two, or in some cases three, ministries or departments.

Like child care, school systems fall under provincial jurisdiction, but their separate legislative frameworks have evolved over the past hundred years to become quite similar, effectively ensuring all Canadians equal access to similar educational services. It is hardly surprising, then, that in 1986 a federal task force on child care recommended the development of 'complementary systems of child care and parental leave that are as comprehensive, accessible and competent as our systems of health care and education.'[16] More than ten years later, with the exception of Quebec, Canada still lacks the element of public entitlement to child care that characterizes public education.

Some small progress is being made. In April 1998 the Minister of Education and Minister for Families and Children in Quebec, Mme Pauline Marois, announced an eight-year program to increase access to child care by funding new spaces and limiting cost to parents to $5 per day, beginning in September 1997 with four-year-olds (and full-day kindergarten for five-year-olds), and lowering the eligibility annually until 2001 when children under one year of age will have access to care at this rate.[17] The $5-per-day rate was extended to three-year-olds in 1998 and two-year-olds in 1999. But such initiatives require inter-jurisdictional cooperation to be successful. Several provinces have provided capital grants for the construction of child care facilities in new schools. Ontario, however, recently moved in the opposite direction by excluding child care from calculations of school facility operating costs. In that province, concern is growing that existing child care spaces may be reassigned to education programs, as school boards cope with the new funding regulations. Even in provinces where capital grants for child care centres have been made, difficulties in securing commitments for fee subsidies may arise if the priorities of departments of education and social services are not the same – an example of jurisdictional conflict within a single level of government.[18]

Doherty et al. have confronted these jurisdictional issues in their proposal for a comprehensive, universal, and affordable national child care system that tests the new social union.[19] They identify various models that respond to the constitutional division of powers:

- Individual provinces and territories working alone
- Joint federal-provincial programs with federal leadership exercised through spending powers and the establishment of principles
- Collaboration between the federal government and the provinces and territories to develop a Canada-wide framework
- Cooperation by the provinces and territories in the absence of federal participation
- A single province with federal funding adopting a strong child care initiative as a lighthouse project for the rest of the country.

These options have been available since at least the early 1970s, when the first call for enhanced government involvement in providing day care services was made by the Royal Commission on the Status of Women. Some twenty-five years later, during which time the needs for regulated child care have continued to escalate, both the political will of provinces (except Quebec) and the policy levers of the federal government have diminished.[20] To date, calls for political and jurisdictional leadership, for enhanced funding mechanisms, and for an increase in shared responsibility, coordination, and integration have been in vain. It is time for a new approach.

IN SUPPORT OF SCHOOL-BASED PROGRAMS

It is important to distinguish at the outset between school-based child care and child care that is fully integrated into the public school system. In school-based systems, community or private corporations operate programs that occupy school space according to a formal tenant arrangement. Fully integrated programs are operated directly by the school board on an equal footing with other school programs. Table 11.1 summarizes the differences between school-based and integrated child care systems. To date, there are no examples of fully integrated programs in Canada, although in some cases hybrid models have been developed. Within this context, Daniel Keating distinguishes between collaboration with public schools and appropriation by them, making a case against full integration by arguing that the public school system should not be the sole controller of all education programs.[21] There are forces, however, that place child care services at risk when they are *not* fully integrated into and maintained by strong infrastructures.

In most currently operating child care models in Canada, whether school-based or community-based, public investment is targeted to the working poor, making it vulnerable to deficit reduction and other cost-saving targets of federal and provincial governments. In a radical departure, Cleveland and Krashinsky propose a model of child care that provides programs for *all* children. They argue that, given its social and economic benefits, 'funding for high quality child care would seem to be a natural extension of the reasoning that led originally to funding for public schools.'[22] It may be worth noting here that the extension of free and compulsory secondary education arrived on the scene much later than elementary education and that even now late secondary education is voluntary, much as early childhood education is voluntary (but not yet free except for kindergarten, where it is provided).

As indicated at the opening of this chapter, the public school system has already assumed a de facto role as a child care provider for much of a school-aged child's day. As a result of changing social and economic conditions, the public provision of education has expanded since its inception to cover both younger and older children. New Brunswick, for example, has reduced the age of mandatory school attendance from six years to five. Senior kindergarten for five-year-olds is available in all jurisdictions except Prince Edward Island, with full-day programs in Quebec and New Brunswick. Junior kindergarten for four-year-olds is an option in several provinces.[23] While these programs have been intro-

Table 11.1. Key features of school-based and integrated child care

Feature	School-based	Integrated
Owner/operator	Not-for-profit, community-based corporation / for-profit providers	School board, school authority
Policy formulation	Provincial enabling provisions, local school board	Provincial mandate, local school board implementation
Standards setting	No change required	Education departments or ministries
Employer of child care staff	Community corporation	School board
Administrative infrastructure, including services	None or voluntary provision by school board	School board
Capital costs	Continued provincial responsibility and community corporation	Education departments or ministries and school boards
Role of parents	Governing boards	Advisory
Occupancy	Tenant	Equal status with other school programs
Liability	Corporation	School board

duced or made mandatory within the context of public schooling and formal education, their impact on and overlap with child care are obvious, and they appear to invite consideration of the public school system as a natural repository for child care services, especially given the advantages to children of a so-called seamless transition from care to education.

At the same time as their reach has extended to a larger segment of the population, public schools have become favourite targets for public and government disapproval. The various reasons for this apparent lack of confidence are beyond the scope of this chapter. It is fair to note, however, that the education of young people has never been a more complex endeavour and that the same changing expectations that are driving government education reform agendas across Canada have created a climate of dissatisfaction among many families and students. That said, it is important to distinguish between the cyclical (and, I believe, healthy) education reform movements driven by changing public expectations and the confidence that families feel in sending their children into school buildings and classrooms, into the care of individual teachers and principals. When we contemplate a further extension of the child care system into the schools, we should keep in mind the public opinion surveys that show that whatever dissatisfaction parents may feel with academic programs or bureaucracies, they continue to be supportive of their children's teachers and believe that their children receive appropriate care in the school setting.[24]

Such an extension of the role of schools is consistent with societal trends that often go unnoticed, according to Carnoy and Castells in a critique of strategies used by selected member countries of the Organization for Economic Cooperation and Development (OECD) to deal with the 'work crisis.' They write that such strategies "fail to recognize that in the global information economy, the very nature of the work system is changing — *away from permanent jobs as the locus of work toward a complex network of learning institutions, including the workplace, families and community schools*' (original emphasis). They argue that the family and community in the information age should also be organized around the centrality of knowledge and information in order to support new forms of work and to foster human development. They define communities in terms of learning networks, including child development centres, educational institutions, and municipal organizations.[25] Clearly this vision requires a substantial leap that could carry us far beyond the discussion at hand. But Keating narrows the concept to focus on schools themselves, arguing that they must be reconfigured as a focal community and family resource and restructured to play a leadership role in increasing community and family participation.[26] The role of schools as child care providers fits nicely within this more modest paradigm.

Although Canadian schools are not there yet, we may not be as far away as some would have us believe. Current provincial reforms that establish community or parent councils suggest an openness to the expansion of the school's role in the community. The range of family and community resources already developed by some school boards is impressive: parent resource and drop-in centres, public health services, parent drop-in centres, settlement services and language classes for immigrant families, toy libraries and access to school libraries, informal computer classes for parents, child care services for attendance at school events, and clothing exchanges. Service development has indeed reflected community needs when resources have been available. Unfortunately, many of these services are under threat as budget constraints reach crisis proportions.

In their *Early Years Project* Johnson and Mathien identify several factors that point to the school as an obvious choice for the provision of child care, as well as education, for young children:

- Staff training may be more important than group size for four- and five-year-olds.
- A school location makes integrated programs more acceptable than a non-school location.
- Full-day kindergarten already requires that attention be given to the content and quality of the 'care' portion of the child's day.
- Parents and practitioners have similar expectations for the nature of the child's learning in both kindergarten and child care.
- There was a desire on the part of parents and practitioners for close ties to education with respect to both location and jurisdiction.
- A preliminary analysis indicates that an integrated approach is cost-effective.[27]

Johnson and Mathien recommend a cautious approach to the development of an integrated model of care and education for young children, noting that such a model will find favour with parents only if it allows participation for variable lengths of the day, avoids increased bureaucratization, addresses the anxieties of practitioners (possibly through cross-training), and provides sufficient resources to support coordination and integration.

Few would argue with the proposition that the ideal child care model should be anchored in the community and responsive to the needs of families. Disagreement may arise as to the extent to which schools have the potential to meet those requirements. I would argue that by working to enhance the school as a flexible and approachable venue for child care, we will simultaneously be making it a more flexible and approachable institution for the education of all children and for the support of all families. There is ample evidence that school systems can incorporate child care into their operations and that in doing so they strengthen the bond between family and school, which has as profound an influence on later student success as any other single factor.

The interests of education authorities in the development of child care in schools has mirrored changes in the policy environment over time. One of the earliest recorded interventions was that of Hester How, a Toronto elementary school principal who, in 1888, petitioned the school board to grant $25 to a group of charitable citizens intent on establishing a day care centre. The impetus for the centre came from a truancy officer's report that pupils were losing school time to care for younger siblings while their mothers worked. During the Second World War, schools were the logical places to set up temporary child care and feeding centres for the children of women who were employed as replacement workers. Two provinces, Ontario and Quebec, passed legislation providing financial support for families with mothers employed in essential wartime industries and for the development of child care programs. The dominion and provincial governments withdrew funding for these day care services soon after the end of the wartime emergency, and at least one school board joined the protest against the reluctant return of mothers to the 'non-remuneration of work at home.'[28]

The next wave of program development occurred in the 1970s when declining enrolment led school boards to establish community use policies. A high priority for a number of boards was the use of school space for not-for-profit child care programs. Some boards provided staff for coordination and advisory services. Some provided free space but charged for caretaking services; some charged a nominal rent of $1 per annum; others established a rental fee at a lower rate than for profit-making services; still others made no distinction among potential users of school space. Concern for the economic futures of teenaged mothers led at least one school board to organize infant care programs for the babies of high school students to make the mothers' completion of secondary education and the healthy development of their infants more likely.[29] Although there were, and continue to be, some school boards that 'don't believe in day care,' or regard it as a policy for which they have no responsibility, most are prepared to facilitate the establishment of child care centres provided no 'education dollars' are required – that is, provided they are not required to bleed monies away from their educational programs.

While there are no current comprehensive studies of the support for child care by school authorities in Canada, a partial survey of school boards conducted by the Canadian Education Association in 1982 identified child care programs operating in elementary and secondary schools in eight of the ten provinces and one territory.[30] Half of the 170 respondents indicated that child care facilities were housed in their schools, but very few had adopted policies regarding the provision of child care. Thirty-four school boards indicated that they provided some level of administrative oversight to child care centres.

A survey of current child care policies in large urban school boards conducted for the preparation of this chapter suggests that little change has occurred on the policy front since the 1980s, but that both the range of program types and the number of centres have expanded dramatically.[31] Preschool, including infant care, before- and after-school care, supervised lunch programs, and summer programs are found in school districts across the country, with the largest concentration in urban areas. Johnson and Mathien reported that by 1995 almost half of all child care centres in Ontario were located in schools.[32] Recognizing the benefits to both parents and students, education authorities have made a variety of accommodations within existing policy and funding frameworks to support the provision of a broader set of services to families, particularly for children of mandatory school attendance age, usually six to twelve.

While most school districts have allowed child care programs to creep into their schools without formal policy recognition, there are several notable exceptions, in particular, the Carleton Catholic School Board, the former Toronto and City of York boards of education, and the Durham Board of Education. During the past decade, these boards have actively expanded the provision of child care services, parent education programs, and the coordination between child care and kindergarten.

The Ottawa-Carleton Catholic School Board has acted on a commitment to provide high-quality child care within its schools in the absence of a formal mandate to do so. It has established a not-for-profit corporation, the Carleton Roman Catholic Child Care Corporation, which administers child care centres in the board's schools with direct support from the board through its governance structure and its Child Care Services Department that provides a number of administrative services to the corporation through a purchase of services agreement.[33]

The Toronto District School Board has made a clear statement in support of an integrated model through its Child Care in Schools Policy which clearly reflects the current focus of educators and education policy makers on the importance of early childhood learning to later success. This policy emphasizes the importance of high-quality child care to the intellectual, physical, emotional, and social well-being of children; the importance of child care to school readiness and long-term educational success; the value of a continuum of care and learning between child care and school programs; the opportunity for integrated programs to provide support for parents and to encourage partnership with schools; and the importance of access to regulated child care programs for student parents.[34]

The level of engagement reflected in the policies and practices of these three boards is the exception rather than the rule, and there is reason for concern that the current political climate will make it difficult to maintain. The lack of clear authority of the boards, inadequate financial support for start-up and administrative functions, and an agenda of significant reform to education that does not incorporate child care objectives combine to put existing programs at risk.

A NEW VISION FOR CHILD CARE IN CANADA

Policy makers in Canada continue to skirt around the edges of the child care imperative, despite incontrovertible evidence that a consistent, universal, high-quality system would be advantageous to Canadian children, families, and society as a whole. And yet, an infrastructure exists to provide the leadership, the policy frameworks, and the research base needed to develop a national child care system to meet the needs of our youngest citizens and their parents. Notwithstanding the lack of federal jurisdiction in education, the educational opportunities available to communities across the country are more similar than they are different. What is lacking is the federal-provincial policy framework and financial commitment to stabilize and expand existing services to incorporate child care programs.

To date, school-based child care has depended on the availability of space, the support of principals, permissive school board policies, and a private provider or organized community initiative. Concerns have arisen about lack of permanency, inadequate financial management, program standards, voluntary cooperation between child care and school, and inexperienced management. In addition, school-based centres, like community-based and private centres, have been at the mercy of subsidization policies that exclude many members of the community from participation.

While a model of fully integrated care raises the spectre of intensive bureaucratic control and concern over issues like qualifications and child-teacher ratios, it does acknowledge the growing public acceptance of child care and early childhood education as an essential social service. Since the 1970s school authorities in many areas have worked hard with little leverage to make the school a 'hub' for family and child services and have arguably made greater progress in responding to cultural and linguistic diversity than any other public system in Canada. The extension of authority for the further development of a high-quality child care system is a logical next step. To that end, I recommend the following policy initiatives:

- All school boards in Canada should be required to provide child care within schools in all communities with demonstrated need.
- Child care facilities in schools should be established as not-for-profit operations, funded by provincial budgets.
- Parents should be expected to pay partial costs (20 per cent), but subsidized spaces should be guaranteed where required to ensure that care is within the reach of all families.
- School boards should assist in the establishment of centres and provide services including financial management, access to professional development, and quality monitoring.
- Child care centres and schools should be required to coordinate program provision.
- Community corporations should be the preferred governing structure, but where not feasible, school boards should be empowered to operate centres directly with a parent advisory committee.
- Flexible provision of programming should include full child care, kindergarten, and nursery school for children from two years of age to kindergarten, and parent resource centres where needed.
- Implementation should be gradually extended downward from the current age of universal access (between four and six years of age) to infants.

Of course, jurisdictional boundaries plague public schools as well as child care, and the implementation of national policy is, strictly speaking, impossible. However, the public education sector has forged a very Canadian solution to the need for a pan-Canadian presence. Since 1967 provincial and territorial education departments have collaborated on research and policy initiatives through the Council of Ministers of Education Canada (CMEC). The council has responded effectively to national interests, spearheading policies like the Victoria Declaration on Education, the Student Achievement Indicators Program (SAIP), a national curricular Framework for Science, and the development of a pan-Canadian Education Research Agenda. It has a proven capacity to collaborate with federal departments; it could ensure that a national agenda is pursued in concert with provincial and local level innovation; it could draw on the first-hand experience of member provinces that have experience with innovative policies and approaches to early learning; it has the capacity to develop frameworks and national expectations, as well as program and training standards; it is connected to provincial and territorial policy and implementation structures; and it is capable of monitoring progress.

This educational infrastructure is unique in Canada, respecting the constitutional division of powers between federal and provincial or territorial jurisdictions, while acting as a national voice and stimulus for national and pan-provincial policy development. Its role — or the role of similar bodies — may become even more important in related social policy fields with the emergence of the new social union.

The CMEC could reasonably be expected to provide the political and administrative leadership necessary for a breakthrough in the formulation of a national child care system. Twelve national organizations representing parents, teachers, principals, trustees, school administrators, and advocates for special populations, child care, and child health, have called on the council to take the lead in ensuring quality educational programs for four- and five-year olds, supporting holistic, coordinated, and integrated approaches to preschoolers, and emphasizing the importance of publically funded preschool programs.[35]

For thirty years Canadians have been talking about the need for universal, affordable child care. At the turn of the century, our inability to convert talk into public policy has created a crisis that is impoverishing families and leaving many children without adequate care and unprepared for formal learning. Perhaps it is time to move away from the social service model and embrace a model that we know is capable of delivering a universal, high-quality service. By building on the local, provincial or territorial, and national mechanisms for management and collaboration that now ensure universal, high quality educational programs across Canada, child care policy makers could implement a national child care service in a relatively short time. By extending the concept of universality for schooling from six-year-olds to child care for two-year-olds, in annual increments, Canada could solve its child care crisis in five years.

Notes

1 Ministry of Education and Training, *Johnson Announces Assistance to Families Affected during Teachers' Illegal Strike* (Toronto: Ministry of Education and Training, Ontario, News Release, 24 October 1997).

2 Michael Valpy, 'Payment to Parents Treated as Refund,' in *Globe and Mail* (26 January 1998), A10.

3 Alan R. Pence, S. Griffin, L. McDonnell, H. Goelman, D.S. Leco, and L.M. Brockman, *Shared Diversity: An Interprovincial Report on Child Care in Canada* (Ottawa: Canadian National Child Care Study, Statistics Canada, 1997).

4 P. Milton, *Innovations for Effective Schools: An Introduction to the Pan-Canadian Experience* (New Zealand Country Paper for the Organization for Economic Cooperation and Development Conference in Christchurch, New Zealand: Combating Failure at School, 1998).

5 Martin Carnoy and Manuel Castells, *Sustainable Flexibility: A Prospective Study on Work, Family and Society in the Information Age* (Paris: Organization for Economic Cooperation and Development, 1997), 26.

6 Organization for Economic Cooperation and Development and Statistics Canada, *Literacy, Economy and Society: Results of the First International Literacy Survey* (Ottawa: Authors, 1995), 73.

7 Judy E. Florian, Lawrence J. Schweinhart, and Ann S. Epstein, *Early Returns: First Year Report of the Michigan School Readiness Program Evaluation* (Ypsilanti, MI : High/Scope Educational Research Foundation, 1997), 8–9, quoting Schweinhardt, Barnes, and Weikart, *Significant Benefits: The High/Scope Perry Preschool Study through Age 27* (Ypsilanti, MI: High/Scope Press, 1993).

8 P. Wolfe and R. Brandt 'What Do We Know from Brain Research?' in *Educational Leadership* (1998) 56(3): 8–13.

9 Florian et al., *Early Returns*, 9.

10 G. Cleveland and M. Krashinsky, *The Benefits and Costs of Good Child Care: The Economic Rationale for Public Investment in Young Children* (Toronto: University of Toronto, Child Care Resource and Research Unit, 1998).

11 Peter Moss and Helen Penn, *Transforming Nursery Education*, reviewed by Martha Friendly, in *Canadian Journal of Research in Early Childhood Education* (1998) 7(1): 191–3.

12 Pence et al., *Shared Diversity*, 93–4.

13 Child Care Resource and Research Unit, *Key Points about Early Childhood Care and Education* (Toronto: University of Toronto, Child Care Resource and Research Unit, 1999). (www.childcarecanada.org/research/stats/keypoints.html)

14 Gillian Doherty, Martha Friendly, and Mab Oloman, *Women's Support, Women's Work: Child Care in an Era of Deficit Reduction, Devolution, Downsizing and Deregulation* (Ottawa: Status of Women Canada, 1998), 18–30.

15 Laura C. Johnson and Julie Mathien, *Early Childhood Services for Kindergarten-Age Children in Four Canadian Provinces: Scope, Nature and Models for the Future* (Ottawa: Caledon Institute of Social Policy, 1998).
16 Pence et al., *Shared Diversity*, 17, quoting K. Cooke, J. London, R. Edwards, and R. Rose-Lizee, *Report of the Task Force on Child Care* (Ottawa: Status of Women Canada, 1986).
17 Mme Pauline Marois, Ministre de la Famille et de l'Enfance, *Québec Communiqué*, 1 April 1998.
18 Personal communication with Tom Rich, executive director, Nova Scotia Department of Education and Culture.
19 Doherty et al., *Women's Support*, 18–30.
20 Ibid., 39–44.
21 Daniel Keating, 'Families, Schools and Communities,' in *Family Security in Insecure Times* (Ottawa: Canadian Council on Social Development, 1996), 164.
22 Cleveland and Krashinsky, *Benefits and Costs*, 12.
23 Paula Dunning, *Education in Canada: An Overview* (Toronto: Canadian Education Association, 1997), 24.
24 For example, Education Quality and Accountability Office, *Ontario Provincial Report on Achievement in 1997–98* (Toronto: Queen's Printer, 1998), 38.
25 Carnoy and Castells, *Sustainable Flexibility*, 33.
26 Keating, 'Families, Schools and Communities,' 164.
27 Johnson and Mathien, *Early Childhood Services*, 57–60.
28 Penny Moss, *Comprehensive Care for Children Programs* (Toronto: Toronto Board of Education, 1981).
29 Ibid.
30 Canadian Education Association, *Day Care and the Canadian School System* (Toronto: Author, 1983), 15.
31 Penny Milton, *Canadian Education Association Survey* (Unpublished,1998).
32 Johnson and Mathien, *Early Childhood Services*, 9.
33 Milton, unpublished survey.
34 Ibid.
35 Council of Ministers of Education, Canada, *Preparation for Learning: Preschool Education*, discussion paper for the CMEC Third National Forum, 1998 (www.cmec.ca).

12. The Case for Community-Governed Child Care Services

Susan Prentice
Department of Sociology, University of Manitoba

Once the case has been made and accepted that child care is a public good and an essential human service, planners must develop mechanisms to deliver care.[1] With the very limited exception of the years during the Second World War, Canadian policy makers have never accepted these propositions, and as a result policy debates over child care have rarely needed to question implementation models. In the absence of an organized system of child care, services in Canada have basically grown ad hoc, reliant on volunteer non-profit corporations or the commercial sector to establish and deliver care, whether licensed or unlicensed.[2] Aside from a very small number of government-operated programs, all regulated child care spaces in Canada are provided by the market as either non-profit or proprietary enterprises.[3]

In this context, 'community delivery' has become synonymous with the absence of comprehensive coordinated care and the lack of a public policy framework, and as such it is often rejected. Advocates have turned to other social services, especially the personal social services, to propose that child care ought to be incorporated into the welfare state. The current model of delivering public services, however, raises valid concerns about the bureaucratization and unresponsiveness of care – part of what fuels conservatives who object to 'institutionalizing' young children in group settings. This history has understandably created the perception that one must choose either the devil or the deep blue sea; that is, if we are to have a universal child care system, it must inevitably be characterized by *either* unresponsive but public services *or* locally democratic but unfunded voluntary services. In this chapter, we want to recuperate community-governed publicly funded child care from both its progressive and conservative critics.

Margaret O'Brien-Steinfels points out that questions of parent and community control may seem like marginal details about administration. 'But,' she argues, 'the question of parental and community involvement is in fact the single most important, albeit acrimonious discussion about child care. It asks, in effect, "Who will raise our children?"'[4] We answer her question this way: we envision a delivery model that provides child care through an organizational and administrative structure accountable to the local community. Such a community-based delivery system must operate within a well-defined and well-resourced public policy framework. From public policy, we look for legislated entitlement for all children to quality early childhood care and education programs, for funding to ensure adequate provision of service, and for high public standards that promote quality care. Within this overall public policy context, child care services should be delivered at the local level. We emphasize that this public policy framework is essential if 'community control' is not to become an excuse for public inaction.

WEAKNESSES AND STRENGTHS OF CURRENT DELIVERY SYSTEMS

Regulated child care in Canada is currently provided through a complex array of regulated and quasi-regulated services. Some are straightforward, such as licensed group child care centres; others are more ambiguous, for example, Quebec's school-age child care which is publicly-funded by the education system yet has no regulations or Saskatchewan's part-day preschool programs for three- and four-years-olds. Family home day care, which provides approximately 15 per cent of the total national number of regulated spaces, is generally offered as a home-based private business, although it can scarcely be considered a profit-making enterprise.[5] Most family home day care providers are individually licensed, although in four jurisdictions family home day care is regulated through licensing of agencies, which may be non-profit, commercial, or directly operated, as in Ontario. The vast majority of children in alternate care are using services in the unregulated sector, generally informal, in-home care provided in caregivers' houses, often virtually indistinguishable from individually licensed family homes. This diversity makes it difficult to analyse and compare models of service delivery across jurisdictions.

Nevertheless, it is possible to generally sketch out four broad delivery routes.[6] First, and most prevalent is the non-profit voluntary sector, which through stand-alone and parent-operated centres, multiple-site single-purpose child care societies, multi-service neighbourhood agencies, child care hubs, and religious or cultural societies provides about two-thirds of centre spaces. What unites all of these services is the statutory obligation to be governed through a board of directors. The second delivery route is the commercial sector which provides about 30 per cent of licensed centre care through independent centres, small chains, and franchises. Like other businesses, commercial child care is operated by its owners, although some jurisdictions require some parental input – a requirement which may act as a brake on the expansion of commercial services in some parts of the country. The third method of delivery is the public sector, with less than 5 per cent of centre spaces directly delivered by municipalities, recreation departments, and school boards. The final mode of delivery is family child care. Of Canada's 429,000 licensed spaces in 1997–8, 66,532 are family child care spaces; these are mainly individually licensed private businesses.[7]

There is no coordination among these models of service delivery and no statutory requirement that child care be provided. Instead, there is fragmentation, lack of integrated services, and significant variations in levels of quality – all manifestations of the absence of child care planning capacity. Canada lacks accountability for public investment in child care and suffers from a missing infrastructure for administrative efficiency and effectiveness. Correspondingly, there is a low public visibility to the child care system, and child care suffers from diminished political support. The dysfunctions of our essentially voluntary system of child care are glaringly evident.

There are, however, some unintended benefits to the current fragmented patchwork of services. One such benefit is that child care services reflect and respond to local diversity, offering a range of choices and options. Most of Canada's statutory social services (we think particularly of health and education) tend to impose a monolithic model of uniform service – the dreaded 'cookie-cutter.' In the case of education, there are generally province-wide standards and program expectations, compulsory attendance, and bureaucratization; in health care, control and accountability are many steps removed from users, who are marginalized in a highly professionalized environment. Child care is quite unlike health or education in both these respects.

Another benefit of the current system is that its size and scale rarely prevent a direct relationship between users and caregivers. Many statutory services suffer from the problem of a size and scale that prevent such a direct relationship. ᒣChild care services, in contrast, are often too small – within a single neighbourhood there may be several stand-alone, board-run child care centres, without coordination, each inefficiently duplicating administrative and other tasks, and without integration with other child, family, and related services. Rita Chudnovsky's work on management and governance structures for child care centres in the City of Vancouver suggests that a size of 350 child care spaces for one administrative structure is the maximum optimal size from a combined efficiency and participation standpoint; a maximum which Quebec will also apparently apply.[8] Some experimentation will be required to establish desired parameters, which may vary across differing communities, but our overall point is that maintaining direct relationships mitigates against bureaucratization, centralization, and overprofessionalization – all tendencies that occur in statutory social services as they are currently delivered, to the detriment of users and care providers alike.

One of the most significant weaknesses with the current situation is that it places an enormous burden on volunteers, mainly overstressed parents and particularly overstressed mothers.[9] About three in five of Canada's licensed regulated centre spaces is offered by a non-profit organization, usually a single centre with a board of directors. Non-profit centres rely on volunteer boards of directors to run complex organizations and manage budgets frequently in the hundreds of thousands of dollars annually. In the current situation, parents who may or may not have the expertise, skills, resources, or time are left responsible for the service they and their children use. Such participation is laudable in principle, but it is frequently reduced to an imposition in practice, as users have more responsibility than knowledge or expertise. In fact, in several jurisdictions in Canada, parents are required by law to 'volunteer' to run their services.[10] The commendable goal of 'parent involvement' too rarely revolves around policy and program decisions and too often manifests as the burdensome request that users supplement scarce resources through donations of time or money or both.

We are acutely aware of the problems of the current voluntary sector model. Still, it has strengths we want to retain and enhance. Notwithstanding the significant shadow side of volunteer-run, non-profit boards, this model does create an important degree of responsiveness to local communities, and a high level of community ownership – and it is an important bulwark against free-enterprise child care. In jurisdictions where there are high expectations of parental involvement, the degree of commercial care tends to be lower and the quality of care tends to be higher.[11]

One of the greatest strengths of the current system is its political autonomy. Community-based child care services have the ability to be advocates for the constituencies they serve. They can speak with an independent voice. This is a capacity that is traditionally absent in public services that lack arm's-length distance from government and are therefore unable to criticize public policy. While an inherent tension remains between publicly funded, community-governed services and the state which funds them, we maintain this tension is potentially fruitful and productive. The independence and autonomy of community-delivered care means that it can (and does) challenge public policy to become more responsive. Moreover, this independent sector can mobilize and build a constituency to ensure that public policy meets local needs. ⌋

PARTICIPATORY, USER-RESPONSIVE, COMMUNITY-GOVERNED SERVICES

Since the 1970s there has been a growing awareness that child and family programs should respond to community needs and values, rather than impose a monolithic or agency-centred model of program and service delivery. This trend has emphasized the importance of democratic administration and responsiveness to the needs of intended and actual participants. We share a belief in the importance of participatory and community-governed service, and we draw on this local democracy perspective in advocating for a decentralized delivery system. Obviously, then, it matters who the participants in child care are.

To ask who is the user of a child care program is to grapple with one of the thorniest questions in the field. By most common-sense definitions, child care is a service for children and children are therefore its users. This seems so obvious that it hardly bears elaborating: it seems self-evident that children are the consumers of a high-quality service that contributes to their multiple social, cognitive, educational, and other developmental needs. This case is sometimes narrowed in claims that the real clients of the service are poor or otherwise needy children; certainly, this is the formal as well as informal assumption of Head Start in its many guises, as well as the premise of all targeted programs based on need. Whether narrowly or expansively conceived, it generally remains that children are understood to be the clients (in the supplicant model) or consumers (in the more expansive version) of child care service. On closer examination, however, other users of child care service emerge.

Although child care services are 'consumed' by children, the case can equally plausibly be argued that parents are the users. Since they are substitutes for parental care, child care services can be seen to be purchased and/or consumed because parents are not directly minding their children. After all, the vast majority of children use child care because their parents work, and parents need to ensure that their children are happy and thriving – or at least safe – while they are on the job. In this light, it can be argued that the client of child care is a particular kind of parent; namely, an employed parent – and so, perhaps, the paradigmatic user should be seen as a worker. Again, this position can fracture along income and class lines. Mainstream policy approaches presume that child care is normally a private parental responsibility, and the only role for public intervention is on behalf of low-income working parents. This is why in Canada, for example, fee subsidies are generally restricted to parents who work or study.[12] Whether only for low-income or for all working parents, it is easy to argue that child care is as much for working mothers and fathers as for children.

But to state the case this neutrally, however, is to miss much of what is really going on. In most households, women continue to have the practical and daily responsibility for parenting, whether or not they work for pay outside the home. Even though women are a growing percentage of the paid labour force, a gender division persists within the home and in caring work.[13] From this perspective, it can be argued that women are also users of child care. Mothers purchase care to replace themselves when they are unavailable to be with their children. The chronic lack of affordable, licensed child care is rooted in ideologies about motherhood, the family, and the role of government. Lack of child care generally deters or transforms maternal, not paternal, participation in the labour force – indeed, we lack the very concept of a 'working dad' or the 'labour force participation rate of fathers.'[14] Certainly, women's equality is compromised when services for children are treated as only a private family responsibility.

Some claim that it is families who are the participants in child care because child care supports the family. There is considerable truth to this, since families are composed of both parents and children. However as well as strengthening families, child care also plays a positive role in helping to challenge the delegation of care to the 'private' sphere. Child care thus also challenges much of what is troublesome about the modern nuclear family.[15]

Recent economic research has created a new awareness that society is also a direct beneficiary of child care services. Gordon Cleveland and Michael Krashinsky have shown that there are clear and direct public benefits to good child care. There is thus a generalized social interest in high-quality child care, since 'Canadian society has a continuing and abiding interest in the care of its young children.'[16] It can be argued that society, or communities more specifically, must be considered in the design of child care programs.

The complicated reality is that the participants in child care are inextricably and simultaneously children, parents, workers, women, families, and communities. Child care services need to be responsive to these multiple users and their diverse needs – and in doing so, the centrality of children and their unique social and developmental care and education needs must be brought to the fore. The child care system must be of high quality to meet the needs of all children; it must recognize and respond to the realities of all parents; and it must acknowledge the gendered nature of women's particular and situated needs. Child care services need to support and extend the care and education of all children, within and beyond private families, with or without working parents. Participatory, user-responsive child care must be designed with these many users in mind, prioritizing their needs and being accountable to them and their communities.

PRINCIPLES FOR COMMUNITY-GOVERNED CHILD CARE

It is common, particularly in these deficit-driven times, to examine public services for quality and accountability – and to primarily consider these in financial terms. We propose that we must also assess equity, social solidarity, and meaningful democracy. We see a community-based model of child care being able to provide such social solidarity to children, workers, parents, women, and families. Such child care is an important element of community development, helping to improve the quality of, and increase the choices in, people's lives.

We see a community-governed child care delivery system as one that ensures a direct relationship between users and caregivers. This relationship is essential to build the trust required for the consistent care and nurturing of children. A community-based delivery system that is tailored to the size, composition, and character of each community is better able to maintain its operation at a scale and size that ensures this direct relationship between parents, children, and caregivers. Such service goes beyond just meeting simple child care needs: we believe that child care services are community builders, helping to empower local populations.

In a community-governed child care system, the major part of social expenditures for care should come from public funds. Government should also have primary responsibility for planning to ensure that adequate levels of service are provided, so that the absence of community involvement does not mean local children are without service. We believe governments should assume virtually 100 per cent of the costs, with either no or a sliding parent fee up to a maximum of 20 per cent of the cost of care. We also propose high public standards and guidelines for quality care, based on best early childhood care and education practices. The delivery of this publicly funded, planned care should be decentralized in such a way that users have self-determination within a democratically accountable and well-resourced infrastructure. The goal of local delivery is that users should have the power to shape services to meet their own diverse and multifaceted needs: such flexibility can best be accomplished by decentralized community governance.

We propose that within an established framework of public policy and funding, child care services should be coordinated at and by the local level. They can be delivered through a mandated, adequately resourced community delivery system that brings together, within one delivery system, a full continuum of care including full, part-day, and occasional care, centre and family-home based services, and programs for infants, toddlers, preschoolers, and school-aged children (including children of every age with special needs). This local delivery agency can also incorporate additional child, parent, women's, family, and related resources, permitting a seamless set of services.

A local delivery agency would need an accountable governance structure (probably a board with a parent majority) that brings together all of the current and prospective users, caregivers, and other community members. Such an agency requires an administrative staff to support the governance structure and its community members. We believe it will be important to unload infrastructure while preserving community control for the specifics of local responsiveness and accountability. Examples of infrastructure support can be found, for example, in the Netherlands, in well-staffed Dutch voluntary agencies that do not depend on volunteer activities except on their management boards.[17]

There are some key principles we wish to affirm about the management and delivery of a community-based child care system. First, it must work hand-in-glove with a strong public policy framework and adequate funding. Within a community-based model, we would insist on a mandate and authority to plan, develop, and deliver a comprehensive range of services that reflect and meet the needs of the specific community being served. We would envision wide diversity in such a system – for example, what works in rural and northern areas, for immigrant communities, for First Nations peoples, among heritage language populations, for shift workers, and in small and mid-sized urban centres, would vary widely. This diversity and specialization is a feature we wish to affirm and promote. The authority and mandate to plan, develop, and deliver comprehensive services needs to be accompanied by public funds and reliable budgets to ensure adequate provision of services, and (like the Child Care Advocacy Association of Canada), we see this being supported by federal-provincial cost-sharing to ensure regional equity.

Among its many benefits, this model of service delivery would mitigate the isolation currently faced by caregivers, as well as end the fragmentation confronting parents and children. The local administrative agency would maximize organizational and financial viability, and avoid the duplication of time and energy that currently occurs when each individual centre or family care home must individually plan such things as professional development training, provision of benefits, co-ordination with neighbourhood services, and liaison with other social service agencies. Such benefits could, of course, be achieved in other models of coordination and integration; what we are specifically advocating are services delivered through participatory measures within a decentralized system of local accountability and local empowerment.

We appreciate that our comments raise questions about welfare pluralism, and resonate with discussions elsewhere about the privatization of the welfare state. We would prefer not to be caught by this paradigm, and wish to distinguish ourselves from it in two ways. We make two simple observations. First, child care services cannot be 'privatized' in the way other social services can and have been, for the simple reason that child care has basically never been publicly provided. Second, our support for decentralization and democratic control does not derive from opposition to the welfare state or public delivery, as is the case in discussions of the presumed superiority of the voluntary over the public sector. It is as proponents of participatory democracy and community development that we propose a community-governed child care system.

TWO EXAMPLES OF COMMUNITY CONTROL: BRITISH COLUMBIA AND DENMARK

Canadians rarely assume that one can have both responsive universal public services and locally democratic services. To the contrary, we know of two examples that demonstrate that this combination of values and practices is viable. In Denmark, 'community controlled' child care exists as part of the public sector of the welfare state.[18] In British Columbia, the provincial government enters into contractual relationships with non-profit societies (and private enterprises) for 'community-based delivery' of statutory and non-statutory services. These non-profit societies are publicly funded and operate within a public policy framework, yet are part of the officially non-state sector. The Danish and British Columbian models offer insights into a delivery structure for child care that brings together the strengths of both public and community controlled services.

In Denmark, child care services have a highly decentralized administrative structure, and are delivered as a matter of universal entitlement.[19] They are organized locally and local government pays virtually all costs in Denmark's 275 municipalities.[20] Broad national legislation requires that public day care facilities must be available to all children: local control determines the exact ratios, program, operation, and other characteristics of service, and municipal governments are responsible for providing, administering, and inspecting all forms of publicly funded child care provision. There are, as a result, no national standards or regulations, yet Denmark's services offer high-quality care. Denmark's public early childhood programs are open to all children and are used by most.[21] Fees to parents cannot exceed 30 per cent of the operating costs, and they are often much lower. Teachers in early childhood education programs are required to have three and a half years of theoretical and practical training, and their starting salaries approximate those earned by Danish elementary school teachers.[22] Even family home day care providers are unionized municipal employees, supported by five weeks of paid vacation annually, sick leave, and pension benefits, and they are part of an organized system run by the social services department of the municipalities.[23]

Staff, parents, and children are involved in the running of centres. Parents have legislated formal influence in centres, and since 1993 they have enjoyed majority control on parental boards.[24] Danish arrangements provide users with significant control and input, similar to well-staffed Dutch voluntary agencies that do not depend on volunteer activities except on their management boards.[25] Boards have significant responsibilities, with control over pedagogical principles, activities, and budgets, and they make recommendations to the local authority committee on staff appointments. Denmark's tradition of cooperation extends to children, who have a legislated right to an age-appropriate voice in the planning of activities. They are further constitutionally protected by minority rights, which recognize that the interests and needs of the child are not always necessarily identical to those of the mother and father – just another reason to carefully think through the question of who is the user of a child care program.[26]

Denmark has a population of less than six million, and in many other ways it is vastly different from Canada. Nevertheless, it offers a practical and existing example of a mode of delivering child care services that combines the best of the public welfare state with the best of what North Americans only expect from the voluntary sector: namely, universal entitlements outside the fee-for-service model, high quality, local control, local democracy, responsiveness, and good working conditions all at once.

Denmark's experience of innovative provision of social services is very different from Canada's, or other liberal regimes such as the United States.[27] In Canada, fear and loathing of the welfare state by conservatives and critiques by social democrats and other progressives have converged in a peculiar agreement that the welfare state is not viable. That some welfare states can work well, however, shows us that public provision can be enabling, positive, and enhancing – the welfare state need not be abandoned as an irretrievable site of social coercion or deadening bureaucracy. We do not inevitably need to trade off access, public funding, and entitlement against quality, innovation, local responsiveness, and community control.

The experience in British Columbia's social service delivery system over the last fifteen years provides another interesting example of community-delivered services. In British Columbia, non-public agencies enter into purchase-of-service contracts with the provincial government and deliver services that were formerly provided publicly.[28] To a degree unmatched in Canada, B.C.'s voluntary sector adopts a public agent role and increasingly delivers care on behalf of government, playing an integral role in the delivery of social services. In the early 1980s, as part of a provincial fiscal restraint program, the Social Credit government of the day began a process of 'privatizing' the delivery of social services. Services previously delivered directly by government employees were now to be delivered by independent societies, proprietors, or companies, with government still responsible for overall program 'deliverables' and funding. This restructuring has not been without significant problems. Given that its original intent was to reduce public expenditures and limit government's long-term obligation to its labour force, community services in British Columbia have continued to experience inadequate levels of funding and a lack of long-range planning. Despite significant weaknesses, the model that has emerged in British Columbia does challenge some pre-existing conceptions about the organization of the welfare state. It bridges the public-private split through a system in which public funds underwrite 'private' provision.

The 'partnership' model of the voluntary (or non-profit – the terms are used interchangeably) sector on the West Coast provides a vehicle through which public funds are administered by private agencies. The evolution of this relationship and the organizational structure of the voluntary agencies that deliver services offer some important advantages for consideration. First, as smaller, more flexible corporations, non-profit societies can quickly mount new programs to meet emerging needs and they can change program direction rapidly. In addition, the non-profit structure governed by a volunteer board of directors has meant that a large number of service users and community residents are directly involved in making decisions about the services in their community. Not only does this increase community cohesion, it also creates an informed, independent advocacy voice that plays an important role in shaping public policy. Further, the B.C. model allows for the development of a range of diverse services that reflect and respond to the specific cultural, linguistic, and socioeconomic characteristics of communities.

As already mentioned, the model as it currently operates is not without problems. Because they are reliant on government funding, non-profit societies are subject to some government control, and historically they can offer services at more competitive prices than the public sector could. The tendering process that has been used to date to award contracts has aggravated the competitive nature of the model. Many in the sector argue that this 'competitiveness' does not serve the community well and are advocating for reforms to the contracting process that will promote increased cooperation between, as well as stability for, contracted services.

Notwithstanding these issues, in British Columbia a relationship is built between the community agency and the relevant government ministry – through a gradually developing situation of mutual dependency that is neither fully 'public' nor fully 'private.' The non-profit agencies have the expertise, staff, and facilities to deliver services, while government is in the position of authority and is responsible for the services. To date, child care services in British Columbia have not received purchase-of-service contracts from the provincial government. Because child care is the only 'community service' that is primarily dependent on fees, public funding for child care has been delivered through subsidies to individual families and a limited number of grants and contribution agreements for eligible services. For a long time, this fundamental difference kept child care on the margins of the contracted community social services sector. However, since the early 1990s child care has become increasingly involved in the emerging structures of the large community social services sector. Today, many in the B.C. child care community see the extension of the 'contracts for service' model as an essential step in the development of a comprehensive, quality child care system in British Columbia. The announcement in 2000 that British Columbia will move to universally accessible, publicly funded child care services suggests that this model will continue.

The 'public' Danish model and the 'private' B.C. model both offer a way to deliver community-governed services. From a theoretical perspective, they both converge as semi-public–semi-private vehicles: within a framework of public policy and public funds, the two examples show that local control and local democracy can coexist within a framework of legislated service and public funding. We offer them as examples which, whatever their weaknesses, expand our sense of the possible and demonstrate the viability of searching for community-governed delivery of universally accessible service.

CONCLUSION

We have proposed that quality child care should be delivered as a community-governed, publicly funded system, characterized by user control and responsiveness within a decentralized system. We are aware that proposals such as ours to involve people in the services that impact on their lives face numerous obstacles and draw criticism from many quarters. It is frequently argued that such ideas are utopian, impractical, or even a diversion from more urgent work. They are often accused of being ideological, as though other proposals were free from normative assumptions or bias. While our proposal might be idealistic, it is at the very least practical and achievable. Comparative analysis shows that such examples exist, as the Danish and British Columbian cases demonstrate. The question of whether a community-governed system is *desirable* can only be answered with reference to values and priorities – and we maintain that the participatory democracy and community empowerment of such a system make it well worth working towards.

Establishing a community-governed child care delivery system allows us to build on the existing and known strengths of the current system, which is largely based on community delivery. The difference is that in the system we propose, there would be:

- A mandate and authority to plan, develop, and deliver a comprehensive range of quality child care services that reflect and meet the needs of the specific community being served
- Public financing to ensure adequate provision of services and universal access
- An accountable governance structure that brings together all of the users (parents, caregivers, and community members)
- A resourced infrastructure, including administrative staff to support volunteers and implement policy

The central problem facing a social service delivery system that is diffused among many agencies, publicly financed and self-directing, without being subject to the price constraints of an economic market, is control. We acknowledge that a community-based delivery system operating within a well-defined and well-resourced public policy framework will confront such issues. Certainly, there may be a tension between reflecting and responding to diversity and building a common civic society. We also recognize the fundamental requirement that services must be available, even in communities where local governance is not currently organized – another tension in a community-based model.

The current delivery of child care is plagued by a number of serious problems that reflect the lack of coherent public policy, the absence of adequate financing, and a missing administrative infrastructure. The child care community, however, enjoys a window of opportunity in which to consider delivery models – we do not currently confront the challenge of democratizing a professionalized and bureaucratized system, such as faces advocates for participatory health or education services. Child care users – including parents, caregivers, and communities – have invested time, energy, and creativity in growing a child care system that tries to respond to their local needs. We propose to support their work by establishing a delivery system that respects these strengths – building participatory, user-responsive, community-governed care.

Notes

1 This chapter is greatly indebted to extensive dialogue, discussion and debate with Rita Chudnovsky, who takes up these issues in her 'Response.' (Although I am the author, Rita and I jointly considered these questions and so I write in the voice of 'we'.)

2 A small percentage of Canada's regulated spaces are publicly delivered; school-aged care in Quebec is delivered by school boards.

3 Directly government-operated programs are found primarily in Ontario, with some in Quebec (including publicly overseen, but unregulated school-aged care), and fewer still in Saskatchewan. First Nations operate child care programs under enabling legislations, and these directly operated programs are also found mainly in Ontario. The exact amount of service is difficult to ascertain, because of variations in how jurisdictions define, track, and record service.

4 M. O'Brien-Steinfels, *Who's Minding the Children? The History and Politics of Daycare in America* (New York: Simon and Schuster, 1972), 246.

5 Child Care Resource and Research Unit, *Child Care in Canada: Provinces and Territories, 1995* (Toronto: University of Toronto, Child Care Resource and Research Unit, 1997), Table 3.

6 Most care is provided in the informal sector – some 90 per cent or so of children needing alternate care get it outside regulated services. (See *Child Care in Canada: Provinces and Territories, 1995*.) This chapter does not address the informal sector, although we would envision the gradual absorption of (most) caregivers into the regulated system through the benefits of regulation and increasing disincentives to unregulated care.

7 Figures calculated from Tables 3 and 4 of *Child Care in Canada: Provinces and Territories, 1995*. First Nations bands in Ontario can directly provide services in a manner analogous to a municipality, but for the purpose of this chapter we do not consider Aboriginal child care to be publicly

provided. At this point, the best information is that Aboriginal child care more closely approximates the non-profit board of director model of the voluntary sector. Some 40,000 school-aged spaces by Quebec are funded through the education system, but we also exclude them as publicly operated, since they are neither licensed nor regulated.

8 Personal communication with Rita Chudnovsky.
9 S. Prentice and E. Ferguson, '"My Kids Come First": The Contradictions of Mothers' "Involvement" in Childcare Delivery,' in *Child and Family Policy: Struggles and Options*, J. Pulkingham and G. Ternowetsky, eds. (Halifax: Fernwood,1997), pp. 188–202.
10 E. Ferguson and S. Prentice, 'Exploring Parent Involvement in Canada: An Ideological Maze,' in *Landscapes in Early Childhood Education*, J. Hayden, ed. (New York: Peter Lang Publishing, 2000), pp. 219–37.
11 Ibid.
12 Some recent welfare and workfare programs expand subsidy eligibility to parents involved in such programs (sometimes for regulated care, other times for informal care). Parental eligibility for a subsidy is generally restricted to employment-support or preparation for employment. Only a small number of subsidies are allocated for general prevention and child protection reasons.
13 E. Ferguson, 'The Child-Care Debate: Fading Hopes and Shifting Sands,' in *Women's Caring: Feminist Perspectives on Social Welfare* (2nd Ed.), C. Baines, P. Evans, and S. Neysmith, eds. (Toronto: Oxford University Press, 1998), 191–217.
14 S. Prentice, 'The Politics "Of" and "Behind" the Text,' paper presented in the 'Reading Documents' session of the Canadian Sociology and Anthropology Meeting, University of Victoria, BC, June, 1990.
15 L. Lind, and S. Prentice, *'Their Rightful Place': Children, Families and Child Care in Canada* (Toronto: Lorimer, 1992).
16 G. Cleveland and M. Krashinsky, *The Benefits and Costs of Good Child Care: The Economic Rationale for Public Investment in Young Children* (Toronto: University of Toronto, Child Care Resource and Research Unit, 1998), 6.
17 M. Brenton, 'Changing Relationships in Dutch Social Services,' in *Journal of Social Policy* (1982) 11(1): 59–80, 60–1.
18 Thanks to Martha Friendly and the marvellous staff at the Child Care Resource and Research Unit for drawing the Danish research to our attention.
19 See, e.g., P. Oberhuemer and M. Ulich, *Working with Young Children in Europe: Provision and Staff Training* (London: Paul Chapman Publishing, 1997), and V. Polakow, 'Who Cares for the Children? Denmark's Unique

Public Child-Care Model,' in *Phi Delta Kappan* (1997) April 78:8, pp. 604–10.

20 Ministry of Social Affairs, *Child and Family Policies: Social Policy in Denmark* (Copenhagen: Ministry of Social Affairs, 1995), 4.

21 Ninety-five per cent of mothers of newborns to six-year-olds are enrolled in the workforce. See General Accounting Office, *Early Childhood Programs: Promoting the Development of Young Children in Denmark, France and Sweden*, briefing report to the ranking minority member, Subcommittee on Children and Families, Committee on Labor and Human Resources, U.S. Senate, Feb. 1995, 11; and O. Langsted and D. Sommer, 'Denmark,' in, *International Handbook of Child Care Policies and Programs*, M. Cochran, ed. (Westport, CT: Greenwood Press, 1993), 145.

22 One study reports wages of 90 per cent (GAO, *Early Childhood Programs*, 25). Others claim starting salaries are equal. (Oberhuemer and Ulich, *Working with Young Children*, 67.)

23 See, e.g., Oberhuemer and Ulich, *Working with Young Children*, and Polakow, 'Who Cares for the Children.'

24 Oberhuemer and Ulich, *Working with Young Children*, 56.

25 Brenton, 'Changing Relationships,' 59–80, 60–1).

26 Langsted and Sommer, 'Denmark,' 148.

27 G. Esping-Andersen, 'The Three Political Economies of the Welfare State,' in *Canadian Review of Sociology and Anthropology* (1989), 10–36.

28 For a critical review of how the Social Credit government's mid-1980s' privatization policies spurred the growth of the voluntary sector, see J. Rekart, *Public Funds, Private Provision: The Role of the Voluntary Sector* (Vancouver: University of British Columbia Press, 1993).

13. How Should Child Care Be Provided?

Julie Mathien
Social Policy Consultant

There are many ways that a jurisdiction can provide early childhood services that meet goals of quality and access better than those in North America have managed to do. For example, France has split provision. With a strong central government, it provides optional full-day kindergartens called *écoles maternelles* through the national education system for children ages three to six. Virtually all children of that age group attend, as do many two-and-a-half-year-olds. Younger children (20 per cent to 25 per cent of them) attend *crèches*, most of which are operated by municipalities with a mix of local and national public funding and employer payroll taxes.[1] The north of Italy, with a history of Communist government and intense local political discourse, situates all types of early childhood education programs for children six and under in the regional education system but delivers programs with a high degree of local, even neighbourhood, autonomy. Sweden, which until recently had a highly developed system of care and education programs for children six and under in the social welfare system, has recently unified the programs under national education. The Netherlands has a history of funding early childhood services via collective agreements with provision through voluntary associations, either religious or secular, but it is currently in transition and appears to be looking at Sweden as a model.[2]

Although most of the European Union has better supports for under-three-year-olds and their parents than we do in North America (for example, better parental leave, more ability for parents to work part-time, more child care spaces, and no one pays the full cost of care), provision for children over three is where we see the most marked difference: in all countries, nearly all four- and five-year-olds and many three-year-olds are in publicly funded kindergarten programs, most of which operate for at least a regular school day.[3] Increasingly, these programs are situated in the education system and children attend irrespective of parent participation in the labour force. Although there are national differences, these countries, with the exception of the United Kingdom, are more like each other than they are like North America.

Canada and the United States, on the other hand, with our vast land mass, heterogeneous populations, a liberal, somewhat individualistic approach to child and family policy, an emphasis on personal choice in virtually all matters either private or public, and a government based on relatively loose federations (for example, neither country has nor is ever likely to have a national education system), have a diffuse mix of public and private provision. Programs and services for young children outside publicly funded schools (for children below the age of four or five and, for older children, during hours outside the regular school day) are largely funded by parent fees and reside in social services. Public funds are directed to schools and, for programs like child care, to poor families. Quebec, with its more European approach to social programs, is the only jurisdiction on this continent that provides large per child support for early childhood programs in both education and social services.

Child care in Canada is plagued by problems with access, affordability, and, in some places, quality. Those working for reform have long had a vision of a system of early childhood education and care characterized by high-quality, flexible and affordable programs rooted in communities. While it is important to understand the value of lessons learned from other countries, it is equally important to examine closely the Canadian social and political landscape when looking for appropriate solutions. Cultural roots around child-rearing run deep and our population is much less homogeneous than nations in the EU. The question becomes: how can we build a system of early childhood care and education within a diverse population, a neo-liberal political context, and a federal-provincial separation of powers that provides potholes at every turn?

The chapters by Penny Milton and Susan Prentice agree that early childhood education and care in Canada must be a part of 'a well-designed and well-resourced policy framework'[4] and governed by a structure that operates within a democratic context and supports communities in their efforts to provide services for all children. Milton argues that the education system (assuming local accountability via elected school boards) provides the most effective way to achieve these goals, while Prentice opts for the voluntary sector kept accountable by an undefined governance structure.

I said at the outset that there are many ways to provide high-quality and universally accessible early childhood education and care. Furthermore, many would argue that resources, not method (that is, jurisdiction or the vehicle for provision) are key to achieving our goals. While resources are crucial, it is as important to find the vehicle that, given the Canadian cultural and political imperatives, is most likely to generate the support essential to gaining the necessary resources. The arguments presented in the two chapters, plus the historical and contemporary trends in early childhood education and care in Canada, lead me to agree with Milton in her support of the education system as that vehicle, particularly for children over the age of three. Let me explain why.

If we wish to make early childhood education and care available to all children whose parents wish them to participate, it makes sense to situate such a program in the system that already provides programs and services for children on a universal basis. In Canada, since the middle of the nineteenth century, the school system has done so. To those who would argue that a compulsory system is not an appropriate home for early childhood programs that parents would choose rather than be compelled to use, I would respond that education also supports publicly funded kindergartens in which attendance is compulsory in only one province – New Brunswick.

Both history and current experience show that when programs are affordable and non-stigmatizing, almost all eligible children attend. In 1881 the City of Toronto school board became the second in North America to establish public kindergartens. They were popular immediately and soon spread across Ontario, so that, by 1900, ten cities, twelve towns, and three villages had started 119 kindergartens with an enrolment of over 11,000 children.[5] Toronto provided kindergarten in forty-six of its fifty schools, and kindergarten children were 15 per cent of total school enrolment.[6] This strong trend continues. Kindergarten is available on a universal basis for five-year-olds in all but one Canadian province (Prince Edward Island), and over 95 per cent of children are enrolled. Ontario, the only province with near-universal provision for four-year-olds, reports an enrolment of 92 per cent where junior kindergarten is available. Kindergartens are firmly within mainstream childhood experience.

In addition to providing the education environments where most of us spend large parts of our childhood, many school boards, especially in the last twenty years, have taken leadership in a number of areas that lead to more equitable outcomes. These vary in presence and intensity across the country and include inner-city, gender equity, anti-racist, and parent empowerment initiatives. In addition, as Milton points out, a number of school authorities have, since the 1970s, housed child care centres and other community-based programs for children and families in schools, at times providing coordination and advisory staff. A few boards have provided the policy frameworks and support to create and strengthen the links between schools and community programs, especially initiatives like child care centres, breakfast and lunch programs, and parenting centres.

In all provinces, education provides infrastructure – physical, bureaucratic, and political – for children's programs. None of these are small considerations if the goal is developing a more systematic service. Elementary schools are built for children. The space is readily converted for child care purposes, and, as the province of Ontario found between 1987 and 1995, building child care centres as a part of new schools is a cost-effective way of providing purpose-built child care space – a rare commodity in Canada. A bureaucracy is, in fact, necessary to support the operations of decentralized programs like schools and child care centres, including the delivery of curriculum and program. Political oversight is an important component of accountability for public resources. Elected school boards are the first level of local democratic representation and have the advantage of governing programs that, again, deal specifically with children. This infrastructure can either support or prevent reform and part of our political effort should involve pushing it towards new, continued, and expanded support.

Prentice paints a picture of universal health and education systems as imposing a 'monolithic model of uniform service' – the dreaded 'cookie-cutter,'[7] remote from users and lacking in sufficient autonomy to advocate for their constituencies. This does not describe the activity of public sector employees over the past few years. While compensation issues have formed a part of the increased politicization of groups like nurses and teachers, advocating for patients and students has been in the forefront of their activity. Teachers, in particular, have been particularly successful in forming alliances with parents and students.

All of this provides an important foundation for entrenching and extending early childhood care and education to the extent that it becomes as important to families as our current health and education systems. Truly public services are the strongest defence against privatization. Although neo-conservative governments have attempted to privatize all manner of public services, in Canada, they have been much less successful in their attempts with public services than they have with private services that receive some level of public funding – for example, in Ontario, home care, nursing homes, and child care.

Neither chapter discusses parent views on early childhood education in any detail. Any attempts at early childhood reform will not succeed without their support. The Early Years Project, which included recent exploratory work on parent preferences concerning programs for kindergarten-aged children in four provinces, showed that three-quarters of the over 300 parents in the study (and over two-thirds of the teachers and child care staff) felt that children are ready for a full school day prior to age six, when most children in Canada go to school all day. Further to this, three-quarters of the parents supported the idea of programs that combined kindergarten and child care in an integrated program taught by teams of teachers and early childhood educators. Over two-thirds of the parents in the study sample were more favourable to the program if it was located in a school.[8] Parents are ready for a new kind of service for their kindergarten-aged children.

By contrast, in Canada, social services are not seen as a mainstream experience, either for adults or children. At the same time as Hester How, principal of Louisa Street School was supervising her kindergarten, she was working to found Victoria Crèche, Toronto's first child care centre, established for the children of destitute women who worked as domestics. Kindergarten was for all children; child care was for poor children. Denmark, on the other hand, has a strong postwar commitment to universality of a broad range of services within a community-based social welfare structure. It has been able to use this system to provide early childhood programs. Nonetheless, while national enrolment rates for three- and four-year-olds (60 per cent and 80 per cent respectively) in Danish public early childhood education programs far outstrip those in Canada and the United States, they are below those in countries like Belgium, France, and New Zealand, where most programs are delivered through education.[9]

Canada does not have the same broad social services history, organization, or clientèle as Denmark and is therefore less likely to achieve even these participation rates in programs delivered outside what is generally accepted as a service available to and used by everyone. This is not to say that social services in Canada are not essential to our well-being as a society and requiring of broad-based support. They most emphatically are and do. This is also not to say that social services staff do not work hard, often in very difficult circumstances, to provide quality services in communities. However, with their history of dealing with marginalized populations, social services in this country are not the appropriate home for early childhood programs with a goal of access to all. Child care's current location in social services has impeded its progress in this regard. What Prentice describes as autonomy in social services is often a type of marginalization that allows the government to ignore both the service and its users. A case in point is child care in New Brunswick, where it is considered sufficiently unimportant that there is no requirement to employ any staff qualified in early childhood education. The impact on program quality is predictable, leading to a low level of public engagement both in terms of support and use.

To thrive, early childhood programs need the participation of children from all social classes. Over the past thirty years, many advocates in Canada have laboured long and hard to reform child care as we know it within a social services context. Although public engagement on issues around child care has increased, substantive success has been slight. With the exception of Quebec, and particularly since the mid-1990s, public funding for early childhood programs situated on the child care side has become increasingly targeted and seen as the preserve of low-income families.[10] This trend will not result in the kind of broad-based support that will generate the necessary resources for programs for young children. Continued efforts in this direction fall into the category of what I refer to as swimming upstream.

Not only are comparisons between Canada and Denmark of limited use in the actual development of policy and program, Prentice's chapter is not entirely clear in its description of how the Danish child care model works. Child care under the Danish social welfare model is delivered in programs that are decentralized in terms of operations within a municipal governance, policy, and funding structure. In fact, the Danish system looks more like Canada's provincial education systems with schools funded and governed by local school boards than the independent social services in British Columbia which, as the chapter points out, provide programs and services on behalf of the government.[11]

To return to the question asked at the outset: how can we build a

Canadian model of early childhood education and care? First, this will take time. Where organization and funding is concerned, child care now is roughly at the same stage as public education in 1850 – with less coverage. The countries that we so admire for their comprehensive services are more homogeneous in outlook and have been at the task since at least the end of the Second World War. This observation is made to set a context for strategic staging, not defeat. The Canadian reality leads to a gradual approach to integrating child care and education. Instead of the 'either' of education or the 'or' of social services, perhaps using both would work, at least in the short and medium term.

From the results of the Early Years Project, there appears to be a greater consensus among parents regarding appropriate programs for their kindergarten-aged children than exists for younger children. The school system provides an environment for integrating the two early childhood education tracks for this age group: kindergarten and child care. The infrastructure to do so exists, and there is some evidence that an integrated program is more cost-effective[12] on a per child basis than the current split provision. Provinces could start with four- and five-year-olds and work downwards to three-year-olds as resources and parent preference allows. Quebec and New Brunswick, with universal full-day kindergarten for five-year-olds, are already part-way there.

There is a good deal less consensus around appropriate settings for infants, toddlers, and preschoolers. While programs for younger children might reside in schools and, where desired, be governed and operated via the education system, their needs might also be met with a greater diversity of early childhood programs and supports, including much improved, publicly funded parental leaves. Funding reform will be necessary to improve access, affordability, and in some provinces, quality of service. However reform takes place, it will be necessary to walk a fine line between supporting parent and community participation in implementation and completely imposing the responsibility of making reform work on already hard-pressed volunteers.

A number of cautions arise from the results of the Early Years Project:

- At this time, neither parents, kindergarten teachers, nor child care staff support extending the integrated day model to include three year-olds.
- All three groups strongly favoured gradual implementation with ongoing input from parents and staff.
- The concern regarding choice remains. Parents were somewhat

concerned at the effect that an integrated day program for kinder-garteners might have on choice and wanted the program to be available for a half-day, a full school day, an extended day, and during school holidays.

- Teachers and child care staff are less enthusiastic than parents are regarding an integrated day. Workforce resistance will have to be overcome with sensitivity and respect.

- An integrated day may, in fact, be essential to maintaining quality throughout the entire day. The Early Years Project found that full-day kindergarten programs (which last for a full school day of about six hours) meant that the separate before – and after – child care programs suffered. In an integrated day, quality could be main-tained.

- Resources are crucial. Although an integrated day may be cost-effective, it will not succeed if parents and staff believe that it is simply an enforced, less expensive add-on to already beleaguered school systems.

Finally, leadership and partnership from all levels of government will be necessary, all the more daunting given the shoals of Canadian federal-provincial relations and the fact that early childhood education reform as described in this discussion involves elementary education, a solely provincial jurisdiction.

Notes

1 See Kathy O'Hara, *Comparative Family Policy: Eight Countries' Stories* (Ot-tawa: Canadian Policy Research Network, 1999), 10.
2 Ibid., 14.
3 Organization for Economic Cooperation and Development (OECD), *Lifelong Learning for All* (Meeting of the Education Committee at the Minis-terial Level, 16–17 Jan. 1996), 51.
4 Susan Prentice, 'The Case for Community-Governed Child Care Services,' this volume.
5 ARUC 1901 Statistical Report, as cited in Julie Mathien, *School Progress for Young Children in Ontario and Toronto, 1830–1900*, 32.
6 *Toronto Board of Education. Inspector's Report, 1900* (Toronto: ARUC, 1901). Statistical Report, as cited in Mathien, 25.
7 Prentice, this volume.
8 Laura C. Johnson and Julie Mathien, *Early Childhood Services for*

Kindergarten-Age Children in Four Canadian Provinces: Scope, Nature and Models for the Future (Ottawa: Caledon Institute of Social Policy, 1998), 16–18.

9 OECD, *Lifelong Learning for All*, 51.

10 Gillian Doherty, M. Friendly, and M. Oloman, *Women's Support, Women's Work: Child care in an Era of Deficit Reduction, Devolution, Downsizing and Deregulation* (Ottawa: Status of Women Canada, 1998), 31–8.

11 Prentice, this volume.

12 Cited in Johnson and Mathien, *Early Childhood Services*, 59.

14. The Need for Public Commitment and Coherent Policy

Jane Beach
Child Care Consultant

Why, in Canada, do we have such a struggle with the provision of early childhood services? After decades of public kindergarten, private pre-school, and child care, and ongoing debate on policy, funding, and responsibility, we are mired in endless contradictions. Many countries are matter of fact in their view that good early childhood experiences are good for children and families and that these services are worthy of public involvement in planning, funding, and delivery to make them available. They do not agonize over whether or not children will have poor attachment if they are away from their parents for part of the day or if programs will help children be better widget-makers of the future.

In Europe we see successful early childhood programs within a variety of different delivery systems. Some are delivered entirely through the education system, some through the social welfare system; others have a combination, depending on the age of the child. Experiences in Europe would lead us to believe that public funding, public support, and well-trained and compensated staff may be as important or more important than the method of delivery.

DISCUSSION

The two chapters on how child care should be delivered, by Penny Milton and Susan Prentice, cover different ground in their arguments, but are quite similar in their assumptions, identification of issues, and even in their proposed delivery approaches (services provided by and in community-owned facilities).

Both chapters note that working parents are the norm, child care is an essential service, programs for young children need to provide both care and education, and that current services are characterized by program fragmentation and lack of a policy framework. They both call for a strong government role in planning, for non-profit ownership and delivery, and for programs that are responsive to community need. Though not specifically stated in either chapter, it may be assumed that staff would consist of employees of the non-profit boards or agencies. Both chapters are silent on how or if child care services should fit into a broader family policy framework, and Milton's chapter is silent on whether family child care would be part of the model.

There are two interesting points of difference – who should pay and who is entitled to service. The 'community' model calls for public funding and an entitlement to service for all children. Milton's 'education' model calls for a user-pay approach, with subsidies where needed. It is not clear what constitutes 'need' – all families, regardless of employment status, or primarily working parents.

Both chapters suggest reforms that would improve the current ad hoc approach to service delivery. Would one delivery model be more likely to succeed? Would one be more likely to get adequate funding? Would one be more likely to get political and public support? Each chapter speaks eloquently to the benefits of a particular approach; it might be useful to also consider the potential drawbacks.

If child care, as Milton describes it, is not a fully integrated part of the publicly funded and delivered education system, it lacks any statutory entitlement to be in the school. The proposed user fee and subsidy approach restricts access, requires policies to define 'need,' and does not create a sense of entitlement. The lack of the federal role in education may be a significant stumbling block to moving forward. With most provincial education budgets under increasing pressure, it is unlikely that adequate resources within a provincial budget could be found, especially when having to compete with a statutory program.

The education system does have a strong infrastructure, and access to services is not tied to parental employment or income. In theory, it has the potential to play a major role in the development and delivery of early childhood programs, but given some of the recent history, how likely is that to happen? Granted, several child care centres were constructed with provincial dollars in Ontario schools in the 1980s, and through the late 1970s and 1980s the former Toronto Board of Education supported and facilitated the development of both non-profit child care centres and directly operated family resource programs in its schools. However, these programs have never been on an equal footing with education, and now with changes to the education formula, they are fighting for their continued existence. As long as child care is considered separate from and an add-on to education, it is likely to remain a poor cousin.

In some provinces, preschool programs are being established and operated by school boards in high-need communities, which view them as something quite different from child care. For example, in 1997 Saskatchewan Education released a report on its prekindergarten program.[1] Included in the section of what prekindergarten is, there is a description of 'experiential learning through play ... child-centred ... focused on the development of the whole child.' In the section of what prekindergarten is not is 'playschool/daycare.'

The delivery model described by Prentice uses the contract-for-service model in British Columbia as an example of successful community-based delivery. However, many of the programs funded under this approach do not necessarily depend on the users of the program for their operation. The bidding process also assumes that there are competent agencies to compete for delivery. These factors can result in uneven service provision. The success of a parent-run child care program relies on particular parents' expertise, ability, willingness, and time. What happens in communities without that resource? What happens when programs experience parent burn-out and are constantly having to re-invent themselves with regular turnover of boards?

Flexibility and parent choice are put forward by Prentice as critical pieces of a quality program. But how flexible are they? How much choice is involved? Too much of either may work against the best interests of parents and children. Parent choice is often the mantra of government as an excuse for inaction. The government of British Columbia often uses it as the reason for continuing to allow fee subsidies to be used in any type of care the parent wishes, so long as it is not illegal. There are no requirements for any form of monitoring, programming, or caregiver training or support in these care arrangements. (Currently, more than half the expenditures on subsidy are spent on this unmonitored type of care.) Flexibility can be used against parents to meet unreasonable demands of the workplace. Split shifts, overtime, and on-call work can all be met by flexible, twenty-four-hour, drop-in care whether your child is well or ill. Flexibility does need to be balanced with, for example, program stability and continuity.

So what is the solution? Would one delivery model work better than the other? Either approach probably *could* work and each has particular strengths and weaknesses. I would argue that there other factors to consider before reaching any conclusions.

It may be useful to step back and look at the current context in which programs and services are being developed and delivered. What exactly are we talking about? Depending on the words we use, whether 'child development programs, child care programs, nursery schools, kindergarten, early intervention programs, playgroups,' we often get different reactions about who they are for and who should pay for and operate them.

THE CONTEXT

Over the past twenty years we have seen successive federal governments undertake major reviews and studies, all calling for the development of widely available child care services,[2] yet we have seen instead the development of targeted programs for particular populations. We know the importance of the quality of early childhood experiences on children's development, and we fund child development programs for disadvantaged children. Yet if a child's parent is on social assistance and wishes to try and get back into the labour force, we often hand out vouchers to buy child care of unknown quality. Alberta, for example, requires parents participating in employment programs to use the cheapest form of care available.[3]

In its recent report, the National Council of Welfare concludes that 'many social programs support families, but child care is the backbone of them all.'[4] There are other views, such as those of Reform MP Lee Morrison, who made this comment in the House of Commons on 21 November 1996: 'What does subsidized day care mean to you? I will tell you what it means to me as a country boy. It means that a professional couple in Toronto can load their child into a BMW and take it to the Silver Spoon Happy Centre for Lucky Tots.'[5]

We hear the call for changes to the tax system to help parents stay at home full-time with their young children, at the same time we hear the call for targeted child care dollars to get single mothers off social assistance and into the workforce. We still hear some argue that child care is not good for children, yet we do not hear the same concern over nursery school and preschool programs, which for the most part, operate under the same regulations, standards, and funding arrangements as regulated child care. What is the difference? Could we not have one program with the option of full-time or part-time attendance? Why do spacious, well-equipped kindergarten rooms sometimes sit empty for half the day while the same group of children who attended kindergarten in the morning, attend child care somewhere else in the building?

The reality is that today we have an increasingly complicated array of programs, policies, and government transfers that often work at cross-purposes. Public policy in recent years has limited the growth of needed services, has made many programs too expensive for most families, and yet governments spend millions in a manner that neither creates programs nor offers any guarantee of quality, such as through the Child Care Expense Deduction. The various child development and child care programs and benefits do seem to fall into two major categories: those called 'child care' usually have, as their primary purpose, the attachment of parents to the labour force. These programs operate on a user-pay system, with some subsidies for low-income parents. Their flexibility is often to meet the changing demands of people's employment situations, but they may not necessarily be in the best interest of the child. Programs referred to as 'child development' usually are seen to be educational in nature, and they often are structured in a way that does not support, and even sometimes precludes, the labour force participation of mothers. They may be universal and publicly funded, such as kindergarten programs; targeted and publicly funded, such as Aboriginal Headstart; or fee-for-service, such as nursery schools.

This segregation of children by parental income and employment status often confuses the discussion of what early childhood care and educations programs are, who they serve, and into whose jurisdiction they fall. It also has often pitted the interests of employed mothers against those not in the paid labour force.

Why should child care, kindergarten, and nursery schools all be viewed as something different? Could and/or should they be developed within a single integrated policy framework and delivery structure? Assuming that public kindergarten programs are here to stay, and that the majority of mothers with young children will continue to participate in the labour force, how can we better deliver and make available affordable, quality, early childhood programs?

We know that all children benefit from positive, enriching early childhood experiences; the current trend towards increased targeting of funding and services to the neediest children denies most children access to such programs. For any delivery system to be effective, the confusing array of disjointed programs and approaches to early childhood services needs to be organized within a coherent policy framework and appropriately resourced. For programs to be effective within a single policy framework, they need to meet multiple objectives. Services need to simultaneously:

- Support the optimal development of children
- Support the labour force participation of parents
- Support and strengthen the parenting role
- Provide additional resources and supports for children living with conditions of risk

Is one delivery model more likely to achieve these objectives than another? Is the particular delivery model even a critical factor? We know successful models in several European countries operate under each and sometimes both delivery models. One common thread in the early development of those various systems was strong central control over standards and policies, followed by greater local autonomy and decentralization as programs became integral parts of community life.

CONCLUSION

There is much to learn from examples in European education-based delivery of *écoles maternelles* in France and the social welfare delivery of early childhood services in Denmark, to name but two. Both have strong public support, public funding, and public delivery. In the Canadian context, the lack of federal involvement in education may be a major limitation to this delivery option. In the current Canadian climate, I would argue, however, that there is little support for increased public delivery. What *may* be feasible is increased federal spending, a federal policy framework developed in collaboration with the provinces, a broader range of family policies, and community-based nonprofit delivery. This is not perfect, but a start.

The leadership shown by the Government of Quebec is an exciting example to watch. It is a program developed within a context that is close to home. It is not perfect, but far ahead of what most of us experience as provincial policy. The Quebec family policy calls for strengthened and expanded maternity and parental leaves and benefits. It also includes kindergarten extended to the full school day; a strong government role in the planning of early childhood services, with targets for growth; multiple services to meet local needs; a greater number of trained staff and a new pedagogical curriculum in ECE training; significant public funding; and access not tied to parental employment. The Confédération des Syndicats Nationaux (CSN), the union representing child care workers, has successfully negotiated a major wage increase; and the program appears to be on target for implementation. Quebec's is certainly a delivery model worth emulating.

Notes

1 Saskatchewan Education, *Better Beginnings, Better Futures: Best Practices, Policies and Guidelines for Prekindergarten in Saskatchewan Community Schools* (Regina: Author, 1997).
2 See, e.g., Royal Commission on the Status of Women, *The Status of Women in Canada* (Ottawa: Author, 1970); R.S. Abella, *Equality in Employment: A Royal Commission Report* (Ottawa: Royal Commission on Equality and Employment, 1984); K. Cooke, J. London, R. Edwards, and R. Rose-Lizée, *Report of the Task Force on Child Care* (Ottawa: Status of Women Canada, Special Committee on Child Care, 1986); *Sharing the Responsibility* (Ottawa: Queen's Printer, 1987) – to name but a few.
3 Child Care Resource and Research Unit, *Child Care in Canada: Provinces and Territories, 1997* (Toronto: Author, 1997).
4 National Council of Welfare, *Preschool Children: Promises to Keep* (Ottawa: Author, 1999).
5 Reform Watch Analysis, *Childcare Program: A Waste of Money* (on-line document: http://www.vcn.bc.ca/refwatch/policy/child.htm)

15. Aboriginal Perspectives on Child Care

Margo Greenwood
University of Northern British Columbia

Perry Shawana
Barrister and Solicitor and University of Northern British Columbia

For Aboriginal people child care is viewed as a vehicle for the transmission of culture and preservation of their languages. Generally, Aboriginal people are reluctant to endorse a pan-Canadian child care policy because of their historical experience with government assimilation policies. Aboriginal people view child care as a community responsibility. Quality child care services are developed in and for the community. Quality, then, is a fluid concept defined by the community.

Identity and cultural realization derived from the family and community is fundamental to providing quality care. It is imperative that child care services instill identity in a child. Professionally trained (i.e., university or college trained) caregivers may not be the best caregivers when viewed in this context of community responsibility. Services should always consider children first within the context and reality of their community.

Child care is often discussed as being a service for working parents or for school readiness. For Aboriginal people it is a matter of cultural survival in both worlds. The question then becomes how can child care best reflect diversity: diversity of the user, diversity of the caregiver, and diversity of the community in which they want to survive.

The community governance model is currently the most appropriate means to enable Aboriginal communities to achieve their objectives in child care. To be effective the model ought to embrace standards that are outcomes-based so that regulations are not prescriptive but defined and implemented by the community. It should be cautioned that this model does not ultimately achieve Aboriginal desires for political autonomy or jurisdiction and authority in child care.

Authors' Responses

Penny Milton

The prospect of providing care and early education programs for young children in schools raises significant spectres in the minds of some observers. All young children require high-quality, age-appropriate programs. The elements of such programs are well known to the early education specialists in the public education sector. This implementation model is predicated on the assumption that the location of programs is not, in itself, a determinant of either the nature or quality of such programs, except that a publicly accountable system operating within a provincial mandate can be expected to ensure that appropriate curricular and qualified staff are in place. The school system is sometimes described as bureaucratic, but elementary schools are not. The experience of school boards that have actively built child care in the schools are sufficient demonstration that schools can be deeply rooted in community and responsive to a wide diversity of ethnic and linguistic groups. The proposed model does not preclude the use of locations other than school, nor does it remove or diminish the role of parents in shaping the child care centre's direction and policy. It simply ensures that a legitimate public authority is charged with the responsibility to provide accessible and appropriate child care and early learning programs.

Authors' Responses

Rita Chudnovsky
Douglas College

(This 'Response,' while authored by Rita Chudnovsky, follows up on the arguments and issues presented by Susan Prentice in her chapter. As this response is greatly indebted to collaboration with Susan Prentice, it is written in the voice of 'we.')

At the policy symposium, panelists and participants raised a number of important and provocative ideas related to optimal child care delivery systems. Some of these ideas strengthened and confirmed our belief in a community-governed delivery system; others challenged us to clarify our thinking, and still others suggest that the discussion and debates must continue. In this 'afterword' we can only take up some of the key questions and issues raised – others will be the topic of work in the future.

A PUBLICLY DELIVERED SYSTEM?

Presenters supporting both a community-based and education-based delivery system were challenged by some who viewed us as hesitant to call for a publicly delivered system. Yet, our chapter clearly calls for legislated entitlement for all children to quality early childhood care and education programs; public funding to ensure adequate provision of service; and public standards which promote quality care. For us, these elements are at the heart of any definition of publicly delivered services. (Our chapter also pointed to the system in Denmark as an example of how community-controlled child care can exist as part of the public sector of the welfare state.)

The question, then, is not whether or not the system is publicly delivered, for clearly in our view an effective community-governed delivery system meets this definition. Rather the question is: How can public delivery be actualized in a way that best meets the needs of the full range of child care users?

Here we face two fundamental options. We can look to existing publicly delivered systems – like education or health – and address the challenges facing these systems, or we can build on the strengths of services that have been created by communities and work to integrate these into a publicly delivered, coherent system. In either case, we face challenges. While we strongly support the need for maintaining and strengthening our public education and health systems in Canada, we treat critiques that argue for fundamental changes in these systems seriously. We know that many educators and health care providers are working hard to make their services more responsive (and we may have understated this in our chapter); but we still have serious concerns about the high level of professionalization, centralization, and bureaucratization that continue to characterize these systems. As a model for child care services, we are particularly concerned about the structural 'distance' that exists between the users and providers in these models.

On the other hand, and in spite of the lack of adequate public policy and funding, most existing child care services support and encourage a direct relationship between users and caregivers, reflect the diversity of cultural and philosophical approaches to child-rearing, provide families (given they can afford the fees) with options from within a range of services that are delivered in diverse settings, and offer unique programming.

The fundamental problem is that these services are not supported through legislation and do not receive public funding. This problem exists whether or not the services are currently delivered by municipalities, school boards, non-profit societies, or individual caregivers. For these reasons, we think that all those who use and benefit from early childhood services will be best served by incorporating the current strengths of existing child care services into a coherent public policy and funding framework. Rather than shying away from calling for a publicly delivered system, we believe that the community-governed system of early childhood education and care we envision should and could become a model for the way in which other public services are structured and delivered in communities and regions across Canada.

WHAT ABOUT GOVERNANCE STRUCTURES?

In addition to calling for a legislated entitlement for children to quality early childhood education and care, a public mandate for planning and delivering a comprehensive range of responsive services, and adequate public funding to ensure universal access to services, our chapter also called for 'an accountable governance structure that brings together all users [and] a resourced infrastructure ... to support volunteers and implement policy.'[1]

We choose not to focus on recommending a specific governance model for two reasons. First, we feel that legislation and resources are a prerequisite for any effective governance structure. As we stated in the panel discussion – give us the money and we will work out the details. Second, a community-based delivery system implies that there are a number of possible governance models and structures that could be considered. While we strongly believe in moving towards 'hub models' that bring together a full range of coordinated early childhood services and supports, we recognize that there are a variety of existing and developing governance structures that could be used to accomplish this goal.

If the fundamental principles of community governance are respected, it is possible to look to existing child care organizations; newly created child care boards, or existing governing bodies (e.g., municipalities, school boards, multi-service agencies) to deliver the early childhood mandate. As Aboriginal contributors have made clear – strategies and programs to support early childhood development are part and parcel of their self-governments.

WHAT ABOUT THE EDUCATIONAL SYSTEM?

As noted above, we accept that, in some cases, local school boards might be an appropriate governing and administrative structure for delivering child care services. In fact, we think that there are a number of practical reasons why school boards could be responsible for full-day services for kindergarten children and before- and after-school care for children up to the age of twelve years.

However, some issues were raised throughout the symposium that pose fundamental questions about the downward extension of the 'educational model' to early childhood. First, we are increasingly concerned about the implications of the 'readiness to learn' arguments.

While we recognize the short-term public and political appeal of this paradigm, we believe that children have an inherent right to be valued for who they are now – and not only for who or what they may become. If the current research teaches us anything, surely it is that some of the most significant learning that occurs in the life cycle happens during the early years. Thus, young children are not getting 'ready to learn,' they are actively engaged in learning.

The 'readiness to learn' approach suggests that 'real learning' does not begin until children enter the formal educational system. Not only is this incorrect, it may well serve to entrench a residual and targeted approach to early childhood services by focusing public attention only on those children who are seen as 'disadvantaged' or 'lagging behind' in their school readiness. The strength of quality early childhood practice is in its ability to nurture and care for each child holistically – respecting and supporting each one's physical, social, emotional, cultural, and intellectual needs. We are left with a fundamental concern about whether 'caring and nurturing' will be lost in the 'readiness to learn' approach.

A third fundamental question about the 'downward extension of the educational model' was raised by some Aboriginal participants at the symposium who spoke about the central role their child care programs play in transmitting Aboriginal cultures and preserving languages. Given the legacy of forced assimilation policies for Aboriginal peoples, these comments referenced Aboriginal peoples' mistrust of and alienation from the formal education system and highlighted the importance of acculturation of young Aboriginal children into their own cultures. We fully support the right of Aboriginal peoples to design, direct, and deliver their early childhood programs, and we look forward to learning from their experiences. We remain interested in the response to this perspective from those who see educational systems exclusively as the appropriate child care delivery system.

We believe that the role of child care in supporting and promoting children's cultural identity has broader implications. As compared with many countries that have well-developed early childhood systems, Canada is a vastly diverse country. If we are going to do more than give lip-service to respecting and celebrating this diversity, we need policies that support both that which is general and that which is unique. While all children and families have a right to equitable access to services, we agree that child care has a particular role to play in supporting all children's cultural identity and remain convinced that a community-based delivery system, operating within a strong public policy framework, offers the best chance of achieving this goal.

HOW DO WE MOVE FROM HERE TO THERE?

A sound child care policy needs to acknowledge that we are not starting from a 'clean slate.' The reality is that most children in Canada are already participating in some form of non-parental care. Many of these children attend centre-based group programs, only a small number of which are located in schools, and the overwhelming majority of children receive care in family-based services. The expertise that exists in these services is an essential building block of the child care system we envision. To a large degree, then, the success of implementing new child care policy will depend on finding ways to integrate these services and service providers into a coherent system. We note that public funding will come with increased expectations for accountability and coordination and some existing service providers may choose not to participate.

Here we look to the child care initiative in Quebec where the government has chosen to work with existing providers. Quebec's child care centres and family child care agencies have been given five years to extend their services to offer both types of care, and there is an expectation that these organizations will further expand their services to deliver other types of care. For the most part, these organizations are non-profit societies with parent and/or community boards of directors. Over time, then, the evolving Quebec child care system will be delivered by community-governed organizations that deliver a range of child care services within a public policy and funding framework. We think that this offers a respectful and practical way forward.

We remain uncertain about how one would move 'from here to there' within the educational system. Our chapter and positions supporting this view imply a single delivery model – school-based group programs. Our question is – how will existing centre programs not located in schools and how will family child care providers be integrated into a school-board-based model? Or, does a school-board-based mandate imply that existing services would be phased out as new school-based services are developed? We note that it would be possible to develop networks of community- and family-based services attached to schools but have not heard this option discussed to date.

COMMUNITY EMPOWERMENT OR
COMMUNITY DOWNLOADING?

Jane Beach, one of the responders to our chapter, raises significant concerns about the impact of a community-governed model where there may not be the resources or capacities to develop, and deliver a comprehensive range of services. We share her concern about a two-tiered system in which affluent, organized communities have the services they need and communities where the need may be greater are left behind. In fact, this is currently the case. This is why we argue for a public 'mandate and authority to plan, develop, and deliver a comprehensive range of quality child care services that reflect and meet the needs of the specific community being served.'

There is no question that government will need to maintain responsibility for ensuring equitable access to services and that a community development approach will be required to support the capacity of communities to govern and deliver their own services. We do not see this as the job of volunteers – which is why we argue for 'a resourced infrastructure, including administrative staff to support volunteers and implement policy.'

With these resources in place, we believe that a 'community-governed, publicly funded system, characterized by user control and responsiveness within a decentralized system' can strengthen and empower communities – and that is one of its greatest strengths.

Discussion

The presentations in this session did not in the end propose wildly different visions of how to organize child care. However, the issue of whether to rely on the institutional structure of the school system or to build community-based non-profit organizations generated a wide set of reactions from the floor.

One set of issues was raised by two Aboriginal representatives at the symposium, Margo Greenwood and Perry Shawana. They pointed out that central control was problematic for a group that viewed child care as a critical way to communicate Aboriginal values. Rita Chudnovsky suggested that we needed to learn from the Aboriginal response. The vision of child care as a vital part of building communities and cultures, which is critical in the Prentice chapter, is both particularly relevant for Aboriginal communities and critically important for many other cultural groups and communities. Another questioner echoed this sentiment, arguing that the Prentice view would be most relevant where the school was seen as an external, potentially hostile force. Julie Mathien, one of the discussants, suggested that some of the Aboriginal concerns might be resolved under local self-governance. However, she saw some potential difficulties in exempting Aboriginal child care from provincial regulations.

A second set of issues arose over the concern about whether school boards could be effective advocates for child care. One questioner suggested that Ontario school boards had functioned that way before their recent losses of autonomy. Penny Milton responded favourably, suggesting that autonomous school boards had originated a number of useful initiatives and that this might be expected to continue now that the educational leadership was becoming increasingly concerned about early education. Rita Chudnovsky pointed out that child care was a useful way for schools to avoid closure when enrolment was declining, but that the natural extension of that was that child care would be pushed out when enrolment went back up. Furthermore, recent cost pressures within the public school system might lead schools to charge child care centres more for space, adversely affecting child care. She reminded the group that in British Columbia, child care could enter the schools only if both the principal and the school board agreed.

Another questioner came to the defence of school boards, suggesting that junior kindergarten had been a great success and that school boards could be effective in initiating child care programs, especially where the community did not have other resources that could easily be mobilized to deliver such a service. The questioner asked why we are so afraid of a publicly delivered system, and what had caused Canadians to be so alienated from their own public services? Penny Milton picked up on this to argue that the school system was functioning relatively well and was hardly as bad as was sometimes suggested. Julie Mathien picked up on the junior kindergarten point to argue that we should build on the general public consensus in favour of that kind of schooling.

PART 5

What Family Policies Are Needed to Complement
Universal Child Care?

Introduction

The fourth session of the symposium turned to the broad issue of family policy. Governments construct their social and economic policies so that they provide different kinds of financial and services support for different kinds of families. Government policies towards early childhood care and education services are, in many countries, a key part of family policy. In any country, the appropriate design of the child care system depends critically on the other policies that affect young children and their families. To choose an obvious example, the type of child care required by the four-year-old children of working parents depends on whether junior kindergarten is provided within the public school system, and whether it lasts for half or full days. The type of child care services needed will also depend on the degree of income inequality in society, which will be affected by tax, family allowance, and social assistance policies.

The issues in this area are both tricky and unresolved. One revolves around the care of infants. There is considerable agreement that organized, good quality child care for children two to five years of age is generally beneficial. On average, children in that age range cared for in good quality full-day child care develop as well, and sometimes better, than children cared for full-time at home. Organized child care does provide socialization and educational experiences that are invaluable to children; children cared for at home will do as well, especially if they receive part-day early education experiences (as do children in many upper-middle class families). Although good child care is quite expensive, the benefits outweigh the costs for most children and mothers.

The results for infants are less clear. High-quality infant child care is extremely expensive. Research results on whether infants do better at home or in organized care are less conclusive. Although we are pretty sure that infants are not harmed if their mothers work and make high-quality care arrangements, just how much quality is 'enough,' and how quality should be defined is not a settled issue. The alternative to an extensive infant child care program is a significantly expanded system of parental leave and benefits, or a combination of infant services and parental benefits. Determining which policy route to take will depend on knowing a lot of different things. What is best for children? What do parents want? What will be the cost of each alternative? Can parents rely on holding high-quality jobs if they take extended leaves, and are employers likely to discriminate against young parents who take (or are likely to take) such leaves? Designing an optimal policy is likely to be a complicated matter, and will undoubtedly require elements of both child care and parental leave.

That these issues are unsettled is reflected in the wide variety of approaches internationally to 'family policy' – by which we mean the variety of public programs that have an impact on families with young children. Sweden's family policy is strongly geared towards maintaining labour market attachment. France's is geared towards supporting parental choices – either maintaining labour market attachment or supporting mothers who care for young children. Other countries choose a different mix.

It seemed to us overly ambitious to anticipate that we would be able to resolve these issues at this time. Instead, we believe that it would be a step forward to define the issues systematically and to position Canada's present policy accurately within the international framework. That is, we took this session to define the issues and determine what Canada is doing on them in comparison with other countries.

The two presenters were chosen because of their knowledge of Canadian policy relative to the rest of the world. Anne Gauthier is currently an assistant professor of sociology at the University of Calgary. She has worked and written extensively in the area of comparative family policy and has written an acclaimed book comparing family policies in a variety of industrialized countries. Maureen Baker is a professor and department head of sociology at the University of Auckland in New Zealand; she was formerly at McGill University. She has written ten books on various aspects of social policy, the most recent of which is a cross-national study of low-income mothers and the restructuring of social policy in Canada, Australia, New Zealand, and Britain.

The two discussants also have an interest in cross-national research in family policy. Kathy O'Hara began working in the federal public service in 1973, and has worked in a number of departments with an interest in family policy. From September 1996 to June 1998 she was a research fellow at the Canadian Policy Research Networks, where she wrote papers and organized roundtable discussions on the social union; she also wrote an influential paper on family policy in eight countries. Since June 1998 she has been the assistant secretary of the Social and Cultural Sector in the Treasury Board Secretariat. Shelley Phipps is a professor of economics at Dalhousie University. Her current research interests include the economic well-being of children, decision making within families, and international comparisons of social policy, poverty, and inequality.

Anne Gauthier looked at how Canada ranked within the group of industrialized countries, both on policy and spending, and on outcomes for families. This is, of course, a heroic task, given the assumptions that must be made to engage in meaningful cross-national comparisons. Her conclusion is that Canada generally ranks from the middle to the bottom in most aspects of family policy. Canada fares well on health, but poorly on educational and child care policies, as well as on parental leave and child poverty. Overall, Canada has made a series of political choices that have not favoured families with young children.

Maureen Baker focused on the experience in Australia and New Zealand relative to that in Canada. She concluded that very few jurisdictions have a systematically formed coherent family policy. Instead, what is called family policy is usually the result of a series of disjointed political decisions, taken by different governments over time, for a variety of political reasons. The situation may be worse in federations where the states may act in different ways than the federal government.

In New Zealand, for example, despite a general commitment by recent governments to market-oriented policies, family policy has generally assumed that mothers would care for their young children at home. Changes in family policy have come as a result of intense trade-offs within Cabinet, especially given the recent minority governments. Australia takes a similar approach to family policy, in that mothers are generally assumed to be at home, yet social benefits are more generous. Parental leave provisions are also more generous, but were won through central collective bargaining rather than through explicit government legislation. Child care policy has varied over time, with a recent devolution of child care support from the federal to the state governments.

In general, both Australia and New Zealand have offered less support for child care than has Canada, and they have also integrated their programs for children with employment initiatives less effectively than has been done in Canada.

Both discussants drew on the material from other countries to draw conclusions about the Canadian experience. Kathy O'Hara looked at the evolution of the child care policy debate, which has shifted in Canada from employment support to a more general orientation towards the care of children. We value child care both in and out of the home, and this complicates our formation of family policy. To advance child care policy, advocates will have to position themselves to reflect Canadians' emerging values.

Shelley Phipps suggested that the chapters in this part emphasize how important it is to look at child care policy as part of a set of policies affecting families with young children. And even if countries set aside the same amount of resources per child, it matters how those resources are disbursed. For example, resources that end up in mothers' hands are more likely to help children than resources that are given to fathers, especially in the area of child care, and in-kind programs are more likely to funnel resources to children than programs that give support to their parents.

16. Family Policies and Families' Well-being: An International Comparison

Anne H. Gauthier

Department of Sociology, University of Calgary

What is the level of support provided by governments for families in industrialized countries? Where does Canada rank from an international perspective? And what is the impact of family policy on families' and children's well-being? These are important questions, especially in the context of budget constraints and welfare reforms. This chapter addresses these questions by comparing the support provided for families by governments in some twenty countries. The comparisons are aimed not only at the level of support provided by governments, but also at the type of support provided, as well as the impacts of these policies on families.

The chapter reveals major differences across countries. In particular, it reveals the dominant position of countries such as Austria, Belgium, France, and Luxembourg in terms of cash support for families, and the dominant position of Finland and Sweden in terms of support for working parents. Canada appears among the middle to low providers of support for families. Cash benefits are limited, the child poverty rate is very high from a cross-national perspective, maternity and parental leave schemes are below average, and support for child care facilities is very limited. Only on indicators of education and health does Canada appear in a favourable position. These results raise major public policy issues: issues of the public willingness to support families with children, issues of equity, and issues of intergenerational transfers of public resources. While I do not intend to resolve these dilemmas, the chapter aims at shedding light on Canada's effort in supporting families with children.

The chapter is divided into six sections. In the first section, I discuss the notion of family policy and raise some of the methodological difficulties involved in comparing family policies across countries. The second section is devoted to a review of trends over time in family policies in industrialized countries. The next three sections examine, respectively, cash support for families, services for families, and support for working parents. The concluding section discusses the implications of the findings for Canada's family policy.

FAMILY POLICY PACKAGE

What do we mean by family policy and family support? It is important to stress that there is no established definition of family policy. Some scholars have adopted very broad definitions that encompass nearly all types of public policies that directly or indirectly affect families, while others have adopted much narrower definitions, limiting them to the core public policy programs directly targeted at families with children.[1] Consequently, some scholars include in their definition of family policy legislation and programs related to public transport, pollution control, and the protection of the environment, while others restrict their analyses to programs earmarked for families with children such as family allowances, maternity leave, and child care subsidies. While not denying that legislation related to public transport and the environment has a potential impact on the quality of life of families and children, here I will adopt a narrower perspective.

The list of programs and policy sectors included in my definition of family policy appears in Table 16.1. The list is obviously long, and, moreover, obviously cuts across several ministries – even in countries that have a ministry for the family.[2] This very fundamental nature of family policy has numerous implications. First, it complicates the coordination of the different components of family policy. In lieu of a comprehensive and well-coordinated policy, family policy is often fragmented and has been referred to as an amalgam of elements[3] or simply as a cash-benefit package.[4] Second, the cross-ministerial nature of family policy also means that the government ministries involved in the provision of family benefits will compete for public monies. Since in the fight for larger budgets, a win for one ministry is usually associated with losses for others, the overall consequence for families may therefore be expected to be mixed. That is, in an analysis of trends over time in family policies, one may expect different trends across the different types of benefits. Finally, the cross-ministerial nature of family policy makes it difficult to measure precisely the overall level of support

Table 16.1. Components of family policy

Component	Specific measure
Income support	Family/child allowances, means-tested family benefits, food subsidies, tax relief for children, benefits for disabled children
Work	Maternity/parental leave, flexible working hours, part-time work, leave for sick children, child care facilities
Education	Educational provision and subsidies, including preschool education, educational grants and loans
Health	Pre- and post-delivery care, general health services, dental services, prescription rebates, family planning services, vaccination programs, infertility treatment, abortion services
Housing	Rent subsidies, provision of affordable housing, low-interest mortgages, subsidies on renovation
Social services	Family counselling, child welfare
Family law	Divorce, child support, adoption, family violence, inheritance

provided by governments for families. Not all ministries report the share of their expenditures or efforts devoted to families, and not all ministries report the information in a comparable way. For this reason, the data presented in the chapters will not cover the whole range of policies listed in Table 16.1, but will be restricted to data that are readily available and comparable across countries. In particular, the analysis will focus on income support programs and work-related benefits.

Three further points should be raised. First, it should be made clear that there are several ways of analysing and describing policies. For instance, one may analyse policies from the point of view of governments, or one may analyse policies from the point of view of families. The first approach consists in analysing the institutional settings and the components of family policies. For instance, one may analyse the bodies responsible for the provision of family allowances, the eligibility criteria, and the value of family allowances, or one may analyse the total money spent by governments on various programs. This was the approach adopted in several recent cross-national family policy analyses.[5] The second approach consists in analysing the level of support provided by governments from the point of view of families. This may involve an analysis of the level of support received by an average family,[6] or by different family types.[7] There is no single best method. Instead, these two approaches shed different light on the level of support provided by governments for families. In this chapter, I will use both approaches to compare the support provided by governments for families across countries.

The second point that should be raised is that family policies are obviously not static. Governments regularly revise, add, cut, and expand programs. In this chapter, I will focus on current family policies. But it has to be kept in mind that the current policies result from different trends across countries, and that although there is a certain level of stability and inertia in programs, their future is always vulnerable.

Finally, beyond the description and analysis of the policies themselves, it is also important to consider the impact of policies on the well-being of both families and children. Such a link between policies and outcomes is rarely done in the comparative literature on family policies. Yet, it is important to assess the extent to which policies achieve their objective of enhancing family well-being.[8] Methodologically, the measurement of the impact of policies is not easy. It requires access to reliable and meaningful indicators of families' well-being, and it requires being able to isolate the effect of policies from the myriad of other factors that may affect families' well-being. Despite these difficulties, I attempt, in this chapter, to capture some of the possible effects of family policies by comparing across countries indicators of family policies and indicators of families' well-being. The approach is, however, strictly descriptive and simply compares the ranking of countries on various indicators of policy and well-being.

A BRIEF HISTORY OF FAMILY POLICY[9]

Although I stated earlier that I would be concentrating on current family policies, it is nonetheless important to see these policies from a historical perspective. Part of the current intercountry differences in governments' support for families can only be understood as a result of differential trends over time.

In most industrialized countries, the first elements of family policies were introduced prior to the Second World War. These included policies regarding maternity leave, financial support for families, and the provision of services for families. In most cases, these programs had a limited coverage and were targeted at families in specific occupational groups, or at the poorest families.

The situation changed entirely after the Second World War when the new policy era emphasized the provision of universal social welfare benefits. Universal family allowances were introduced in most countries in the 1940s, and maternity leave schemes were strongly expanded (in coverage and benefits) as of the 1950s. Canada joined other countries in introducing universal family allowances in 1944. Canada, however, appeared as an outlier in adopting a paid maternity leave scheme only in 1971, that is, several decades after all European countries. It is beyond the scope of this chapter to explain the lagging position of Canada with regard to paid maternity leave. It should, however, be kept in mind that family policy in Canada has had a different trajectory than that of other countries.

The first major change of direction in governmental support for families took place in most industrialized countries as of the mid-1960s, when evidence of persistent poverty forced governments to add programs targeted at low-income families. While the immediate postwar period emphasized universal programs, designed for all families, the 1960s 'rediscovery' of poverty led to the adoption of targeted programs. At a time of rapid economic growth, these targeted programs were simply added to the existing universal programs, rather than substituted for them. For example, the United Kingdom introduced a family income supplement scheme in 1970, and New Zealand adopted a means-tested family maintenance allowance scheme in 1968.

The other major change to take place during this period was the development of measures in support of women's participation in the labour force. Maternity leave schemes had been in place for several decades, but, until the 1960s most family policies assumed the presence of the mother at home (with the exception of Eastern European countries). They were, therefore, modelled after a very traditional gender division of labour. From the late 1960s the rapid entry of women, with and without children, in the labour force challenged this situation. Governments did not stay indifferent. Although some governments initially resisted the implementation of further support for working mothers, others more readily endorsed the new trend and even encouraged the entry of women into the labour force.

Sweden and Finland are good examples. While so far their maternity leave schemes had been lagging behind those of most other European countries, these schemes were strongly expanded as of the 1960s. As will be seen later in this chapter, maternity leave policies in Sweden and Finland rapidly became, and still are, more generous than those of other countries.

Finally, the trends in family policies since the 1980s have been mixed.

While support for working mothers – and fathers – has been expanded in all countries, financial support for families has been cut in several countries or has been targeted at the poorest families. I will come back to these divergent trends in the next sections.

CASH SUPPORT FOR FAMILIES

How do countries compare in terms of their cash support for families? There are various ways of measuring cash benefits for families. None of the indicators are perfect, and countries are often ranked differently. Results for two such indicators, as of 1993–4, appear in Table 16.2. The first indicator measures governments' expenditure on family benefits, expressed per child, as a percentage of the gross domestic product per capita. Family benefits, as measured in this indicator, comprise family allowances and other cash benefits.[10] This is a relatively reliable indicator of cash benefits, although it may be criticized for failing to take into account the coverage of benefits.[11] According to this indicator, cash support for families is higher in Luxembourg, Austria, and France, and lower in Portugal, Ireland, and Italy. Canada appears among the countries providing the lowest level of support for families (ranked thirteenth out of seventeen countries).

The previous indicator measures direct transfers to families, but ignores indirect transfers in the form of tax relief for children. An alternative index is the disposable income index (column 3 of Table 16.2). It compares the amount of direct and indirect cash transfers received by an average family with those received by a single person – an unattached individual – earning the same income. For this comparison, the average family is defined as a two-parent family with two children with only one of the parents in the paid labour force. Both the single earner in this family and the unattached individual earn the average manufacturing wage. A single-earner family is, of course, no longer the predominant family type, but it is the only type for which we have cross-national, comparative data at the time of writing.

The disposable income index expresses the additional disposable income (after taxes, social security contributions, and family benefits) of the average family as a percentage of the disposable income of a single person (i.e., with no spouse or children) who earns the same pretax, pre-transfer income. For instance, an index of 12 per cent indicates that the average two-child, one-earner family in that country has a disposable income that is 12 per cent higher than that of a single

Table 16.2. Indices of cash support for families, 1993–4

	Expenditure index 1993	Rank	Disposable income index 1994	Rank
Australia	8.3	(7)	10.5	(16)
Austria	10.9	(2)	25.1	(4)
Belgium	9.9	(5)	39.2	(1)
Canada	4.0	(13)	14.6	(12)
Denmark	5.9	(11)	27.2	(3)
Finland	6.0	(10)	20.2	(7)
France	10.8	(3)	18.9	(8)
Germany	4.2	(12)	24.3	(5)
Greece	n.a.	–	n.a.	–
Ireland	2.8	(16)	16.2	(10)
Italy	2.1	(17)	12.5	(14)
Luxembourg	11.6	(1)	34.6	(2)
Netherlands	8.2	(8)	18.0	(9)
New Zealand	3.6	(14)	0.0	(20)
Norway	9.8	(6)	21.7	(6)
Portugal	2.9	(15)	10.4	(17)
Spain	n.a.	–	8.4	(19)
Sweden	10.2	(4)	14.2	(13)
Switzerland	n.a.	–	16.1	(11)
United Kingdom	6.3	(9)	12.1	(15)
United States	n.a.	–	9.4	(18)

n.a. = not available
Notes: The expenditure index is the expenditure on cash family benefits, expressed per child (age 0–14 years old) as a percentage of GDP per capita. The disposable income index is the additional disposable income (after taxes, transfers, and social security contribution) of a one-earner, two-child family with earnings equal to those in manufacturing, as compared with the disposable income of a single earner with equivalent earnings.
Sources: Computed by the author, based on data from ILO and OECD. International Labour Office, *The Cost of Social Security Expenditure* (1999) (on-line database: http://www.ilo.org/public/english/110secso/css); Organization for Economic Cooperation and Development, *The Tax/Benefit Position of Production Workers, 1991/1994* (Paris: Author, 1995).

unattached individual earning similar wages. Of course, families with children typically have higher expenses than unattached individuals, a point that the index does not address.

According to this index, cash support for families is higher in Belgium and Luxembourg, and lower in the United States, Japan, and New Zealand. Benefits provided in Belgium are in fact very large, reaching nearly 40 per cent higher for families than for unattached individuals.

Canada appears with a slightly better ranking (twelfth out of twenty) as compared with the previous indicator. In Canada, a family with two children receives an additional income (as a result of direct transfers and taxes) equal to 15 per cent of the income of a single earner at the same wage level. According to this indicator, Sweden ranks below Canada. This is partly explained by the fact that this index refers to a single-earner family and therefore is affected by the amount of financial support available for a dependent spouse. Using the expenditure index, Sweden ranks above Canada.

Although this chapter focuses on the current support for families, it is important to mention that cash support for families has been threatened by major cuts in recent years, as part of government efforts to curb public expenditures. In several countries, universal family allowances have been abolished and replaced by means-tested schemes. Such a reform was introduced in Australia, Greece, Italy, and Spain. The abolition of universal family allowances in Canada in 1992 is, therefore, not an exception. On the other hand, several other governments have resisted such a cut and have instead continued to acknowledge families' universal entitlement to family allowances. Under Prime Minister Margaret Thatcher, for instance, the British government attempted to abolish the universal child benefit in the mid-1980s. The opposition to this plan was, however, very strong, and led the government to withdraw it.[12]

What is the impact of these cash benefits on families and children? To answer this question, we can only rely on an indirect indicator. But, as will be seen, this indicator correlates very well with the ranking of countries in terms of cash benefits. In Figure 16.1, I compare the index of disposable income with the poverty rate among children after governmental transfers and benefits. For the purpose of this comparison, poverty is defined as having an income that is less than 50 per cent of the median income. The poverty index refers to two-parent families.

The countries have been ranked according to their level of cash support. The relationship between these two indicators is unmistakable – although not perfect. Countries with high levels of cash support tend to have low levels of child poverty. The United States obviously ranks very badly on these two indicators, with more than 20 per cent of children being poor and a low level of cash support for families. At the other end of the distribution, Finland, Sweden, and Denmark fare very well, with low levels of child poverty and medium to high levels of cash support. Canada's ranking is not enviable. It has the third highest level of child poverty, after government support is included, and a low

Figure 16.1. Cash support and child poverty, 1980s–1990s.

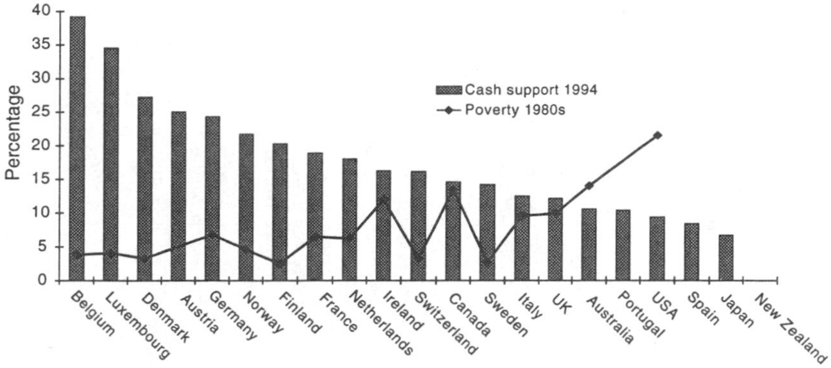

Note: The index of cash support is the disposable income index (see Table 16.2). The data on child poverty refer to poverty after governmental transfers and taxes. Poverty is defined as having less than 50 per cent of median income. The value of cash support for New Zealand is zero. There are no data points on child poverty for either Austria or Poland. Sources: Organization for Economic Cooperation and Development. *The Tax/Benefit Position of Production Workers, 1991/1994* (Paris: Author, 1994); L. Rainwater and T.M. Smeeding, *Doing Poorly: The Real Income of American Children in Comparative Perspective* (Luxembourg: Luxembourg Income Study, 1995).

level of cash support. Canada's policies appear to be successful in partly reducing the level of pre-transfer child poverty, but the reduction is far less impressive than that of other countries (data not shown). It should be noted that these data refer to the late 1980s, that is, prior to the Canadian reform of family allowances and the child tax benefit system. Recent estimates of child poverty, however, suggest that the reform has not succeeded in significantly lowering child poverty.[13]

SERVICES FOR FAMILIES

The cash benefits considered above represent one form of governmental support for families. Governments also devote large fractions of their budgets to the provision of education, health services for families, and housing subsidies. Data on these categories of benefits are, unfortunately, limited as they often refer to the total population of recipients and do not distinguish the fraction of benefits or expenditure devoted to families with children.

One policy indicator is the total expenditure on education as a percentage of GDP, as of 1994. This indicator is not a very satisfactory one, as it does not distinguish between the different levels of education, and between public and private institutions. Nor does it control for the

Figure 16.2. Education expenditures and math scores, 1994–5.

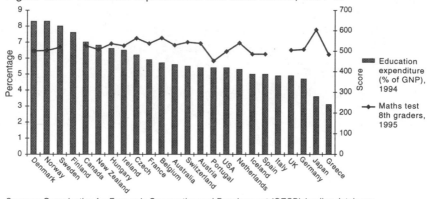

Sources: Organization for Economic Cooperation and Development (OECD) (on-line database: www.oecd.org/els/stats/edu-db/edu_db.htm); and OECD, Education at a Glance: OECD Indicators, 1998 (Paris: Author, 1998).

quality of education. But, it is the best data available on a cross-national basis.[14] These data are compared with an outcome indicator, the mean mathematics score of eighth graders on the Fourth International Mathematics and Science Study. This last indicator has been widely used in comparative analyses and has pointed to strong disparities across countries. Results appear in Figure 16.2.

If we focus first on the expenditure data, we see that expenditure on education is highest in the Nordic countries and lowest in Germany, Greece, and Japan. Canada appears among the leading countries. The observed relationship between the expenditure indicator and the outcome indicator is somewhat puzzling. In theory, we would expect students in countries where governments spend more on education to fare better on the international test. This is not the case. The highest mathematics score is, in fact, observed in Japan where the least is spent on education. One possible explanation lies in the quality of education: a factor that is not necessarily correlated with the level of expenditure. What the data suggest is that countries spending high amounts on education do not do so efficiently – or at least, do not get the educational returns or payoffs that could be expected. For instance, 1998 data from the OECD suggests that the rate of high school graduation in Canada is below the average in industrialized countries, despite relatively high expenditure on education (data not shown here).[15]

Health services is another major component of support for families.

Figure 16.3. Expenditure on health and child mortality, 1993–4.

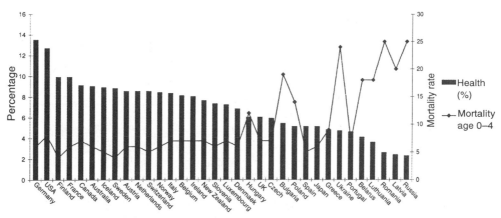

Source: World Health Organization (1998).

Unfortunately the available data do not allow us to compute the share of health care expenditures provided for families with children. The data refer to the whole population and are therefore partly distorted by intercountry differences in the age and sex structure of the population.[16] Our indicator is the expenditure on health services as a percentage of GDP, as of 1993. Once again, the indicator does not control for intercountry differences in the quality of services, nor in the actual cost of services, nor in the coverage of the services. The outcome indicator is the child mortality rate (number of deaths of children under the age of five per 1,000). In most Western countries, the child mortality rate is relatively low. It is, however, much higher in Eastern Europe. Results appear in Figure 16.3.

Germany and the United States spend the largest amount on health, while Romania, Latvia, and Russia spend the least. The leading position of the United States needs some qualification. That country spends a large amount of money on health but the coverage of the population is limited. According to the U.S. Bureau of the Census (1998), 15 per cent of children in the United States were not covered by any health care insurance in 1996. Furthermore, public health expenditures in the United States, as captured in Figure 16.3, refer only to services provided to low-income families and elderly people under the Medicare and Medicaid programs.

Is there a relationship between the level of expenditure on health and child mortality? What we observe is a mild inverse relationship. Countries spending a large amount of money on health tend to have lower levels of child mortality. The relationship is, however, mainly because of the high levels of child mortality observed in some Eastern and Central European countries. In most Western countries there is, in fact, little relationship between the two indicators. Canada ranks relatively well, having a relatively high level of expenditure on health care and a relatively low level of child mortality.

Child mortality is, however, not necessarily the best outcome indicator since it has reached very low levels in most countries. Data from the Health Behaviour of School-Aged Children of the World Health Organization may eventually provide more satisfactory measures of health and well-being.[17]

SUPPORT FOR WORKING PARENTS

Support for working parents has been at the core of government family policies since the 1970s. It has aimed at protecting the health of mothers and children, but has also been part of government efforts towards bringing greater gender equality in the labour force. As suggested earlier, the differences across countries are large.

Table 16.3 provides information on two types of leave: maternity leave and child care leave. Looking first at maternity leave, information on both the duration of the leave and the cash benefits paid during the leave (expressed as a percentage of wages) is provided. Furthermore, an index combining the duration and the level of cash benefits is also provided. The index expresses the equivalent number of weeks fully paid for. For example, fourteen weeks of leave paid at 80 per cent of regular earnings is equivalent to 11.2 weeks fully paid (14 weeks multiplied by .80). Data refer to 1997.

Finland and Sweden dominate the other countries in providing the most generous maternity leave scheme, when both the duration and the pay are combined. The index corresponds to about forty weeks fully paid for. At the other extreme, Greece, Ireland, and the United Kingdom provide the least generous schemes. Canada ranks below average, in view of its relatively short leave and its limited cash benefits. It should be noted here that the comparison ignores the eligibility criteria which may be very stringent in some countries.

Table 16.3 also provides information on child care leave. Also known as parental leave, this is an optional leave (paid or unpaid) that may be taken after maternity leave, that may be shared between parents in some countries, and that usually guarantees return to work in the same or equivalent position. Since the 1970s a large number of countries have adopted such a scheme. While in 1975 only Austria and Italy were offering a child care leave, by 1997 most countries were doing so. In several countries the leave is very long and extends until the child's third birthday. This is the case in the Czech Republic, Denmark, Finland, France, Germany, Russia, Slovakia, Spain, and Ukraine. The leave is, however, not paid in Spain. Canada introduced a paid parental leave scheme of ten weeks in 1990. This scheme still leaves Canada behind most European countries. (As this book goes to press, there are plans to extend paid parental leave in Canada.)

To provide an overview of the support for working parents, I have combined in Figure 16.4 information on the total number of weeks provided by the different schemes: paid maternity leave, unpaid child care leave, and paid child care leave. The height of the bars in Figure 16.4 refers strictly to the duration of the leave and does not factor in the value of the cash benefits. According to this indicator, Germany, France, Finland, and Denmark appear in a leading position. Canada, conversely, appears among the lagging countries.

Policy surrounding childbirth is obviously only one form of support for working parents. Other ways of supporting parents include the provision of child care facilities, subsidies for child care, opportunities for part-time and flex-time work, and leave for sick children. No cross-nationally comparable data on all these forms of support are available. Table 16.4 reports data on child care provision and early education. The data express the percentage of children enrolled in publicly financed institutions as of the late 1980s and covers children enrolled both full-time and part-time, as well as children enrolled in preprimary schools, day care centres, kindergartens, crèches, and family day care – as long as these services are partly or fully publicly funded.

The differences among countries are enormous. While 95 per cent of children age three to school age were enrolled in a publicly financed institution in Belgium, France, and Italy, this was the case for less than 60 per cent of children in Canada, Finland, Ireland, Norway, Portugal, and the United Kingdom. The coverage of children under the age of three also varies significantly across countries, and is generally very low (the exception being Denmark). These data are, however, not perfect. For one thing, they refer to the total population of children and not

Table 16.3. Maternity and child care leave and benefits, 1997

	Maternity Leave			Child Care Leave	
	Duration (in weeks)	Cash benefits (% wages)[a]	Index	Duration of paid leave (in months)	Duration of unpaid leave (in months)
Australia	–	–	–	–	12b
Austria	16	100	16.0	24b	–
Belgium	15	77	11.6	12	–
Canada	15	55	8.2	2	3
Denmark	28	100	28.0	12	–
Finland	63	70	44.1	36b	–
France	16	100	16.0	36b	–
Germany	14	100	14.0	36b	12b
Greece	16	50	8.0	–	6
Ireland	14	70	9.8	–	1
Italy	22	80	17.6	12b	–
Japan	14	60	8.4	12b	–
Luxembourg	16	100	16.0	12b	–
Netherlands	16	100	16.0	–	6
New Zealand	–	–	–	–	12b
Norway	42	100	42.0	–	12b
Portugal	21	100	21.0	–	24
Spain	16	100	16.0	–	36b
Sweden	64	62	39.7	–	18
United Kingdom	18	45	8.1	–	7b
United States	–	–	–	–	3
Eastern Europe					
Albania	52	65	33.8	–	–
Belarus	18	100	18.0	–	–
Bulgaria	17	100	17.0	24b	12b
Croatia	26	100	26.0	12b	–

Table 16.3. (Continued)

	Maternity Leave			Child Care Leave	
	Duration (in weeks)	Cash benefits (% wages)[a]	Index	Duration of paid leave (in months)	Duration of unpaid leave (in months)
Czech Rep.	28	69	19.3	–	–
Estonia	18	100	18.0	–	–
Hungary	24	100	24.0	24[b]	–
Latvia	16	100	16.0	–	–
Lithuania	18	100	18.0	12[b]	–
Poland	16	100	16.0	24	–
Romania	16	85	13.6	12[b]	–
Russia	28	100	28.0	18[b]	–
Slovakia	28	90	25.2	36	–
Slovenia	52	100	52.0	–	–
Ukraine	18	100	18.0	36[b]	–

– = No benefit.

[a] In most countries, the cash benefits are proportional to earnings or wages. In countries where this is not the case (e.g., where flat-rate benefits are paid), an equivalent percentage was computed on the basis of female wages in manufacturing.

[b] Total duration from the birth of the child, including months covered by the paid maternity leave.

Notes: Belgium: The leave is part of a general career interruption leave of 6 to 12 months. Canada: The maternity leave is of 17 weeks, but only 15 weeks are paid; up to 24 weeks of parental leave may be taken, but only 10 weeks are paid. Czech Republic: Prior to 1993 there was a 36-month paid parental leave. Denmark: The maternity flat rate benefits represent slightly more than 100 percent of female wages in manufacturing; the parental leave is of 13 to 52 weeks. Greece: A 3-month unpaid leave is available to each parent (not transferable). Hungary: The child care leave and allowance was eliminated in April 1997. Luxembourg: A parental leave of 2 years is available for families with three and more children. Netherlands: The 6-month leave is a part-time leave that allows parents to reduce their hours of work when they have young children. New Zealand: There is also a 14-week unpaid maternity leave. United Kingdom: 29-week unpaid leave.

Sources: A.H. Gauthier, The State and the Family: A Comparative Analysis of Policy in Industrialized Countries (Oxford: Clarendon Press, 1996); Social Security Administration, Social Security Programs throughout the World, 1997 (Washington, DC: Government Printing Office, 1997).

Figure 16.4. Maternity and child care leave arrangements, 1997

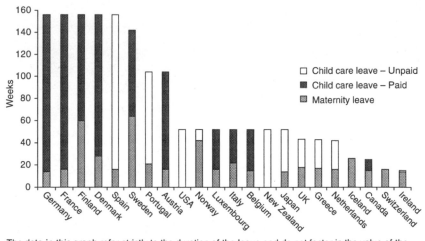

The data in this graph refer strictly to the duration of the leave and do not factor in the value of the cash benefits. For data on cash benefits, see Table 16.3. Sources: Computation by the author from United States, *Social Security Programs throughout the World – 1997* (Washington: Social Security Administration, 1997).

to children in need of care (i.e., children whose parents are in the labour force). Furthermore, the data ignore other types of subsidies and support related to child care (e.g., tax relief for child care), and they ignore intercountry differences in the quality of child care.

Results on the overall support for working parents appear in Figure 16.5. This index was computed by Gornick, Meyers, and Ross and is based on eleven indicators of family policy including maternity leave and child care facilities.[18] Canada appears again near the bottom of the distribution. It is followed by the Netherlands, the United Kingdom, Norway, and Australia. Norway's position among the least supportive countries may be surprising. Its provision of child care facilities, and the expenditure on such facilities, differ substantially, in fact, from those of the other Nordic countries.[19]

What is the impact of these policies on families? The impact may be wide-ranging. Working parents benefiting from higher levels of governmental support may find it easier to combine work and family responsibility; they may be less prone to stress and mental health problems, and they may experience lower rates of absenteeism. Mothers may, furthermore, experience less career disruption for family rea-

Table 16.4. Percentage of children in publicly funded care and education services, 1993

	Children age 3 to school age	Children under the age of 3
Austria	75	3
Belgium	95	30
Canada	59	5
Denmark	79	50
Finland	43	27
France	99	23
Germany	65[a]	5[a]
Greece	64	3
Ireland	52	2
Italy	97	6
Luxembourg	68	2[a]
Netherlands	69	8
Norway	50[a]	10[a]
Portugal	48	12
Spain	84	5
Sweden	79	33
United Kingdom	53	2

[a]1988 data.

Note: The European data come from the European Commission Network on Childcare. They cover children in preprimary schools, day care centres, kindergartens, crèches, and family day care – as long as the service was partly or fully publicly funded. No fully comparable data for Canada are available. The data for Canada refer to children enrolled in day care centres (publicly or not publicly funded) and in preprimary schools. The data for day care come from Human Resources and Development Canada; they refer to the number of spaces available in day care centres in 1995. For the purpose of this table, spaces in family day care were excluded, as they mostly consist of non-funded spaces (the exception being the province of Quebec). The data on preprimary schools come from the UNESCO on-line database; they also refer to 1995. The index for children age 0–2 in Canada was computed by dividing the number of spaces in day care centres for children age 0–2 by the population of that age in 1995 (the population data come from Childcare Resources and Research Unit). The index for children age 3–5 in Canada was computed by dividing the number of spaces in day care centres for children age 3–5, plus the number of children enrolled in preprimary school, by the population of that age in 1995. The numerator of this index is likely to overestimate the provision of care and education facilities, since a child may be enrolled in a day care centre on a part-time basis and be enrolled in a preprimary school, also on a part-time basis.

Sources: W. Tietze and D. Cryer, 'Current Trends in European Early Child Care and Education,' *Annals of the American Academy of Political and Social Science*, 563 (May 1999) 175–207. Childcare Resource and Research Unit, 'Child Care in Canada: Provinces and Territories' (Toronto: Author, 1995). Human Resources Canada, *Status of Day Care in Canada 1995 and 1996: A Review of Major Findings of the National Day Care Study 1995 and 1996* (Ottawa: Human Resources Development, 1997). UNESCO online data website: http//unescostat.unesco.org/stats/stats0.htm.

Figure 16.5. Support for working parents, late 1980s

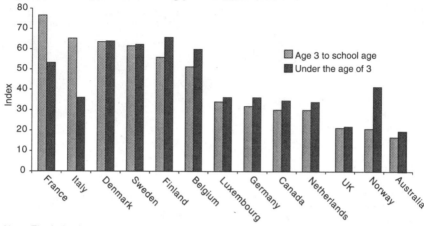

Note: The index is based on 11 indicators of family policy, including maternity leave and child care facilities. Source: J.C. Gornick, M.K. Myers, and K.E. Ross, 'Public Policies and the Employment of Mothers: A Cross-National Study,' in *Social Science Quarterly* (1998) 79(1): 35–54.

sons. Data on the labour force participation rates of women, with and without children, provide us with a first look at the potential impact of family policies. The data in Figure 16.6 show the labour force participation rates of married women from thirty to thirty-nine years of age, in various countries, by age of the youngest child. Data refer to 1997.

The impact of young children on participation of women in the labour force appears to be especially strong in Austria, Germany, Ireland, Luxembourg, and the Netherlands. In all these countries, women with young children have significantly lower labour force participation rates than women who do not have children under the age of fifteen. At the other extreme, the impact of young children appears to be minimal in Belgium, Denmark, and Portugal. The ranking of Portugal on this indicator may be surprising and may possibly be explained by the availability of grandmothers and other relatives to care for children. Canada appears in an intermediate position. Although the results are not clear-cut, women in countries with high levels of support appear to be able to minimize the potentially negative impact of children on their labour force participation rates. The data are, however, slightly misleading as they combine women at different stages of their life cycles.

Figure 16.6. Employment rates of married women age 30–39 by age of the youngest child,1996–7

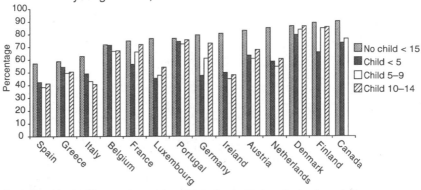

Note: The data for European countries refer to the employment rate of married women 30–39 years of age by age of the youngest child in 1997. No fully comparable data for Canada were available. The data for Canada instead refer to employment rates of married women (spouse present) 25–34 years of age by age of children (no children at home, children under 6 years only, youngest child 6–14 years of age) in 1996. Sources: European Union, *Employment Rates Report, 1998: Employment Performance in the Member States* (http:/europa.eu.int/comm/employment_social/empl&esf/emplgg/rates_en.htm). Statistics Canada, *Census Data*, 1996 (special tabulation from on-line database).

The data do not tell us the full and genuine impact of children on women's careers.

To get more precise information on the impact of children on women's employment, we have to rely on retrospective information on the history of women's participation in the labour force. Two surveys provide such information: the special module of the 1991 Eurobarometer survey on the employment of women and the 1984 Canadian Family History Survey.[20] The data in Figure 16.7 indicate the percentage of women having ever experienced a work interruption of at least one year among those who have ever been in the labour force. Of course, childbirth and child care may not be the only reasons for such job interruptions, but the data suggest that these two reasons account for more than 60 per cent of the job interruptions for women. In Figure 16.7 I have also added data on the percentage of women who experienced downward mobility after returning to work following a job interruption.

The data reveal very large intercountry differences. Women in the

Figure 16.7. Work discontinuity and downward mobility, late 1980s.

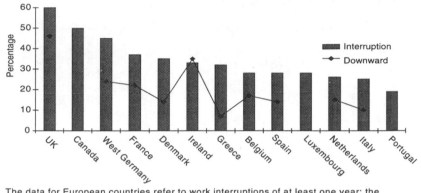

The data for European countries refer to work interruptions of at least one year; the data refer to women aged 22–60 years who have been employed for at least one year. The data for Canada also refer to work interruptions of at least one year by women 18–64 years of age. Sources: M. Kepeneers and E. Lelievre, *Emploi et famille dans l'Europe des douze* (Brussels: European Communities, 1991); Statistics Canada, *Family History Survey: Preliminary Findings* (Ottawa: Author, 1985).

United Kingdom score very high on both indicators. They have the highest percentage of interrupted careers and the highest percentage of downward mobility among returnees. If we recall, the United Kingdom also scored very low on indicators of maternity leave and child care facilities. Canada comes second on the indicator of job interruption. At the other end of the distribution, Italy, Luxembourg, the Netherlands, and Portugal have the lowest percentages of interrupted careers. One should, however, not lose sight of the fact that these four countries have relatively low levels of women's labour force participation. The few women who joined the labour force apparently have a high degree of labour force attachment and job continuity.[21]

CONCLUSION: A LESSON FOR CANADA?

Before discussing the main conclusions that may be drawn from the results described in this chapter, it is worth reminding the reader about some major methodological considerations and warnings. First, it should be re-emphasized that we are dealing with imperfect data. Despite the increase in the literature on comparative family policies, the available data are still limited in term of their scope and cross-national comparability. For example, data on cash benefits cover means-tested benefits imperfectly, data on maternity leave ignore the coverage of benefits and the eligibility criteria, and data on health expenditures do not distinguish the share of expenditures devoted to families with children. The second methodological warning concerns the evaluation of the impact of policies on families' well-being. The analysis presented here provides only a rough indication of the possible impact of policies. More sophisticated analyses, involving multivariate statistical techniques, would be needed to isolate the impact of policies from other determinants of families' well-being.

There are two further methodological points. First, the analysis presented here clearly demonstrates the multidimensional nature of family policies and the importance of looking at a whole range of benefits and services. Countries tend to rank differently on different indicators of family policies, and no country appears to excel in all sectors of family policies. As stressed at the beginning of this chapter, family policy is an amalgam of benefits and services, and no country has yet developed a completely comprehensive package of family benefits. The second methodological point is that while family policies may be described and analysed on their own, the analysis of their impact on families' well-being is essential. Family policy is costly and ought to be considered in relation to the goals, needs, and inequalities of societies.

Bearing in mind these warnings, the main conclusion that may be drawn from the previous results is that Canada does *not* rank among the high providers of state support for families. At best, it ranks in an average position, at worst, in a very low position. From an international perspective, Canada appears to have placed a lower value on public support for families than other countries have. This result is not new. Esping-Andersen, in his analysis of welfare states, placed Canada among the low-spending countries, that is, among countries that give preference to market forces over governmental intervention.[22] This situation raises major public policy issues, especially in the context of tight governmental budgets, economic globalization, international competition, and population aging. Canada is today confronting major decisions about the allocation of its limited public resources. These constraints are not specific to Canada, but Canada has undoubtedly made choices that have, so far, resulted in lower support for families than is found in most European countries. There is obviously a cost associated with such choices, namely, that Canada has one of the highest levels of child poverty and that families in Canada are left largely on their own when it comes to finding ways of combining work and family responsibilities.

Should we, as a society, care about this situation? If so, are we willing to devote more resources to families with children? Are we even willing to increase taxes to finance a more generous family policy? These are major questions. Equally important is the question of whose responsibility is it? Since the 1950s governments have emerged as the sole providers of family benefits. In an era of universality of welfare programs, governments have been given the responsibility to allocate public resources to different subgroups of the population. But what about the role of other actors? While there may be little public support for a shifting of the responsibility from governments to families, or from governments to charity organizations, one may legitimately raise the issue of employers' responsibilities. In Europe this issue has attracted much attention in recent years. The European Commission has been devoting large efforts to the identification and promotion of benefits provided by employers for working parents, on the grounds that they help reduce the incompatibility between work and family responsibilities, they contribute to greater gender equality, and they result in lower rates of absenteeism and higher rates of retention among employees.[23] In Canada, such employer-sponsored benefits have not received much attention. While one has to agree that employer-provided benefits may not eliminate the need for state-provided ones, the involvement of employers in the provision of family benefits may help us to create a more family-friendly society.

Notes

1 A.H. Gauthier, *The State and the Family: A Comparative Analysis of Family Policy in Industrialized Countries* (Oxford: Clarendon Press, 1996).

2 In 1996, in Western Europe, five countries had a ministry of the family: Austria, Germany, Italy, Luxembourg, and Norway.

3 J. Aldous, W. Dumon, and K. Johnson, eds., *The Politics and Programs of Family Policy: United States and European perspectives* (Leuven, Belgium: Leuven University Press, 1980).

4 S. Kamerman, and A.J. Kahn, eds., *Government and Families in Fourteen Countries* (New York: Columbia University Press, 1978).

5 For example, Gauthier, *State and Family*; Kamerman and Kahn, *Government and Families*; J. Kurczewski, and M. Maclean, eds., *Family Law and Family Policy in the New Europe* (Aldershot, UK: Darmouth, 1997); A. Leira, *Welfare States and Working Mothers: The Scandinavian Experience* (Cambridge: Cambridge University Press, 1993); M. Maclean, and J. Kurckewski, eds.,

Families, Politics, and the Law; Perspectives for East and West Europe (Oxford: Clarendon Press 1994); G. Therborn, 'The Rights of Children since the Constitution of Modern Childhood: A Comparative Study of Western Nations,' in *Social Exchange and Welfare Development*, L. Moreno, ed. (Madrid: Conejo Superior de Investigaciones Cientificas, 1993); K. Scheiwe, 'Labour Market, Welfare State and Family Institutions: The Links to Mothers' Poverty Risks,' in *Journal of European Social Policy* (1994), 4(3): 201–24.

6 For example, D. Blanchet and O. Ekert-Jaffé, 'The Demographic Impact of Family Benefits: Evidence from a Micro-Model and from Macro-Data,' in *The Family, The Market, and the State in Ageing Societies*, J. Ermisch and N. Ogawa, eds. (Oxford: Clarendon Press, 1994), 79–104; O. Ekert, 'Effets et limites des aides financières aux familles: une expérience et un modèle,' in *Population* (1986) 41(2): 327–48; I. Wennemo, 'The Development of Family Policy: A Comparison of Family Benefits and Tax Reductions for Families in 18 OECD Countries,' in *Acta Sociologica* (1992) 35(3): 201–17.

7 For example: S. Kamerman, and A.J. Kahn, 'Income Transfers, Work and the Economic Well-being of Children: A Comparative Study,' in *International Social Security Review* (1982) 3: 345–82; and J. Bradshaw, J. Ditch, H. Holmes, and P. Whiteford, 'A Comparative Study of Child Support in Fifteen Countries,' in *Journal of European Social Policy* (1993), 3(4): 255–71.

8 H.L. Wilensky, G.M. Luebbert, S.R. Hahn, and A.M. Jamieson, *Comparing Social Policy; Theories, Methods, Findings* (Berkeley: University of California Press, 1985).

9 This section draws heavily from Gauthier, *State and Family*.

10 We have very little information on the degree of intercountry comparability. Using a similar data set compiled by OECD, Kamerman and Kahn identified some cross-national differences in the definitions of family benefits. S.B. Kamerman and A.J. Kahn, *Government Expenditures for Children and Theiur Families in Advanced Industrialized Countries, 1960–85* (Florence: International Child Development Centre, 1991).

11 E. Amanta, 'The State of the Art in welfare State Research on Social Spending Efforts in Capitalist Democracies since 1960,' in *American Journal of Sociology* (1993) 99(3): 750–63.

12 Gauthier, *State and Family*.

13 Data from the Canadian Council on Social Development, e.g., suggest an increase in child poverty between 1990 and 1996 (see http://www.ccsd.ca/factsheets/fscphis2.htm).

14 The OECD has compiled some other indicators, notably indicators of expenditure per student and per level of education. Unfortunately, data for some countries including Canada were not available.

15 Organization for Economic Cooperation and Development (OECD), *Education at a Glance: OECD Indicators 1998* (Paris: Author, 1998).
16 We know, e.g., that elderly people typically receive a higher share of health care services than younger citizens.
17 A. King, *The Health of Youth; A Cross-National Survey* (Copenhagen: World Health Organization Regional Office for Europe, 1996).
18 J.C. Gornick, M.K. Meyers, and K.E. Ross, 'Public Policies and the Employment of Mothers: A Cross-National Study,' in *Social Science Quarterly* (1998) 79(1): 35–54.
19 A.H. Gauthier, '*Historical Trends in State Support for Families in Europe (Post-1945),' Children and Youth Services Review* 21: 11/12, 937–65.
20 Results of the Eurobarometer survey were reported in Kempeneers and Lelievre. Results of the Canadian survey were reported by Statistics Canada. M. Kempeneers and E. Lelievre, *Emploi et famille dans l'Europe des douze* (Brussels: European Communities, 1991); Statistics Canada, *Family History Survey: Preliminary Findings* (Ottawa: Author, 1985).
21 Kempeneers and Lelievre, *Emploi et famille.*
22 G. Esping-Andersen, *Three Worlds of Welfare Capitalism* (Cambridge: Polity Press, 1990).
23 M. Thozet-Teirlinck, 'The Network Families and Work and the Social Innovation Award,' in *Reconciling Work and Family Life – A Challenge for Europe?* B. Arve-Pares, ed. (Stockholm: Commission of the European Communities and Swedish National Committee on the International Year of the Family, 1995).

17. Child Care Policy and Family Policy: Cross-National Examples of Integration and Inconsistency

Maureen Baker
Department of Sociology, University of Auckland

Several years ago, when I still worked in Canada, I participated in a multicountry project concerning Family Change and Family Policies,[1] involving about twenty-five member nations of the Organisation for Economic Cooperation and Development (OECD). The Canadian report, which I completed with Shelley Phipps, was published as part of a book edited by Sheila Kamerman and Alfred Kahn called *Family Change and Family Policies in Great Britain, Canada, New Zealand and the United States*.[2] In preparing this report, we were asked to consider the historical roots, politics, and institutionalization of family policy in our country. After struggling with these issues for about a year, many of the participating researchers argued that there is no coherent 'family policy' in their country.

Instead, we concluded that a variety of family-related policies had been formulated, altered, and expanded throughout the years by different governments, often with conflicting philosophical ideas about how the state should support family life and women as mothers and workers. The governments that developed these social programs over the past century had different political agendas and had made concessions to various pressure groups that influenced the final outcome of their policy initiatives. Furthermore, federations such as Canada, Australia, and the United States have two or three levels of government involved in policy formulation, and these government do not always agree on the relationship between families and the state, family entitlements, or parental responsibilities.

Governments tend to label a particular set of policy decisions or social programs as 'family policy' or 'family benefits,' while excluding other social and economic decisions that affect families just as much. A

Canadian example would be calling the Child Care Expense Deduction an 'employment deduction' from income tax rather than acknowledging it as a 'family benefit.' Furthermore, if we look at broader policy changes that affect families, we could certainly argue that the establishment of block funding under the Canada Health and Social Transfer will have considerable impact on families. Yet this is not considered by government to be 'family policy.' So, what governments label as family policy and what researchers perceive to be policies impacting on families are often discrepant.

The researchers in this multicountry project discussed the historical development of the myriad policies and programs related to families with children and noted that these policies and programs were often poorly integrated and sometimes contradictory. In Canada, inconsistencies exist among provincial family laws and social welfare regulations, and federal divorce law and income tax regulations relating to families with children. For example, the 'man in the house' rule in welfare law assumes that low-income women are men's dependents, but divorce law now assumes that most sole mothers are capable of supporting themselves with a small amount of child support from the children's father.[3]

There are at least two broad approaches to policies involving families and child care in OECD nations. One approach continues to focus on the male-breadwinner family, supporting child care by mothers at home and making only a gesture towards the needs of employed mothers. The other promotes the mother-worker with varying degrees of public support for child care, parental benefits, and leave for family responsibilities. This second approach can be divided into two further categories: nations such as United States that have pushed mothers into paid employment with few public supports and nations such as Sweden and Denmark that have provided more generous benefits and services for employed mothers.[4]

In this chapter I focus on the integration (or lack of integration) among child care programs, income support, and employability programs in New Zealand and Australia in comparison with Canada. I explain the inconsistencies and contradictions by discussing the models of family implicit within family policies and by focusing on political pressures affecting policy formulation. For the past two years, I have been comparing four 'liberal' welfare states (Canada, Australia, New Zealand, and the United Kingdom) that have made recent attempts to move low-income mothers off social benefits and into the paid work force. I use some of this research – especially the restructuring discourse and program changes from these nations – as examples of policy variation and the political nature of policy formulation. In the conclusion, I discuss the lessons that Canada can learn from this cross-national research.

Welfare state theorists such as Esping-Andersen have classified nations depending on the generosity of their social provision and how they see the role of the state, compared with markets and voluntary organizations, in ensuring well-being. Esping-Andersen classified Canada and the English-speaking countries (such as United States, United Kingdom, Australia, and New Zealand) as 'liberal' welfare states because they provide low-level and mainly means-tested benefits.[5] In contrast, corporatist nations such as France and Italy have maintained social well-being through social insurance programs mainly for labour force participants, and social democratic states such as Sweden and Denmark have focused on universal benefits and services. I have argued in my book *Canadian Family Policies: Cross-National Comparisons* and in my book with David Tippin that many variations are apparent among so-called liberal welfare states.[6] In this chapter, I highlight some of the differences relating to family policies and child care, and I will start with an overview of recent policy changes in New Zealand.

FAMILY POLICY AND CHILD CARE IN NEW ZEALAND

Internationally, New Zealand has been used as an example of a welfare state that has undergone extensive market-oriented restructuring, involving deregulation and privatization in many state sector activities, electoral reform, and social program cuts. Furthermore, this has been accomplished with unprecedented speed and minimal public opposition.[7] Yet despite these dramatic reforms to economic policy, changes to family and child care policy have been minimal.

New Zealand's policies relating to families have been implicit and imbedded within labour market and wage policies, income support programs, and taxation regulations.[8] Historically, the male-breadwinner family has been a central concept behind labour market policy. Early in the twentieth century the government and unions supported the 'family wage,' giving a man enough pay to support himself, his wife, and two or three children. Since 1938 unemployment benefits have been based on the idea that men are breadwinners and women are

primarily wives and mothers. Consequently, eligibility for unemployment benefits has always been based on family income and unemployed people (mainly men) are paid a supplemental benefit for their
'dependents.' This contrasts sharply with Canada's Employment Insurance, which is based on individual entitlement and does not consider
the income or economic needs of the members of the unemployed
worker's household.

To maintain income security, the New Zealand government has provided three main categories of means-tested support: unemployment
benefits (targeted at men and unattached childless women), sickness
benefits, and the Domestic Purposes Benefit (DPB). The DPB was developed in the 1970s to enable lone mothers to care for their preschool
and school-aged children at home. Until 1996 this was paid until the
children reached adulthood, but now it is paid until the youngest child
reaches fourteen. This benefit is based on the cultural understanding
that 'good mothering' includes physical care and emotional support,
but it does not necessarily include paying for children's upbringing
through wages. In fact, women who work outside the home are sometimes considered to be neglecting their children, somewhat like the
1950s and early 1960s in Canada.

The consequence of these labour market and income security policies
is that employment rates for mothers have been extraordinarily low in
New Zealand. Although these rates have been increasing in recent
years, especially as male unemployment rises, a relatively low percentage of mothers are employed, especially full-time. As Table 17.1 indicates, only 17 per cent of New Zealand's lone mothers and 31 per cent
of partnered mothers work full-time, compared with 32 per cent and 41
per cent of Canadian mothers with children under sixteen years old.[9]
About 89 per cent of lone mothers are on social benefits (compared with
44 per cent of lone mothers on social assistance in Canada).[10] New
Zealanders still see themselves as a rural people (even though almost
one-third of the population lives in Auckland), who support 'family
values,' including mother at home caring for three children. Fertility
rates have been higher in New Zealand than in many industrialized
countries. For example, the total fertility rate in 1995 was 2.04 in New
Zealand compared with 1.64 in Canada.[11]

Cross-national research, such as the studies from the Family Policy
Studies Centre in the United Kingdom, identify the absence of affordable child care as the major factor explaining differential employment
rates of lone mothers.[12] In addition, the attempt to leave social assist-

Table 17.1. Employment rates for mothers with children under 16, 1994–5 (%)

	Sole mothers			Partnered mothers		
	Employed	F-T	P-T	Employed	F-T	P-T
Canada	57	32	25	74	41	33
Australia	43	22	21	51	27	24
New Zealand	27	17	10	58	31	27

Sources: Maureen Baker and David Tippin, *Poverty, Social Assistance, and the Employability of Mothers: Restructuring Welfare States* (Toronto: University of Toronto Press, 1999).

ance for paid work is often made difficult by high taxback rates and the loss of other 'passport' benefits associated with social assistance (such as subsidized health care). These have clearly been factors in New Zealand as well as Canada.

More so than in Canada, child care services in New Zealand have been geared to children's development, preschool education, and parent-run play schools rather than full-time employment of mothers. In this respect, income support policy and child care policy have been integrated. I am not suggesting that child care is not well developed in New Zealand. Community preschools exist in the form of child care centres, kindergartens, play centres, Maori preschools (*Te Kohanga Reo*), and Pacific Island Language Groups. Over 93 per cent of four-year-olds and about 83 per cent of three-year-olds participated in some form of early childhood service in 1996. These services, however, usually operate only a few hours a week. Licensed child care centres (both for-profit and not-for-profit) comprise about 40 per cent of available spaces for preschool children, yet children attend for only 15 hours per week on average.[13] After-school care is not developed, as most mothers with school-aged children are at home during the day.

Political support for public child care is stronger within the political left, but New Zealand is run by a right-wing government. Shortly after assuming office in 1990, the National Party government rolled back child care support. Child care subsidies for children under two years of age were reduced substantially, the proposed increases in overall funding were abandoned, and an initiative called 'Parents as First Teachers' was introduced to encourage parents to take primary responsibility for early childhood education.[14] Given the prevailing division of labour within households,[15] this initiative involved new responsibilities for mothers and a further disincentive to seek paid work outside the home.

Affordable child care remains an obstacle to paid work for low-income mothers, particularly as user fees have risen with neo-liberal reforms. The existing child care subsidy helps to fund child care services for children under the age of five from low-income families who are citizens or permanent residents. To qualify, the child must attend licensed care for at least three hours a week. If the parents are unemployed, they may be entitled to only nine hours of child care subsidy; if they are employed, studying, in a training program, or ill or disabled, they may qualify for up to thirty hours a week. Yet, unlike the Canadian system, the subsidy does not support full-time work.

As in Canada, the child care subsidy is paid directly to the early childhood service rather than to the family, but in New Zealand it can be claimed for only twelve months at a time. Furthermore, if the child's care centre is changed, the parent has to reapply for the subsidy.[16] The value of the subsidy varies with the parents' income and the number of children in the family, and the maximum rate in May 1998 was about $56.70 Canadian[17] a week (NZ$70) if the parents worked thirty or more hours a week, earned up to $421.20 a week (NZ$520), and had one child.[18] Rules for the subsidy reflect the ambivalent messages about unpaid caring and paid work in New Zealand.

In 1998 the National government introduced a 'workfare' program called 'The Community Wage,' which emphasized the importance of self-sufficiency and work incentives for recipients of social benefits. At the same time, the government changed the name of the welfare office from 'Income Support' to 'Work and Income New Zealand' (WINZ). Yet the child care subsidy was not altered to support full-time work. Its partial nature and the relative lack of after-school care for older children reinforce the status of low-income mothers as part-time workers who retain responsibility for dependent care. Full-time employment is seen as interfering with mothering in a society with weak support for public child care.

The underdevelopment of flexible employment policies augments the problems of full-time employment for mothers, and childbirth usually means withdrawal from the labour market, as there are no statutory maternity or parental benefits in New Zealand.[19] Under the Parental Leave and Employment Protection Act 1987, pregnant women and adoptive mothers (who have been employed full-time or part-time for twelve months) are entitled to fourteen weeks of unpaid maternity leave. New fathers are entitled to two weeks of unpaid leave at the time of birth.[20] In 1998 a private member's bill to introduce 12 weeks of paid parental benefits (funded primarily through employers' contributions) was introduced into the House of Representatives and debated for several months. Paid parental benefits have been as controversial in New Zealand as they were in the United States in the early 1990s.[21] New Zealand opponents of paid parental benefits use low U.S. unemployment rates and the relatively strong U.S. economy as reasons to reject the proposed 'payroll tax' that would 'kill jobs.' In the May 1999 budget, the National government attempted to side-step the issue by introducing a modest eight-week 'baby bonus' for new parents with middle and low incomes, paid both to families with employed mothers and to those with mothers at home. This means that New Zealand still does not offer employed parents paid parental leave.

The political left (the Labour Party and the Alliance Party) support paid leave, arguing that New Zealand is one of two OECD countries (other than the United States) without it. The political right oppose paid leave, arguing that employers cannot afford the extra costs. Right-wing parties and interest groups support an allowance and tax incentives for full-time parental child care (Christian Coalition), or regard children as the product of parental choice and their exclusive responsibility (Association of Consumers and Tax-Payers). The ruling (right-wing) National Party prefers the status quo, although there has been recurring pressure from the Treasury to reduce child care expenditures further.[22] The political right is concerned that too many lone mothers rely on costly social benefits instead of working for pay. At the same time, their opposition to public child care reflects concern that greater participation by mothers in the workforce might increase unemployment rates (now about 7 per cent), that public child care will be too expensive, and that non-family care will in some way harm children.

Despite the National Party's restructuring of the New Zealand economy and of many government services, their efforts to include lone mothers in the Community Wage program have failed. This is what happened. In the May 1998 budget, the government announced 'a radical change in welfare direction,' to strengthen the work test in all means-tested benefits by establishing the Community Wage program. For recipients of the Domestic Purposes Benefit, the idea was to ask lone mothers to look for part-time work when their youngest child was between seven and fourteen, and full-time work when the youngest child reached fourteen. The government promised $2.6 million (NZ$3.2 million) over three years for out-of-school child care and to extend the child care subsidy for low-income families with children aged five to thirteen.[23] Yet the subsidy still would not have covered full-time work. Objections to extending the work test to low-income mothers came from within the National Party (by an influential female MP) and from community groups who argued that mothering is a 'full-time responsibility.' Faced with both internal and external opposition, the government quietly withdrew the portion of the budget proposals relating to the DPB but tightened work requirements for male beneficiaries. Both social activists and conservative women's groups objected to making lone mothers with school-age children accept paid work when the full-time job market is shrinking, relative wages are declining, and quality child care is limited.

The current New Zealand government now requires most social beneficiaries to search for paid employment, but neither compels mothers with children under fourteen to do so nor offers employed mothers much public support for combining paid work and child care. The preferred policy option is part-time employment while receiving the Domestic Purposes Benefit, which reinforces the image that low-income women remain primarily responsible for unpaid caring and domestic duties.

For other New Zealanders using child care services, the government offers a maximum income tax rebate (or credit) of $251.10 per year (NZ$310).[24] This benefit is much less generous than the Canadian deduction of $7,000 per preschool child. In fact, New Zealanders are amazed that the Canadian government is so 'generous.'

POLICIES RELATING TO CHILD CARE IN AUSTRALIA

Australians and New Zealanders are similar in their attitudes about employed mothers and their expectations that government will provide income support for mothering at home, yet social provision is more generous in Australia.[25] Australia also based unemployment benefits on family income and always paid unemployed men a supplement for their 'dependents.' In 1995–6 (after Canada had eliminated its Family Allowance), the Australian government established the Parenting Allowance to allow all parents caring for children at home (mainly mothers) to receive an income of their own, with a substantial supplement for those with low incomes. The Partners Allowance was also created in 1994 for low-income older women without children but living with an unemployed man.[26] Formerly, the husband would have received an additional amount to support his wife and children.

Since the late 1980s the Australian government has also provided the Sole Parent Pension to enable low-income lone parents (mostly mothers) to care for their children at home until the youngest child reached adulthood. Now, the age of the youngest child has been reduced to sixteen years old (with much opposition from feminists), and about 94 per cent of sole mothers receive this benefit.[27] Although the government initiated a voluntary employability program at the same time (called Jobs, Education and Training, or JET), government officials have continued to voice their intention to maintain income support for mothers caring for their own children at home, as well as for public child care.

In contrast to Canada, Australians first gained maternity and parental benefits through union negotiations, which were then generalized into national 'awards' for other employees. In Canada, provincial and federal legislation covers these issues. Since 1973 twelve months of *unpaid* maternity leave have been available to all federal government employees in Australia (temporary and part-time as well as permanent). In addition, these employees received twelve weeks of paid leave if they have one year of continuous service. In 1979 this entitlement was extended to many private sector workers when the Australian Council of Trade Unions brought its Maternity Test Case to the Australian Industrial Relations Commission (AIRC).[28] In 1990 the AIRC's Parental Leave Test Case replaced gender-specific maternity leave in most awards with twelve months of unpaid leave shared between parents (with one week at birth overlapping). In addition, provision was made for parents to work part-time until the child's second birthday, if the employer agrees. By 1992 parental leave had been inserted into 280 federal awards and adopted by most state awards and legislation.[29] The Industrial Relations Reform Act, proclaimed in March 1994, prohibits termination because of family responsibilities. Employers are now required to provide twelve months of unpaid leave (which can be shared between parents) as a minimum employment entitlement, although casual and part-time employees who have not worked for the employer for twelve continuous months are exempt. In Canada, eligibility for unpaid leave varies by province but maternity benefits under Employment Insurance entitle pregnant women to fifteen weeks of benefits paid as a percentage of previous earnings (55 per cent up to a maximum level) with an additional ten weeks of paid parental benefits.

In August 1994 the first stage of the test case decision on family leave from the AIRC stated that employees may use their own sick leave for the care and support of sick family members.[30] This decision allowed greater flexibility in the workplace for family needs and formally recognized caring responsibilities within households. Yet it did not grant any additional leave time. Stage two of the Personal/Carers Test Case (in 1995) allowed employees to combine sick leave and bereavement leave for family leave purposes, and provided a maximum of five days of carers leave that can be accumulated. It also allowed carers leave to be taken as a portion of the workday rather than an entire day.[31] Many employees, however, are ineligible for carers leave. These include the 23 per cent of employees and 30 per cent of women employees who were 'casual' workers in 1994. Also, 24 per cent of women have been in their jobs less than twelve months and are therefore ineligible for paid parental leave.[32]

Australian statistics (like those from other jurisdictions) indicate that mothers rather than fathers are taking parental and family leave, even though it was meant to be gender-neutral. Among workers with children under twelve who have been absent in the previous two weeks, 9 per cent of women and 2 per cent of men were on maternity or parental leave. There is no special sick leave to take care of family members except for the decisions of the AIRC test cases in 1994 and 1995 (noted above). Furthermore, whatever advances have been made could be halted in the future by the recent move from centralized to enterprise bargaining, even though the award system has been retained.[33]

Since the Child Care Act in 1972, public day care centres have been funded through cost-sharing arrangements among federal, state, and local governments, but as in Canada, parents must pay fees for these services.[34] The federal government pays an operating grant for each approved child care place. Since 1988 it has also offered tax deductions to private companies providing child care services,[35] but only recently to individual taxpayers. The Australian Council of Trade Unions (ACTU) supported public funding for private centres, but this was opposed by the community child care lobby[36] and other supporters of universal access who want all child care to be not-for-profit.[37] The number of private day care centres has increased since they became eligible for government assistance, yet a shortage of child care spaces exists in Australia.[38]

Although the Child Care Act initially focused on children 'in need,' the Labour government established a policy of universal access to child care when they assumed power in 1983. Despite this policy, priority continued to be given to employed lone parents, two-income families, and children with special needs.[39] Child care became a more political issue with higher employment rates for mothers throughout the 1980s, and funding increased steadily.[40] Child care places funded by the federal government were increased from 46,000 in 1983 to 253,000 by the end of December 1994.[41] Yet the employment rates of Australian mothers lag behind Canadian figures, as Table 17.1 indicated, although a higher percentage of lone mothers are employed in Australia compared with New Zealand.[42]

Just before the 1993 election, the Labour party promised a social benefit to recognize the income loss experienced by mothers who forgo full-time employment to care for their children at home. Clearly, this policy was designed to capture the conservative women's vote. In 1994, after Labour's victory under Paul Keating, the government introduced the Child Care Cash Rebate (CCCR) to help families meet work-related child care costs. This rebate, providing $27.94 per week (A$28.80) for one child and $60.67 (A$62.55) for two or more children, covers both formal and informal care (including care by a family member), and payments are made through the medicare office. The Labour government also introduced a new child care accreditation scheme in the same year.[43]

Several conservative women's groups (such as Women's Action Alliance) continued to lobby for a payment for mothers at home, reminding the government that the Lavarch Report (*Report of the Inquiry into Equal Opportunity and Equal Status for Women*) had recommended it in 1992.[44] In response to this lobby, the Keating Labour government replaced the Dependant Spouse Rebate (DSR) with the Home Child Care Allowance (HCCA). The HCCA was an non-taxable allowance, means-tested on the carer's income, while the DSR had been a tax rebate paid to the husband based on family income. The maximum HCCA was $58.20 every two weeks (A$60), a small increase over the former DSR, but the money was directed to mothers as carers rather than fathers as principal taxfilers in the family.[45]

Although both the Home Child Care Allowance and the Child Care Cash Rebate successfully captured the women's vote, the allowance remained controversial with other interest groups. In the past, the trade unions had objected to the idea of converting a tax benefit for (male) breadwinners into an allowance for (female) caregivers, as this would represent a loss of income and power for male wage earners. Yet as women's employment rates and union membership increased, and economic globalization forced unions to make concessions to government, the unions eventually supported Labour's child care reforms. In fact, the unions began to place greater emphasis on the 'social wage' to counter the loss of income caused by declining real wages under 'the Accord.'[46] (The Accord was an agreement negotiated by the governing Labour party with employers groups and the unions about economic policy and how restructuring would take place during the 1980s.)

Australian lobby groups continued to debate these new child care benefits. Conservative groups (as well as the opposition political parties) argued that the Labour government was favouring employed women over homemakers. They also noted that the tax rebate for child care was distributed at medicare offices while the allowance was directed through social security, giving it a 'welfare' connotation. The conservative Women's Action Alliance objected to the fact that the HCCA but not the CCTR was targeted to lower-income families. The National Council for the International Year of the Family argued to amalgamate the two benefits and target them to families with a child under six years of age, but they also wanted the payment increased. The Australian Council of Social Service argued that the allowance should be directed to carers of preschool children rather than targeted to lower-income families.[47]

The controversial HCCA lasted for only nine months before the government abolished it in order to establish the Parenting Allowance. The Parenting Allowance offers all parents caring full-time for children at home a benefit of $59.36 (A$61.20) per fortnight, but low-income families are entitled to additional support up to $263.84 (A$272) per fortnight. In creating this benefit, the Labour government argued: 'The Parenting Allowance recognizes the value of the caring work performed by parents who choose to stay at home to care for their children.'[48]

Despite these initiatives, Australians have been slower than Canadians to accept the idea of non-family child care to enable mothers to enter or remain in paid employment. Traditional gender-segregated views persist, personal independence is still highly valued, and employed mothers tend to work part-time and retain the major responsibility for housework and child care. Any convergence in the time that men and women spend in housework and child care since the 1980s has occurred because women are spending less time on housework and not because men are spending more.[49]

When the conservative coalition government came into power in 1996, they introduced additional changes to the funding of child care. These included the removal of operating subsidies from community day care, beginning July 1997, but with the guarantee that four years of funding would be available for family day care, occasional care, outside school hours care, multifunctional services, and multifunctional Aboriginal services. The government also extended accreditation to family day care, but offered no new funds.[50] These changes represented a move from subsidizing group care to privatization by offering parents a tax rebate to purchase their own care. The government rationalized this reform as necessary 'to support choice for parents,' but it also accompanies a devolution of child care support from the federal to state governments.

As in Canada, the state premiers, represented by the Council of Australian Governments, want social services (including child care) to be delivered by states and territories rather than by both levels of governments. In 1996, the federal government regulated family day care,[51] but this will be devolved to the states in the future. Organizations such as National Family Day Care Council of Australia (NFDCCA) object to these changes because they want common federal goals to be retained to help the states administer services. NFDCCA believes that it is in the 'best interest of Australia's children for the Commonwealth government to maintain responsibility for delivery of child care services, that the National Children's Services Program be maintained and expanded, and that there be allocation of sufficient resources to enable the delivery of high quality care to all those children requiring it.'[52]

NFDCCA also argued that providing more government support for one-earner families with the mother at home sends a double message to women. On the one hand, women are being told that they do not need to work for pay, yet there is more emphasis on 'employability' in other social benefits (such as the Sole Parent Pension). The Labour Shadow Minister for Aged, Family and Community Services (Jenny Macklin) asked: 'Is this an attempt to solve unemployment problems by removing women from the labour force?'[53]

A continued focus on deficit reduction remained a priority for the Australian government, despite opposition from community groups and the political left. Yet in the October 1996 budget, the coalition government allocated $35.6 million (A$36.7 million) more than in the previous year for caregivers, established the National Respite for Carers Program, and announced the creation of Carers Resource Centres across the country. The government also increased the number of respite days available to carers from forty-two to fifty-two days per year, and carer pensioners can now spend twenty hours a week (up from ten) in work or study without losing benefits. Furthermore, the government announced an allocation of $30.1 million (A$31 million) more for children with high levels of need (such as children with disabilities) who would normally be placed in federally funded child care services.[54]

In the May 1997 budget, the same coalition government announced further cuts to child care expenditures. A limit was imposed on new private sector places in 1998 and 1999, which is expected to save over $200 million (A$206.9 million) over four years.[55] As the level of unmet need among children under five years old is estimated to be about 72 per cent, this announcement is unlikely to win support from parents who cannot find a place for their child. Despite the emphasis on employability, the coalition government also limited to twenty hours a week access to child care assistance for parents who are studying or searching for work. If parents require more hours, they must use their own money. The government also reduced operating subsidies for after-school care in centres. After 1 January 1998, all funding for child care outside school hours has been paid directly to low-income parents (with annual family incomes under $25,220 or A$26,000) in the form of an enhanced child care assistance payment.[56] Despite these cuts, the coalition government has promised to increase the number of family day care places by 2,500 from 1997 to 2001, primarily to alleviate pressures in rural and remote areas. Yet in the May 1998 budget, the two-year freeze on child care assistance payments was extended for another year despite an increase in centre fees.[57] The private sector is now the main provider of centre-based child care and non-profit services remain precarious.[58]

Although the Australian government introduced an employability program (JET) for social beneficiaries in the late 1980s, mothers were never compelled to work for pay on a full-time basis. The state's encouragement of more women to see themselves as actual or potential paid workers is mediated by ambiguous and contradictory attitudes about women's appropriate roles and responsibilities. As in Canada, government reforms to social programs are attempting to reconstruct and rebalance the identities of low-income women – including those of mother, paid worker, unpaid carer, and more frequently head of household.[59] Distinctive from Canada, however, is the continuing social and political unease in Australia about the idea of leaving young children in non-family child care, especially when they are preschoolers. Australian restructuring has retained the social emphasis on the concept of 'care' and 'carers,' but the issue is framed within traditional assumptions of gender segregation and responsibilities of women for providing this care.

In Australia, gender segregation is reinforced by three important factors.[60] First, the greater presence of part-time employment in women's lives allows more time for caring activities. Second, official discourse and policy offers women (but not men) the 'choice' of paid work or family caring work. Third is the continuing ambivalence of the Australian feminist movement over women's caring and labour market roles when children are young. In Canada, the unstated objective of employability programs seems to be to create the 'worker-mother' as a new citizenship ideal for low-income women early in their child-raising period. The focus in Australia continues to be on unpaid caring work while a mother has young children, with moderate incentives to move into paid work when all her children are grown.

Australia has not restructured the state and government programs along neo-liberal lines to the same extent as New Zealand has. One reason is that the trade union movement and left-wing lobby groups are stronger in Australia, and they have been a consistent voice for the maintenance of social programs. Second, Australia has legislated compulsory voting and this means that governments must be more cognizant of the wishes of all citizens, including those on social benefits (who are less likely to vote in non-compulsory elections). Third, like Canada, Australia has a federal system and a bicameral parliament which make rapid policy change more difficult, while New Zealand is a unicameral state with one central government which has allowed the Cabinet to make major reforms in a short time period. These factors contribute to the differences between the two countries, which many Canadians see as similar. Yet one similarity that remains is the strong emphasis on mothering at home, although this is diminishing in both nations.

CONCLUSION

This chapter provides some evidence from New Zealand and Australia that creating policies to support families with children is a political exercise involving trade-offs and compromises among political parties and advocacy groups. Government policy analysts may design new programs to resolve certain social concerns only to find that they conflict in some way with existing regulations or programs designed by another government with a different political philosophy. Furthermore, citizen groups and opposition parties often force governments to amend their proposed legislation to coincide with their interests. This means that the initial design of family policy and child care policy may have been consistent, but by the time of implementation, inconsistencies become apparent in social programs.

Since the 1980s most governments have been gradually integrating labour market policy with income support programs, and new employability programs have elevated paid work into an ideal to be attained by most social beneficiaries. This has coincided with a transition from social policy based on the male-breadwinner model of family to a more gender-neutral one that focuses on the individual earner. This in itself could be emancipatory for women, except that gendered work inside the home has not changed much over the decades, especially in Australia and New Zealand, which means more mothers are now expected to work for pay while retaining their caring roles.[61] Furthermore, the labour market in most liberal welfare states is producing mainly low-paid and part-time positions, which do not necessarily pull people out of poverty, especially if they have to purchase child care on the open market. In addition, not all countries have provided statutory maternity benefits, leave for family responsibilities, pay equity, or affordable child care, which means that many women are disadvantaged in an already tight job market.[62]

Recent research on employability programs suggests that expecting beneficiaries to enter paid work in the present economic climate is increasingly complicated and risky for low-income mothers and may result in a net financial loss for them and their families.[63] These complications are not always recognized by policy makers, as they call into question the insecurity and low pay of available jobs, the shortage of training positions to allow workers to move to better positions, and the psychological damage caused by dead-end and low-paid work. Recognition of these complications also requires an acknowledgment of the lack of child support from some non-resident fathers and the inaccessibility of affordable public child care.

Comparative research indicates that providing statutory supports and services for parents attempting to combine paid work and child-rearing is essential to their labour market equity, but this also requires careful government coordination, regulation, and public money. Greater integration between family policy and labour market policy always requires effective lobbying and coalition building, but especially in an era of neo-liberalism and demands for smaller government and lower taxes. New programs such as expanded child care services require additional public money or the reallocation of public expenditures, and competition will be stiff for shrinking resources. Yet the day care lobbies in many countries are demanding that governments acknowledge the need for improved child care both as an equity issue for employed mothers, as women's employment rates rise, and as an investment in children as a future national resource.

My comparative research indicates that Canadian governments have integrated programs for child birth and care with employment initiatives in a more effective way than New Zealand and Australia have. Canadian governments have provided broader social protection for employees who are new parents and more generous subsidies and tax relief for employed parents using child care services. Yet Canadian governments have been less successful in viewing child-bearing and child-rearing as something that parents do for themselves, but also for the good of the nation.

My cross-national research indicates:

1 Employability programs for recipients of social assistance will be unacceptable to parents and ineffective as public policy without government financial support for child care. This support could be in the form of subsidies paid directly to care-providing organizations and individuals, or tax rebates to parents, but public support must cover the cost of child care for parents in *full-time* employment (as it does in Canada).
2 Over the past decade, appreciation of the importance of public child care services has been building. Yet this acceptance has been set back in some jurisdictions by public concerns over child abuse in centre care, the lack of regulations governing the quality of care, the possibility that national unemployment rates will rise if more mothers are encouraged into paid work, and perceptions of inequality in government support for caring work within the home, and services for employed parents.
3 Governments cannot afford to ignore parents (mothers) caring for children at home as they remain an important political constituency who want and deserve public recognition for their work and government assistance to defray their costs. Australia has been the most cognizant of this constituency (compared with Canada and New Zealand) and provides more effective support for them. Canada used to provide more recognition of the costs of rearing children

through the former Family Allowance and the Child Tax Exemption, but had eliminated both these benefits by 1993.

In conclusion, governments need to be seen to be fair and equitable in the subsidies and tax relief they provide for caring work. At the same time, the child care lobby needs to recognize that caring work is done inside the home as well as in public child care services. My research indicates that governments need to ensure that both kinds of caring work provide children with high-quality care and their care providers with financial support and employment options.

Notes

1 This project was coordinated by the Mannheim Institute of European Social Research.
2 Maureen Baker and Shelley Phipps, 'Canada,' in *Family Change and Family Policies in Britain, Canada, New Zealand and the U.S.*, Sheila Kamerman and Alfred Kahn, eds. (Oxford: Oxford University Press, 1997), 103–206.
3 Maureen Baker, 'Gender Inequality and Divorce Laws: A Canadian Perspective,' in *Family Matters* (1997), issue 46: 51–5.
4 Maureen Baker, 'Social Assistance and the Employability of Mothers: Two Models from Cross-National Research,' in *Canadian Journal of Sociology* (1996), 21(4): 483–50.
5 Gøsta Esping-Andersen, *The Three Worlds of Welfare Capitalism* (Cambridge: Polity Press, 1990).
6 Maureen Baker, *Canadian Family Policies: Cross-National Comparisons* (Toronto: University of Toronto Press, 1995), and Maureen Baker and David Tippin, *Poverty, Social Assistance and the Employability of Mothers: Restructuring Welfare States* (Toronto: University of Toronto Press, 1999).
7 Jane Kelsey, *Economic Fundamentalism* (London: Pluto Press, 1995).
8 Ian Shirley, Peggy Koopman-Boyden, Ian Pool, and Susan St John, 'New Zealand,' in *Family Change and Family Policies in Britain*, 207–304.
9 Baker and Tippin, *Poverty, Social Assistance, and Mothers*.
10 Ibid.
11 Jean Dumas and Alain Bélanger, *Report on the Demographic Situation in Canada 1996* (Ottawa: Ministry of Industry, 1997), 19.
12 Jonathan Bradshaw, Steven Kennedy, Majella Kilkey, Sandra Hutton, Anne Corden, Tony Eardley, Hilary Holmes, and Joanne Neale, *Policy and Employment of Lone Parents in 20 Countries* (Brussels: Commission of European Communities, 1996).

13 Ministry of Education, Education Statistics *News-Sheet*, vol. 7, no. 2 (New Zealand: Ministry of Education, April 1997).

14 Sue Kedgley, *Mum's the Word: The Untold Story of Motherhood in New Zealand* (Auckland: Random House,1996), 304.

15 Statistics New Zealand, *Unpaid Work* (Wellington: Statistics New Zealand, 1998).

16 New Zealand Government, *Childcare Subsidy: A Guide for Parents and Caregivers* (Wellington: New Zealand Government, 1996).

17 All figures are in Canadian dollars, calculated according to the exchange rate on 12 March 1999. $1 New Zealand = $.81 Canadian, and $1 Australian = $.97 Canadian.

18 New Zealand Government, *Budget: Work Focused Welfare* (Press Release, 14 May 1998.

19 Maureen Baker, 'Restructuring Welfare States: Ideology and Policies for Low-Income Mothers,' *Social Policy Journal of New Zealand* 8 (March 1997), 37–48.

20 Statistics New Zealand, *New Zealand Official Yearbook 1998*, 327 (Wellington: Author, 1998).

21 Maureen Baker, 'Advocacy, Political Alliances and the Implementation of Family Policies,' in J. Polkingham and G. Ternowsky (eds.), *Child and Family Policy: Struggles, Strategies and Options* (Toronto: Fernwood Publishing, 1997).

22 Kedgley, *Mum's the Word*, 335.

23 New Zealand Government, *Budget*.

24 Statistics New Zealand, *New Zealand Official Yearbook 1998* (Wellington: Statistics New Zealand, 1998), 575.

25 Baker and Tippin, *Poverty, Social Assistance, and Mothers*.

26 Bruce Bradbury, *Income Support for Parents and Other Carers* (Sydney: University of New South Wales, Social Policy Research Centre, 1996).

27 Ibid.

28 Ilene Wolcott and H. Glezer, *Work and Family Life: Achieving Integration* (Melbourne: Australian Institute of Family Studies, 1995), 145.

29 Ibid., 146.

30 Baker and Tippin, *Poverty, Social Assistance, and Mothers*.

31 Australia Department of Industrial Relations, *Work and Family Resource Kit* (Canberra: Australia Department of Industrial Relations, Work and Family Unit, 1996).

32 Australian Bureau of Statistics (ABS), *The Labour Force Australia* (Canberra: Department of Industrial Relations, ABS, Catalogue #6203.0, 1994).

33 Wolcott and Glezer, *Work and Family Life*, 147.

34 Y. Ergas, 'Child-Care Policies in Comparative Perspective: An Introductory Discussion,' in *Lone-Parent Families. The Economic Challenge* Organization for Economic Cooperation and Development (OECD), ed. (Paris: OECD, 1990), 201–22.

35 Gay Ochiltree, 'Child Care in the English-Speaking Countries with Reference to Australia,' in *Child Care in Context: Cross-Cultural Perspectives*, M.E. Lamb, K.J. Sternberg, C. Hwang, and A.G. Broberg, eds. (Hillsdale, NJ: Lawrence Erlbaum Associates, 1992).

36 Represented by the National Association of Community Based Children's Services.

37 Jennifer Curtin and Marian Sawer, 'Gender Equity in the Shrinking State: Women and the Great Experiment,' in *The Great Experiment: Labour Parties and Public Policy Transformation in Australia, and New Zealand*, F. Castles, R. Gerritsen, and J. Vowles, eds. (Auckland: Auckland University Press, 1996), 149–69; and Gisela Kaplan, *The Meagre Harvest: The Australian Women's Movement 1950–1990s* (Sydney: Allen and Unwin, 1996), 54.

38 Australia, Child Care Task Force Interim Report, in *Future Child Care Provision in Australia* (Canberra: Australian Government Publishing Service, 1996).

39 Ergas, 'Child-Care Policies.'

40 Ochiltree, 'Child Care in the English-Speaking Countries.

41 Wolcott and Glezer, *Work and Family Life.*

42 Baker and Tippin, *Poverty, Social Assistance, and Mothers.*

43 Curtin and Sawer, 'Gender Equity.'

44 Baker and Tippin, *Poverty, Social Assistance, and Mothers.*

45 Ibid.

46 Paul Henman, *Constructing Families and Disciplining Bodies: A Socio-Technical Study of Computers, Policy and Governance in Australia's Department of Social Security* (Unpublished doctoral thesis, University of Queensland, 1996).

47 Baker and Tippin. *Poverty, Social Assistance, and Mothers.*

48 Paul Henman, *Constructing Families.*

49 Michael Bittman and Jocelyn Pixley. *The Double Life of the Family: Myth, Hope and Experience* (Sydney: Allen and Unwin, 1997).

50 National Family Day Care Council (NFDCC), *Jigsaw: The Magazine for the NFDCCA*, issue 3 (Australia: Author, 1996).

51 Regulated child care in the providers' home of several children, often in addition to her own.

52 NFDCC, *Jigsaw*, 11.

53 Ibid., 13.

54 Baker and Tippin, *Poverty, Social Assistance, and Mothers.*
55 Michelle Gunn, 'Suffer the Children as Care Slashed,' *Australian Online* (14 May 1997).
56 Ibid.
57 Tom Allard, 'No Relief from Soaring Child-Care Fees,' *Sydney Morning Herald* (13 May 1998); available at http://www.smh.com.au/cgi-bin/archive.cgi
58 Deborah Brennan, *The Politics of Australian Child Care* (Melbourne: Cambridge University Press, 1998).
59 Baker and Tippin, *Poverty, Social Assistance, and Mothers.*
60 Ibid.
61 Bittman and Pixley, *Double Life of the Family*; and Maureen Baker, 'Marginalizing Unpaid Work: Employability and Social Assistance,' keynote address presented to the Sociology Association of Aotearoa / New Zealand, Napier, New Zealand, 28 November 1998.
62 Baker, 'Marginalizing Unpaid Work.'
63 Patricia Evans, Lesley A. Jacobs, Alin Noel, and Elisabeth B. Reynolds, *Workfare: Does it Work? Is it Fair?* (Montreal: Institute for Research on Public Policy, 1995); Eric Shragge, ed. *Workfare: Ideology for a New Under-Class* (Toronto: Garamond, 1997); Baker and Tippin, *Poverty, Social Assistance, and Mothers.*

18. Canadian Values and the Evolution of Child Care Policy

Kathy O'Hara
Treasury Board

This chapter explores the ways in which Maureen Baker's and Anne Gauthier's chapters reflect the evolution in the policy discourse or debate on child care, at least in Canada, since the mid-1980s. Material presented in the two chapters is supplemented by my own research on family policy in eight countries which is presented in the Canadian Policy Research Network study entitled *Comparative Family Policy: Eight Countries' Stories*.[1] I will argue that the debate on child care has evolved considerably over the past fifteen years in a direction that is more consistent with Canadian values and preferences, but that to achieve progress on child care, the issue must be clearly positioned in a way that reflects that evolution in the debate and thus is seen to resonate with Canadians' values.

THREE THEMES IN THE EVOLUTION OF THE DEBATE ON CHILD CARE IN CANADA

It can be argued that the way in which we think and talk about child care, at least in Canada, has evolved significantly in the past fifteen years in three ways:

1 Child care is no longer discussed exclusively as an employment support policy, but is seen as a multidimensional policy that provides support to families balancing work and family responsibilities as well as early education and child development opportunities, which are increasingly viewed as vital investments in children at a key point in their life cycle.

2 There is increasing focus on the need to value both the caring for children in the home by a parent and the care provided in public child care facilities, although this may be expressed through different policy instruments.
3 Child care is increasingly seen as one policy in an extensive inventory of policy instruments that governments can use to address the needs of families and children, whose scope reflects the wide range of choices that Canadians make about caring for their children.

With respect to the first change in our thinking, Maureen Baker's chapter indicates that the orientation of child care services to child development and preschool education rather than employment support for mothers has always been more evident in New Zealand than in Canada, although it is less clear whether the same conclusion can be drawn with respect to Australia. Although Anne Gauthier's chapter does not deal directly with this issue, the comparative family policy literature provides evidence that many countries in Western Europe, such as Italy and Spain, have high levels of children's attendance in public child care facilities despite having relatively low female labour force participation rates. In these countries, the provision of child care is linked to early childhood development, so much so that child care services are often delivered by ministries of education rather than social services. France has a high female participation rate in the labour force, but this alone cannot account for the statistic quoted in the Gauthier chapter that 95 per cent of children age three to school age are enrolled in *écoles maternelles* which are operated by the Ministry of Education.

In Canada, throughout the late 1980s and early 1990s, child care tended to be discussed by both advocates and governments as an employment support strategy. For example, the federal government's discussion paper entitled 'Improving Social Security in Canada,' which was released in 1993, discussed child care in the chapter on working, under the heading 'Meeting the Needs of Working Parents,' rather than in the learning chapter or the security chapter that dealt with a number of other children's issues.[2] (Nonetheless, it should be noted that the document did include in the security chapter the notion of linking child care and child development, and the section on child care in the working chapter described child care as lying at the heart of the three areas – working, learning, and security – addressed in the discussion paper.) In the late 1990s the accumulating evidence about the importance of investing in child development in the first five years of a child's life has ensured that the discourse around child care consistently integrates the policy objective of child development.

The second way in which the debate on child care has evolved in Canada is in the increasing focus on the need to value care for children provided in the home as well as in public child care facilities. Baker's chapter describes the pressure in both New Zealand and Australia for support for parents who care for their children at home which led to the introduction of the Parenting Allowance in Australia for parents caring for children at home, and appears to account for the Domestic Purposes Benefit in New Zealand which provides income support to enable lone parents to care for their children at home. As Baker notes, efforts in both countries to introduce employability programs for lone parents on welfare were resisted in both countries on the grounds that full-time employment would interfere with mothering.

The debate in Canada on support for parents who stay at home to care for children has recently intensified. Unlike New Zealanders and Australians, however, Canadians tend to be ambivalent with respect to lone parents, often simultaneously calling for income support for stay-at-home parents and increased emphasis on employment for lone parents on welfare (despite the lack of affordable child care). As Baker concludes, however, the child care lobby needs to recognize the value of care provided in the home, and governments need to ensure that both care in the home and public child care services are supported.

One particular experiment that is worth following is the recent introduction in Norway of a child care allowance for families that do not have a space in a child care facility. As of August 1998 these families receive a grant that corresponds to the government subsidy for a full-day care space. A similar allowance was introduced in Sweden and subsequently abolished, although many expect that this issue will return to the public debate there. This approach allows families to use the grant to purchase a child care space or to supplement the income of parents who choose to provide care for their children at home.

The third and most significant way in which the policy discourse on child care has evolved in Canada is reflected in the very fact that a major child care symposium such as this asks what other policies are needed to complement child care. This reflects a growing recognition that families with children have a wider range of needs and make a wider variety of choices about caring for their children than can adequately be addressed in a single policy instrument. Both chapters describe the range of policies used by other countries to support families and children, including income support, maternity and parental leave policies, spending on education and health, and child care services.

Canadians, like many Western Europeans, express a high level of ambivalence in their attitudes about mothers participating in the labour force and the impact of this on their children. While values studied in the eight countries included in my research showed that a majority of people in these countries believe that both the husband and wife should contribute to the household income, a majority also believe that a preschool child is likely to suffer if his or her mother works. The data for 1995 show 70 per cent of Canadians supporting dual-earner families, but 55 per cent (up from 52 per cent in 1991) agreeing that preschool children are likely to suffer in such families. Kamerman and Kahn, two experts in comparative family policy, have argued that this ambivalence explains the limited development of infant and toddler care in the United States.[3]

In Canada, unlike some other countries, this ambivalence has combined with low support for government intervention in the family to inhibit the development of family policies, including child care. Gauthier's chapter concludes that Canada ranks at best in an average position, and at worst in a very low position, in the level of support provided by the state to families, the exception being the province of Quebec which does have a family policy in place, unlike the rest of Canada. Interestingly, one of the speakers at the symposium argued that positioning child care in the context of a package of family policies in Quebec was critical to its success. Given Canadians' ambivalence about dual-earner families and the impact on children, if the issue of child care is to resonate with Canadians' values, it should be positioned as part of a broad package of family policies which reflects the research on early child development, the preferences of some parents to care for their children at home, and the wide range of choices that parents make about caring for their children.

Notes

1 Kathy O'Hara, *Comparative Family Policy: Eight Countries' Stories* (Ottawa: Canadian Policy Research Network, 1999).

2 Human Resources Development Canada. *Improving Social Security in Canada: A Discussion Paper* (Ottawa: Author, 1994).

3 S.B. Kamerman and A.J. Khan, eds., *Family Change and Family Policies in Great Britain, Canada, New Zealand and the United States*, vol. 1 from the series *Family Change and Family Policies in the West* (Oxford: Clarendon Press, 1997), 333.

19. How the Composition and Level of Support for Families Affects Children

Shelley Phipps
Department of Economics, Dalhousie University

This section compares the package of family and child care policies available in Canada with those available in a variety of other relatively affluent countries. Maureen Baker focuses upon Canada in comparison with Australia and New Zealand, while Anne Gauthier compares Canada with a much wider set of countries (mainly adding European countries to the comparison). The advantage for Canadian policy analysts of looking at what exists elsewhere is that it can help us to remove our 'blinkers' and to see entirely new ways of doing things – some of which may be suitable for application to Canada, and others which may not. For example, Canada is 'younger,' geographically larger, and more ethnically diverse than many of the European countries with which it is compared.

The set of countries examined by Baker are all from what Esping-Andersen has labelled the 'liberal' cluster of welfare states.[1] However, while these countries share a concern with maintaining work incentives and tend to prefer targeted to universal transfers, Baker's discussion demonstrates that there is nonetheless substantial variation in the policy mix available in the three. (The United States is typically also included in this cluster, and as Canadians are aware, offers a different blend of programs for families with children than is available in Canada.) Gauthier's set of countries ranges more widely across 'social democratic' welfare states (such as Sweden, Finland, and Norway) and 'conservative-corporatist' states such as Germany and the Netherlands. Focusing on a smaller set of countries has the advantage of allowing for a more detailed analysis; ranging more widely has the advantage of opening up the range of alternatives that exist. We benefit from having both sorts of approaches.

In reading the two chapters, I was struck that it is very important to think about the full 'package' of child care and family policies available in any country – it is unfair and incomplete to talk about only one aspect of the package in isolation. What follows is an informal synopsis of alternative ways in which countries can allocate resources to child care and/or family policy. Funds can be specifically allocated for child-care-related purposes: (1) through publicly supported child care; (2) through vouchers enabling parents to make their own choices among private child care options; (3) through tax exemptions for expenditures on child care; and (4) any combinations of (1) to (3).

Funds can be allocated to families through the general tax and transfer system in a way that is not specifically earmarked for child care, but that could nonetheless be used for child care (at least indirectly by freeing up resources from other purposes). Major ways in which resources are allocated to families with children in the countries studied by Gauthier and Baker include (1) tax exemptions and/or non-refundable credits for dependant children; (2) universal family allowances; and (3) refundable child tax credits (effectively a family allowance payment that is targeted to lower-income families rather than universally available).

A third key component of the family policy / child care package available in any country is the way in which the state acknowledges the needs of parents and children, not just in terms of financial resources, but in terms of time. Thus, both Baker and Gauthier discuss the maternity and parental leave provisions available in different countries in addition to other forms of time off such as days off for sick children or rights to part-time employment while a child is young. When we are talking about such leave provisions, we are very much at the interface between the family and the labour market. Such policies are particularly relevant for countries in which mothers are very likely to work for pay outside the home.

As mentioned above, it is important to think about the entire package of programs available in a country in order to give a fair picture of support for families with children. For example, one country may offer little in the way of public child care, but offer significant general income support for families with children, which could be used to purchase child care, among other things. Of course, it is also true, as Gauthier points out, that the overall *level* of support offered families with children in most other countries studied is much higher than is currently available in Canada. Thus, it is not just the case that some countries offer more in the way of publicly provided child care; it is also true that these same countries offer more in the way of income support and more in the way of time off to accommodate family responsibilities (e.g., Sweden, Finland, and France).

But, suppose that two countries devoted the same level of resources to each child, though packaged differently. For example, suppose that one country offered more publicly provided day care and less in the way of tax exemptions for dependant children. Would this make any difference from the perspective of mothers, fathers, or children? An emerging literature in economics on the distribution of resources *within* families suggests that it can matter very much *how* resources are allocated to families. First, there is evidence that money given to the mother is more likely to be used to benefit the child than money given to the father. For example, Lundberg, Pollak, and Wales present an econometric study of the implications of a major policy shift in the United Kingdom in the late 1970s, when a tax exemption for dependant children, benefiting the father, was changed into a sizable family allowance, benefiting the mother.[2] This policy shift was associated with an increase in the ratio of children's clothing to father's clothing. Of course, expenditures on children's clothing are not the best proxy for children's well-being (are babies really better off with designer sleepers?), but the evidence is consistent with folk wisdom in Canada that funds intended to benefit children should be given to mothers (dating back to the 1940s and debates about family allowances going to mothers).

An additional piece of econometric evidence indicates that, among couples in which both mother and father work full-time, full-year, and controlling for occupations, education and other relevant socio-demographic characteristics of the family, increases in mother's income were associated with increases in child care expenditures while increases in father's income had no statistically significant relationship with child care expenditures.[3]

Janet Currie presents additional evidence that from the perspective of the child's well-being, it can make a difference how resources are directed to the family. Currie's conclusion, using data for the United States, is that in-kind transfers 'deliver' more than cash transfers in terms of improving child well-being.[4] This contradicts conventional wisdom among economists that it is better to give people income and let them choose how to spend it than to give them in-kind transfers that constrain their choices. Of course, children can't be given income directly. Income must be given to their parents, and some of any income transfer will presumably be used to benefit the child, but some of it will be used for other purposes.

In summary, a growing literature in economics indicates that the implications for individual family members of alternative policy packages can be quite different and that, in general, it may be better to give cash to mothers than to fathers; better to give in-kind transfers to children than cash transfers to parents.

Since different countries do offer rather different combinations of policies, we might therefore expect to see that outcomes for children vary across the countries. For me, one of the most interesting things we can try to learn from cross-national comparisons is whether there is a different way of doing policy in Canada that would help to improve outcomes for children and parents. (Gauthier's chapter takes the same theme.) Unfortunately, it is very hard to draw definitive conclusions about the relationship between very complicated combinations of policies and very complicated measures of well-being for parents and/or children.

Still, the descriptive evidence is at least not inconsistent with the idea that children do fare better in many countries than they do in Canada, and that countries in which children do better are the countries that spend more on programs for children. First, as Gauthier points out, children are more likely to be poor in Canada than in almost any other country (the United States and United Kingdom excepted), and this is largely a result of more generous systems of taxes and, especially, transfers available elsewhere. Second, in terms of measures such as infant mortality or low-weight births, Canada's record is not as good as many of the European countries. Third, my own research using the new National Longitudinal Survey of Children and Youth (NLSCY), as well as comparable micro-data sets for Norway and the United States, indicates that children are sometimes but not always better off in Canada than the United States.[5] My research also indicates that children are quite consistently better off in Norway than in Canada (e.g., in terms of experience of asthma, accidents requiring medical attention, fear, anxiety, and limitations on their activities.

Why is this so? This is a hard question to answer definitively at this stage, though it is clear that Norway offers much more in the way of cash transfers and tax benefits for families with children, particularly single-parent families. It is also clear that Norwegian policy is much more supportive of the dual role of parent and employee than is Canadian policy. Rates of participation in the labour force participation are not dissimilar across the two countries, but a more supportive interface between family and labour market may, in fact, be the reason Norwegian children are so much less anxious than Canadian children. More research in this area is clearly warranted.

Note

1 G. Esping-Andersen, *Three Worlds of Welfare Capitalism* (Cambridge: Polity Press, 1990).
2 S. Lundberg, R.A. Pollak, and T. Wales, 'Do Husbands and Wives Pool Their Resources? Evidence from the U.K. Child Benefit,' *Journal of Human Resources* 32:3 (1997), 463–80.
3 S. Phipps and P. Burton, 'What's Mine Is Yours? The Influence of Male and Female Incomes on Patterns of Household Expenditure,' *Economica* 65:260 (1998), 599–613.
4 J. Currie and D. Thomas, 'Does Head Start Make a Diference?' *American Economic Review* 85:3 (1995), 341–64.
5 S. Phipps, 'An International Comparison of Policies and Outcomes for Young Children,' *CPRN Study No. F05* (Ottawa: Canadian policy Research Networks, 1999).

Discussion

The family policy session, because of its focus on the array of policies affecting children and families, generated several broad questions. These tended to bring out some of the basic trade-offs implicit in the design of a comprehensive child care policy.

The first question raised the issue of whether the interests of children and parents might ever be in conflict. The benefits to children from good child care are generally phrased in terms of child development, while the benefits to working mothers revolve around the gains that accrue to adults because of permanent attachment to the labour force. Yet the pure child development function might require less than thirty hours of care each week, while most jobs require significantly more care than that.

Maureen Baker responded by noting that this conflict comes out in systems that require children to move from one kind of service to another (from nursery school to part-day day care centre, for example). Since, in general, these kinds of moves are bad for children, we need more integrated services. Anne Gauthier responded by observing that the conflict is less between parents and children than between employers and parents. This occurs because the law in some countries may require employers to accommodate the work disruptions that affect the parents of young children.

A second question raised the issue of parental leave and how it fits into a comprehensive child care policy. One questioner suggested that there seemed to be a difference of opinion over whether parental leave benefited or harmed families (relative to child care for very young children). Another questioner, while admitting the need for a variety of different programs for families, cautioned the group against buying in to the notion of offering too wide a menu of choices to families, since this would undercut the designing of a comprehensive policy.

In response, Baker reminded the group that the provisions of unpaid parental leave posed serious problems for some families. Gauthier commented that although Sweden allows either parent to take parental leave (to a maximum of four hundred and fifty days), fathers took less than 5 per cent of the leaves. In contrast, Norway provides parental leave for both parents, but does not allow transferability between parents. Yet it is unclear whether Canadians would tolerate such an arrangement. She suggested that we should allow individual parents to judge whether parental leave helps or hinders them.

Shelley Phipps developed this point, suggesting that although women's careers were clearly hurt by being out of the labour force, the damage was much less in Sweden than it was in Canada, despite the much longer leaves at the birth of a child. This seems to be linked to the design of Sweden's parental leave policy, which guarantees the mother's right to reclaim her job after an absence caring for young children. This result also is consistent with our findings that the loss in future wages caused by a temporary absence from the labour force was greater for those who changed jobs than for those returning to the same job. Phipps reminded us that in Canada, maternity and parental benefits were provided in large part through the Employment Insurance Act, so that every time policy on employment insurance changed, there was an accompanying (and often unforeseen) change in maternity and parental benefits.

Gauthier then suggested that some mothers might be helped by the option of continuing to work, but reducing hours. Yet, as she pointed out, this works only if part-time child care is available in any comprehensive policy.

Underlying this discussion was the issue of values. Several questioners returned to Kathy O'Hara's warning against relying on polls to determine values, since often the more subtle polls revealed that there were underlying conflicts in individual's views on child care. Maureen Baker reminded us that poll results suggesting that mothers want to be at home with their children may reflect social pressures that result in working mothers continuing to do all the housework while being made to feel bad about being away from their families.

PART 6

Single Parents, Child Poverty, and Children at Risk:
What Special Child Care Policies Are Needed?

Introduction

The fifth session of the symposium looked at the special needs and circumstances of some families who use child care. A comprehensive child care policy such as that proposed in the Cleveland and Krashinsky monograph tends to look at child care in an integrated way. Child care services would be provided universally to all young children who want to use them. Yet, in Canada to date, much of the direct public funding for child care has focused on children from poor families – largely those with single parents – and on other children at risk. Providing funding for all children will represent a break from this focus. However, the needs of disadvantaged children or children in poor families may be different and more intense, and their parents may require different types of assistance. Future child care policy will have to meet these needs within the context of a more universal early childhood program.

The Cleveland and Krashinsky proposal assumed that parents would contribute 20 per cent of the cost of a reformed child care program, yet the current structure of welfare in Canada would make this kind of contribution difficult for most recipients of social assistance to afford. Such a fee could result in a serious disincentive for poor parents to enter the labour force and to use child care. How might the parental contribution be structured to avoid this difficulty?

Disadvantaged children will likely require different and more intensive types of programming than other children in child care. Research shows that most children are helped by good child care, but that the largest pay-offs exist for resources directed towards the most disadvantaged children. How could these children and these programs be integrated into a comprehensive child care system, and what effects might we expect from this?

The presenters were chosen because of the research work they have done on the design and effects of child care programs. Michael Krashinsky is a professor of economics and Gordon Cleveland is a senior lecturer in economics in the Division of Management at the University of Toronto at Scarborough. They have a long-standing interest in child care, wrote the monograph that served as the background for the symposium, and were the organizers of the symposium. They both have done significant research on welfare systems and child care funding.

Gina Browne is a professor of nursing and clinical epidemiology and biostatistics at McMaster University. She is founder and director of the System-Linked Research Unit on Health and Social Service Utilization. In this capacity, she shapes proposals and executes projects that seek to inform the priorities of various health and social service planning and provider agencies. She has served as principal or co-investigator on approximately forty-five different projects. Her report 'When the Bough Breaks' presents the results of one experiment in intersectoral service strategies.

The three discussants have had considerable involvement in child care and social assistance issues. Richard Budgell is the national manager with Health Canada of the Aboriginal Head Start program for urban and northern communities; he was involved in the initial development of the program. Michael Goldberg is the research director at the Social Planning and Research Council of British Columbia. He has developed a variety of child care programs and been involved in a number of studies of child care while with SPARC. Donna Lero is an associate professor in the Department of Family Relations and Applied Nutrition at the University of Guelph and co-director of the university's new Centre for Families, Work, and Well-being. She has been co-director or principal investigator on a number of child care studies, including the Canadian National Child Care Study and the You Bet I Care! project.

The principal contributors to this part come at the topic from different approaches. Krashinsky and Cleveland look at how parental payments for child care might be integrated with the social assistance system. The current Canadian welfare system has serious disincentives for work because of the rate at which benefits are reduced when recipients enter the labour force. Current proposals for a national child care system often involve parents making a significant contribution towards the cost. Such a child care fee would worsen work disincentives to the point where few welfare parents would participate in the child care program. Krashinsky and Cleveland suggest that a graduated scale of fees would have to be used to restore some work incentive to the system of child care payment. Such a scale would typically charge no fee to families with low incomes, and would raise the fee gradually so that median income families would make a more significant contribution to the program. The trade-offs in such a program design can be quite dramatic, so that there are significant relationships between the maximum fee charged to wealthier parents and the minimum income at which fees begin to be assessed. In any case, Krashinsky and Cleveland suggest that special developmental child care programs would have to be offered to disadvantaged children within the system.

Gina Browne's chapter, co-authored with Joanne Roulston of the National Council of Welfare and a number of other authors, presents research on providing special services, including child care, to lone mothers on welfare. By comparing those who received these special services with a control group who received no services, they were able to show that all of the special services had very large pay-offs. The key, they argue, is to look at all public services being used by the families. Although it costs money to help these families, the result is that they make use of fewer other services, so that the public sector as a whole saves money. In most cases, public spending on special services for these families would pay for itself within two years. Of course, this looks only at public spending, leaving aside improvements in well-being that are not reflected in reduced public expenditures. The study did, however, examine a wide range of health-related public expenditures. The moral is that public spending on child care aimed at disadvantaged children will pay for itself, even if one takes a more limited view of costs and benefits than did the original Cleveland and Krashinsky monograph.

The three discussants approach these issues from somewhat different perspectives. Richard Budgell suggests that it is important to look at the particular cultural characteristics of poor children, since this would inform the ways in which child care programs were designed. For example, large numbers of poor children in Canada's cities are either Aboriginal or recent immigrants to Canada. Thus, we need to be sensitive to the cultural characteristics of participants.

Donna Lero argues that the focus on labour force participation for poor lone parents might be problematic. Many of these recipients are not employable, and full-time employment may increase stress and degrade outcomes for both the mothers and the children.

Michael Goldberg focuses on the benefits of child care, especially for disadvantaged children. This being the case, fees make little sense if they discourage use. Furthermore, if the problem is the work disincentive built into welfare programs, then it makes more sense to reform the programs themselves instead of designing a national child care system around those flaws.

20. What Special Arrangements Are Necessary for Lone-Parent Families in a Universal Child Care Program?

Gordon Cleveland and Michael Krashinsky
Division of Management, University of Toronto at Scarborough

There have been, until recently, three different approaches to providing child care assistance in Canada. The first, beginning in a coordinated way in 1966, was provision of subsidies to low-income families using licensed child care services. Although these subsidies were cost-shared between federal and provincial (or federal and territorial) governments, they were not available to most families. The income eligibility criteria restricted them to use by lone-parent families, to a very significant extent. In Ontario and the Northwest Territories, a needs test for subsidy eligibility was used, with similar effects. The intent of these subsidies, which typically required the parent to be in the labour force or in preparation to enter the labour force, was primarily to provide an alternative to social assistance for some low-income mothers of young children. A secondary objective was to provide good quality developmental opportunities for children of lone-parent families during the working day.

The second form of government assistance to child care has been the provision of tax relief to parents paying for child care, based on the amount of their child care expenses. The intent of the Child Care Expense Deduction, beginning in 1972, was to remove income which pays for employment-related child care expenditures from being subject to taxation and therefore to reduce otherwise punitive levels of effective taxation on mothers entering the labour force. This type of assistance has only been available to the lower income earner in a family and only to those who were able to obtain a receipt for child care expenses from their caregiver. It has covered users of all different types of paid child care, both licensed and unlicensed.

The third form of governmental assistance to child care, in different provinces and territories at different amounts at different times in the 1980s and 1990s, has been the provision of direct operating grants to providers of licensed child care services. Typically, the stated intent of governments providing operating, maintenance, and wage-enhancement grants was to improve the quality of care and the remuneration of caregivers in licensed facilities.

These different types of child care assistance have had different objectives and have been targeted at different groups of families. The question we wish to raise in this chapter is whether a new form of child care funding will still effectively address these objectives and help these groups of families. The new form of funding is universal funding, along the lines of the proposal discussed in our recent study *The Benefits and Costs of Good Child Care: The Economic Rationale for Public Investment in Young Children – A Policy Study.*[1] A broadly similar model of funding has been adopted recently by the Quebec government, covering licensed child care services for children from zero to five years of age (being implemented in stages). In both cases, there is an important parental contribution (20 per cent in our study, $5 per day in Quebec), but the lion's share of the funding is provided by the public purse.

On the face of it, it would seem as if the issues addressed by the Child Care Expense Deduction and by operating grants are largely resolved by a move to universal funding. In our study, we calculated the average price of full-day, high-quality child care to be $8,500 per year; parents using full-day care would pay, on average, 20 per cent of this, or $1,700 per year. Part-time users of child care would pay less. In any case, the burden of child care expenses, for high-quality care, would be much less than that faced by many families at present. The Child Care Expense Deduction might stay in place after the commencement of universal funding to address the needs of those families, perhaps with unusual work schedules, who continue to use expensive in-home forms of care. However, the role of the deduction would be greatly diminished by the general fall in parental child care expenses.

Operating grants have been designed to improve the quality of child care and/or enhance wages in licensed facilities. Our universal funding proposal is premised on excellent staff-child ratios, extensive use of staff with considerable training and education in early childhood care and development, and a corresponding increase in wages or salaries and benefits. In Quebec, the ratio of trained to untrained staff has been doubled (for four-year-olds at least), and the premier has promised substantial wage enhancements soon. Although there may be important transitional problems with the quality of care in some places in Quebec, universal funding would appear to supersede the role of operating grants.

The question we wish to address is whether the special needs of lone parents and their children would be adequately addressed in a system of universal funding of child care. If not, what special arrangements should be provided to address these needs? Should existing subsidy programs continue to exist? If not, should they change or be abolished as redundant?

It is our view that a comprehensively funded child care program would involve a fundamental shift in the way child care and working women are viewed in our society – or, at least, in public policy. Policy towards young children in Canada has, in a very basic way, lagged significantly behind the economic realities facing working mothers and their families. In 1967 only 17 per cent of women with children under the age of six years participated in the labour force. By 1997 that number had risen to 67 per cent. The labour force participation rate of women with young children is now higher than the participation rate for all adult women, suggesting that what has occurred is a generational shift in attitude. Even as late as the 1960s, women with young children generally stayed at home and cared for them unless some unusual circumstance made work either personally desirable or economically necessary. It is now apparent that a clear and growing majority of young women with children regard lifelong attachment to the labour force as a natural state of affairs, and the regular use of some kind of paid arrangement for young children as a natural implication.

Unfortunately, the current arrangements being made for those young children are, overall, less than is desirable. We have proposed that policy must evolve to provide affordable high-quality child care to all families with young children. This kind of policy, which views provision of subsidized child care services as the norm, is clearly very different from the child care subsidies currently provided to lone parents based on need. How the latter policy would have to evolve is the subject of this chapter.

In the next section, we discuss some issues of how a comprehensive child care system is likely to affect lone parents and their employment. We recommend special child care subsidies for low-income parents, especially lone parents. These subsidies would, as a condition of eligibility, require parents to be engaged in training for employment or in employment itself, in the same way that current subsidy programs do.

Then we consider the special needs and programs that might be required for children at risk, or children needing enriched care, within the context of a general program of assistance to child care. Our conclusions are summarized in the final section.

LONE PARENTS, EMPLOYMENT, AND CHILD CARE ASSISTANCE

If a comprehensive child care system were designed along the lines of the proposal in our 1998 study, each family, whether having two parents or one parent, would be eligible for highly subsidized, high-quality early childhood education for preschool children. If parents were working full-time, they would be expected, on average, to contribute 20 per cent, or $1,700 (about $7 per day), of the total expected $8,500 annual cost of care. Should all such parents pay the same contribution, or should low-income parents, especially lone parents, contribute less?

One way to approach answering this question would be purely from an equity or social justice point of view. From this standpoint, no one with low income should be expected to pay for child care. Since we have argued in our earlier work that various types of market failure require that all families require a significant subsidy to encourage them to use high-quality child care, this would naturally suggest some kind of sliding scale (i.e., graduated fee). For example, families below a certain annual income – say $20,000 – might be required to pay nothing for child care. All other families might pay 12 per cent of family income above that cut-off, to some maximum which includes a significant subsidy – that maximum might be $8 or $10 per day per child. If we take $10 per day as the maximum charge and 12 per cent as the tax-back rate, we would find a family with an income of $30,000 paying $1,200 (about $5 per day) for child care; at $35,000, a family would pay $1,800 (about $7 per day); at $41,667 and above, a family with one child would pay the maximum of $2,500 per year (or $10 per day). Families with higher incomes could pay more if they had more than one child two to five years of age, but not more than the lesser of 12 per cent of income over $20,000 or $2,500 per child.

Since $45,000 to $50,000 is roughly the median family gross income in Canada, this would mean that special subsidies were available only to those families with incomes below the median. The low cut-off for full subsidy ($20,000) would mean that virtually all two-parent families would have to pay something for child care. And the numbers that we have chosen were designed to generate approximately the average payment of $7 per day necessary to cover 20 per cent of the cost of the program (see below for some discussion of this).

Notice that this scheme was apparently evolved with only equity in mind. But there are several important market considerations that suggest that such extra subsidization of the child care costs of lone-parent families would be appropriate. In particular, there are two special issues with respect to lone-parent families that should affect the amount they are charged for child care services. First, the available econometric evidence suggests that the employment behaviour of lone mothers is highly sensitive to economic variables. In other words, small differences in the costs of care, and of the take-home portion of the lone mother's wage, are likely to have important effects on the employment of lone mothers. Second, the design of social assistance systems in Canada gives very little monetary incentive to lone parents to be employed and stay employed.

These two issues are not unrelated. Lone mothers often cannot rely on financial assistance from other individuals, so that their families' well-being depends critically on the decision to enter the labour force. Naturally, then, these mothers would have to be far more sensitive to short-term economic considerations than would mothers in two-parent families. As will become clear, the design of social assistance systems in Canada is a considerable part of those 'short-term economic considerations.' We explore these points and their implications below.

We have summarized the evidence about lone mothers and employment in our earlier work this way:

> There is a distinct economic literature on the effects of child care on lone mothers.[2] It is virtually a consensus in this literature that the effects of child care costs (and availability) are strong; the decisions of lone mothers are likely to be more sensitive to changes in child care policy than are the decisions of married mothers. So, for instance, Cleveland and Hyatt, using data from the Canadian National Child Care Survey, find that a 10% rise in child care costs would lower the employment rate of lone mothers by about 6% (about 2 percentage points). In the US, Connelly finds that use of social assistance would fall from 20% to about 11% if child care costs were fully subsidized for unmarried mothers. In self-reported evidence, lone mothers in the Canadian National Child Care Survey who are currently working and paying for child care were asked whether they would change child care arrangements or leave their employment situation if the price of child care were to rise by 25% or more. Nearly 70% of single mothers

reported they would change child care arrangements under these circumstances, while nearly 40% reported that they would quit their jobs. On both counts, lone mothers were found to be considerably more sensitive than married mothers. Similarly, on both counts, never-married mothers were found to be more sensitive than divorced, separated or widowed mothers.

The effects of child care costs and availability on lone mothers may be strong but so too are numerous other factors; there has been a dramatic decrease in employment rates of single mothers in the last number of years in Canada, while the employment rates of married mothers have continued to rise. Many lone mothers with young children are potentially eligible for social assistance and other federal and provincial tax benefits. These payments are not exceedingly generous; for a single parent with one child, and ignoring the Yukon and Northwest Territories, they varied from about $11,000 in Alberta, New Brunswick, or Manitoba to about $16,000 in Ontario in 1995 (National Council of Welfare, 1997). Nonetheless, many lone mothers do not have extensive job experience or education and many have spent time out of the labour force with young children. Their anticipated employment earnings may supplement these social assistance and other payments, but given the almost punitive rates at which employment income is taxed-back from welfare recipients, the returns to employment will be meagre unless hourly wages are quite high. Child care costs may well be the straw that breaks the lone mother's back; unless child care expenses are fully subsidized, there will be little incentive to work for most lone mothers.[3]

Social Assistance and Employment

The importance of social assistance in the decision to work requires some discussion. Social assistance systems in Canada have a common design. All of them provide a basic income guarantee to those who have no other means of support; then they reduce this income payment dramatically as the family develops alternative means of support, such as a job. The rate of reduction of payments (the so-called tax-back rate) is usually very high (75 per cent to 100 per cent), so the incentive to get a job (generally a low-paying job) is very small, because the lone parent gets to keep very little of her new earnings. If we expect child care users to pay any significant fraction of the cost of child care, then this cost will represent a disincentive to work for lone parents requiring this kind of care. Adding this disincentive to the already significant work disincentives built into the current social assistance systems in Canada can be overwhelming.

For this reason, most welfare systems designed under the Canada Assistance Plan did not charge lone parents very much for child care, as long as any welfare payments were being received. Once the family ceased to be eligible for welfare, child care charges typically rose at some proportion (often half) of any increase in net income. The effect of this rule, however, was to extend the 'tax-back' range on lone-parent incomes to very high levels, and to further reduce the incentive to work. This problem can be illustrated simply in the following numeric example. Assume that a lone-parent family is eligible for $12,000 per year in social assistance. If the parent goes out to work, earned income is of course subject to normal taxes. Assume a simplification of the Canadian tax system, in which wages are subject to a 6 per cent payroll tax (Canada Pension Plan and Employment Insurance) and a 25 per cent joint federal and provincial income tax on earnings above $12,000 (roughly the amount of the personal credit and the equivalent-to-spouse credit) and below $30,000 (the tax rate rises to about 40 per cent on income over $30,000). Welfare payments are reduced by 75 per cent of net earnings (after the taxes discussed above), after subtracting an earnings exemption of $2,400 ($200 per month). We also assume work-related expenses (transportation, clothes, lunches) of $2,400 per year. Finally, we ignore other types of assistance received by the family (it is worth observing that many provincial welfare systems provide a variety of programs to welfare recipients, including drug and dental benefits, which often disappear when the family goes off welfare, and which thus represent a significant and often ignored obstacle to participation in the labour force – these have been the subject of recent federal-provincial discussions related to enhancement of the Canada Child Tax Benefit). We also model all other types of tax relief (the Child Tax Benefit and the GST credit, for example) as a simple transfer to the family of $2,400 per year, taxed back at the rate of 5 per cent for earned income above $20,000 (the actual structure of these programs is far more complicated, and do represent significant income for poor families; their reduction as earned income increases represents a significant further work disincentive; for simplicity we assume that these credits and the welfare system operate independently, even though this is not entirely the case). Cleveland and Hyatt offer a detailed discussion of the various programs available to low-income, lone-parent families.[4]

The simulation shown in Table 20.1 indicates the (lack of) work

Table 20.1. Family disposable income, after work expenses (in dollars)

Hourly wage	Annual wage	All taxes	Social assistance payment	Take-home income, after work expenses, before child care
0	0	−2,400	12,000	14,400
6	12,000	−1,680	5,340	16,620
8	16,000	−440	3,270	17,310
10	20,000	800	1,200	18,000
12	24,000	2,240	0	19,360
14	28,000	3,680	0	21,920
16	32,000	5,420	0	24,180
18	36,000	7,460	0	26,140
20	40,000	9,500	0	28,100

Notes: 1. Assume 40 hours of work per week, 50 weeks per year. 2. Taxes include payroll taxes of 6% of earned income, income taxes of 25% on income above $12,000 and 40% on income above $30,000, as well as refundable tax credits of $2400 minus 5% of income over $20,000. 3. Welfare payments are equal to $12,000 minus 75% of net earnings over $2400; net earnings are earned income minus payroll taxes and income taxes, but do not take account of refundable tax credits. 4. Welfare payments cease when earnings are $22,319.

incentives in a typical social assistance program, even before we consider any child care costs. The implications of this table are clear; social assistance recipients have little obvious reason to work if their wages are under about $12 per hour. All families who are eligible for social assistance could decide to stay out of the paid labour force. In that case, the hourly wage would be zero and the annual take-home income (final column) would be $14,400. At $12 per hour, the individual earns a gross wage of $24,000, but family disposable income rises (relative to not being employed) by less than $5,000 (to $19,360), after paying for work expenses, but before paying for child care. This $5,000 difference is a small incentive to go out to work, especially when one considers the additional loss of eligibility for other programs, and the risk of losing a job and then having to negotiate one's way back onto welfare again. Adding on any significant fee for child care will make full-time work all that much more unattractive, since even with free child care, the current welfare design provides little reason for single mothers with low wage expectations to join the labour force.

Yet there are lots of long-run reasons why work might be advantageous for these families, just as it is for two-parent families. First, we know that a mother's future wages will depend on the development and evolution of skills that can only be achieved through ongoing attachment to the labour force. For many individuals, a long stretch of time out of the labour force will erode skills and remove the worker from any possibility of promotions and wage increases. For that reason, continuing labour force participation can be vital for lone parents and highly advantageous for society in the long run.

Second, parents who participate in the labour force can serve as a role model to children. These children can also benefit from the kinds of experiences that we would expect in good quality child care and early childhood education. Thus, for a variety of reasons, children in lone-parent homes are likely to be better off in the long run when their mothers are in the labour force.

The design of child care subsidies for lone parents makes sense to us. To recap: we would propose a flat rate charge for good quality child care of $10 per child per full-day (this could vary by province, because of the different levels of average cost). We propose a flat rate, rather than a full sliding scale of fees in order to have full participation by all working parents. In other words, it is important that the maximum charge not be too high, even for parents with relatively high incomes. This presumes a specific public value in having the children of wealthier parents in child care, as opposed to using nannies or babysitters.

We would also propose a subsidy system, or sliding scale of fees, available to lower-income families. All families annually earning less than $20,000 (with income verified in some fashion, probably through income tax returns) would pay zero for child care. As gross income rises above $20,000, a fraction of the increase in income would be used to eliminate the extra child care subsidy, until the point where the family pays the maximum charge of $10 per child per day, or about $2,500 per year. (All income figures are stated before taxes, rather than after taxes; gross rather than net income.) We have not considered the exact mechanisms most appropriate for administering this subsidy arrangement.

Table 20.2 shows the impact of this proposal and several alternatives on the income of lone parent families with one child. Four possible fee arrangements are shown. Fee #1 simply charges all families with employed mothers the average fee of $1,700, independent of income. As can be seen from the table, this further erodes the work incentive for these mothers. For example, the mother who can earn $10 an hour ($20,000 per year) sees a benefit of less than $2,000 a year ($16,300 minus $14,400) from working, after paying for child care and other work expenses, and after taking into account taxes and the reduction in welfare benefits. Clearly, the impact on poor lone-parent families is

Table 20.2. Family disposable income, after child care costs, lone-parent families only (in dollars)

Hourly wage	Annual child care fee #1	Income after child care	Annual child care fee #2	Income after child care	Annual child care fee #3	Income after child care	Annual child care fee #4	Income after child care
0	0	14,400	0	14,400	0	14,400	0	14,400
6	1,700	14,920	0	16,620	0	16,620	0	16,620
8	1,700	15,610	0	17,310	0	17,310	0	17,310
10	1,700	16,300	0	18,000	0	18,000	0	18,000
12	1,700	17,660	2,000	17,360	1,000	18,360	480	18,880
14	1,700	20,220	2,500	19,420	2,000	19,920	960	20,960
16	1,700	22,480	2,500	21,680	2,500	21,680	1,440	22,740
18	1,700	24,440	2,500	23,640	2,500	23,640	1,920	24,220
20	1,700	26,400	2,500	25,600	2,500	25,600	2,400	25,700

Notes: The annual child care fee is the fee charged to the family under the various possible subsidy arrangements. Income after child care is the family's disposable income (income available for various consumption purchases) after work expenses and day care costs, as well as taxes and social assistance reductions are applied. Assume 40 hours of work per week, 50 weeks per year.

Taxes include payroll taxes of 6% of earned income, income taxes of 25% on income above $12,000 and 40% on income above $30,000, as well as refundable tax credits of $2400 minus 5% of income over $20,000. Welfare payments are equal to $12,000 minus 75% of net earnings over $2400; net earnings are earned income minus payroll taxes and income taxes, but do not take account of refundable tax credits. Welfare payments cease when earnings are $22,319.

Child care fees are computed based on ability to pay. Computations are performed for four possible fee arrangements: Fee #1 = $1,700 flat fee. Fee #2 = $0 fee for incomes below $20,000, rising at 50% of income to maximum of $2,500. Fee #3 = $0 below $20,000, rising at 25% of income to maximum of $2,500. Fee #4 = 0 below $20,000, rising at 12% of income to max of $2,500.

deleterious, both from an equity standpoint and in terms of the incentives to enter the labour force.

Fees #2, #3, and #4 all provide full subsidies to poor employed lone parents and vary only in the rate at which they reduce the subsidy as income rises. Clearly there is a trade-off to be considered here. For instance, if the subsidy is removed more quickly (Fee #2 = 50% tax-back rate), the effective tax rate on recipients earning just above $20,000 annually (or $10 per hour) is significant; however, this reduces the number of families receiving subsidies and thus would allow us to set a lower maximum on the fee charged to all families (as well as increasing the administrative convenience of this plan).

Trade-offs in Designing a Sliding Scale

To examine the various policy trade-offs in designing a sliding scale of child care fees, we looked at some data on the current income distribution for families with preschool children and computed what these families would pay on average per child under different subsidy rules. We used data on family income for mothers employed full-time in the labour force from the 1988 Canadian National Child Care Survey. There are problems with this calculation because of weaknesses in the underlying data, so the following should be considered an approximate example. However, these calculations can give us some flavour of the trade-offs that exist. Five alternative designs would raise the required revenues of close to $7 per child per day:

1 No fee below $10,000; clawback at 10 per cent; maximum fee $10 per child: raises $7.19 per child.
2 No fee below $15,000; clawback at 15 per cent; maximum fee $10 per child: raises $8.17 per child.
3 No fee below $20,000; clawback at 15 per cent; maximum fee $10 per child: raises $7.33 per child.
4 No fee below $20,000; clawback at 12 per cent; maximum fee $10 per child: raises $6.76 per child.
5 No fee below $20,000; clawback at 12 per cent; maximum fee $12 per child: raises $7.47 per child.

Looking at the first two calculations, we can see that increasing the fee more quickly as income rises (the clawback rate) allows us to raise more money, which in turn allows us to reduce the number of parents

paying fees by raising the minimum income at which fees begin. Similarly (looking at calculations 2 and 3) simply raising that minimum
income clearly reduces the amount of money raised by the fee, while
simply lowering the clawback rate (calculations 3 and 4) also reduces
what the fee will generate. Finally, increasing the maximum fee (calculations 4 and 5) obviously increases revenue. The scheme we have
focused on in our discussions above (Fee design #4) raises revenues
very close to the desired average of $7 per child.

We also calculated the percentage of families, all of whom are engaged in full-time employment, who would pay the minimum fee
under each program design and the average fee paid by each family.
The results are shown in Table 20.3. Clearly most of these 'special'
subsidies go to lone-parent families, because of their low family incomes. Of course, all families, whether one-parent or two-parent, are
assumed to receive good quality child care at a fraction of its full cost
under the proposed program.

Employment or Training Requirement

We have what is clearly an anomaly in the labour force participation of
mothers. Over the past two decades, while the labour force attachment
of all women, and particularly of mothers in two-parent families, has
been rising, the participation rates for lone mothers have been staying
constant at a low level. Today, roughly 35 per cent of lone mothers with
preschool children are in the labour force; this is about half of the
participation rate for mothers in two-parent families. The explanation
for this is complex, but the work disincentives built into the welfare
system in Canada are clearly a significant factor.

Let us assume that we cannot effectively modify the current welfare
system. One of the critical underlying assumptions in a comprehensive
child care program is that attachment to the labour force is a desirable
outcome for most mothers. Thus, it is critical that something be done to
counter the work-disincentive effects of the social assistance system.[5]
By itself, low cost (in the case of lone parents, essentially free) day care
will not do the trick. If mothers can use full-day child care while at the
same time staying at home, this compromises one of the significant
benefits in our cost-benefit calculations for the program. In addition,
significant evidence of this would, we believe, erode the political support for child care funding.

We would propose that the program take as its starting point the

TABLE 20.3. Amounts paid by lone-parent and two-parent families under alternative fee scales

Policy design no.	Average amount paid per family – lone-parent families	Average amount paid per family – two-parent families	Average amount paid per child – lone-parent families	Average amount paid per child – two-parent families	Percentage of families paying maximum fee – lone-parent families	Percentage of families paying maximum fee – two-parent families
1	$4.74	$9.87	$4.17	$7.50	8.7	63.1
2	$4.17	$11.35	$3.67	$8.63	11.9	71.9
3	$2.41	$10.34	$2.12	$7.86	7.9	61.8
4	$2.09	$9.55	$1.84	$7.26	8.7	50.7
5	$2.18	$10.57	$1.92	$8.04	2.6	42.6

assumption that women will have a lifelong attachment to the labour force. Work incentives can be made explicit within the day care system. At cost levels that we have discussed, day care will offer significant benefits to young children – developmental, educational, nutritional, and so on. The quid pro quo for this arrangement will be an expectation built into the child care subsidy system that all recipients of special subsidies, above the norm, either participate in or be preparing to participate in the labour force. Of course, some recipients will for a variety of physical or mental reasons, be unable to fulfil this requirement, a situation currently allowed for under most disability programs. But for those who are able to work, there will be a strong expectation of some kind of participation.

We leave unspecified the ways in which this expectation will be enforced. For example, those not working in the paid labour force may be required to engage in some form of educational or training programs as a requirement of receiving extra child care subsidy (by implication, child care without this special subsidy, at $10 per day, would be available irrespective of employment status). We do not believe that this will be seen as a coercive and unfair requirement. The current barriers to participation – day care that is of lower quality and unreliable supply, inadequate training and adult educational experiences, confiscatory tax-back rates – are far more decisive for most of those on welfare, we believe, than an inadequate long-run incentive to work.

Another concern about subsidy programs designed for lone mothers, voiced especially in the United States, is that programs for this group might provide incentives for family break up. This break-up could be real, or could be 'misrepresented' to qualify for assistance. It is worth noting that this would not be much of an issue in the programs we propose. The child care subsidy available to the family depends on family income, so naturally single parents will qualify for larger subsidies than two-parent families. But the maximum value of the subsidy – $2,500 a year – hardly seems like a significant incentive for family break-up!

SPECIAL PROGRAMS FOR CHILDREN OF LONE PARENTS OR CHILDREN AT RISK

In our study of the costs and benefits of child care, we reviewed a series of empirical studies about the effects of child care on the development of preschool children. For children from two-parent families and lone-parent, middle-income families, we found evidence of decreased grade repetition as a result of increased attendance at good quality early childhood facilities and evidence of improved academic and school performance in later grades for those with preschool child care experience relative to those without.[6] For children from low-income, lone-parent families, particularly those with additional risk factors, there is good evidence that early education, especially when combined with supplementary parent programs, can have substantial pay-offs[7]. This is not only confirmed by the well-known Perry Preschool results,[8] but also by a careful evaluation of Head Start's effectiveness[9] and RAND's assessment of reduced incidence of serious criminal activity.[10] One question that needs to be addressed is whether these results are generated by regular early childhood education programs or by specially designed programs targeted at the needs of children from low-income or at-risk backgrounds. In the specific cases of Perry Preschool and Head Start, the answer is that the programs are targeted at children from low-income families. In particular, there was an important component of parent education that accompanied Perry Preschool, and for many Head Start programs there is an important emphasis on parent education: 'In 1992, some 621,000 children attended Head Start programs, mostly for a few hours per day, while some of their mothers attended parent education and skill development classes, often in the same building.'[11] Many Head Start programs have significant health monitoring components, too. As economists, we are not very familiar with other details of the programming in Head Start, but it appears to be tailored to the background of the children.

Our instincts suggest to us that there will be some important differences in programming that meets the special needs of children from low-income families or children otherwise at risk. Although many individuals in the early education field have practical experience that could be called on, the research necessary to answer questions about what kind of programming is needed is, as yet, insufficient. As Michael Lamb writes:

> Unfortunately, little effort has been made to specify the influential aspects of intervention programs so that attempts can be made to fine-tune their effectiveness. As in research on day care, which was mired too long in argumentative responses to the question, 'Is day care bad for children?' proponents and critics have focused on determining whether Head Start is effective, instead of determining which aspects of which programs are of

particular value to which children from which types of families. It is a shocking testament of our inattention to curricular issues that this chapter can offer only the most general conclusions about the beneficial effects of 'high quality' care rather than empirically supported conclusions about the value of particular programs and approaches.[12]

We conclude that it is necessary to design some special programming to ensure that the needs of low-income and at-risk children are met either in the context of integrated facilities or programs designed specifically for such children in particular neighbourhoods. However, we cannot be clearer about the exact nature of these programs. Further, because of the strong evidence of the beneficial effects of good quality care on children from low-income and at-risk backgrounds, we feel compelled to amend the eligibility requirements discussed above for child care subsidy. In particular, we believe that children in low-income families should be eligible for child care subsidy for part-day preschool (two and a half hours per day) irrespective of the employment status of their parents. In other words, the requirement to be employed or in education or training would apply only to low-income families seeking child care for more than two and a half hours per day.

CONCLUDING REMARKS

Not all single-parent families are the same. There is a tendency to treat typical characteristics of many single-parent families as if they are inherent. They are not. Some lone mothers are highly educated, earn adequate incomes, are continuous participants in the paid work force and have children who are not at all 'at risk.'

On the other hand, many young single mothers have the characteristics of many young married mothers – they may have limited educational attainment and only modest work experience, meaning their anticipated employment income is low. Under these circumstances, the work disincentives created by social assistance and child care expenses associated with employment may be a serious problem. Since paid work, while not exactly enobling for the soul is, we believe, an important experience for both lone mothers and their children, the design of a universal system of child care services has to take the issue of work incentives into account.

Reconsidering our earlier work, which recommended that parents pay 20 per cent of the costs of a universal child care program for two- to five-year-olds, we have proposed a sliding scale of fees that would provide additional subsidization for low-income families and a maximum fee of, perhaps, $10 per child (about $2,500 per year), even at high levels of family income. Several alternative designs of a sliding scale of fees were discussed and the related trade-offs were considered.

Unfortunately, given the design of social assistance systems, the incentives to seek paid employment are weak, even with highly subsidized child care services. We conclude that eligibility for the extra subsidization of child care should be linked to an expectation that the parent(s) will be engaged in employment-related training or full-time paid work.

There is a large literature in North America and elsewhere on the effectiveness of early intervention and child care programs in stimulating the development of 'at-risk' children. Good child care is good for children, especially when packaged with family supports and parent training. Many of the positive effects for children and families are long-lived. We expect that universal integrated child care will be beneficial for most children from lone-parent and two-parent families. We also expect that some specialized intervention programs will continue to be desirable for children with multiple risk factors. Specially subsidized half-day child care would be available for all children according to income or need, regardless of the employment status of their parents.

Notes

1 G. Cleveland, and M. Krashinsky, *The Benefits and Costs of Good Child Care: The Economic Rationale for Public Investment in Young Children – A Policy Study* (Toronto: University of Toronto, Childcare Resource and Research Unit, 1998).
2 R. Connelly, 'The Effect of Child Care Costs on the Labor Force Participation and AFDC Recipiency of Single Mothers,' in *Institute for Research on Poverty Discussion Paper no. 920–90* (Madison: University of Wisconsin-Madison, 1990); J. Kimmel, 'The Effectiveness of Child-Care Subsidies in Encouraging the Welfare-to-Work Transition of Low-Income Single Mothers,' in *American Economic Review*, Papers and Proceedings (1995), 271–5; J. Kimmel, 'The Role of Child Care Assistance in Welfare Reform,' in *Employment Research Newsletter* of the Upjohn Institute for Employment Research (Kalamazoo, MI: Upjohn Institute, 1994); J. Kimmel, 'Child Care Costs as a

Barrier to Employment for Single and Married Mothers,' *W.E. Upjohn Institute Working Paper October.* (Kalamazoo, Michigan: Upjohn Institute, 1994).

3 National Council of Welfare, *Another Look at Welfare Reform* (Ottawa: Author, 1997); Cleveland and Krashinsky, *Benefits and Costs of Good Child Care.*

4 G. Cleveland and D. Hyatt, 'Subsidizing Child Care for Low-Income Families: A Good Bargain for Canadian Governments,' *Choices* (Montreal: Institute for Research on Public Policy, 1988).

5 K. Battle and S. Torjman, *The Welfare Wall: The Interaction of the Welfare and Tax Systems* (Ottawa: Caledon Institute of Social Policy, 1993).

6 Cleveland and Krashinsky, *Benefits and Costs;* A.G. Broberg, C.P. Hwang, M.E. Lamb, and R.D. Ketterlinus, 'Child Care Effects on Socioemotional and Intellectual Competence in Swedish Preschoolers,' in *Caring for Children: Challenge to America,* J.S. Lande, S. Scarr, and N. Gunzenhauser (Hillsdale, NJ: Lawrence Erlbaum Associates, 1989), 49–93; A.G. Broberg, H. Wessels, M.E. Lamb, and C.P. Hwang, 'Effects of Day Care on the Development of Cognitive Abilities in 8-Year-Olds: A Longitudinal Study,' in *Developmental Psychology* (1997) 33(1): 62–9; A.F. Osborn and J.E. Milbank, *The Effects of Early Education: A Report from The Child Health and Education Study* (New York: Clarendon Press, 1987); G. Doherty, *The Great Child Care Debate: The Long-Term Effects of Non-Parental Child Care* (Toronto: University of Toronto, Childcare Resource and Research Unit, 1996).

7 L.A. Karoly, P. Greenwood, S. Everingham, J. Hoube, R. Kilburn, P. Rydell, M. Sanders, and J. Chiesa, *Investing in Our Children: What We Know and Don't Know about the Costs and Benefits of Early Childhood Interventions* (Santa Monica, CA: Rand, 1998); National Council of Welfare, *Preschool Children: Promises to Keep* (Ottawa: Minister of Public Works and Government Services Canada, 1999).

8 W.S. Barnett, 'Benefit-Cost Analysis of the Perry Preschool Program and Its Long-Term Effects,' in *Educational Evaluation and Policy Analysis* (1985) 7(4): 333–42; W.S. Barnett, 'The Perry Preschool Program and Its Long-Term Effects: A Benefit-Cost Analysis,' in *High/Scope Early Childhood Policy Papers (no. 2)* (Ypsilanti, MI: High/Scope Press, 1985); W.S. Barnett, 'Benefits of Compensatory Preschool Education,' in *Journal of Human Resources* (1992), 27(2): 279–312.

9 J. Currie and D. Thomas, 'Do the Benefits of Early Childhood Education Last?' in *Policy Options* (1997) 18(6): 47–50.

10 J. Greenwood, C.P. Rydell, and J.Chiesa, *Diverting Children from a Life of Crime: Measuring Costs and Benefits,* Final Report of a project in RAND's

Criminal Justice program, prepared for the University of California, Berkeley, James Irvine Foundation (Santa Monica, CA: RAND, 1996).

11 M.E. Lamb, 'Non-parental Childcare: Context, Quality, Correlates and Consequences,' in I.E. Siegel and K.A. Renninger (vol. eds.), *Child Psychology in Practice*, W. Damon (series ed.), *Handbook of Child Psychology* (5th edition) New York: Wiley, 1998), 117.

12 Ibid., 124.

21. Investments in Comprehensive Programming: Services for Children and Single-Parent Mothers on Welfare Pay for Themselves within One Year

Gina Browne, Joanne Roulston, Bonnie Ewart, Michael Schuster, Joey Edwardh, and Louise Boily
McMaster University, National Council of Welfare, and Health Canada[1]

This chapter represents the growing consensus among researchers and policy makers about the best social policies and programs for very poor families with children. It may be used to guide policies made at various levels of government that affect poor single parents, their children, and the agencies that serve them.

Much of the public funding for children's services in the 1990s focused on children from poor families – primarily those with single parents – and those considered 'at risk' of health and developmental problems. This 'welfare' or 'targeted' approach to funding for children's programs, can be at odds with a more universal approach that extends funding to all children and families. Many recent efforts have focused on the needs of children, particularly very young children, by providing stopgap programs that deliver services to children, while bypassing the needs of parents and the family as a whole. For example, prenatal nutrition, school lunch programs, early child development programs, and many other children's services work directly with the child. Where the parent is involved, she is often just the conduit to getting the services to her child.

What is often missing from strategies for poor children is recognition of the importance of the family in children's lives, especially in the case of children on welfare. Throughout the 1990s many politicians, the media, and government officials engaged in public displays of 'poor-bashing' that promoted negative stereotypes of parents on welfare. Important programs such as welfare, unemployment insurance, and other health and social services that supported very poor people suffered serious funding cuts. More recently, governments have increased their efforts to provide services for children, but they have not restored the important complementary supports to parents through programs such as employment training and job creation.

Let us remember that children are poor because parents are poor. A logical approach to promoting the health and development of very high-risk children living in poverty is to work with children while also working with their parents to increase the chances that the whole family will no longer be poor. One of the most important and effective ways is to help parents find and keep jobs that provide the hours and the pay to lift their families over the poverty line. To paraphrase a familiar saying: 'Give a person a fish, you feed her for a day; teach a person to fish, she can feed herself for the rest of her life.'

Social policies that still assume a pre-1960s family structure in which all families have or ought to have two parents and all mothers are at home full-time simply do not respond to the realities of today. They do not provide the essential work supports for single-parent families such as adequate child care or children's recreation programs, employment training, job creation strategies, and parental leave. They certainly do not provide adequate family supports to help a person raising her children alone without a partner.

It is evident that Canadian social policy remains ambivalent about the relationship of mothers to the labour market. Child care and child care subsidies are in short supply at the same time that welfare programs push to get parents of very young children back into the workforce. Alberta considers single parents on welfare to be ready to return to the labour force when their children are only six months old. Welfare programs across the country have created serious financial disincentives to work for welfare recipients, particularly for single parents whose low wages are unlikely to compensate for the extra work-related costs such as transportation, child care, and work clothes.[2] In Ontario in 1996, a single parent on welfare could earn only $275 a month before the welfare department began to deduct 75 per cent of her earnings from her welfare cheque.

Nowhere in Canada do welfare rates allow anyone to live above the poverty line. Being on welfare is highly stigmatized. For most people, the most practical route out of poverty is a job – if the job provides adequate wages and hours. But over the past decade, federal cuts to transfer payments, and provincial and territorial cuts to social programs including child care have forced the cost of child care up and the availability down.

All of these points move us to ask: just what do we really want single parents to do? Stay at home with their children or get paid work? What would be best for children and parents?

The second policy problem is the way in which Canadian social policy has understood the needs of children and their families. Policy makers have sometimes assumed that child care had to be based on some monolithic institutional model that could never meet the varied needs of children from different parts of the country from families with different strengths and risk factors. Programs for 'high-risk' and 'at-risk' children were targeted at poor families, but often they did not provide the other supports children and the families needed, especially the provision of high-quality child care for children while their parents attended school and re-entered the workforce. In reality, families living in poverty need a combination of services that provide supports to their efforts to get training and jobs while also providing interventions that promote early childhood development.

EVIDENCE ABOUT COMPREHENSIVE PROGRAMMING

A recent randomized control study in Hamilton-Wentworth, Ontario, provides valuable evidence about the kind of programming that appears to work best for all the needs of children and families on social assistance; the results of this study have been fully reported elsewhere.[3] These results, discussed in more detail below, show that it is equally effective, but less expensive, to respond to the needs of mothers and children on welfare with a range of services that are comprehensive and supportive. Proactive, comprehensive health and social services for mothers and quality child care or recreation services for children produce more impressive results than services that leave families on welfare to direct and try to finance their own opportunities.

Within a short period of time, proactive services for mothers and children pay for themselves in reduced use of other public services. In addition, there are important short-term financial gains for the mothers and children and for the public purse along with long-term societal benefits in the form of earlier exit from social assistance.

Most effective of all the programs tested are age-appropriate child care and recreation. Services work even better when they also provide employment supports that help mothers on welfare to re-enter the workforce and provide the support of nursing services. Good, integrated services that provide several types of support for mothers and children are far more effective – both for families and for taxpayers – than leaving families to cope on their own with the existing welfare and social services system.

The study in Hamilton-Wentworth involved 765 households with 1,300 children from zero to twenty-four years of age. All households were headed by single mothers and were collecting social assistance. Each family was randomly assigned to one of two groups. The 'treatment' group received provider-initiated and subsidized services; the 'control' group received self-directed and self-financed services. In particular, the treatment group received age-appropriate child care or after-school recreation opportunities organized by a recreation coordinator. Children of welfare recipients allocated to the self-directed arm of the trial received no additional provider-initiated or financed recreation or child care service. Parents and children in this group were free to enrol in any recreation activity of their choosing and received no subsidy.

Income maintenance, in-home visits by nurses, employment retraining, therapeutically justified quality child care and recreation for children and youth are the most common solutions for parents on social assistance or at risk. (Most of the distinctions between child care and recreation seem redundant. In practice, good child care and good early education are very similar, especially when early education programs cover parents' work hours. For school-aged children, recreation programs provide child care by providing adult supervision while parents are not around). Our empirical evidence documents the value, effects, and benefits of most of these programs. This study examined the outcomes of families that had used several types of programs on their own and together. The study then compared the results with those of parents who had access to services for themselves and their children but had to design the mix for themselves.[4]

Research Outcomes

The sample of families studied had the following characteristics:

- Of those parents eligible for welfare 45 per cent agreed to fill out questionnaires about their health, functioning, and use of services. Those who refused questionnaires, yet were eligible for welfare, were rated by their welfare case workers on a five-point global scale showing that they were in poorer mental health than those who participated.

- Of those parents who participated in this study 45 per cent showed signs and symptoms of major depression; 55 per cent did not endorse clinical depression.
- Depressed parents were more likely to have children with a behavioural disorder or developmental delay. This finding is consistent with other recent Canadian research such as the National Longitudinal Survey of Children and Youth.[5] Depressed parents also had higher annual expenditures for their and their children's use of (public) health and social services.
- The overwhelming majority of parents and children (79 per cent) found quality child care and recreation the most acceptable interventions for the longest period (two years). Contact with a public health nurse was almost as acceptable to families (78 per cent). Some 36 per cent of single parents accepted contact with the municipal employment services. Until the study, these employment services had not even been offered because single parents had been designated unemployable by the municipality and therefore ineligible for these services.

After two years, researchers found that:

- The group of families that remained in the study were a more disadvantaged sample of people, that is, had histories of longer spells on welfare, more mental health problems, and greater use of child protection services.
- Although the sample was a more disadvantaged group, mothers' depression rates dropped from 50 per cent at the beginning of the study to only 20 per cent after two years of involvement in any of the services. The social adjustment scores of parents improved.
- Any of the services for families offered in these studies paid for themselves within a year by decreasing the use of professional services. They were therefore not more expensive than the self-directed use of services.
- Each of the proactive services resulted in a greater exit from welfare (by 10 to 12 percentage points) within the first year compared with the 10 per cent rate of exit by parents directing their own service use.
- When services were combined so that a family could, for example, use child care and recreation as well as nursing visits, families were

15 percentage points more likely to leave welfare (representing a 25 per cent likelihood of leaving welfare). There was no extra cost in providing the combination of services because the cost was offset by the reduction in parents' and children's use of the services of physicians, other professionals, and the child protection system.

The provision of ongoing age-appropriate quality child care and recreation – even with no other supports to families – had many positive outcomes: Parents rated it as the most enduringly acceptable service to both themselves and their children. It paid for itself by decreasing the use of professional public services and was used more by children with a disorder. Quality child care and recreation maintained the academic, social, and vocational competence of children with behaviour disorders at levels equal to those of children without disorders who did not receive subsidized quality child care or recreation. It resulted in improvements in the mental health of parents, and improved the standard of living of parents on welfare by providing children's services, equipment, or transport that was not deducted from their welfare income. There was a decreased the use of food bank services by parents now left with more disposable income. By itself, the provision of child care and recreation generated a 10 percentage point exit from welfare.

After two years, all parents in the treatment group showed these improvements, and there were no trends of reduced improvement associated with subgroups of parents with problems such as affective mental health disorders. Providing any of these services, alone or in combination with one another, reduced the use of other health and social services by both parents and children. Any one of the services alone paid for itself in just one year by reducing costs to the health and social services system.

After just one year, 10 per cent of parents on welfare who directed their own use of services left the welfare roles and did not use welfare again in the following year. By comparison, 25 per cent of parents who were offered age-appropriate comprehensive quality child care and recreation, public health, and employment retraining services left welfare. This 15 percentage point greater exit from welfare translates into an impressive and immediate savings of approximately $20,000 a year for every family that left welfare. The 15 percentage point increase in parents who leave welfare is, therefore, worth $300,000 for every 100 mothers offered comprehensive services.

Comprehensive services to single parents and their children pay for themselves by reduced use of other services and are associated with

Figure 21.1. Comparison of total cost per family on social services: those receiving proactive subsidized recreation (1) vs those in self-directed and self-financed programs (2).

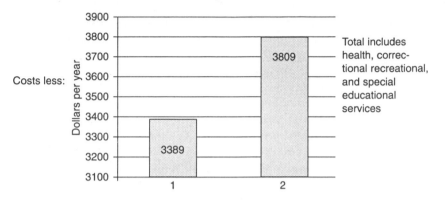

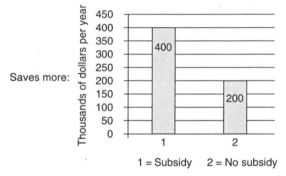

considerable savings to society within a year by fostering the 'financial independence' of parents and the maintenance of childhood competence (see Figure 21.1)

EXAMINING THE EFFECTIVENESS, EFFICIENCY, ADEQUACY, EQUITY, AND RESPONSIVENESS OF COMPREHENSIVE INTERVENTION FOR HIGH-RISK FAMILIES WITH CHILDREN[6]

The criterion of *effectiveness* asks whether a valued outcome has been achieved. For an intervention to be effective, participants must attend often enough for the intervention to have a chance of success.

Based on the findings of our studies,[7] age-appropriate and tailored quality child care or recreation was the most acceptable type of intervention for the greatest number of parents and children on welfare for the longest period, particularly among parents of children with a behaviour disorder. Acceptability meant that the child's enrolment and participation in self-selected activities was maintained. More intense public health nurse visits were provided to parents with poorer social adjustment scores. Some 36 per cent of these mothers were also willing to consider engaging in employment retraining services during the first year on welfare if offered.

The criterion of *efficiency* asks how much expenditure or effort was required to achieve the valued outcomes. The studies show that the costs of all proactive services were more than offset by the lower use of publicly funded health services. It is no more expensive to provide comprehensive services than not to do so, but the investment in family support pays off with a 15 percentage point greater departure from welfare within just one year. The net savings following the first year were worth at least $300,000 *more* than the total cost of serving 100 mothers and their children.

In 1997 there were 429,600 single parents and their children on welfare in Canada.[8] If the take-up rate for a new program of this kind were the same as the take-up rate in this study (45 per cent), this means that about 190,000 would be willing to participate in a program of directed child care, recreation, and support services. For each 100 of these families, we have estimated that there would be social assistance, health, counselling, and other savings of $300,000. Under these assumptions, it would be possible for society to save about $570 million ($300,000 × 1,900) with no new expenditures.

The criterion of *adequacy* examines to what extent the achievement of a 25 per cent exit from welfare solves the most acute problems of children and parents living in extreme poverty on welfare. Families that benefit from proactive comprehensive family supports leave welfare more quickly than families that make do without such services, as families do under current Ontario welfare policy. On the other hand, despite the fact that they were also offered this mix of services, 75 per cent of families were still on welfare after two years. The results of the four-year follow-up will permit an assessment of the enduring effects and the expense of these policies.

The criterion of *equity* asks whether the effects and expense are distributed equitably among different groups. The findings of this study are generalizable to single-parent mothers on welfare residing in Southern Ontario. Further studies are needed to see if these findings would apply to other single-parent families on welfare and to working poor families in other geographically and culturally diverse communities.

The criterion of *responsiveness* asks whether policy outcomes satisfy the needs, values, and preferences of particular stakeholder groups. Our studies showed that comprehensive family support was acceptable to 45 per cent of parents on welfare who consented to be surveyed. The acceptability of the service by the other 55 per cent of consumers can be reassessed when these ideas are implemented as policy.

One persistent question remains. Is there any stakeholder group that would have reasonable ground for objection to the widespread implementation of this policy? Based on the evidence of this study, service providers are unlikely to have reasonable grounds for objection since they are included in the service provision and would suffer no job displacement. Service agencies should not object if the savings were reinvested in services for their clientele. Health professionals should not object since the reduction in use of health services should help to reduce waiting lists and delays in visits to hospitals and specialists. Governments and taxpayers have no reasonable ground for objection to a policy that costs no more, yet saves money.

Finally the criterion of *appropriateness* asks whether the desired outcomes are actually equitable as well as efficient. Comprehensive family supports should be available to both welfare-poor and working-poor families with children, for many good reasons. Many of the difficulties in parenting and child development appear in populations of children who are poor, whether their parents have earned incomes or not.

Many very poor people move on and off welfare regularly. Even when on welfare, many people have at least some earned income, even though it may not raise their incomes enough to take them off welfare. When people move off welfare, they often get work that is not much better paid than welfare, and as a result, welfare-poor families become working-poor families. This is largely because of very low (and shrinking) minimum wages and the increased number of 'bad' jobs that are irregular, poorly paid, temporary, or part-time. Young people – who tend to be the parents of young children – are the most likely to have bad jobs. In many important ways the population of very poor people on welfare and the lowest income working poor share the same risks and vulnerabilities, and need the same kind of supports to ensure that they can take the best possible care of their children.[9]

In our view, some of the savings that come from providing good supports to families on welfare could be invested in extending high-quality children's and public health services for working-poor parents and their children and not just the welfare poor. By extending family supports to low-income working families who are at high risk of needing welfare, parents would be better supported in their jobs (and therefore more likely to be able to continue to work), their children would benefit from the developmental advantages of having working parents,[10] the children could benefit from good child care and recreation, and fewer of these families would be likely to develop the need for welfare.

Research has shown again and again that all families – not just the poorest and most vulnerable – benefit from good family supports, and most children benefit from good quality child care and recreation programs. However, research from many sources also indicates that the poorest and most vulnerable children and families benefit the most from good quality interventions.[11]

In an ideal world, high-quality, comprehensive family supports would be provided publicly to all families. Based on the findings of these studies, however, it is clear that at the very minimum, these services must be provided for the poorest and most vulnerable families with children. Questions of the fairness of giving services to one type of family and not to all obscure the issue of returns on taxpayers' investment. We need to get the incentives right in systems of social and health policy. It costs society more *not* to help poor families than it costs to help them out. The expense is immediate. Any apparent conflict of values is more rhetorical than real.

CONCLUSIONS

Evidence from our study confirms the findings of many other studies:[12] good investments in comprehensive family supports provide rich dividends for the people who use the services as well as for taxpayers. Our study showed that parents benefit enormously from employment supports to re-enter the workforce, children benefit from the opportunity for recreation and development, and families benefit from home visits from nurses. Moreover, when families receive more than one type of support, improvements in their lives are greater and the costs of other supports for them decrease. Clearly, programming that is proactive and comprehensive enough to support families in several facets of their lives works better than any one program on its own.

In our view, policies and programs for families with children must be comprehensive and provide good supports for parents and children, especially during the most sensitive periods of their lives. Our study indicates that the period when families first come onto the welfare rolls is an important time to provide parents and children with strong supports that promote parents' re-entry to the job market and provide children with programming that promotes their health and development.

In all likelihood, even more comprehensive programming to support families – for example, improved minimum wages, wage supplements for parents in the workforce, improved parental leave policies, and a job creation strategy that increased the opportunities for parents seeking to enter the workforce – would provide even greater improvements in the health and development of children and their families. This is an area of research that calls for more study.

In summary, we recommend:

- Supports for all families. Raising children well is a community responsibility, not just a parental responsibility. This is in part a moral question, but evidence from our studies shows that if we do not provide good supports to the highest risk families, the larger community will pay for our failures in increased costs for public health care.
- Comprehensive family policy. Supports for families work best when they work together to support parents *and* children. One support is good, more supports work together to create even greater results. Child care and recreation must be at the centre of strategies to support families with children. Comprehensiveness and coordination are key. Children must be supported in the context of their families.
- Good programming for poor families. Providing universal supports for families may be an ideal, but governments may not be willing or able to provide the funding for them. Even so, providing supports for the poorest of poor families has been shown to be cost-effective.
- Family supports must not create a division between welfare-poor and working-poor families. Poor is poor. The poorer a family is, the worse the results for its children. Good, comprehensive family supports must be extended to all poor families. Ideally, they should be extended to all families, but poor families need the services most.

- Supports must respond to the reality that many families are headed by single women. These families face an extremely high risk of poverty. Poverty and raising children on one's own place an enormous stress on parents that make it very hard for them to provide the high quality of care that we know is so important for the optimum development of children. Because of the low level of financial assistance from welfare, it seems especially prudent to promote the re-entry to the workforce by single mothers on welfare. Welfare and child care policies must be reformed to support mothers in the workforce.
- Research into the effectiveness of family supports must be a priority.[13] Governments must make a commitment to act on the evidence about programs that work for families with children. All levels of government must make and keep their commitments to meeting the needs of children and their families.

Notes

1 Gina Browne, McMaster University: System-Linked Research Unit on Health and Social Service Utilization; School of Nursing; Department of Clinical Epidemiology and Biostatistics. Joanne Roulston, National Council of Welfare. Bonnie Ewart, McMaster University: System-Linked Research Unit on Health and Social Service Utilization. Michael Schuster, McMaster University: System-Linked Research Unit on Health and Social Service Utilization, and Hamilton-Wentworth Regional Department of Community Services. Joey Edwardh, McMaster University: System-Linked Research Unit on Health and Social Service Utilization, and Halton Social Planning Council. Louise Boily, Health Canada, Children's Mental Health Division.

2 National Council of Welfare, *Incentives and Disincentives to Work* (Ottawa: Author, 1993).

3 G. Browne, C. Byrne, J. Roberts, A. Gafni, S. Watt, B. Ewart, M. Schuster, J. Underwood, S. Flynn Kingston, K. Rennick, I. Thomas, and S. Haldane, 'When the Bough Breaks: Provider-Initiated Comprehensive Care is More Effective and Less Expensive for Sole Support Parents on Social Assistance,' submitted to *Social Science in Medicine* (1999); and G. Browne, C. Byrne, J. Roberts, A. Gafni, S.Watt, S. Haldane, I. Thomas, B. Ewart, M. Schuster, J. Underwood, S. Flynn Kingston, and K. Rennick, 'Benefitting All the Beneficiaries of Social Assistance Is "Within our Reach": A RCT of

the 2-Year Effects and Expense of Subsidized Versus Nonsubsidized Quality Child Care/Recreation for Children,' in *National Academies of Practice Forum* (1999) 1(2): 131–42.

4 Browne et al., 'When the Bough Breaks'; and Browne et al., 'Benefitting All.'

5 E. Harvey, 'Short-Term and Long-Term Effects of Early Parental Employment on Children of the National Longitudinal Survey of Youth,' in *Developmental Psychology* (1999) 35(2): 445–59.

6 Dr Mehta, *The Essential Guide to Policy Development and Analysis* (Ottawa: Canada Research Institute, Policy Planning Directorate and Appendix Publishing, 1994).

7 Browne et al., 'When the Bough Breaks'; and Browne et al., 'Benefitting All.'

8 National Council of Welfare, *Profiles of Welfare: Myths and Realities* (Ottawa: Author, 1998), 10.

9 According to the National Council of Welfare's (NCW) *Profiles of Welfare*: 58 per cent of welfare cases were because the head of household is a single parent on welfare for more than 25 months, 14 per cent for 13–24 months, 9 per cent for 7–12 months, 7 per cent for 4–6 months, and 11 per cent for 0–3 months. As for the NCW's *Poverty Profile*, single-parent mothers living under the poverty line: 46 per cent had some earned income, 68 per cent welfare, 8 per cent unemployment insurance, 5 per cent investments, 99 per cent child tax benefit, 4 per cent Canada Pension Plan or Quebec Pension Plan, 2 per cent workers compensation, 18 per cent child or spousal support.

10 M.J. Zaslow and C.A. Emig, 'When Low-Income Mothers Go to Work: Implications for Children,' in *The Future of Children, Welfare to Work* (1997) 7(1): 110–16; T.L. Parcel and E.G. Menaghan, 'Effects of Low-Wage Employment on Family Well-Being,' in ibid., 116–21; K.A. Moore and A.K. Driscoll, 'Low-Wage Maternal Employment and Outcomes for Children: A Study,' in ibid. 122–37.

11 See National Council of Welfare, *Profiles of Welfare*.

12 L.B. Schorr, 'Effective Programs for Children Growing Up in Concentrated Poverty,' in *Children in Poverty*, Aletha C. Huston, ed. (Cambridge: Cambride University Press, 1991).

13 T. Liew, and N. Halfon, E. McGlynn, D. Steinwacks, W. Valentine, (guest eds.), 'Improving the Quality of Health Care For Children: An Agenda for Research: Supplement,' in *Health Services Research* (1998) 33(4).

22. The Needs of Aboriginal Canadians

Richard Budgell
Aboriginal Head Start, Health Canada

I find little to argue with in the broad principles addressed in the chapters by Gordon Cleveland and Michael Krashinsky, and by Gina Browne et al. But both chapters, for me, commit the crime of omission. That is, both fail to describe the characteristics of these faceless poor, whose best interests we are discussing.

The general arguments in the two chapters – in Cleveland and Krashinsky, that some special arrangements may be necessary for lone-parent families, and in Browne, that a comprehensive web of services best addresses children's needs – are well supported with relevant research findings. However, both chapters ignore what differentiates families on welfare, or lone-parent families, in addition to and apart from their income levels. The reality is that poverty in Canada often has colours, languages, and values different from those that are dominant and that this has a fundamental policy and programming implication. The fact that poverty has a gender is noted in both chapters.

For a significant number of Canadians, what makes and keeps them poor and vulnerable is the fact that they are Aboriginal. It would be impossible in this forum to delineate the historical causality and the contemporary reality of discrimination, lower education levels, poorer health, lower employment rates, and higher incidence of incarceration that put Aboriginal people in Canada at the bottom of the socioeconomic pile. But some facts: almost one-third of Aboriginal children under the age of fifteen lived in a lone-parent family in 1996, twice the rate within the general population. In Winnipeg, Regina, and Saskatoon, about one-half lived with a single parent, which meant that 30 per cent of all children in lone-parent families in those cities were Aboriginal.[1] On the issue of income, average earnings of Aboriginal people in 1995 were lower in every age and education category. Average employment income of Aboriginal people living on reserves was $14,055, and for those living off reserves it was $18,463, as compared with the national average of $26,474.[2] In 1995, 44 per cent of the Aboriginal population living off-reserve was below Statistics Canada's low income cut-off level, compared with the national rate of 20 per cent; three out of five Aboriginal children under the age of six years were in low-income families in 1995, compared with the national rate of one in four.[3] In education, although some progress has been made in the past decade and a half, in 1996 Aboriginal people aged twenty to twenty-nine were 50 per cent less likely than non-Aboriginal people to have completed post-secondary studies.[4] Although my interest and expertise is in Aboriginal people, I have to mention, briefly, another group well represented among the poor, recent immigrants. In 1996 rates of poverty for unattached individuals and heads of families who immigrated after 1989, were 47 per cent and 61.2 per cent, as compared with 35.8 per cent and 13.2 per cent for Canadian-born unattached individuals and heads of families.[5]

Where does this bleak picture lead us in relation to services for Aboriginal children and families? For me, it belies the assertion in the Browne chapter that 'poor is poor'; when designing services for families on welfare or children of lone-parent families, if the recipients are seen only through the lens of their poverty, the vital ingredient of their cultural background is missing. The theory on which I premise this is that everyone, whether poor or not, prefers to use services that respect their cultural characteristics. Few of us would choose to be defined solely by our income levels.

Both Cleveland and Krashinsky and Browne et al. advocate for universal programs for all children and families. The danger of universality, though, and the fear of it on the part of many Aboriginal people, is that our distinctiveness will be lost within it. This has, unfortunately, been part of the experience of my Native American counterparts involved with the Head Start program in the United States, where their participation represents only 3 per cent of the total Head Start population. Their values, issues, languages, and preferences are therefore those of a tiny minority within a much larger program context that defines itself primarily as one targeted at low-income families, instead of one that is culturally defined. In contrast, Aboriginal people in Canada have been able to define the nature of the program in which I work, Aboriginal Head Start, which began in 1995. While advocating for comprehensive child care and early education programs for all Canadian children and families, we must not lose sight of the diversity of the population.

Cleveland and Krashinsky imply that some specialization of programs is appropriate: 'We conclude that it is necessary to design some special programming to ensure that needs of low-income and at-risk children are met either in the context of integrated facilities or programs designed specifically for such children in particular neighbourhoods. However, we cannot be clearer about the exact nature of these programs.' Browne et al. also critique a one-size-fits-all model: 'Policy makers have sometimes assumed that child care had to be based on a monolithic, institutional model that could never meet the varied needs of children from different parts of the country from families with different strengths and risk factors.'

The mention of 'strengths' is a heartening one. When I argue against perceiving people solely on the basis of their income levels, a corollary to that is to argue against perceiving people solely in relation to their weaknesses, a.k.a. their 'risk factors.' A thinker whose work I have very much taken to heart, John McKnight, has written eloquently against the pathologization of the poor and the medicalization of their situation; instead, he recommends a focus on human strengths as a route towards empowerment.[6] Within Aboriginal Head Start, we talk about bringing out the 'gifts' of children and parents, to enable people to contribute in a way that maximizes their talents and strengths. This is, for us, not idle psychobabble, but part of an authentic Aboriginal belief system that has great meaning for many of our participants. It is also an example of how involving the recipients of a program in the design of that program can create empowerment and effectiveness.

Neither of the chapters answer the question, who should design and operate early education or child care services for families on welfare or lone-parent families? Browne argues for comprehensive and integrated services and says that 'these services must be provided for the poorest and most vulnerable families and children,' in an imperfect world that so far has not provided the resources to make such programs universal. What is being found to be effective among Aboriginal people are services designed and operated by Aboriginal people themselves. Some Canadians may find this model inherently threatening: it raises the spectre of a form of cultural apartheid or separateness in our midst that, particularly in the context of urban environments, may seem jarring. But, to make a different analogy, do we believe that providing health or educational services to minority francophone populations in French, or minority anglophone populations in English, is inherently threatening? While most Aboriginal people speak one of the dominant Canadian languages, for many Aboriginal people there are layers of difference from other Canadians, and a strong desire to preserve or revive cultural traditions. We know quite conclusively, I think, that forced assimilation did not succeed in creating the desired white people with brown skins. Today's model, of encouraging cultural strength and confidence while fostering the skills to succeed in the dominant society, will, I hope, eventually produce socioeconomic equality for Aboriginal people. There is no doubt that those skills are increasingly necessary to the large majority of Aboriginal people who do not live on reserves: in fact, about three in ten Aboriginal people live in metropolitan areas, and another one-quarter live in other urban areas.[7]

All of us who attended the symposium are no doubt in agreement that early education and quality child care have an immeasurable positive impact on children and families. I was very pleased to note, in the Browne chapter, a criticism of programs that ignore the centrality of family in the lives of children. It is a cornerstone of Aboriginal Head Start, that to be most effective our projects must work with both children and their parents. The program is now serving approximately 3,600 children in urban centres and northern communities every year, in half-day, four-day-per-week programs that run from September to June. The recently announced expansion of the program to First Nations people living on reserves is projected to serve another 5,000 to 6,000 children and families. This is in addition to the estimated 6,000 child care spaces funded by Human Resources Development for First Nations (on-reserve) and Inuit children. When looked at as an agglomeration, this represents a large and growing community of Aboriginal families participating in early education. Unfortunately, it also represents only a tiny proportion of the nearly 200,000 Aboriginal children under the age of ten years (half of whom are under five years of age).

As Cleveland and Krashinsky and Browne et al. make clear, the cost of providing services to those currently unserved or underserved are far outweighed by the cost of doing nothing. This is a conclusion that applies as much to Aboriginal as to non-Aboriginal Canadians.

Notes

1 Statistics Canada, '1996 Census: Aboriginal Data,' in the *Daily*, 13 Jan. 1998.

2 Statistics Canada, '1996 Census: Sources of Income, Earnings, and Total Income, and Family Income,' in the *Daily*, 12 May 1998.
3 Ibid.
4 Heather Tait, 'Educational Achievement of Young Aboriginal Adults,' in *Canadian Social Trends* (1999): Spring, 6.
5 National Council of Welfare, *Poverty Profile 1996* (Ottawa: Author, 1998), 49.
6 C.B.C. Radio, *Ideas*, Program transcript from broadcast 3, 10, 17, January 1994. The program was called 'Community and Its Counterfeits.' See pages 4 and 5 of the transcript.
7 Statistics Canada, '1996 Census.'

23. Learning from Experience: Can We Check Old Assumptions and Categorical Thinking at the Door?

Donna S. Lero
Centre for Families, Work, and Well-Being, *University of Guelph*

The opportunity to engage in serious thinking about a new policy and program approach to better meet the needs of children and families is both exciting and an awesome responsibility. Experiences in Canada, the United States, and many other countries provide important lessons both about what works for children and families, and what creates additional fragmentation and difficulty for families, for service providers, and for communities. Most readers of this volume are well aware of the problems that have been created or exacerbated by not investing dollars, political will, and significant human resources into the development of a comprehensive approach to family-related social policies, including child care policies, that can support families through changing times.

The two chapters opening this part, while quite different in scope and approach, identify the need to ensure that a comprehensive approach is adopted that can meet a variety of needs simultaneously. Both chapters recognize at least three functions that good child care programs serve: enabling parents to be employed or preparing for employment; avoiding financial barriers to good quality care that can sabotage welfare reform efforts; and providing excellent developmental programs that can enrich children's lives and provide effective intervention and support for children and families at risk. Cleveland and Krashinsky have suggested both broader and more specialized subsidy approaches to fund child care and to ensure its accessibility to low-income and single parents. Gina Browne and her colleagues have affirmed the importance and effectiveness of subsidized child care and recreation programs as one component in a broader range of services for children and families with serious economic, social, and health challenges. Both chapters provide an important springboard for reminding us that new approaches must be comprehensive and must avoid the pitfall of putting good child care programs out of reach of those who can benefit from them.

There are three major concerns that the two chapters raise. The first is a philosophical, political, and practical concern about whether or not it is still possible to propose that child care and related services be fully funded without direct parental fees. If not, then clearly there must be alternative or specialized subsidies to ensure that all families can have access to good quality services, regardless of their income, family structure, geographical location, ethnic origin, and the health and abilities of parents and children. The second concern is one based on recognition of the pitfalls waiting if we cannot avoid thinking about child care services in boxes that are static, contrived, and limiting compared with the dynamic circumstances of many children and families. While the days when single male-breadwinner families predominated are long gone, we are continuing to see shifts in family structure, parents' labour force patterns, and communities that are not being considered in current thinking. Assuming that parents and children will fit neatly and consistently into categories of user groups – full-time, full-year child care for employed parents; part-day early intervention or enrichment programs that assume that parents are not or will not be employed as well; or separate programs for teen moms or for post-secondary students – can create many difficulties that need not be created as we attempt to design new systems and services. The third concern is one based on research on child care programs and current practices. Specifically, the concern is that we need to pay serious attention to how policies and funding approaches operate on the ground, if we wish to ensure that high-quality care will be sustainable when conditions change or new, more inclusive approaches are adopted. Current research both in Canada and the United States suggests that such vigilance is warranted.

FULL PUBLIC FUNDING VS SHARED FUNDING: PHILOSOPHICAL AND PRACTICAL ISSUES

Over the years, many Canadian child care advocates have observed systems in Denmark, Spain, Sweden, and France that endeavour to provide early childhood education and care to all children, regardless of their parents' income or employment status as a valuable public service and/or contribution to the quality of children's early years. Our mixed economy of care has been affected in recent years by significant cutbacks and restructuring that have moved current child care provisions closer to being a market service in which government funding is used more often for targeted funding purposes (i.e., subsidies and early intervention). The new social union framework need not preclude federal-provincial cost-sharing for child care and early childhood programs. However, current political thinking seems to have moved away from seeing child care as a potentially fully funded service (such as health and public education for children) and towards a service that must inevitably(?) include a parental contribution (user fee). Public opinion polls and focus groups confirm that Canadians are more supportive of a shared funding approach that includes a parental contribution, as is embodied in the Child Care Advocacy Association of Canada (CCAAC) position and Cleveland and Krashinksy's proposal. The fact that the public views a parent funding component as essential (to ensure that parents take their responsibilities seriously, and perhaps to encourage parental involvement in their children's programs) reflects continued ambivalence about the role of parents (especially mothers) when it diverges from direct care provision and the adoption of a societal responsibility for the well-being of children. Under current circumstances, proposing that child care and early education be fully funded when provision is funded outside of the public education system seems like a lost cause.

Yet *not* providing full funding creates the need to have specialized subsidy mechanisms and systems for implementing them that add additional costs and difficulties. Cleveland and Krashinsky have correctly pointed out that relying on the parental contribution of 20 per cent of child care budgets creates inevitable trade-offs and decisions: what should the maximum fee be? Where should the threshold be for minimum direct payment? How quickly should special subsidies be phased out? There is no one right answer to these questions. Instead, there are other complications: What about families with more than one child? Should subsidy rates be adjusted to account for total child care costs compared with total net family income? Should subsidy expectations be the same in all areas of the country, or a province, regardless of differences in the cost of living? What happens when family structure or family income or the need for full versus part-time care changes (an increasingly frequent occurrence in the lives of young families). How can specialized subsidy systems operate in a flexible and responsive manner, when they are inherently designed on the basis of classifications built on last year's income or last month's child care needs?

Further concerns relate to the continued flow of subsidies from both parents and governments that are essential for the stable funding of programs. During recessions and tough economic times, when unemployment increases and government funds are tight, public education is not greatly affected. But if recent experience is a guide, the times when young families most need public support is the time when child care may be least available, especially if there is less money for subsidies and less stable parental employment. The point, of course, is that funding child care as a support to employment presumes high parental employment as the driver of the need for care, while direct public funding of child care as a developmental service for all children maintains the system in place regardless of downturns in the economy or shifts in the personal lives of individual parents.

AVOIDING THE PITFALLS OF THINKING CATEGORICALLY

I have already referred to the concern that there needs to be flexible, responsive programs and funding arrangements. Families and their circumstances are not fixed, but are more fluid than ever before. Recent studies based on Statistics Canada data confirm that families fall in and out of low income categories; parents lose jobs, find jobs, shift from part-time to full-time work, and experience periods of uncertain and unstable income. Couples separate, common-law unions form and dissolve, children are born. Parents and children experience significant personal and/or health problems. Families move; the school year begins and ends; a province introduces, expands, or ends kindergarten programs or changes welfare policies that affect child care in any number of ways; a community loses its major employer; there is a significant increase in immigration. All of these changes in the lives of children and families and in the resources that are needed in communities are important and substantial. Both programs and funding sources must be flexible enough to ensure continuity in the lives of young children and their parents and to be responsive to changing needs. In fact, the most current research on Canadian child care programs, the *You Bet I Care!* study, indicates that some programs are changing to meet changing needs. We have recently found that most programs (80 per cent) offer both full- and part-time care, often to quite broad age ranges spanning infants under eighteen months to children five years and older. One in eight programs in the *YBIC!* sudy provided at least one service for children at risk or special populations (a Head Start or early intervention program, counselling for teen-age parents, second language learning for children, or consultation and support for other programs on matters such as including children with special needs or other issues). Almost one-quarter of centres represented in our sample have a high proportion of children receiving subsidies and endeavour to provide significant amounts of support to the children and their parents.

Funding for programs that assumes that centres provide full-time or part-time care only, specially designed interventions or 'just' good developmental care, care only for children two to five years of age, or education and care only to certain populations and not to others do not do most programs justice. Furthermore, categorical funding and silo approaches make it very difficult for programs to maintain stable enrolments and even more difficult for parents to be eligible for the programs they need at the time they need them. Any new approach to Canadian child care should particularly avoid situations that block parents from full-time employment. Current experiences with welfare reform efforts in the United States are demonstrating the critical need to meld Head Start with full-day care and to maintain the highest program standards and most affordable fees while doing so.

MAINTAINING HIGH PROGRAM QUALITY ON THE GROUND

Current research demonstrates that there are many factors that affect structural and process aspects of program quality. Recent analyses of national child care data from the Profiles of Child Care Settings Study and the National Child Care Staffing Study indicate that while there are serious concerns about the quality and accessibility of child care across social classes, there are also major inequities in quality of care within services provided to low-income populations. Comparisons across Head Start programs, public school preschool programs, and community-based child care programs indicate major differences in wages and working conditions, staff turnover, observed global quality scores, and measures of the quality of teacher-child interactions. Moreover, in comparisons across child care centres serving mostly upper-, middle-, or lower-income populations, those serving middle-income groups were often the poorest or most variable quality. If we expect Canadian programs to consistently provide good care and family support, and to be more inclusive and more responsive to children with special needs and to families needing additional support, we must ensure that they will have the resources to do so on a consistent basis. These resources include stable funding, opportunities to attract and retain well-educated child care professionals, the capacity to utilize external specialists to ensure quality improvements, and a far more valued place in the social infrastructure available in communities. This cannot be done without leadership and public policy development that recognizes how important child care and early education is – not just for economic benefits accruing from parental employment or enhanced readiness to learn – but as a visible and concrete means of supporting children's development as a public good.

A FINAL NOTE

It is obvious that an enhanced, comprehensive approach to supporting child development and family well-being cannot be done piecemeal. High-quality care and education and/or recreation is also essential for school-age children. Affordable housing is a necessity; stable family income is required for children's well-being and for good family functioning. The best policy approach would be one that really does engage in a fundamental paradigm shift – one that includes the design of good child care within a more comprehensive approach to family and child policy that will be worth our efforts and energy and be consistent with our values and our dreams for the twenty-first century.

24. Why Child Care Fees Are Problematic

Michael Goldberg
Social Planning and Research Council of British Columbia

The two chapters at the beginning of this part explore the type of child care policies that are needed to address the particular circumstances of single parents, child poverty, and children at risk. Both primarily focus on single parents with low incomes, particularly those on income assistance.

Cleveland and Krashinsky present a case for modifying their proposed universal child care program, where parents pay 20 per cent of the cost of quality child care through fees. The modifications are necessary, argue Cleveland and Krashinsky, to address the disincentives of child care fees for those with low incomes, and particularly for those families moving from income assistance to the labour market. The authors convincingly demonstrate the large disincentives contained in the transition from income assistance to the labour market. As they point out, the 'clawback' or 'tax-back' on earned income is usually 75 per cent or greater for each additional dollar earned for those on income assistance. The disincentive effects of child care fees are also illustrated, and the proposed solution is to develop a sliding fee schedule based on parental income. By reducing the fee to zero for families with low incomes, the disincentive inherent in a fee-based system would be ameliorated. I would argue, however, that the problem lies in the income assistance system with its high 'tax-back' rates, and attempts to find solutions must go to the source of the problem, rather than attempting to 'get around the problem.' While I would agree with Cleveland and Krashinsky that this will be difficult to achieve because of the 'politics' of income assistance, an argument needs to be put forward if the problem is ever to be effectively addressed.

The heart of the problem is that income from transfers, either through refundable tax credits such as the Child Tax Benefit, or through direct cash payments, such as income assistance, are treated differently than income from the market. The amount of 'clawback' or 'tax' is determined by the source of income, rather than the total amount of income. The problem becomes even more exacerbated when eligibility for subsidies is added to the mix. This is especially the case when multiple subsidized programs are used. For example, as noted above, earnings from income assistance recipients are generally 'taxed back' at 75 per cent for each additional dollar. Reductions in child care fee subsidies, along with reductions in other transfers such as child tax benefits, can lead to effective marginal tax rates that exceed 100 per cent for additional dollars earned. To reduce such disincentives, Cleveland and Krashinsky propose a sliding scale for child care fees. Higher income earners would pay more (10 per cent of the cost to a maximum $10 per day per child) in order to achieve a balance of 20 per cent of the cost from fees as articulated in their original proposal.

The solution, however, looks at the problem from the wrong end. I would argue that it would be more economically efficient to change the current rules governing income assistance and other transfers in a way where all income is treated the same regardless of the source. This would enable the tax and transfer system to be more truly progressive. Programs, such as child care, that other submissions show is a 'common good,' would be universally available at no fee.

Fees inherently create barriers to accessing a service, particularly for those with low incomes. I agree with the research that early child care and learning are beneficial to all children, and should therefore be available to all children. This can only happen if the service is available without a fee. Having a no-fee system also has the advantage of not requiring additional staff resources to either administer the fee (collecting, receipting, billing, and recording) or requiring staff resources to 'test' if someone is eligible for, and the amount of, the proposed subsidy. The disentangling of income transfers from program subsidies would also eliminate the disincentive issues raised by Cleveland and Krashinsky.

Of course, the question then becomes one of how do you pay for the service. I would suggest that publicly funded services through tax revenues, would, in the long term, cost no more. It simply means that the tax system is used to spread out the cost over the life cycle. That is, we make payments through the tax system over our taxable lifetime, part of which comes back to us in the form of services. The tax system is therefore used to achieve both vertical and horizontal equity in paying for services.

Such an approach is not new. Our health care system and public schooling are two obvious examples. We often do not think of health care as part of horizontal equity, but essentially, it involves transfers (in terms of service use) between those who are free of illness to those who have illness. Similarly, public education transfers benefits from persons without school-aged children to families with school-aged children. In the long term, we all benefit, at various stages, through the provision of universal, publicly funded programs. While those who decide not to have children will ask what is in it for them, the answer is relatively straightforward. Their 'reward' comes later by having a trained workforce that is able to contribute to a publicly funded income security program for seniors. Horizontal equity eventually benefits everyone over the life cycle.

The research by Browne and her colleagues reminds us that single parents with school-aged children also require access to age-appropriate child care and recreation. Their study confirms that, for single parents, entry into the labour market is dependent on having access to the age-appropriate child care. Their study also provides initial evidence on the general benefits, to both the parents and children, when such programs are accessible. These benefits extend beyond parents being able to enter the labour market. Again, barriers that fees imposed on access are identified. While Browne et al. propose a slightly different mechanism than Cleveland and Krashinsky, their solution also calls for subsidized fees for lower-income single parents to access programs. Again, I would argue that if there is a common good, and the evidence suggests that there is, then the programs should be funded publicly and should be accessible to all children.

The debate concerning public provision and private choice is often based on the assumption that we cannot afford a broad range of publicly funded programs. The irony is that we in fact already pay for much of these programs, either through direct fees by those who can afford such programs, or through the additional fundraising where we provide the baking and purchase it at the bake sale. Would it not make more sense to pool these payments in a way that allows us to spread the cost over a longer period of time? If we are already paying for the service, why should we assume that it would actually cost us more?

Given economies of scale, would it not make more sense to have such programs available to all children?

Perhaps the real issue is not one of cost, but rather one of some retaining privilege and advantage that can only be obtained if programs are denied to others.

Authors' Responses

Gordon Cleveland and Michael Krashinsky

Michael Goldberg suggests that we are looking at the problem of designing a sliding scale of fees 'from the wrong end' and that we would be better off avoiding all fees for child care – financing the entire service directly through taxes. It is certainly true that many other services (e.g., medical care, primary and secondary education) are provided without fees. But it is not clear that we should adopt this approach in our advocacy of a national child care system.

One reason for advocating that parents should directly pay 20 per cent of the cost is to increase political support for this new universal program. Many Canadians support better services for children, but feel that full-day child care, which is expensive, provides substantial direct benefits to working parents. These parents might thus be expected to contribute something (above and beyond their share of taxes) to the cost of that care to reflect the financial gains from working. Thus, a 20 per cent fee can be viewed as a political compromise to build the coalition that will enable us to achieve public child care. In fact, as mentioned at the symposium, the idea for a fee was not our original idea, but was initially the public position of the Child Care Advocacy Association of Canada. This is consistent with the findings of Canadian Policy Research Networks[1] that public opinion favours joint financing of early childhood services by government and parents. It is also consistent with parental contributions for early childhood services in many countries (Sweden, Denmark, Finland, Germany), although not others (France, kindergarten in Canada).

Once one accepts the necessity for some kind of child care fee, the need to modify the fee for low-income parents becomes intuitive – these parents cannot pay high fees, and the current welfare system imposes work disincentives that are so dramatic that the added disincentive of a child care fee can be overwhelming and discourage from working those parents who might benefit significantly from participation in the labour force.

Goldberg accepts this argument, but suggests that it would be more obvious and clearly preferable simply to reform the welfare system to eliminate significant work disincentives. He suggests this could be achieved by taxing back welfare payments at the normal tax rates paid by other citizens (25 per cent to 50 per cent approximately), rather than at the punitive 75 per cent to 100 per cent rates that are now common for social assistance recipients. (Despite the commonly used terminology of 'tax-back' rates, really we are talking about 'benefit-reduction' rates of 75 per cent to 100 per cent as income rises above certain levels.)

We believe that welfare reform is harder to achieve than Goldberg suggests. He argues that we can reform the welfare system simply by making welfare benefits taxable and avoiding any special tax-back provisions within the welfare system In effect, we would provide welfare benefits to everyone, but then tax them back at the individual's marginal tax-back rate. Higher-income individuals would thus pay back their welfare through the tax system.

The problem with this approach is both subtle and overwhelming. Goldberg's proposal in essence involves the implementation of a 'negative income tax.' While such a system seems to solve the problems of work disincentives inherent in most welfare systems, it contains a fatal flaw. Because the negative income tax proposal uses the lower tax rates of the income tax system (as opposed to the higher tax-back rates implicit in welfare systems), the costs of the system are much higher. Those on welfare who do go to work pay back fewer of their benefits (using the existing tax system's rates, they would pay back, at maximum, 50 per cent of benefits, even if they earned a high income). Low income earners may end up paying no taxes at all, or paying back much less than they currently do. Unless tax rates were changed, higher income earners would also pay lower net taxes because they receive the welfare payment and pay back only part of it The only way that the government could continue to collect enough tax revenues to pay for this new welfare plan and for its other programs would be to increase dramatically the marginal tax rates faced by all Canadians.

This problem may seem minor, but is not at all trivial. According to Krashinsky, a full negative income tax system for Canada would require marginal tax rates on earned income of 80 per cent or higher for the average tax payer.[2] These kinds of confiscatory tax rates would place efficiency costs on the economy that are undoubtedly more than can be tolerated in the currently competitive world economy. Equally problematic, these kinds of tax rates would be politically unacceptable and would doom this kind of welfare reform from the beginning.

The bottom line is this: the existing welfare system 'works' financially because not very many citizens are eligible for it, and as citizens earn income, they rapidly become ineligible for much or any social assistance. Goldberg's proposal of lowering tax-back rates would 'fix' the welfare system, but it would make the welfare system expensive enough that tax rates themselves would have to rise dramatically. Imperfect though it might be, we are likely to be forced to live with something like the current welfare system into the foreseeable future, and the heavy work disincentives implicit in that system are going to require some kind of differential treatment of child care fees for low-income parents.

Notes

1 Joseph Michalski, *Values and Preferences for the 'Best Policy Mix' for Canadian Children* (Ottawa: Family Network of Canadian Policy Research Networks, 1999).
2 Michael Krashinsky, 'The Role of Workfare in the Social Safety Net,' in *Crosscurrents: Contemporary Political Issues*, 3rd ed., M. Charlton and P. Barker, eds. (Toronto: ITP Nelson, 1998), 488–505.

Discussion

The discussion on the papers in this session tended to highlight the uneasiness felt by some in the child care community about charging fees for the use of child care services. As well, participants felt uneasy about separating out lone mothers and about expecting them to work.

On the first issue, several questioners pointed out the cost of administering a fee system, and one questioned whether it was wise to use fees to restrict use, even if parents were out of the labour force. In response, Mike Krashinsky reiterated his argument that disincentives to work built into the welfare system required some counterbalancing incentives in the day care fee. Gordon Cleveland reminded participants that the notion of charging most parents a fee had originated with the Child Care Advocacy Association of Canada.

On the second issue, several comments focused on the ways in which we place special expectations on single parents. Although we emphasize choice for most mothers, we expect lone mothers to work. In effect, we may be pathologizing single-parenthood. One questioner asked whether it was better to encourage single parents to stay out of the workforce. Another responded that part-time work might be a more realistic expectation, especially given the variety of stresses on those parents. A third reminded us that programs for lone parents were generally inadequate. But another comment raised the issue of whether we might not risk developing a problem with successive generations within a family on welfare.

Gina Brown renewed her call for an intersectoral approach, focusing on programming that would save money overall. She also reminded the group that lone parents often move out of that state by marrying.

PART 7

Child Care Workers: What Qualifications, Pay, and
Organizations Should They Have?

Introduction

The final session of the symposium shifted its attention to the people who would work in the expanded child care sector. Services such as child care are labour-intensive. The skills, knowledge, experience, and efforts of the caregivers are the primary determinants of the quality of care and the developmental effects on children. To design a national child care system without paying attention to the characteristics, pay, working conditions, and long-term career path of those workers would be foolish.

Furthermore, the wages and benefits of child care workers and the staff-child ratios in day care centres are the primary determinants of the public and private cost of care. The wages of workers involved directly with children account for about 70 per cent to 75 per cent of the cost of child care; when the wages of administrative and supervisory staff, cleaners, and other staff are factored in, that number can rise well over 80 per cent. This means that anything that affects wages, benefits, or ratios will have a dramatic and immediate impact on cost. What government policies and human resource policies will maximize the benefits from good child care while keeping costs within reason? What, approximately, should the pay, benefits, and responsibilities of child care workers be? What should the 'occupational ladder' of child care workers look like, and what should be the educational and experience requirements of different rungs on that ladder?

It is also important to keep in mind the current state of organization of the child care sector. Most children are currently cared for in informal child care arrangements. About 20 per cent of children aged two to five years are cared for in formal supervised facilities (mostly in day care centres), but these facilities are, for the most part, small non-profit institutions with non-unionized staff. While it is certainly possible that a national child care program might preserve the elements of local control implicit in the non-profit form, it is also likely that child care workers will be far more organized under such a program, whether child care is provided though local non-profit institutions or through large publicly controlled organizations. Given this reality, what is the role of unions and professional associations in determining compensation and other conditions of work? What is the role of child care workers and their organizations in defining and maintaining quality child care services, and what is the role of regulation, policy, and funding initiatives? How do we handle the difficult issues that are likely to arise during the transition as children inevitably move from informal to formal forms of care? Specifically, many of the workers in the informal sector lack the credentials and perhaps the inclination to secure employment within a regulated child care sector. How are these workers to be treated during the transition, and how are new workers to be found for the dramatically expanded formal sector?

The presenters in this session were chosen because of their knowledge of the child care workforce and of the impact of training and standards on outcomes in the child care sector. Jane Bertrand is a faculty member in the early childhood education diploma program at George Brown College in Toronto. She has been active in shaping child care policy over the past twenty years, and most recently she has been involved in studying Canada's emerging early childhood workforce and its future directions. She recently assisted with the Ontario study of early childhood services authored by Judge Margaret McCain and Fraser Mustard – *Reversing the Real Brain Drain: The Early Years Study Final Report*.[1] Annette LaGrange is an associate professor at the University of Calgary and is currently dean of the Faculty of Education. Her research focuses on early childhood education and teacher education. She is a member of the research team for the You Bet I Care! project.

The two discussants also have significant expertise in the child care workforce. Douglas Hyatt is associate professor of management, economics, and industrial relations at the University of Toronto at Scarborough, at the Rotman Faculty of Management, at the Centre for Industrial Relations, and at the Institute for Policy Analysis (all at the University of Toronto). He is also senior scientist at the Institute for Work and Health, and in 1998 was research director for the Royal Commission on Workers' Compensation in British Columbia. He is currently studying the impact of child care policy on the labour market activities of parents, and on child life course outcomes such as health, educational attainment, and labour force attachment. Marta Juorio has an ECE degree and is currently director of the YWCA Child Care Centre in Saskatoon. She is co-chair of the Child Care Advocacy Association, and she advocates for accessible affordable child care as a support service for families, as a developmental tool for children, and as an essential service for the advancement of women in society.

The session featured two very different presentations. Jane Bertrand focused on the need for standards for professional education and development that would create a well-trained and coherent child care workforce. Currently the profession is fragmented and disorganized. But post-secondary training in human development is essential to the preparation of a competent early childhood workforce. This will require higher wages. But it will also require the articulation of agreements between colleges and universities to ease the preparation of that workforce. Other things will follow – unionization, professionalization – but the development of a set of national standards for the child care workforce is the critical first step.

Annette LaGrange argued for at least two or three years of post-secondary preparation for workers in the sector, and for higher wages, at the level now being paid to nurses. She also suggested that unions would play a critical role in the emerging sector, especially in mobilizing support when child care programs were threatened.

Doug Hyatt commented largely on the contribution by Bertrand. He suggested that the child care workforce is currently largely in the unregulated informal sector. Because of this, it forms what economists call a secondary labour market. Higher educational standards will fundamentally alter the nature of this market, which will displace current workers at the same time as there is a shortage of trained personnel. There is an intellectually compelling argument for a common credential, but selling this to the public will probably require us to develop some way of measuring outputs in the sector, a problematic task.

Marta Juorio also is an advocate of higher levels of education for child care providers. This education gives child care workers the tools to find answers to everyday problems. But these higher standards will require ways to transfer credits and credentials between institutions and jurisdictions. She also supports unions in child care as a way to raise salaries and improve working conditions.

Notes

1 (Toronto: Ontario Children's Secretariat, 1999).

25. Working with Young Children

Jane Bertrand
George Brown College

Margot works at a regulated child care centre located in an office tower in downtown Toronto. She completed an Early Childhood Education (ECE) diploma at George Brown College three years ago. After graduating from college, Margot was hired to replace a staff member on maternity leave. When that contract was complete, she was able to move into a full-time position in the toddler room. Recently, she has moved into the infant group, where she works with two other staff members. The workplace child care centre includes children from three months to five years.

Sonja is a coordinator of a family resource program located in a rural community in eastern Ontario. Ten years ago, she worked as an assistant in a regulated child care centre in Kingston and enrolled part-time in an ECE diploma program at St Lawrence College. Sonja moved to a farm forty-five miles north of the city a couple of years ago. She started a half-day playgroup for preschool children and their parents which is located in a local church. Now Sonja has expanded the playgroup to a family resource program that offers activities for both children and adults including family literacy groups, a toy-lending library, respite care, and caregivers' support groups. The program receives funding from the federal Community Action Program for Children.

Ayesha provides family child care in her own home in Halifax. She completed an ECE certificate at Nova Scotia Community College five years ago. Ayesha worked in a nursery school for two years before having her own child. When her baby was six months old, Ayesha began offering family child care to three preschool children. Twice a week, Ayesha takes all of the children to a neighbourhood family resource program located in a public school.

Anna is a kindergarten teacher in a public school in Calgary. She completed an ECE diploma and worked for two years in a child care centre. Anna returned to school at the University of Alberta and completed a Bachelor of Arts in psychology. She then completed a one-year Bachelor of Education degree program. Anna is now completing a primary specialist program offered by the university during the summer months.

Corrine works in an early intervention program in Winnipeg for children with developmental delays which includes a part-time group program, individualized programs plans, and regular home visits to work with parents and other family members. She completed an ECE diploma six years ago at Red River Community College and then worked with toddlers in a child care centre. Corrine completed a Special Needs post-diploma certificate offered in the evenings.

All five of these women are working with young children and their families in early childhood settings. They earn a living caring for and educating young children who have not yet entered the formal school system. They also work with the children's families. They have different job titles, earn different salaries and benefits, and work in different environments but the core of what they do each day is similar.

Canada's fragmented approach to early child development services and programs for young children and their families creates an isolated, unconnected workforce. Individuals who work with young children are spread across regulated (governed by child care, children's services, or education legislation) and unregulated early childhood settings. Their employers may be in the private or public sector or they may be self-employed. Professional education and development opportunities are delivered through different streams of post-secondary education that, typically, do not recognize each other's credentials or offer full transfer of credits. The workforce, then, becomes an element in maintaining the fragmentation of early childhood care and education programs.

Integrated early childhood care and education programs for young children require a competent early childhood workforce. Such a workforce will evolve at the intersection of a number of events including a coherent public policy, legislation and funding framework, professionalization, and unionization. The role of professional education and development is central in creating an early childhood workforce that both supports and stimulates the evolution of an early childhood system of care and education. A common post-secondary credential is one key component. Another important consideration is the recognition and inclusion of the collective skills and abilities of those currently working with young children, in spite of their disparate qualifications and working environments.

This chapter argues that professional education and development are the critical underpinnings to both an early childhood system and an early childhood workforce. The first section summarizes the arguments for the importance of competent staff to work with young children and their families during the early years; the arguments point to post-secondary education qualifications based on a continuum of human development as essential to the preparation of a competent early childhood workforce. The second section examines the current work environments and professional education and development opportunities for individuals who work with young children. The third section proposes post-secondary professional education needed to support and promote an early childhood care and education system. The fourth section discusses the challenges post-secondary education programs in colleges and universities face in offering coordinated preparation programs for an early childhood workforce. The concluding section calls for coherent public policy, leadership from post-secondary professional education programs, research, and a national human resource network.

THE QUALITY CONNECTION

The period from conception to entry into the formal school system sets the stage for learning, behaviour, and health risks in later life. Early development, particularly the organization of the brain and its neural networks, is most rapid during the first three years. The competence and coping skills of the future labour force, future citizens, and future parents are set during this period. The social and physical environments a young child experiences determine, to a large extent, the course of early brain development. The quality of care and stimulation – parental and non-parental – a young child receives during this period is the critical environmental component that embeds experience into the brain's structure.[1]

Canadian and international studies report that staff are a key factor in the quality of care that children receive and how well they do (based on measures of cognitive, social, and emotional development). Children do better in language development, cognitive abilities, social skills, and emotional well-being when they are stimulated and nurtured by individuals with knowledge and skills in early child development.[2] Doherty reviewed the literature on quality child care settings and found that individuals with post-secondary education in child development are more likely to 'behave in desirable ways.'[3] She points out that this is not surprising because education in child development and early childhood education practices contributes to an understanding of children's developmental needs, helps the adult make appropriate responses to a child, and assists the adult in working with the group dynamics inherent among unrelated small children.

Research studies point in the direction of professional education at the post-secondary level as an important contributor to quality environments for young children. In an educational research environment where 'multiple perspectives, diverse methodologies, and conflicting and contradictory results are the norm, it is rare for researchers to be in unanimous agreement.'[4] However, there is a strong consensus among researchers that quality early childhood care and education programs for children are best supported by staff members who have completed related post-secondary education programs.

There are a number of further questions that arise in determining what format, duration, and content are optimal in preparing individuals for early childhood care and education settings.

- What kind of post-secondary education curriculum is most effective? Is a more theoretical orientation better than one that is practical?
- Is there a difference between practitioners who have completed two-year college-level diploma programs and those who have completed four-year university degrees?
- Should all adults who are working with young children have completed professional education?

Of course, one could assume that more is better and propose that all staff working with young children should have at least an undergraduate university degree in an area of study related to early child care and development But the additional costs – of both the post-secondary education itself and higher salary costs – must be justified in terms of differences in performance that affect children's outcomes and experiences.

The answers are less definitive but do suggest some possible directions to setting qualification policies and professional education programs for an early childhood system. The findings from the Atlantic Day Care Study indicate that the child care director's general education level and specialized early childhood education are associated with overall centre quality.[5] A U.S. study identified the child care centre director's level of formal education as the strongest predictor of quality and the director's specialized training in early childhood education and program administration as the second most significant predictor.[6] A Canadian study of kindergarten practices reported that kindergarten teachers with a background in early childhood education and an undergraduate university degree were the most effective teachers with four- and five-year-old children.[7] Only a few studies of family child care have been completed. A recent review of these studies identified the caregiver's formal education in early childhood education or child development as a possible key factor in contributing to high-quality family child care.[8]

Leaders and advocates in the field of early child care and education in Canada promote ECE certificate or diploma requirements for all staff working with young children and their families in child care centres. This suggests a preference for college-level ECE qualifications for everyone in centre-based programs. For example:

- The recent Canadian child care sector study recommended the establishment of educational requirements for all caregivers in regulated settings: 'Requirements should include a two-year post-secondary ECE [diploma] or equivalent for centre-based caregivers.'[9]
- Early childhood care and education organizations across Canada recommend ECE-related post-secondary education qualification (usually a two-year ECE diploma) for all program staff who are working in child care centres.

The National Family Day Care Training Project involved key national and provincial organizations and caregivers in a study of the training and professional development issues in family day care.[10] Their findings indicate strong support for accessible training for regulated and unregulated family child care providers. Caregivers, trainers, researchers, and government representatives supported a definition of training that includes post-secondary education: 'Training includes any opportunity provided to caregivers to learn new skills or enhance existing skills, or to learn information that builds caregivers' competence, self-

Table 25.1. Work with young children and their families

Environment	Workers
Unregulated family child care	155,000
In the child's home	115,000
Centre-based care	42,000
Regulated family child care	15,000
Unregulated school-age care	6,000
Kindergarten	21,000
Family resource centres	4,000*
CAP-C, early intervention	1,600*

Source: J. Beach, J. Bertrand, and G. Cleveland, *Our Child Care Workforce: From Recognition to Remuneration* (Ottawa: Child Care Sector Study Steering Committee, 1998).

confidence, personal empowerment or network of support. We see training as an ongoing process of professional development or lifetime learning. By this definition, training and learning opportunities include a range of activities such as home visits, written or audio-visual materials, mentoring, workshops and certificate courses.'[11]

WORK IN CANADIAN EARLY CHILDHOOD SETTINGS

The recent Canadian study of the child care sector found that more than 300,000 individuals work with young children and their families.[12] The majority (over 95 per cent) are women (see Table 25.1).

The working environments vary across different early childhood care and education settings. In both centre-based and home-based programs, compensation levels remain low, and a lack of respect from parents and society in general is a significant problem.[13] Compensation levels in early intervention and family support programs vary according to the funding base and organizational structure of a particular program. In contrast, kindergarten teachers working within the school system, receive higher salaries and benefits. These early childhood settings are publicly delivered and financed.

You Bet I Care! is a recent survey of staff in regulated child care centres. It provides an updated overview of working conditions in these settings.[14] The findings are discussed in other chapters in this volume.

Education Qualifications

Educational backgrounds of practitioners vary. A 1991 study of licensed child care centre staff found that 58 per cent of those in centre-based programs had completed an ECE certificate, diploma, or degree.[15] About 30 per cent of child care centre directors and 13 per cent of all child care centre staff had a university degree.

It is more difficult to obtain information about the educational levels of home-based caregivers who may be self-employed family child caregivers or caregivers employed to work in the child's home. Three recent surveys of home-based caregivers suggest that about 10 per cent have ECE credentials.[16]

The majority of kindergarten teachers have completed a university degree and a teacher education program; a proportion of those have either teacher education or a degree program with a focus or specialization in early childhood education. A number of staff in family resource programs and in early intervention programs have also completed studies in early childhood education.

Overview of ECE Post-secondary Education and Development

Post-secondary education in Canada is provided by eighty-eight universities and over 200 community colleges. Approximately 120 institutions deliver Early Childhood Care and Education credentials through community colleges, CEGEPS, universities, and private institutions. A 1996 survey of ECE programs offered in Canadian post-secondary institutions, completed for the recent child care sector study, reported that:

- Approximately 20,000 individuals are currently enrolled in ECE certificate and diploma programs. About 12,000 ECE certificate and diploma students are enrolled in continuing education and distance education models, while another 8,000 students are enrolled in full-time ECE programs.[17]
- Curricula of ECE certificate and diploma programs contain similar content that reflects a broad core of knowledge and skills. All programs include a supervised field placement component and course content in child development, behaviour guidance, and ECE methodology. The age range of children and the program delivery focus does vary. There is a trend towards expanding the scope of ECE post-secondary education programs to include children from zero to

twelve years of age in a variety of home-based and centre-based settings.[18]

- While the overall differences in curriculum content are minimal, there are significant differences in how the content is structured, and this contributes to difficulties in transferring ECE academic credits and in the portabilitly of ECE credentials. There is considerable variation in the length of the program, length of field placements, and the organization of courses.[19]

There are also approximately twenty ECE-related degree programs and Bachelor of Education programs with a preschool or ECE specialization offered at universities and university-colleges.[20] Most offer some advanced standing to students with college-level ECE credentials. In some instances the degree programs are geared towards preparation for employment in specialized early childhood settings (e.g., early intervention programs); in other instances the programs are geared towards entry into a Faculty of Education program. The Bachelor of Education programs prepare teachers for employment in public school systems. It appears that most graduates do not pursue careers in centre-based early childhood programs (such as child care centres or nursery schools) outside of the education system.

There are about twelve family child care certificate programs in British Columbia, Ontario, Quebec, and the Yukon Territory. Individuals who have completed these certificates receive little recognition for advanced standing if they enter a college-level ECE certificate or diploma program. Also various specialized post-diploma programs are offered through community colleges. Colleges and universities do offer some professional development to early childhood practitioners, but a much larger proportion is delivered by ECE professional and advocacy organizations through conferences and workshops. Family child care agencies and family resource programs offer professional development, often specifically designed for caregivers in family child care.

Career Pathways

The recent studies and reports summarized above suggest that individuals who work with young children and their families:

- Have a range of educational credentials from less than high school completion to university degrees

- Use different routes to acquire early childhood related training
- Seek out ongoing opportunities for professional development

Individuals often pursue a career working with young children and their families (as opposed to a short-term, stopgap employment. They appear to enter the field from one of three points:

1 Preservice college ECE diploma or certificate program followed by employment in an early childhood care and education setting.
2 Employment as an assistant in a centre program or as a caregiver looking after children in the home, followed by attendance in related workshops or networks, and part-time or full-time studies in ECE or a Family Child Care Certificate program.
3 University degree or college diploma (not directly related to early child development) and employment in an early childhood care and education program, followed by additional professional education in early childhood education. Once individuals have acquired early childhood education credentials, they may change settings – for example, seek employment in a kindergarten or a specialized setting, and require further education and development.

The individuals who choose to work with young children identify it as a career (as opposed to short-term employment on the way to something else or helping out a friend or relative). They make a commitment to formally or informally acquire related skills, knowledge, and abilities, and are members of an emerging early childhood workforce.

AN EARLY CHILDHOOD WORKFORCE

A new system of early childhood care and education for young children before they enter the formal school system will require a competent early childhood workforce that draws on those working in child care settings, early intervention programs, family support programs, and kindergarten classes in the school system. The effectiveness of an infusion of funding and integration of the current fragmented array of early childhood programs will depend on competent staff members who have the capacity to work with young children and their families in a variety of settings.

Defining the Early Childhood Workforce

Regardless of the setting, a competent early childhood care and education practitioner promotes the health, safety, and well-being of the child; establishes partnership with parents; supports parenting abilities; develops and maintains a positive relationship with each child and with the group; plans and provides daily learning opportunities that promote positive child development; observes and responds to children's activity and behaviour; supports learning within a context of the family, culture, and society being mindful of principles of fairness, equity, and diversity; and works in partnership with community members and organizations.[21]

An early childhood workforce includes competent practioners who are working with young children and their families in centre-based and home-based settings. They are committed to their work and seek out opportunities to expand their core knowledge, skills, and expertise. They have completed ECE post-secondary programs, or their competencies have been assessed as equivalent through a credentialling process. Inclusion in the early childhood workforce is determined by an individual's educational background and expertise, not by her specific work setting.

The implications of an early childhood workforce for those who work with young children include a broader view of early childhood programs; increased job opportunities; better coordination to ensure flexibility and mobility; and the need for more inclusive and flexible approaches to both content and delivery of early childhood care and education. This workforce will bring increasing pressure for higher levels of post-secondary education and greater participation in professional development activities.

Professional Education for An Early Childhood Workforce

Professional education can be defined as post-secondary education programs that prepare individuals for a specific occupation. They include a core body of knowledge, skills, and expertise needed to enter or participate in the occupation. Typically there are opportunities to apply theoretical learnings through guided practice.

ECE certificate, diploma, and degree programs are professional education. They prepare individuals to participate in various early childhood care and education settings – particularly in regulated child care centres and nursery schools. The curriculum centres on core knowledge and supervised field practice. However, the focus is not a broad enough preparation to meet the needs of an early childhood workforce. Professional education for an early childhood workforce to staff an expanded system of early child care and education requires an integration of ECE certificate, diploma, and degree programs with early intervention specialization programs and a primary teacher preparation program.

The breadth of such a qualification signals the need for a common university degree program. The reality of the costs of the preparatory education and the remuneration of an early childhood workforce fully educated to this level is probably prohibitive. But such a credential could serve two purposes. First, it would be a unifying element in a fragmented sector. Second, it would provide a goal or benchmark. Diploma- and certificate-level programs could then be realigned to provide a clear route for individuals who could transfer their credentials towards a degree program if they wished to pursue further education.

The degree program could qualify individuals to work in kindergarten programs within the school system, as directors of early childhood care and education programs (including child care centres and family resource programs), and as early intervention specialists. The diploma and certificate programs could qualify a core group of program staff in child care centres, nursery schools, and related early childhood settings to meet minimum adult-child ratios. The program staff could guide the work of additional assistants, volunteers, students, and parent participants who can complement the human resources and ensure optimal adult-child ratios. Providers in family child care, who do not have related qualifications, could be offered access to post-secondary certificate courses tailored to the family child care setting. The credits could be recognized for a transfer of credit towards the diploma or degree program.

An integrated early childhood care and education system for young children will require competent early childhood staff – both at the degree and diploma level. The professional education and development requirements for such an early childhood workforce will require the transformation of current post-secondary education programs to offer integrated degree and diploma programs. The new integrated degree and diploma credentials would be designed to be recognized qualifications for early childhood care and education programs delivered through education, health, and social service sectors across provincial and territorial jurisdictions.

BETWEEN VISION AND IMPLEMENTATION

The creation of linked college-level and university-level early childhood credentials would propel an early childhood system forward. But the implementation of post-secondary professional education programs will have to build on the existing programs and current levels of education among individuals who work with children. This also means dealing with the array of barriers to articulation among programs and credential mobility across provincial and territorial boundaries.

The challenges in professional education and development for an early childhood workforce include the following:

- *Inconsistent educational qualifications*
  The range of academic requirements for qualified staff in licensed centre-based child care settings vary across provincial and territorial boundaries. There are no formal post-secondary qualification requirements or recognition for individuals working in family child care. There is also considerable variation in the academic qualifications needed to work in other types of early childhood care and education settings.[22]
- *Gaps in ECE certificate and diploma and teacher education post-secondary programs*
  In the past, most ECE programs focused on centre-based programs for preschool-aged children. In recent years, there are noticeable steps to include more curriculum content and field experiences with both younger and older children, although gaps continue in course content in the care for children with special needs and in cultural, racial, and linguistic diversity. Kindergarten teachers working within public school systems must have university-level education qualifications plus teacher certification as required by that provincial or territorial jurisdictions. No jurisdiction in Canada requires that kindergarten teachers have education or expertise in early child development or early education practices. In a few instances, teacher education qualifications do include early child development and early education practices, but most do not.[23]
- *Expanding the scope of early childhood care and education*
  Broadening the scope of early childhood care and education to

include much more than centre-based, regulated programs presents challenges to existing post-secondary programs. How can programs increase the breadth of their curriculum content without diluting the depth? What is appropriate entry-level knowledge and skill competency?

- *Barriers to credit and credential mobility*
  There are both provincial or territorial and institutional barriers to the mobility of early childhood care and education credits and credentials. At the present time there are only a handful of post-secondary education qualifications that are recognized credentials in the school system and in regulated child care programs.[24] At the provincial or territorial level, it is often difficult to transfer the recognition of an early childhood care and education credential from one province to another. Some provinces offer equivalency for all credentials from specified institutions while others review credentials on an individual, course-by-course basis. Although the overall content of ECE post-secondary certificate and diploma programs is similar, the transfer of credits between institutions is often difficult. There are differences in the delivery format (e.g., length of field placements, sequencing of courses, and organization of curriculum content) and institutional autonomy. The transfer of credits between colleges and universities is another area of difficulty.
- *Effective field practice*
  Faculty members in ECE college programs seem to agree that field practice is an essential component of ECE professional education. However, there are large variations in field practice in terms of hours, structure, and supervision, and there is very little information-sharing among ECE programs about these matters. Most field placements take place in traditional centre-based settings. There is very little in the literature about what are the characteristics of effective field practice experiences.
- *Family child care*
  There are unique needs for training in family child care that are not accommodated within traditional early childhood education post-secondary programs. At the same time, colleges are not providing much in the way of credit or non-credit opportunities for providers in family child care. There is agreement that much of the curriculum content is similar but delivery format and structure must meet the needs of family child caregivers.

- *Increased credential requirements*
  Some provinces are increasing the proportion of staff requiring early childhood academic qualifications. This presents several challenges to the post-secondary ECE programs to rapidly increase the numbers of qualified staff.
- *Access*
  Barriers to professional education and development include financial cost, time, and scheduling constraints, as well as geographical location. There are ethnocultural and linguistic barriers. Delivery models and curriculum content must respond to these challenges.
- *Training for the trainer*
  As ECE programs expand their focus and scope, it will be critical to ensure that appropriate education and training is available to individuals who are teaching these courses.

MOVING FORWARD

Canada is in the midst of somewhat chaotic and uneven developments towards expanded early childhood care and education programs. But the overall trend is unmistakable. There is considerable activity within regulated child care programs, public education systems, and a tangle of family support and early child development initiatives. There is also considerable momentum to bring these different programs together and to integrate functions and formats in order to offer seamless services to young children and families.

Three major reports have recently recommended similar directions:

- The requirement is for centres available to children from an early age, where preschool children from all backgrounds can come together.[25]
- The federal, provincial, and territorial governments must create a national system of child care and early childhood education.[26]
- The framework for early child development and parenting centres draws together and expands the full range of programs and services for children and their families from conception to age six years.[27]

An integrated system of early childhood care and education programs for young children will come together because:

- There is growing recognition that the early years of life set the base

for learning, coping, competence, and well-being throughout the life cycle.
- Maternal labour force participation will remain high and is necessary to sustain family incomes and to sustain the economy.
- Early childhood care and education programs both support positive child development and encourage parental (particularly maternal) labour force attachment.

In Canada, as in European countries[28] and the United States, the provision of organized programs for young children usually precedes professional education programs to prepare staff for work in these settings. As new models of early child care and education emerge, there are changes in the related training of staff. For example, after kindergarten classes were introduced into Toronto and then Ontario schools, a kindergarten course was added to the teacher preparation program at the Normal School.[29] College early childhood education certificate and diploma programs shifted from a focus on half-day nursery school to full-day child care centres over the past couple of decades as the employment market for graduates shifted. New definitions of the work led to a redefinition of professional education.

The expansion of early childhood care and education programs in different jurisdictions in Canada offers possible solutions. For example, when New Brunswick introduced public kindergarten, the ECE teachers in the former private kindergartens were allowed to work in the school kindergarten programs and complete their teacher education degree through a part-time eight-year program.[30]

European countries are further along in the provision of publicly funded programs to young children before school entry. The specific organization and availability of programs varies, but most offer extensive provision to children from age three years on. A recent survey of staff training for publicly funded programs in the European Union reported that the professional education requirements in most countries have been reorganized and upgraded over the past twenty years.[31] In Finland, France, Greece, Ireland, Spain, and Sweden the required training takes place at universities. Belgium, Denmark, Greece, the Netherlands and Portugal offer training at vocational higher learning institutions, equivalent to Canada's post-secondary community colleges. (Greece is the only European jurisdiction with parallel systems of training and two systems of early childhood care and education for children before they enter the formal school system, which is common in most Canadian jurisdictions.) The minimum length of training is three years. France requires fully qualified staff in its *écoles maternelles* to have a three-year university degree, followed by a two-year professional course of training equivalent to a Master's degree in education. In France, Ireland, United Kingdom, and the Netherlands, the credential also qualifies individuals to work in primary schools.

The preparation of individuals to work across the array of existing early child care and education programs will prepare a workforce for integrated early childhood settings. A redefinition of professional education could also be a compelling influence on the overall quality, organization, and management of early childhood care and education programs.

In Canada, it is unlikely that (outside of Quebec) any jurisdiction will bring in dramatic public policy and funding reforms to rapidly transform the patchwork of early childhood care and education services into a coherent system. In all likelihood the transformation will evolve incrementally, step by step. In this environment coherent, coordinated professional education qualifications that cross between service and geographical jurisdictions are an important lever in moving the evolution along.

The first step could be the development of a national framework to develop coherent, articulated post-secondary programs to prepare the early childhood workforce. A pan-Canada network that includes practitioners, unions, professional and advocacy associations, post-secondary institutions, and provincial and territorial, as well as national governments is a possible mechanism to begin the process. Such a group could provide a forum for the discussion and negotiation of common credentials and the linked certificate, diploma, and degree programs.

Common professional education qualifications across Canada will build a competent workforce for early child care and education. Advocacy, professionalization, and unionization will undoubtedly have important roles in the development of such a workforce and an early childhood system. But the creation of common qualifications stands out as a leading strategy.

Notes

1 D. Keating and C. Hertzman, eds., *The Wealth of Nations in the Information Age* (New York: Guildford Press, 1999).

2 S. Kontos, *Family Day Care: Out of the Shadows and into the Limelight*, Research Monograph on the National Association for the Education of Young Children, vol. 5 (Washington, DC: NAEYC, 1992); D. Galinsky, C. Howes, S. Kontos, and M. Shinn, 'The Study of Children in Family Child Care and Relative Care – Key Findings and Recommendations,' in *Young Children* (1994) 50(1): 58–61; S. Helburn, M. Culkin, J. Morris, N. Morcan, C. Howes, L. Phillipsen, D. Bryant, R. Clifford, D. Cryer, E. Peisner-Feinberg, M. Burchinal, S. Kaga, and J. Rusticic, *Cost, Quality and Child Outcomes in Child Care Centres* (Denver etc.: University of Colorado University of California, University of North Carolina, and Yale University, 1995); M. Whitebook, *Who Cares? Child Care Teachers and Quality of Care in America* (Oakland, CA: Child Care Employee Project, 1990).

3 G. Doherty, *The Great Child Care Debate: The Long-term Effects of Non-Parental Child Care* (Toronto: University of Toronto, Childcare Resource and Research Unit, 1996), 43.

4 P. Jorde-Bloom, 'Staffing Issues in Child Care,' in *Yearbook in Early Childhood Education*, vol. 3: *Issues in Child Care*, B. Spodek and O. Saracho, eds. (New York: Teachers College Press, 1992), 143.

5 M. Lyon and P. Canning, *The Atlantic Day Care Study* (St John's NF: Memorial University of Newfoundland, 1995).

6 P. Jorde-Bloom, 'Professional Orientation: Individual and Organizational Perspectives,' in *Child and Youth Care Quarterly* (1989) 18: 227–40.

7 C. Corter and N. Park, eds., *What Makes Exemplary Kindergarten Programs Effective?* (Toronto: Ministry of Education and Training, 1993).

8 D.A. Boisvert, *Literature Review of Training and Family Day Care: A Background Paper Prepared for the Family Day Care Training Project* (Ottawa: National Family Day Care Training Project, 1997).

9 J. Beach, J. Bertrand, and G. Cleveland, *Our Child Care Workforce: From Recognition to Remuneration* (Ottawa: Human Resources Development Canada / Canadian Child Care Federation, 1998), 141.

10 L. Dunster, *Synthesis Report: A Summary of the Findings of a National Study on Training for Family Day Care* (Ottawa: National Family Day Care Training Project, 1998).

11 Ibid., 3.

12 Beach et al., *Our Child Care Workforce*.

13 Ibid.

14 G. Doherty, D.S. Lero, H. Goelman, A. LaGrange, and J. Tougas, *You Bet I Care! A Canada-Wide Study on: Wages, Working Conditions, and Practices in Child Care Centres* (Guelph: Centre for Families, Work, and Well-Being, 2000).

15 Canadian Child Care Advocacy Association / Canadian Child Care Federation, *Caring for a Living – Final Report: A Study on Wages and Working Conditions in Canadian Child Care* (Ottawa: Authors, 1992).
16 The three surveys by Goss-Gilroy Inc., Management Consultants, in 1998 found that approximately one-third of each group of caregivers had completed a college or university program (11 per cent of unregulated family caregivers and 9 per cent of in-home caregivers reported an ECE qualification. Based on 1991 Census data, the sector study reported that 30 per cent of caregivers in family child care and 22 per cent of in-home caregivers had post-secondary education qualifications (Beach et al., *Our Child Care Workforce*). A number of unregulated caregivers are not recorded by the census, and the reported data may reflect this bias. The selection of the respondents to the surveys through random telephone calls may have resulted in a bias in the sample; the number of caregivers who declined to participate is not reported.
17 Beach et al., *Our Child Care Workforce*.
18 Ibid.
19 Ibid.
20 J. Bertrand and J. Beach, 'Mobility of Early Childhood Care and Education Credits and Credentials in Canada,' *Research Connections* 2:101–140 (Ottawa: Canadian Child Care Federation, 1999).
21 Adapted from Beach et al., *Our Child Care Workforce*.
22 Bertrand and Beach, *ECCE Credit*.
23 J. Bertrand, *ECCE University Degree Programs* (Ottawa: Association of Canadian Community Colleges / Canadian Child Care Federation, in press).
24 Ibid.
25 T. Kent, *Social Policy 2000: An Agenda* (Ottawa: Caledon Institute of Social Policy, 1998), 20.
26 National Council of Welfare, *Preschool Children: Promises to Keep* (Toronto: Author, 1999), 20.
27 M. McCain and F. Mustard, *Reversing the Real Brain Drain: The Early Years Report* (Toronto: Ontario Children's Secretariat, 1999), 152.
28 P. Oberhuemer and M. Ulich, *Working with Young Children in Europe* (London: Paul Chapman Publishing, 1997).
29 J. Mathien, *School Programs for Young Children in Ontario and Toronto* (Unpublished manuscript, 1990).
30 L. Johnston and J. Mathien, *Early Childhood Services for Kindergarten-age Children in Four Canadian Provinces: Scope, Nature and Models for the Future* (Ottawa: Caledon Institute of Social Policy, 1998).
31 P. Oberhuemer and Ulich, *Working with Young Children*.

26. Thoughts on Child Care Workers

Annette LaGrange
University of Calgary

POLICY

The context of the work and the nature of the field influence the way that those who work in the field are prepared, compensated, and valued. There is considerable diversity in the way child care is provided in Canada, and this makes the formation of policy complex. This complexity is further complicated by the ambivalent public view of child care, and the difficulty in establishing a clear identity for those who work in the field.

Qualifications and Standards of Care

While other caring professions (such as nursing or teaching) have increased the minimum education required of caregivers, child care has lagged behind. International standards suggest two or three years of post-secondary education should be the norm. Our goal ought to be to get to the level of three years of preparation. There is some argument, at least at the beginning, for differentiating roles within the child care centre. Some workers might be required to have more years of preparation than others, a strategy that has worked in nursing, but not in teaching.

We have not yet reached closure on the precise nature of the training that child care workers should receive. While there is certainly a role for highly technical training, oriented around psychology and science, many caring professions are moving towards a more philosophical orientation that amplifies various concepts of care.

Wages and Support for Child Care Workers

Child care workers are not well paid relative to other care providers. If we expect workers to achieve higher levels of training, we will have to pay them appropriately. This is probably the biggest challenge for an emerging national policy.

A reasonable goal would probably be to pay child care workers on a par with nurses. One way to achieve this would be to begin by raising the salaries of the most qualified workers in child care, using differentiated staffing models. Over time, this can be used to raise the qualifications and standards of all workers. Eventually, child care should move to a relatively undifferentiated wage structure, like that for teachers. The only way to achieve that is through public funding, since as long as pay increases must be passed on to parents, there will be barriers to decent wages.

Higher wages must flow out of a greater appreciation by Canadians for the work of those employed in child care. This appreciation will also improve morale in the field and provide the basis for political support for a national child care system.

Unions and Associations

Traditionally, unions have not always supported professionalization Nevertheless, the experience in education and nursing suggests to us that unions will be essential in raising wages. Professional associations are also critical in developing the standards essential in child care. But these professional organizations must also serve a critical advocacy process. Again, the experience in teaching and nursing suggests that these functions can all be carried out effectively by a single association.

THE ALBERTA EARLY CHILDHOOD SERVICES PROGRAM

In Alberta, in 1973, Early Childhood Services (ECS) was a specific program developed to provide integrated services to children from zero to eight years of age, and separate from child care services. At that time, it was deliberately developed not as a kindergarten program, but as a community-based set of services to children. The goal was to begin with special services to disadvantaged children, then implement enrichment programs for kindergarten, and finally to have the system evolve into an integrated system of child care. We emphasized the interdisciplinary nature of services to children and arranged for the program to be shared by four government ministries.

Of course, those who worked in the program required training, but credentialling was through the Department of Education. This attracted the attention of the Alberta Teachers' Association, which lobbied very hard to have all those training in education classified as teachers. The policy adopted was to require a teaching certificate and to also require an early childhood diploma to ensure that the teacher was an early childhood specialist. The teachers' association opposed this ECE credential and fought it for almost twenty years. In 1989 the requirement was eliminated.

The results are clear. In 1989, of ECS workers 97 per cent had an early childhood certificate; in 1995, when the government cuts began, the percentage holding the certificate was down to 40 per cent. One lesson is that when early child care is closely associated with other professions, there is danger of losing a clear and distinct identity. This may erode parental involvement and consequent support and advocacy for child care. And it may lead those in child care to assume that because they are allied with the teachers' movement, they require less parental support. In Alberta, when the cuts came, we did not have the kinds of links with parent groups and the kinds of allies that could have been most helpful.

Furthermore, the support of the teachers' association was not unequivocal. When the cuts came, they affected all parts of the educational system. Since many ECS workers had seniority, they would normally displace teachers with less seniority. At the beginning, the teachers' association was not supportive of this process. However, there was also an advantage in our connection with the teachers' association. In the end, the union did support the principle of seniority. It also launched a strong and effective public relations campaign in favour of early childhood education. The focus on young children worked, and the government was forced to back down and restore some of the program.

So the lesson is a mixed one. We were stronger and less vulnerable in being connected with the teachers' association, but we also lost full control over what constituted an early childhood professional. In hindsight, I would have preferred a looser link to education, but with the protection of a strong professional organization.

Another lesson from the ECS situation is that the focus must not only be on wages, but also on the caring services provided by workers. The emphasis on services is what brings parents and other voters on board.

We have also observed that there are relatively few men in the early childhood profession. At first we thought this was because of the low salaries associated with the field. But even after the link to the teachers' association equalized salaries, men did not seem anxious to do this kind of work. This was true, even when there were lots of potential jobs for men in early education, and jobs elsewhere were relatively scarce. I suspect that this has something to do with issues of 'women's work' and the way we treat and view workers who care for young children.

On balance, I have to come down on the side of the teachers' association, and on an emphasis on the positive things that they can accomplish for child care workers. The most important accomplishment is higher wages. I also have to emphasize the importance of insisting on greater qualifications for child care workers. We need to require at least three years of post-secondary preparation, and we need to ensure mobility across the caring professions. But the issue of who will provide that training is less clear, especially in an era when universities are no longer the sole keepers of diplomas and certificates. I suspect that in ten years we will be looking at a very different combination of experiences and courses that will go into creating a degree or certificate.

In the end, however, the key will be wages. If child care workers are to be respected, then they will have to be paid the same as nurses and teachers. They certainly deserve as much.

27. Issues in the Professionalization of Child Care

Douglas Hyatt
University of Toronto, Institute for Work and Health

Jane Bertrand has assembled a very thought-provoking chapter. To me, at least, at its essence is the basic question, 'Why should Canadian society be willing to accept lesser standards of qualification for those working in all manner of early childhood education settings than it does for teachers of other young children? The evidence that exists, and probably most people's intuition, points to the essential nature of appropriate stimulation of young children in helping to place them on lifelong development paths. The dependency on these paths established at early ages may well end up closing doors for the child later in life, without giving the child the opportunity to decide which doors to walk through.

Young children are exposed to a patchwork quilt of child care experiences, which is mirrored in the patchwork of child care providers. Children should receive a similar (high) quality of care from appropriately trained providers, independent of the setting. Assuming the existence of an otherwise supportive child care public policy environment, the creation of this seamless early childhood care structure is supported by:

1 An inclusive definition of the early childhood workforce. This definition encompasses both formal and informal caregivers, as well as kindergarten teachers.
2 Professional education and career-long development. These are seen to be central to enhancing the abilities of early childhood workers and the quality of care they provide. Further, the commitment to professionalism exhibited by child care workers who clear these educational hurdles provides a signal of quality to those seeking care for their children.

3 An early childhood workforce with a common post-secondary credential. To encourage and support a more professional workforce and career-long learning, post-secondary institutions need to better align their programs (and perhaps attitudes!) to recognize course credits from other post-secondary institutions.

In addition to the potential for providing higher quality care for children, professionalization is a proactive approach to improving the lot of early childhood workers. Early childhood care, to many observers and advocates, is seen as an employment 'ghetto.' Child care workers are often cast as constituents of the 'secondary labour market,' which is characterized by poor remuneration, low occupational status, little opportunity for career advancement, and no investment in continuing training. A concern among those who study secondary labour markets is that they cause workers to exhibit the kinds of qualities that one might expect from those confronted by these conditions: high likelihood of voluntary or involuntary exit; absenteeism; and little upgrading of skills. Secondary labour markets are therefore particularly insidious because they become self-fulfilling – workers become less attractive to employers outside of the secondary labour market as a result of their experiences and therefore find it extraordinarily difficult to leave. It also makes consumers of services purchased by these workers suspicious of the quality they are receiving, and in the child care setting this must influence the attitudes of parents towards child care workers and the value of their services.

In essence, the three supporting mechanisms also represent a 'bootstrap' approach to, at once, raising the quality of care received by Canada's children and improving the perceptions of parents and others who 'pay' for child care services. The systemic undervaluing of child care work that is reflected in low wages, poor working conditions, and barriers to career advancement would be addressed through professionalization.

Bertrand raises a number of provocative issues that will be the fodder for much lively, and no doubt productive debate. However, there are at least three important areas where the debate would benefit from more information.

First, while there is an intellectually compelling argument to be made for child care workers achieving a common core post-secondary credential, it is not entirely obvious from the existing research that this results in better 'outcomes.' Perhaps more to the point, what specifically are the child outcomes we are trying to achieve with a move to professionalization? My own sense is that the citizenry has become weary of programs that measure their success by the quality of inputs rather than the quality of outputs. How will we know if this approach makes a difference? It is the child care research and advocacy community that should lead the way in defining how we measure success. I also believe that there are substantial research opportunities for cross-national studies of contrasting approaches to child care professionalization and to measure the extent to which the different approaches seem to matter.

Professionalization of the child care workforce will likely have two immediate effects. The first is that the supply of qualified child care workers will fall. This is a fairly predicable consequence of raising the bar. The second is that unless a significant phase-in period is allowed (and why should it be if it places children at risk?), then those workers who are suddenly unqualified for their jobs will be displaced. In many respects, this displacement is like any other industrial restructuring, that is, workers become unemployed because they lack the skills necessary to fill existing job openings (termed 'structural unemployment' by economists). We have learned a great deal about the impacts of structural unemployment on workers, particularly older workers. While retraining may help some of those who lose their jobs, it does not have a stellar record. I am no more optimistic about the displaced old guard of the child care workforce to successfully retrain than other displaced workforces, and perhaps even less optimistic if they have been tarnished by their association with the secondary labour market. As part of the plan to professionalize, there must be an accompanying realistic plan for addressing the resulting displacement of workers.

Finally, beginning the process of bringing post-secondary institutions to a common core curriculum is an essential next step. As Bertrand noted, research on what constitutes an 'optimal' curriculum is currently sparse. It appears that post-secondary institutions have filled this information vacuum with different programs – perhaps because of the legitimate differences in how the programs ought to be run, or perhaps as a protectionist marketing strategy. This process could begin with a courageous group from the child care community structuring a very specific core curriculum that recognizes, through the use of specialized courses, the necessity for some institutions to respond to the special needs of the communities they more directly serve.

28. The Need for a Well-Trained Child Care Workforce

Marta Juorio
Director, YWCA Child Care, Saskatoon

THE TRAINING OF THE CHILD CARE WORKFORCE

Working with young children is rewarding and challenging. Caregivers who are well adapted to the job often turn their dedication into a long-term commitment. 'Caregiver' is a term used globally to describe the many individuals who work with children in early childhood settings. In essence, the nature of the work is similar, but the variety of their work environments shows the fragmented nature of child care in Canada. The differences described by Bertrand reflect the wide range of needs families and children have. It is difficult to define the key common features of the 'child care profession.' A teacher teaches, but what does a caregiver do?

Because women bear and nurture their own children, caregiving is seen as a natural extension of this role. The myth persists that to look after the needs of young children requires no training; anybody can do it.

In addition to working in environments that vary greatly, caregivers receive a wide range of wages that are seldom adequate with few or no existing benefits. Different titles describe different caregivers with essentially similar jobs. This is an enduring paradox: this profession employs a multitude of capable and committed individuals providing important services who, so far, have been unable to gain recognition from society, governments, and the public in general.

HOW DO YOU DESCRIBE A CAREGIVER?

A caregiver has the ability to:

• Nurture and understand children

- Foster self-esteem in each individual child as well as tending to her or his health and safety
- Mediate conflicts among children without bruising tender egos
- Discipline with understanding
- Develop programs for age-appropriate activities
- Foster creativity in children through activities
- Provide continuing support to parents

While family life has changed drastically, society's views and (often) parents' views of what a family should be have not been altered. The programs that train caregivers must prepare students to deal with both halves of this complex new reality.

The work environment has also changed, and working parents have more stress, more demands on their time, and less quality time with their children. This has added a new dimension in the life of young children. Caregivers are, then, an essential supplement providing balance and continuity for children while enabling parents to function in their multiple roles. A good quality child care program should be a special place away from home, where a child learns and thrives in trust.

EDUCATING OUR CHILD CARE WORKFORCE

Once we understand that child care is a reality of modern life, beneficial for children, and a positive support for parents, we must insist that children deserve and need services of high quality. This will not happen without a well-defined plan supported by governments. Society's attitudes to the rearing of children and the role of government assistance to families must evolve. A competent and well-educated child care workforce will be instrumental in educating the public and getting the message across. This will not happen automatically. Society does not question the value of having educational standards for schoolteachers; this expectation was established a long time ago. The benefits of teacher education to children and society are accepted. Since new research points out the importance of children's early years, it should now become equally well accepted that having qualified and competent educators is key to determining the quality of care young children will receive.

To have effective and successful early childhood care and education programs, we need a workforce that is capable of meeting this challenge. We need educational standards, but we also need a set of policies that will address the existing inequalities. An educated and talented workforce will have to receive adequate remuneration. While this may be difficult, one thing will not happen without the other. Wages are an important predictor of quality in child care as well as an important factor affecting turnover of staff, which in turn affects quality.[1]

The most valued and lasting gifts a child can get from a quality environment are a secure sense of self, positive socialization, meaningful interactions, creativity, and a deep-rooted eagerness to learn that will last a lifetime. Caregivers must, then, have a sound understanding of children's developmental stages to be able to provide activities that will enhance learning. Activities provided that are above a child's level of development are not only wasted but have the potential of dulling the child's interest in learning.

A combination of theory and practice is favoured in preparing the students for the child care field. I firmly believe, in contrast to some of my colleagues, that theory is most important; practice will come naturally in a job context. Valuable time in the classroom must not be sacrificed to allow for extended practical experience.

The personal attributes of future caregivers are very important. Some people naturally interact well with children, and a solid education in early childhood can only improve their aptitude. On the other hand, no amount of suitable education will improve the interactions of individuals who lack the degree of tolerance and patience needed to work with young children.

I personally believe that professional education for caregivers will not only improve the quality of the care children receive, it will also improve the professional image of caregiving.

THE HIGH COST OF QUALITY CARE

Despite the current inadequate funding and support for child care, we must not give in to the pressures created by the present climate of tight budgets. If we do so, we fail to look at the whole picture and we will close doors to future opportunities for growth, both for children and for staff. How can we justify and argue that child care providers should have undergraduate university degrees? While this may be considered out of the reach of our collective pockets, I would suggest that there would be considerable benefits in offering various levels of education to child care providers. It would offer new opportunities for staff and create a career ladder. In addition, it will prevent people from becoming stagnant and trapped in a field with little opportunity for advancement. It would promote excellence in child care.

Towards a Suitable Child Care Workforce

Early childhood education training programs should be designed to create opportunities for further education and career options.[2] The first step is to standardize present college programs in a way that will allow students to transfer credits to other provinces. The next is to upgrade the content so students can transfer some credits to university, to pursue a degree in education, psychology, speech therapy, or other related fields. A comprehensive system of early childhood education could start with a set of basic child development and psychology classes that could evolve either into a college degree or a university degree.

College degrees could offer specialization in administration, communication skills, and human resources management to prepare students for a director or supervisor position. While caregivers in charge of the children would have post-secondary education, there could be others with more in-depth background in areas of language development, socialization, or special needs. There also could be support staff in charge of routine tasks such as mealtimes and pre-nap routines as well as outdoor play supervision, which are less-demanding tasks. This would allow the primary caregivers to concentrate on the overall learning experiences of the children. I am not particularly favourable to promoting hierarchies in the child care workplace, but the sharing of some duties will make trained staff more capable of important initiatives. Such an arrangement would provide the opportunity for more one-on-one interactions for caregivers in charge of a group of children.

THE NEED FOR A COMPREHENSIVE APPROACH

To meet the diverse needs of children, families, and communities, a competent child care workforce must be equipped to be inclusive. College curricula must prepare students to deal with diversity both of family make-up and ethnicity. Students must have the ability to advise on common health concerns of young children, nutrition, and communicable diseases. Curricula must also include some specialization for infant care as well as school-aged care.

A well-prepared child care workforce would have an important role in the early diagnosis of possible delays by helping parents of children with developmental needs to find suitable professional support.

Infant care needs special training. The whole issue of after-school care needs to be looked after and integrated with a service that meets the needs of children. A whole range of activities could be offered by after-school care such as art, gym, and special projects. These activities could be guided by staff trained to do this and would free valuable school teachers' time.

A narrow scope in the early childhood education curriculum will graduate students afraid to deviate from the limited boundaries of their textbooks and limit their motivation to expand their knowledge. By broadening it, students will have the opportunity to become more confident in their ability to deal with the complex issues facing child care today. Fostering creative and critical thinking must be an essential part of the training. Working with young children requires skills and knowledge that are provided though formal education.

The importance of professional education for caregivers is also emphasized in Annette LaGrange's chapter. Standards in other countries point to the benefits of two to three years of specific education. Given the complex nature of the work, LaGrange favours three years of preparation. In addition to educational standards, she recommends a high-profile professional association that will both educate and advocate for caregivers.

WORKING CONDITIONS

Long hours, demanding work, unsuitable wages, and poor or non-existent benefits such as inadequate pension and dental plans are harsh realities for new graduates. Capable students who have finished their educational programs with excellent marks and high expectations feel discouraged. Not having appreciated the weight of the responsibility that they have to carry once they become staff themselves, they are unable to cope with the stress. Efforts to significantly improve staff salaries have become secondary to the quality of care children receive.[3] Child care staff are a critical determinant of quality in early child care and education programs.[4]

CONCLUSION

In a society that equates success to earning power, it is not then surprising that child care providers command little recognition. A new profession needs to come to life. Considerations of cost are no excuse to keep child care as a second-class job for untrained women. European countries and Quebec have been able to justify the effort and expense of creating services staffed by trained and qualified early childhood professionals. We have a lot to learn from their example.

Well-adjusted child care providers are resilient, enduring individuals with considerable enthusiasm for their chosen occupation. They accept the noisy environment, deal with parents' frustrations, handle emotionally charged situations, deal with children who may kick, bite, and punch. Given the poor compensation, and absence of advancement opportunities, it is not surprising that there is high turnover in the field. Love can only go so far. When positive, well-adjusted staff leave, we lose a major investment in education and experience: a loss for children and for society. The growing evidence supporting the link between trained staff and healthy child developmental outcomes should persuade governments and parents that a custodial solution for child care is not a good enough solution.

Notes

1 M. Whitebook, C. Howes, D. Phillips, *Who Cares? Child Care Teachers and Quality of Care in America. Final Report of the National Child Care Staffing Study* (Oakland, CA: Child Care Employee Project, 1990).
2 J. Bertrand, *Caring for the Children: Putting the Pieces Together. A Child Care Agenda for 90s* (Toronto: Ontario Coalition for Better Child Care, 1994).
3 B. Finkelstein, 'Women and the Dilemmas of Professionalism,' in *Professionalism and the Early Childhood Practioner*, B. Spodek, O. Saracho, and D. Peters, eds. (New York: Teachers College Press, 1988).
4 G. Doherty, *Quality Matters in Child Care* (Huntsville, ON: Jesmond Publishing, 1991).

Author's Response

Jane Bertrand

Canada's youngest children and their families need a comprehensive system to support early child development and parenting. Such a system could include all the fragmented, isolated programs that now exist in isolation. But to bring together child care centres, nursery schools, and preschool programs, family resource programs, kindergarten, early intervention programs, parenting and family literacy initiatives, and family child care is a daunting challenge. An early childhood workforce would help build bridges between programs and services. Common post-secondary credentials and opportunities for ongoing education and development are essential to the development of a competent early childhood workforce.

WHAT WOULD HAPPEN TO THE MANY CAREGIVERS WHO DO NOT HAVE EDUCATIONAL QUALIFICATIONS?

First, I do not argue that all those working with young children will be required to have post-secondary education qualifications. I suggest that there should be a core component of qualified staff available to meet *minimum* adult-child ratios. These individuals would work with assistants, students, volunteers, and parent participants which would provide the optimum number of adults to meet the needs of very young children. I believe that if salaries and benefits were improved and articulated diploma and degree programs were available, many individuals would acquire the credentials.

Second, I do not suggest that family child caregivers would be required to have post-secondary education credentials. Members of an early childhood workforce may opt to provide family child care and could be supports and mentors to other providers.

Finally, just as a comprehensive system will not be created instantly, an early childhood workforce will take time to develop. There are several options to consider that can build on the existing capacities of those who are now working with young children. In-service and distance education delivery models can be adapted to meet the needs of those now working in the sector.

WHAT WOULD BE THE BASIS FOR THE CURRICULUM OF COMMON POST-SECONDARY EDUCATION DIPLOMA AND DEGREE CREDENTIALS?

The curriculum should be developed to prepare individuals to support the early development of young children and parenting abilities. The purpose of a 'professional education' is not to train individuals to acquire a particular set of skills but to develop the ability to be reflective practitioners in their work with young children and their families. Therefore, the common curriculum needs to include opportunities to develop critical thinking, examine multidisciplinary, cross-cultural human development perspectives, and to integrate this framework into practice.

To identify the curriculum content necessary for common diploma and degree programs, we will need to identify what are our goals for young children. I suggest that these goals should include health and well-being, the ability to cope and get along with others in rapidly changing and diverse environments, and basic competence to acquire literacy and numeracy skills. (I hasten to point out that the recognition of the importance of laying the basis for literacy and numeracy during the early years is a reasonable goal in the current Canadian context and this is *not* accomplished by promoting a structured, academic readiness curriculum.) Young children make meaning of their world and acquire coping abilities and competencies through the relationships they have with the adults who nurture their minds and bodies. The curriculum to prepare an early childhood workforce in Canada must be based in the cultural, linguistic, religious, and racial diversity that is part of our Canadian identity. It must respect a wide diversity of child-rearing practices.

Support to parents and other family members includes intentional support to parenting abilities. The most effective strategy to enriching young children's development is to engage parents as active partners who participate in their child's early learning and development.

A degree credential could offer areas of specialization, including administration, leadership, and management for centre directors, or more intensive study related to a particular work environment or age grouping.

WILL PROFESSIONAL EDUCATION CONTRIBUTE TO A PROFESSIONALIZATION THAT CREATES AN ELITE EARLY CHILDHOOD WORKFORCE THAT ALIENATES PARENTS AND OTHER CAREGIVERS?

Early childhood educators in North America have spent considerable energy debating the issue of professionalism over the past couple of decades. Many suggest that a new type of egalitarian professionalism is needed that values both the caring and teaching aspects of work with young children. Some suggest more inclusive opportunities to acquire credentials and recognition than are found in more traditional professions.

The harsh truth must be faced, however. Educational credentials do create barriers between people who are working together and separate those who have the credentials from those who do not. I believe that the critical piece is to work to ensure that we develop accessible postsecondary programs designed for adult learners with diverse educational and life experiences. We also need to think carefully before we take on other characteristics of traditional professions that may interfere with our collective ability to work effectively with parents.

WHAT ABOUT IN-SERVICE EDUCATION AND DEVELOPMENT?

The early childhood workforce will need ongoing opportunities for continuing education and development. Preservice diploma and degree programs should be geared to encourage graduates to seek out formal and informal learning opportunities. We need to consider the infrastructure necessary to ensure this is possible. The ongoing development of a competent early childhood workforce needs to be supported by academic graduate programs and early child development research in Canadian universities.

Many, by necessity or choice, will complete post-secondary education qualifications while working with young children and families.

Others may work as assistants or parent participants for a period of time and will be able to apply their in-service development and experiences towards credits in post-secondary programs if they decide to pursue formal studies.

HOW WILL MORE POST-SECONDARY EDUCATION PROGRAMS SUPPORT QUALITY HOME-BASED CHILD CARE?

Quality in-home and family child care options should be included as part of a comprehensive system. Supported home-based child care offers in-home and family child caregivers opportunities such as networking, workshops, home visits, group playtime for children, community resources, book- and toy-lending libraries, and referrals to other services. An early childhood workforce will be prepared to work in settings that provide these kind of opportunities. Their preparation will include an understanding of adult learning and how to engage parents and caregivers in understanding early child development.

I can think of no better way to conclude, than to quote Helen Penn, one of the keynote speakers at the symposium: 'We need reflective and well-informed practitioners, who do not assume there is one best practice which suits us all, but who are able to recognize, explore and discuss the arc of human possibilities.'[1]

Note

1 H. Penn, *Summary: Values and Beliefs in Caring for Babies and Toddlers* (Toronto: Childcare Resource and Research Unit, University of Toronto, 1999), 4.

Discussion

The discussion on this topic returned to some of the themes that had emerged earlier in the session on quality. Several questioners focused on the problem of how to adjust training requirements to the reality that 70 per cent of the child care now being provided was in the informal sector, where all the workers were essentially unregulated. That being the case, one questioner asked whether further training for the 30 per cent of workers in the formal sector should be our highest priority. Some argued for the need for different standards for family home child care workers. Annette LaGrange suggested that one way to handle this problem would be to give some credit for experience. Others emphasized the value of formal training, since it raised job satisfaction by providing some knowledge of how and why we provide child care. Also, formal education developed the essential skill of learning how to solve problems and to think.

The issue of the long-run fate of family home child care within a comprehensive system was left unresolved.

Other comments focused on the problem of how to make the transition to a more intensively trained workforce. One questioner emphasized the need to link training to wages, and commented that at present, workers faced a problem in raising wages, since these would have to be passed directly on to parents. Another questioner reminded us of the need to grandfather existing workers while providing incentives for them to upgrade their skills. This had occurred in education thirty years ago when degree requirements were introduced. Several questioners reminded us that training was itself no replacement for aptitude and caring (and one suggested that this might be at the heart of some of the resistence among some workers to professionalization). One suggested the importance of considering the additional skills we would require of directors of child care centres. Another emphasized the need for transferability of credits, citing the Quebec system that allowed CEGEP-trained workers to gain credit if they entered university. Yet another emphasized the need for ongoing in-service training.

Concluding the session, Annette LaGrange reminded us that some of the debate arose from the peculiar nature of child care, which lies between the public world of patriarchal education and the private world of home.

Conclusions

We believe, as we concluded at the end of our policy study on the costs and benefits of a universal program of early childhood education in Canada, that there are good reasons to invest considerable public money in child care. The phrase is hackneyed – worn thin by repetition at after-dinner speeches – but still true: children are our future. The benefits of developmental early childhood experiences to children and their families, and through them to society as a whole, are considerable. Many countries already provide extensive early childhood development services for children above two years of age; without any federal financial assistance, Quebec has begun to move in this direction on its own.

When we began planning the symposium, from which this volume is the result, our goal was to move policy discussion on from the 'whether' to the 'how' – that is, to move beyond the debate on whether Canada needs a child care program to a discussion of the details of how such a program might be implemented. We defined a series of key unresolved policy questions that we thought might provoke useful debate among academics, policy experts, and policy advocates committed to child care. We hoped that those debates might help resolve some of the issues of policy design that would have to be decided before Canada could implement a national child care strategy.

Was the symposium successful? Did we feel at the end that those questions had been answered: did we know more about the 'how' of getting a good child care program? What did we learn; how has our thinking been changed; what policy path should child care follow? Alternatively, what do we still not know – that is, what issues remain to be resolved and what concerns still, potentially, lie between a conviction that Canada needs better child care policy and the nuts and bolts of designing a child care policy?

In Part 1, on federal-provincial issues, we learned that the debate over whether child care is a federal or provincial issue, or more specifically, whether the major stumbling block that has prevented the implementation of a child care program has been at the federal or the provincial level, is to some extent a red herring. Especially in the light of Quebec's recent child care reforms (discussed in Part 2) and the proposals in British Columbia, it appears that the problem has been primarily one of political will at all levels, rather than of jurisdiction. Federal money will be essential in building a national program, but expanded political support for a specific set of child care and family policy reforms is the prerequisite, the sine qua non. Bob Rae, and others, reminded us of the necessity of building political coalitions in favour of child care at all levels. He argued, persuasively, that getting at least one provincial government (other than Quebec) to champion a provincial or national program of early education and care is an indispensable part of a political process for advancing child care on the policy agenda. The success and popularity of child care reforms in Quebec suggests that when appropriate coalitions have been built, and when political will is present, progress can be made quickly. Martha Friendly made powerful arguments that there is no inherent barrier to federal leadership on child care issues – the social union agreement and federal leadership on child care policy reform can be entirely consistent with one another. If we are going to have a nation-wide child care program in Canada, the federal government will have to facilitate it by the judicious provision of an important part of the funding.

In Part 3, on quality care, there was substantial agreement, in relation to child care centres, on the benefits of spending additional dollars on staff training. As economists, we tend to focus on the trade-offs among the various ways in which money might be spent. In other words, good quality child care might be achievable in a number of different ways (e.g., lower ratios but more training, higher ratios but less training, or more training for directors and less for staff). From this perspective, a discussion of child care quality might involve an enumeration of the key factors that might affect quality (e.g., various teacher characteristics, such as education, age, and experience; staff-child ratios, group size, and other elements of classroom structure; the size of the centre, type of programming, mix of children, and other aspects of centre structure; characteristics of the director or administration of the child care facility; and auspice and amount of public support). Then, the discussion would proceed to evaluate the relative contribution of each of these factors to quality and the ways in which these factors complement one another or can be substituted for one another in producing good quality child care (e.g., do kindergartens and day care centres, with their very different combinations of staff-child ratios, group size, and staff education, both provide good quality developmental care?). Finally, with an eye to the costs associated with these different factors, we would determine the lowest-cost way of meeting our quality objectives.

Most participants in the symposium felt, however, that at least two or three years of post-secondary training is an indispensable requirement for those people who would care for our children. Put another way, although participants would undoubtedly agree that other factors, like staff-child ratios, group size, and programming, are important, they seemed to agree that the most important next step for increasing quality was a general rise in the training of caregivers. There was considerable discussion of the important benefits of this policy change, with some discussion of the potential costs and techniques for the implementation of these new requirements.

Quite aside from the issue of trade-offs among various quality-enhancing factors within centres, there remains the related issue of the quality and appropriate role for family child care. Should the emphasis be on quality in centre-based facilities, or should quality in family child care be the biggest concern? There was no consensus, nor even agreement on whether family child care providers should meet a formal in-class educational standard in order to improve child care quality. The argument is twofold: these caregivers do not have the time or ability to upgrade in a formal setting, and family child care providers tend to have extra experience in caregiving which can be traded-off against formal education in producing child care quality. This debate, though unresolved, stimulated considerable thought.

What was also clear, both from Part 3 and Part 7, on the labour force, was that it is difficult to deal with the issue of what will happen to the current secondary labour force that now supplies most of the informal care in Canada. While many of these workers are, no doubt, dedicated and caring individuals, it is also true that child care has long been considered one of those jobs that virtually anyone can do. (It is, perhaps, instructive that Statistics Canada's National Occupational Classification groups informal child care providers along with cosmeticians, pedicurists, animal care workers, zoo attendants, astrologers, psychic consultants, colour consultants, weight loss consultants, and home support workers. In other words, Statistics Canada views these different occupations as requiring approximately the same skill type and skill level.) Insistence on post-secondary education would naturally change this. Many of those now working in the sector would, we suspect, not be able to obtain the new credentials. Is it a problem if these workers are displaced from the child care workforce? What kinds of transitional arrangements should be contemplated? At this point, few policy experts have addressed these issues, at least in a public way.

In Part 4, on child care service delivery – community versus school – we learned that the division between experts on this issue is more subtle than we had imagined. Most of the participants at the symposium assume that child care services in the future will be delivered or coordinated by small non-profit community-based organizations. Even those who see the school system playing a major role in the future delivery of child care services envision that in most cases the direct provider of service will be a small non-profit enterprise (under contract to the school system).

It is our suspicion that a Canada-wide set of early childhood care and education services, involving most preschool children, is likely to require a far larger bureaucracy than most of us currently imagine. Just think of the education and health care systems, and the various organizations involved in planning, resource allocation, and decision making in these fields. Most participants at the symposium were united on the importance of a strong measure of local control and direction over local child care services, whether those services are delivered in schools or not. This is a conclusion with which we broadly agree. However, maintaining that local control in the face of a radical expansion of the child care system and its bureaucracy will be challenging.

These feelings are buttressed by the concerns of Aboriginal child care experts. There are fundamental and serious Aboriginal concerns about centralized control of early childhood education, stemming from the role of early education in the preservation and transmission of culture, and from the negative experiences of Aboriginal Canadians with Canada's school system. Concerns about the transmission of culture are likely to be of importance to other communities in Canada as well, enhancing the need for parental involvement in programming decisions and local control of many aspects of child care services.

In Part 5, on family policy, we confirmed our initial belief that child care policy cannot and should not be seen in isolation from other forms of family policy. Child care is only one of a variety of policies that affect families (e.g., parental and maternity leave, taxation, direct financial support for low-income families, and social assistance programs), and designing a good child care program will require us to examine and amend some of those other policies. Furthermore, child care will be more important to some families than others, so that a truly equitable and popular early childhood policy will be one that meets a variety of different family needs within a range of policies.

Cross-national comparison of child care and family policy objectives and programs makes clear the important role of a country's values in developing early childhood policies. No country is politically or socially homogeneous, so there are inevitable value conflicts (e.g., over the appropriate labour force role of mothers of young children, over the role of the state in family life, and over the appropriate assistance to provide to single-parent families). Different family policy packages resolve these social and value conflicts in different ways. Further, the balance of different policies in each country is adjusted frequently through time. It is useful to compare policy generosity and family outcomes in different countries. On balance, when we do this, Canada does not compare favourably with other developed countries, although we are not at the absolute bottom internationally. It was suggested, correctly we believe, that Canada is on the verge of choosing whether, in the case of child care, it will predominantly follow the United States free-market model or the more socially oriented European one. The implications (articulated also in Part 2) are profound for all aspects of policy towards early childhood development and families.

We ourselves are the authors of one of the chapters in Part 6, on lone parents and child care policy. Thus, we had some strong views on the need to adjust any new child care policy to account for the work disincentives built into the social assistance system. We took as given that most families would pay something for child care. This is the norm in Sweden, Denmark, and some other countries for financing their child care systems. It also conforms with findings of the Canadian Policy Research Networks that most Canadians feel more comfortable with government support for child care services if parents share some of the costs directly. Parents' financial contributions have been a key element of the recent child care initiatives in Quebec. Notwithstanding this, there was considerable support at the symposium for the view that no fees ought to be charged for child care services. We suspect that this issue will have to be worked out over time, if only because of its impact on the cost of any comprehensive program.

We were forcefully and frequently reminded that there is no 'typical' lone-parent family and that meeting the various needs of different families will continue to require subtle and complicated program design. Furthermore, recent research in Hamilton-Wentworth, Ontario, has confirmed that good child care can play a key role in meeting the needs of disadvantaged children and their families, while dramatically reducing medical and other public costs. As a result, the social benefits of providing child care and recreation programming for lone-parent families can be particularly high.

Finally, Part 7 emphasized the important role that organized child care workers play in serving as advocates for improved child care. However, as we suggested earlier, the evolving nature of the workforce under a national child care policy will require some hard choices. These apply both to those people currently working in the informal sector, as well as the role of family day care in a centralized system. Currently, centre care accounts for only about 30 per cent of the extra-family care provided to children between the ages of two and five years. It is hard to imagine that this number will not grow dramatically within any comprehensive program. The question still to be resolved is whether there will continue to be much of a role for the informal caregivers now providing the 70 per cent of the care for young children.

So far, this Conclusion has focused on the lessons we learned in each part, rather than on the overall issue of where child care policy should be headed. This focus on specific issues mirrors our bias in setting up the symposium. We believe that advancing the cause of child care requires, at this point in time, as much or more attention to the detailed road map than to the broader advocacy questions of why we need better child care services (we have played our own role in addressing the latter, of course). Nonetheless, we find it impossible to conclude this volume without some reflection on the future – some gazing into the fabled crystal ball. Do we see a genuine possibility of a successful strategy for child care reform in Canada?

These are the best of times and the worst of times for those concerned about policies for young children in Canada. Never has there been more recognition of the importance of good quality developmental child care in the early lives of children, no matter what their parents' work status. Never before have there been provinces willing to commit themselves financially and politically to a universal early childhood